Pathways of Empire
———— ✳ ————

New Perspectives in South Asian History 25

The **New Perspectives in South Asian History** series publishes monographs and other writings on early modern, modern and contemporary history. The volumes in the series cover new ground across a broad spectrum of subjects such as cultural, environmental, medical, military and political history, and the histories of 'marginalised' groups. It includes fresh perspectives on more familiar fields as well as interdisciplinary and original work from all parts of South Asia. It welcomes historical contributions from sociology, anthropology and cultural studies.

Series Editors

SANJOY BHATTACHARYA *Reader in History, The Wellcome Trust Centre for History of Medicine at University College London*

PETER CAIN *Professor of History, School of Cultural Studies, Sheffield Hallam University*

MARK HARRISON *Professor, History of Medicine, and Director, Wellcome Unit for the History of Medicine, University of Oxford*

MICHAEL WORBOYS *Director, Centre for the History of Science, Technology and Medicine, and Wellcome Unit for the History of Medicine, University of Manchester*

Editorial Advisory Committee

Clive Dewey *Formerly Reader, Department of Economic and Social History, University of Leicester*

Paul Greenough *Professor of History and of Community and Behavioural Health, Director, South Asian Tsunami Research Program, University of Iowa*

Biswamoy Pati *Reader, Department of History, Sri Venkateswara College, Delhi University*

Douglas M Peers *Professor of History and Dean of Graduate Studies, York University*

Peter Robb *Pro-Director and Professor of the History of India, School of Oriental and African Studies, University of London*

Tan Tai Yong *Associate Professor of History, National University of Singapore*

Pathways of Empire
Circulation, 'Public Works' and Social Space in Colonial Orissa (c. 1780–1914)

———— ✳ ————

RAVI AHUJA
School of Oriental and African Studies
London

Orient BlackSwan

ORIENT BLACKSWAN PRIVATE LIMITED

Registered Office
3-6-752 Himayatnagar, Hyderabad 500 029 (A.P.), India
e-mail: centraloffice@orientblackswan.com

Other Offices
Bangalore, Bhopal, Bhubaneshwar, Chennai,
Ernakulam, Guwahati, Hyderabad, Jaipur, Kolkata,
Lucknow, Mumbai, New Delhi, Patna

First Published
Orient Blackswan Private Limited 2009

Series cover and book design
© Orient Blackswan Private Limited 2009

ISBN 978-81-250-3527-5

Printed at
Graphica Printers
Hyderabad 500 013

Typeset by
Line Arts
Pondicherry 605 003
in Bembo (Aldine) 10.5/12.5

Published by
Orient Blackswan Private Limited
3-6-752 Himayatnagar
Hyderabad 500 029 (A.P.), India
e-mail: hyderabad@orientblackswan.com

The external boundary and coastline of India as depicted in the
maps in this book are neither correct nor authentic.

For Nici and Shilu

Contents

List of Tables and Charts ix
List of Maps x
Acknowledgements xi
Abbreviations xiv

Introduction 1

PART I: Space–Circulation–Infrastructure: Conceptualising the Social History of Transport in Colonial India

2 Space–Society–History 19
   Hypothesis 1: Production 25
   Hypothesis 2: Conflict 30
   Hypothesis 3: Historicity 36
   Hypothesis 4: Relativity 40
   Hypothesis 5: Compression 48
   Hypothesis 6: Disparity 53
   Hypothesis 7: Rhythm 61
3 Circulation and Infrastructure 66
   Circulation, Communication and Transport 66
   Infrastructure, 'Public Works' and 'Productivity' 79

PART II: Circulatory Regimes and 'Public Works': The Case of Colonial Orissa in the Long Nineteenth Century

4 Patterns of Circulation and Modes of Transport in *Ancien Régime* Orissa 119
   Along the Coast, Across the Plains and Uplands: The NE-SW Axis 125
   Following the Rivers: The W-ESE Axis 127
   Points of Intersection and the Network of Circulation 130

Contents

Rhythms of Circulation	134
The Intensity of Circulation	144
An *Ancien Régime* of Circulation	151

5 Who Needs a Road? Circulation, Society and the East India Company — **154**
Colonial Priorities: Securing Communications and Quelling Insurgency — 156
Exigencies of Local Power: The Uses and Dangers of Roads — 162
Plebeian Perspectives: Circulation and Coercion — 175

6 Early Colonialism, 'Public Works' and the Orissa Famine — **186**
The Orissa Famine and the Problem of Circulation — 186
'Free Communication': Infrastructure Policy before the 1850s — 196
Imperial and Cotton Roads of the 1850s and 1860s — 204
Reconceiving a Circulatory Regime: 'Public Works' before the Famine — 216

7 Circulation and Infrastructure in the Times of Colonial Capitalism — **224**
Commercialisation and the Circulatory Regime — 225
'Public Works' and the Reorganisation of Social Space: Roads and Canals — 237
'Public Works' and the Reorganisation of Social Space: Railways — 247
Pilgrims and Railways: An 'Unreasonable' Appropriation — 258

8 Kings, Commerce and Corvée in the Tributary States — **270**
Commercial Kingdoms and Improving Rajas — 270
Unsanctioned Mobilities and the Violence of 'Public Works' — 283
The Reinvention of Bethi — 290

Conclusion — **301**

Glossary	324
Bibliography	327
Index	351

Tables and Charts

Table 1: Seasons of climate, production and circulation in Orissa, c. 1800 — 136

Table 2: Interregional trade of Chhattisgarh in Central India: Routes and estimated volume, 1862 — 146

Table 3: Interregional trade of Chhattisgarh in Central India: Regional distribution of estimated trade volume, 1862 — 147

Table 4: Road construction in the Bengal Presidency, 1848–1858 — 205

Table 5: Roads in 1864, Cuttack Division and Bengal Presidency — 217

Chart 1: Local roads in the Bengal Presidency, 1864 — 218

Chart 2: Orissa's maritime imports, exports and rice trade, 1868–69 to 1909–10 — 227

Chart 3: Orissa's maritime rice exports, 1865–66 to 1897–98 — 228

Chart 4: Orissa's maritime passenger traffic (1873–74 to 1890–91) — 236

Table 6: Variations in the population of selected areas of eastern India, 1891–1921 — 281

Maps

Map 1: Railway networks of India and Britain around 1900 — 308

Map 2: Plan and realisation of the railway network of India (1845 and 1881) — 310

Map 3: Axes of Orissa's *ancien régime* of circulation (c. 1780 to 1860) — 312

Map 4: "A Map of the Province of Cuttack", 1804 — 314

Map 5: Roads in 1804 (Mahanadi Delta and Chilka Lake) — 316

Map 6: Orissa according to Rennell, 1788 — 318

Map 7: Berar–Chhattisgarh–Orissa routes, 1862 — 320

Map 8: Major channels of circulation in Orissa, c. 1900 — 322

Map 9: Orissa in 1909 — end of volume

Acknowledgements

Research for this book was undertaken in 1999 and 2000 as a contribution to the "Orissa Research Programme" (ORP) and funded by the German Research Council. This institutional context has not only provided the material basis for my study, but also an inspiring intellectual environment. I am especially grateful to Hermann Kulke, Jürgen Lütt, Georg Pfeffer and Heinrich von Stietencron for their support, critique and encouragement. Various other colleagues involved with the ORP have generously shared their regional expertise with this interloper into Orissan studies—Georg Berkemer, Martin Brandner and Biswamoy Pati immediately come to my mind, but there were many others. Special thanks are due to Chandi Prasad Nanda for instructive discussions at Bhubaneshwar tea stalls and for his help in getting access to the fascinating local records in the Orissa State Archives.

The attentive staff of this small but rich archive as well as the librarians and archivists of the National Archives of India, of the Nehru Memorial Library (both in New Delhi), of the British Library's Oriental and India Office Collections in London, of the Bodleian and Indian Institute Libraries in Oxford, of the South Asia Institute's Library in Heidelberg and of the State and University Library in Göttingen were extremely helpful and patient in tracing material on long-forgotten hinterland roads.

In the year 2000, I had to move on to a seemingly unrelated area of investigation. Yet surprisingly the intensive and fruitful discussions of the 'Indian Ocean Research Initiative' of the Center for Modern Oriental Studies in Berlin also shed new light on my earlier research on Orissa's social history of circulation. Our probings into the problem of historical space enabled me to develop the conceptual framework elaborated in chapters 2 and 3 of the present study. I wish to thank Katrin Bromber, Jan-Georg Deutsch, Margret

Acknowledgements

Frenz, Friedhelm Hartwig, Patrick Krajewski and Brigitte Reinwald for many hours of unpretentious and stimulating debate.

Neeladri Bhattacharya, Sabyasachi Bhattacharya, Harald Fischer-Tiné, Chitra Joshi, Ian Kerr, Michael Mann, Ganeshwar Nayak, R. K. Nayak, Dietmar Rothermund, Sumit Sarkar and Jayeeta Sharma encouraged me at various points to persevere with a project the realisation of which was far from smooth. Early results of my research were presented and critically discussed on various workshops and conferences in Bad Salzau, Berlin, Cambridge, Edinburgh, Kiel and Leiden. I recall with particular pleasure a very lively and instructive discussion in the history department of the Open University in Hagen.

Moreover, I could not have returned to writing down the monograph in 2004 without the whole-hearted support I received from the history department and the directors of the South Asia Institute in Heidelberg. Gita Dharampal-Frick generously and unbureaucratically supported my applications for academic leave. Georg Berkemer, Claudia Theis-Passaro and the department's student research assistants helped me to solve numerous small but essential problems.

An earlier version of chapters 4 and 5 was accepted for publication as an essay despite its excessive length: "Opening up the Country'? Orissan Society and Early Colonial Communications Policies (1803–1866)" in *Studies in History* (new series), 20, no. 1, 2004. The last section of chapter 7 is a revised excerpt from a contribution to a volume of essays edited by Harald Fischer-Tiné and Michael Mann (*Colonialism as Civilizing Mission: The Case of British India*, London: Anthem Press, 2004, pp. 195–216). I thank the editors for their permission to reuse this material.

This study could not have materialised without the hospitality of family and friends. My cousin Aarti Rawla, her husband Anup and their daughters Jaya and Pallavi have made me feel so very much at home on the terrace of their Delhi house. My late aunt Vimla, her sons Ravi and Munish Khanna and their families made archival trips to London much more enjoyable. And my friend Jan-Georg Deutsch generously put me up in his cosy Oxford house.

Others helped me in the final stages of this study. Nils Harm produced sophisticated maps in a laborious process without losing his characteristic patience. Franziska Roy's thorough copy editing and

Acknowledgements

critical reading of the manuscript were more helpful than she is ready to accept. My editor Veenu Luthria's competent work further increased the readability of this text. Ahmad Azhar assisted me with the index.

Furthermore, there are heavy debts incurred with my family in Germany. Margret Schreiber-Ahuja's and Surindra Ahuja's parental confidence in my abilities was surely biased but nevertheless encouraging. Wolfgang Mayer and his early deceased wife Sieglinde may not always have been convinced whether my work made sense, but their unfailing support was essential in solving many practical problems. But my greatest obligations are, as so often before, to Nicole Mayer-Ahuja who did not ditch me despite my months-long disappearance to various archives immediately after our wedding, whose help was crucial in overcoming several crises in the production of this work and who has been my most ruthless critic and closest intellectual ally for many years. Finally, there is Sheela Ahuja, who entered and shook up our lives when this book was in the making. Being witness to her infectious *joie de vivre* and irrepressible keenness to expand her world has helped me to maintain a sense of proportion. It has also turned the time of writing into an unforgettable experience. It is to Nici and Shilu that I dedicate this book.

Abbreviations

BoR	Board of Revenue
BNR	Bengal–Nagpur Railway
CE	Chief Engineer
CoCD	Commissioner of Cuttack Division/Commissioner of Orissa
Com.	Communications
Dpt.	Department
EE	Executive Engineer
GoB	Government of Bengal
GoI	Government of India
HMSO	Her Majesty's Stationary Office
Offg.	Officiating
OIOC	British Library, Oriental and India Office Collections
OSA	Orissa State Archives, Bhubaneswar
PWD	Public Works Department
Secry.	Secretary
SE	Superintending Engineer
Sess.	Session (as of Parliament)
SI	Superintendent

1
Introduction

This study has two objectives. The first is to forge conceptual tools for the examination of a hitherto neglected area of South Asian social history: the history of how people and goods circulated through the subcontinent and of the infrastructures that facilitated such movements. The second objective consists in an empirical reconstruction of major tendencies in the social history of transport in one Indian region: the transformation of Orissa's circulatory regime from the final decades of the precolonial era in the late eighteenth century through World War I. The two objectives require two distinct approaches: the first is systematic and abstract, the second sequential and concrete. Corresponding to this dual approach, the study is organised in two parts. Though they can be read separately, each of them is no more than one arm of a pincer. Empirical studies of South Asia's social history of transport will remain prisoners of particularity and of their sources (which are inevitably colonial to a large extent) without the smelting process of conceptual abstraction. Conceptual tools, in their turn, will remain blunt in their generality and of limited investigative use unless edged and differentiated in a working process of historical concretisation. Since each of these parts is preceded by a short outline, this introduction is confined to a brief critique of the relevant historiography, followed by a definition of the scope of this study, by an explication of its theoretical and methodological approach and, finally, by an overview of the questions examined in the chapters.

Historiography

Students of South Asia's history of transport can draw upon a stream of substantial and sometimes sophisticated historical writings since the late nineteenth century.[1] Yet much of this historiography of transport has three major drawbacks that have impeded the development of a *social history* of circulation and infrastructure: (i) a lack of critical reflection on basic concepts, (ii) the failure to assume a *longue durée* perspective on the history of circulation spanning both the precolonial and colonial eras, and (iii) a narrow focus on railways.

The first drawback originates from the propensity of most historians of South Asian transport to operate from the assumption that more and 'improved' roads, railways and canals are under all circumstances in a usually unspecified 'public interest'. "Let us travel over all the countries of the earth," wrote the Abbé Raynal in the late eighteenth century, "and wherever we shall find no facility of trading from a city to a town, and from a village to a hamlet, we may pronounce the people to be barbarians."[2] The general structure of this argument has been recycled time and again, not only in the official historiography of British imperialism but also by postcolonial writers. The availability of transport facilities, particularly for commercial purposes, has thus been variously declared an objective, technical measure of human "civilisation", of universal "improvement", of a people's material and moral "progress", of "national unification" and of regional "development".[3] Indian

---

[1] For a detailed official, yet still useful history of 'public works' up to the early 1890s, see G. W. MacGeorge, *Ways and Works in India: Being an Account of the Public Works in that Country from the Earliest Times up to the Present Day* (Westminster: Constable & Co., 1894). For a more recent, uncritical but well-documented overview of colonial transport history up to the 1880s, see K. E. Verghese, *The Development and Significance of Transport in India, 1834–1882* (New Delhi: N. V., 1976). For an excellent survey of the historiography of Indian railways and its problems, a collection of significant contributions to this field and a useful commented bibliography, see Ian J. Kerr ed., *Railways in Modern India* (New Delhi et al.: Oxford University Press, 2001). More detailed references to relevant literature can be found in chapter 3 of the present study.

[2] Guillaume T. F. Raynal, *A Philosophical and Political History of the Settlements and Trade of the Europeans in the East and West Indies* (London: W. Strahan and T. Cadell, 1783 [1st French ed. 1770]), 8: 36.

[3] For samples of the imperialist and Indian nationalist varieties of this argument, see John Strachey and Richard Strachey, *The Finances and Public Works of India from 1869 to 1881* (London: Kegan Paul & Co., 1882), 3; S. K. Srivastava, *Transport Development in India* (New Delhi: Chand, 1964), 98–100. For more detailed evidence, see chapter 3.

Introduction

nationalist critics of colonial railway policy did not question, for instance, the general utility of 'public works' as such, but merely what they considered to be colonial perversions of a project that was universally beneficial in its essence (see ch. 3). The question of whether the railways benefited the British or the Indian nation or both has also been at the centre of the debates of postcolonial economic historians, while the premises on which the primacy of this question was based were rarely reflected. Many studies of transport history thus combine technocratic progressivism with methodological nationalism. A social neutrality, linearity of technological change and priority of the national scale are assumed, while conflicting social interests that emerge from concrete historical contexts and entail diverging needs, preferences and practical alternatives with regard to transport policy are considered only in passing if at all.[4] The implication is that concepts like 'public works' or "infrastructure" have hardly been put into question and are still used as if they had no history and no specific social content. The illusion of self-evidence is reinforced by the quotidian experience that roads and railways are open to the 'general public' or, more precisely, cater to needs of a wide range of social actors. Only a critical reflection of the seemingly commonsensical basic concepts of transport history permits us to perceive historical constellations of social forces behind supposedly timeless technical necessity and to discern a plurality of distinct and potentially conflicting appropriations behind

---

[4] These limitations are particularly visible in works of the 1960s and 1970s. For instance, see Verghese, *Development and Significance of Transport*, and Srivastava, *Transport Development in India*. However, even the most sophisticated contributions to the history of Indian railways have revolved around notions of a given and unitary national interest in infrastructure development. The hierarchical and contradictory constellation of interests that constitutes any nation is only implicitly acknowledged in these studies insofar as it is sometimes admitted that the gains of the revolution in transport and of the accompanying commercialisation were unevenly distributed. Consider for instance the centrality of the concept of "social rates of return" in Hurd's important survey essay; see John M. Hurd, "Irrigation and Railways: Railways", in *The Cambridge Economic History of India*, c. 1757—c. 1970, ed. Dharma Kumar (Cambridge: Cambridge University Press, 1982), 2: 737–61 (especially pp. 741 and 743). For a perceptive historical examination of the notion of economic nationhood in the Indian context, see Manu Goswami, *Producing India: From Colonial Economy to National Space* (Chicago: University of Chicago Press, 2004), especially chapter 7.

the appearance of consensual utilisation. This kind of theoretical spadework is a precondition, therefore, for any serious attempt to investigate the transformations of circulatory practice and transport infrastructure as social and historical phenomena.[5]

With regard to the second drawback, it is evident that so far little effort has been made to take a long view of the history of circulation and transport infrastructure in South Asia. There is a limited corpus of studies in precolonial modes and patterns of transport, the most significant being Jean Deloche's magisterial and painstaking survey.[6] And there is a far larger amount of literature on India's transport revolution in the age of steam locomotion.[7] Yet attempts to understand the long-term transformation of the specific circulatory regimes of South Asia or any of its regions have been both rare and limited in scope. Historians interested in 'modern' transport have largely contented themselves with dealing most casually with the precolonial history of circulation: either by denying its relevance altogether or merely alluding to the importance given to roads in ancient normative texts like the *Arthashastra*. Some of their writings contain random (and often rather anachronistic) references to the "public works departments" of precolonial rulers.[8] In more

---

[5] The lack of theoretical groundwork has recently been noted by the most perceptive historian of Indian railways: "Clearly, there is much in the conceptual, definitional and methodological realm that needs to be cleared away and developed before the role of the railways in the making of modern India can be properly addressed." Ian J. Kerr, Introduction to *Railways in Modern India,* ed. Kerr (New York: Oxford University Press, 2001), 14.

[6] Jean Deloche, *Transport and Communication in India Prior to Steam Locomotion*, 2 vols. (New Delhi: Oxford University Press, 1993–94). See also chapter 3 of the present study.

[7] For railways, see Kerr, Introduction. Literature on Indian steam shipping is more disparate. However, see Frank Broeze, "Underdevelopment and Dependency: Maritime India during the Raj", *Modern Asian Studies* 18, 1984, 429–57; Frank Broeze, "From Imperialism to Independence: The Decline and Re-emergence of Asian Shipping", *The Great Circle* 9, no. 2, 1987, 73–95 and, for a recent introductory overview, see Ravi Ahuja, "Lateinsegel und Dampfturbinen: Der Schiffsverkehr des Indischen Ozeans im Zeitalter des Imperialismus", in *Der Indische Ozean: Das afro-asiatische Mittelmeer als Kultur-und Wirtschaftsraum*, ed. Dietmar Rothermund and Susanne Weigelin-Schwiedrzik (Vienna: Promedia, 2004), 207–25.

[8] For the latter variety, see, for instance, Srivastava, *Transport Development in India*, 241. For detailed evidence on colonial representations of transport infrastructure in pre-nineteenth-century India, see ch. 3 of the present study.

Introduction

sophisticated studies, certain aspects of early modern modes of transport have been isolated for comparative purposes, such as the citation of the carriage costs of pack bullocks as a baseline for calculations of "social savings" achieved by the railway.[9] Comprehensive analyses of spatial, temporal and social patterns of precolonial circulation in specific regions or in the subcontinent as a whole appear, however, to have been considered dispensable in investigations of the social effects engendered by the construction of an extensive railway network and the rise of steam navigation in the latter half of the nineteenth century. Many historical writings seem to have been afflicted by the cavalier attitude of most colonial accounts with regard to transport and infrastructure in pre-nineteenth century India (see chapter 3 and 4). The view that India had been a *tabula rasa*, an empty space in terms of transport facilities before British rule did not merely satisfy the legitimatory need for imperial self-aggrandisement, but was also a one-sided, coloured and magnified reflection of the radicality of a transport revolution that could indeed be experienced in parts of India since the 1850s. The depth or shallowness of this transformation can only be fathomed, however, on the basis of a reconstruction of long-term processes, in which patterns of circulation were replaced or reinforced, remoulded or overlaid.

Coming to the third drawback, a review of the relevant literature leaves no doubt that South Asia's more recent historiography of transport under colonial rule is as yet, with a few notable exceptions, merely a historiography of Indian railways.[10] This remarkable one-sidedness is particularly evident in what is still the authoritative

---

[9] See, for example, Hurd, "Railways", 740.

[10] Among the notable exceptions is an interesting geographical thesis on the development of transport infrastructure in the region of Awadh: Robert G. Varady, "Rail and Road Transport in Nineteenth-Century Awadh: Competition in a North Indian Province" (Ph.D. diss., University of Arizona, 1981). Some recent studies of regional economic development and particularly Anand Yang's commercial history of Gangetic Bihar also take a somewhat broader view of problems of transport, without, however, exploring this field systematically; see Anand A. Yang, *Bazaar India. Markets, Society, and the Colonial State in Gangetic Bihar* (Berkeley: University of California Press, 1998). Earlier comprehensive narratives of transport history have never reached the sophistication of studies in railway history. See, for instance, Verghese, *Development and Significance of Transport*, and Srivastava, *Transport Development in India*.

synthesis of South Asia's economic history: extensive (and no doubt important) chapters on railways and (partly navigable) irrigation works are all *The Cambridge Economic History of India* offers on problems of transport for the post-1850s period—as if the availability or non-availability of roads, river navigation and maritime infrastructure had been of no significance for the subcontinent's economic development.[11] This bias echoes probably unwittingly the post-1840s preference of India's colonial administration for so-called 'productive public works', that is, infrastructure projects providing profitable investment opportunities for British capital (as opposed to 'unproductive public works' like roads). It also reproduces the attitude of early Indian nationalists, who generally did not question the preference given to these 'productive public works' but debated *which category* of 'productive public works'—railways or irrigation—should have priority (see ch. 3). Hence, while colonial sources are unproportionately rich with regard to railways and canals, it requires a deeper dig to recover information on roads and natural waterways. This unevenness in documentation however, merely reflects the perspective of particular (though dominant) social interests. Meanwhile the circulatory regime in its entirety, some of its most pervasive quotidian features and divergent perspectives remain concealed. Moreover, historical turning points, where the realisation or non-realisation of equally possible trajectories of infrastructural development was decided according to the prevalent field of social forces, cannot be distinguished by the same token.

Criticising the corresponding bias of historical writing does not, however, deny that major advances in understanding the economic history of Indian railways have been made since Daniel Thorner's seminal study of 1950.[12] Nor can we ignore the fact that the written history of Indian railways is no longer narrowly confined to aspects of political economy. Ian Kerr's contributions have been particularly important for widening the scope of research and for encouraging a new generation of historians to look into cultural and social

---

[11] Dharma Kumar, ed., *The Cambridge Economic History of India*, c. 1757—c. 1970, vol. 2 (Cambridge: Cambridge University Press, 1982).

[12] Daniel Thorner, *Investment in Empire: British Railway and Steam Shipping Enterprise in India, 1825–1849* (Philadelphia: University of Pennsylvania Press, 1950). For an overview of the historiography of Indian railways, see Kerr, Introduction.

Introduction

implications of railway development.[13] As will be seen in subsequent chapters, the present study is heavily indebted to the achievements of the historians of Indian railways. What is suggested here is merely that social and cultural implications of the railways will be more clearly distinguishable and that exaggerations as well as oversights can be avoided if the railways are examined not as isolated phenomena, but in the context of the overall patterns and modes of transport. That geographer Sunil Kumar Munsi has explored the potential of a comprehensive approach to transport history as early as in the 1980s in an important study on eastern India, has unfortunately generated little interest among historians.[14]

Scope

The scope of the present study is determined by the need to transcend these limitations of earlier historiography. The early bias on railways can be overcome only if all modes and infrastructures of overland and water transport, even inconspicuous bullock trails and rough timber rafts, are taken into consideration. The point is to examine how all these modes and infrastructures affected each other in their development and how various social agencies generated a circulatory regime—a complex pattern of interdependent practices and institutions—in the process.

Moreover, assuming a long-term perspective requires a comparatively long period of review. It commences, in this study, with the final decades of the eighteenth century, when the East India Company turned into a strong territorial power on the subcontinent. The *ancien régime* of circulation prevailing in the late precolonial

---

[13] See especially Ian J. Kerr, "Representation and Representations of the Railways of Colonial and Post-colonial South Asia", *Modern Asian Studies* 37, no. 2, 2003, 287–326; Kerr, "Reworking a Popular Religious Practice: The Effects of Railways on Pilgrimage in Nineteenth- and Twentieth-Century South Asia", in *Railways in Modern India,* ed. Kerr (New York: Oxford University Press, 2001), 304–27. Kerr has also edited another volume on Indian railway history, which includes a number of essays by younger cultural historians: Kerr, ed., *27 Down: New Departures in Indian Railway Studies* (Delhi: Orient Longman, 2007).

[14] Sunil K. Munsi, *Geography of Transportation in Eastern India under the British Raj*, CSSSC Monograph 1 (Calcutta: K. P. Bagchi, 1980).

period persisted without much qualitative change in most parts of India until the mid-nineteenth century. It was only in the following half-century that another circulatory regime emerged that was predominantly determined by the exigencies of colonial capitalism. The study traces this development up to about World War I, when the new circulatory regime and its contradictions had fully unfolded and the rise of new technologies of transport (especially of motorised road transport) brought about further changes mainly within the bounds of this regime. However, the very fact that the history of circulation is to a large extent a history of the *longue durée* renders it necessary to draw the boundaries of the period under review not too strictly.

Finally, whereas the first part of the study takes a broad view of conceptual and material developments in and beyond the Indian subcontinent, the second part focuses on one particular geographical area of South Asia on the assumption that, at the present state of historiography, a regional perspective is most adequate: there is not enough material to permit generalisations for the whole subcontinent and not enough analysis of broader processes to provide the context for in-depth micro-histories. This study examines the transformation of that area of eastern India, where the Oriya language is spoken by a majority of the people—an area largely coextensive with the present Indian State of Orissa. This region consists of coastal plains including the vast delta of the Mahanadi River (which were annexed by the East India Company as early as in 1803) and of extensive hill tracts in the interior (which continued to be ruled in the main by tributary rajas and chiefs). Unlike most of the regions that have so far caught the attention of historians of transport,[15] Orissa was clearly no major target of colonial infrastructure policy and has a rather loosely meshed circulatory network according to subcontinental standards even today.[16] This choice

---

[15] For detailed references to such works, see chapter 3, in this study.

[16] For a conventional but well-researched study of Orissa's transport development after 1866, see Ganeswar Nayak, *Development of Transport and Communication: A Case Study* (New Delhi: Anmol, 2000). Also see B. N. Sinha, "Transport and Communications Problems in Orissa", *The National Geographical Journal of India* 3, no. 1, 1957, 27–45; B. N. Sinha, "Railway Transport and Its Problems in Orissa", *The National Geographical Journal of India* 3, no. 2, 1957, 93–103. For further literature on the regional history of transport, see chapters 4–8 of the present study.

brings contradictions of the colonial circulatory regime into sharp focus and is especially useful for investigating the contribution of public works policies to the creation of regional disparities.

Theory and Methodology

In order to overcome the three general drawbacks of India's historiography of transport (the assumption of general utility, the inattention to long-term processes and the narrow focus on railways), the present study approaches its subject by generating a wider theoretical framework. This framework ties up to philosophical conceptualisations of the "production of social space" by Henri Lefebvre.[17] The heuristic potential of these conceptualisations for the writing of South Asian history has been successfully explored and demonstrated in recent research on cities and nationalism.[18] In the present study, the notion of a "produced social space" is adapted to and concretised for the analysis of problems of circulation and transport infrastructure. The starting point for this concretisation is the recognition that roads, railways and other forms of infrastructure should be perceived, not as isolated and neutral technical "facts", but as materialisations of social relations in space. They should be seen simultaneously as results and preconditions of "circulation", that is, of potentially cyclic spatial practices of social groups. A procedure of theoretical and historical reflection aimed at extracting specific tools of analysis from these still rather abstract ideas is the methodological approach of the first part of this study.

This approach has intrinsic limitations: it can help to discern general patterns and dynamics of circulatory practices and infrastructural development in certain periods, but the level of analysis is still too general to do justice to the concrete dynamics of transformative processes in a particular region at a specific time. For representing the contradictory tendencies of such processes, their conflicting currents and undercurrents, their rich historical possibilities the 'fields of force' where these possibilities are realised or discarded and

---

[17] Henri Lefebvre, *The Production of Space*, trans. Donald Nicholson-Smith (Oxford, Cambridge, MA: Basil Blackwell, 1991) For a more detailed discussion of the relevant theoretical literature, see chapter 2 of the present study.
[18] Janaki Nair, *The Promise of the Metropolis: Bangalore's Twentieth Century* (New Delhi: Oxford University Press, 2005); Goswami, *Producing India*.

the contemporaneity of the non-contemporaneous, a fundamentally *sequential format* is required. The temporal order of social acts matters if we wish to understand which social forces determined the general direction of such processes to what extent, by which means and for which reasons. The question of whether the transformation of Orissa's precolonial regime of circulation set in before or after the catastrophic famine of 1866 is, for instance, crucial to the understanding of the historical configuration of social agencies, of the field of force where this process was shaped (see ch. 6).

Moreover, emphasising problems of space in a historical study always bears the risk of spatial reductionism, that is, of a reductionist conversion of four-dimensional history to a two-dimensional depiction. This risk is further exacerbated by current trends in the writing of South Asian social history. For it seems that an understandable uneasiness with earlier historical narratives of unilinear progress and 'development' has created among historians an increasing tendency to replace processual forms of representation with complex 'freeze images' of particular historical situations or with a largely unconnected series of such images. The preference for such 'situational' modes of representation is linked to a reluctance to address problems of historical causation and a propensity to suppress questions about historical tendencies by condemning them summarily as teleological.[19] The often unintended and unperceived result seems to be that quietist contemplation is confirmed as the professional historian's code of conduct. Resisting these pressures and preserving the critical, possibly even prognostic potential of social history[20] requires, however, that spaces be conceived of as inextricably intertwined with historical processes. The critical historian's turn to problems of social space demands careful attention

---

[19] For a preliminary critique of such approaches in the field of South Asian labour history (which I hope to develop more systematically and expand to other areas of research at a later stage), see Ravi Ahuja, "Erkenntnisdruck und Denkbarrieren: Anmerkungen zur indischen Arbeitshistoriographie", in *Konfigurationen der Moderne: Diskurse zu Indien* (Soziale Welt, Sonderband 15), ed. Shalini Randeria, Martin Fuchs and Antje Linkenbach (Baden Baden: Nomos, 2004), 349–66. See also chapter 2 of the present study.

[20] For a thoughtful essay on this unfashionable and important subject, see Eric J. Hobsbawm, "Looking Forward: History and the Future", *New Left Review* 125, 1981, 3–19.

to problems of chrononology, sequence and tendency. If the outline of the second part of this study is largely sequential, therefore, it is not so out of deference to increasingly outmoded historiographical conventions. It is a conscious methodological choice with regard to the task at hand and a contribution to the debate on historical methodology.

While the first part of this study relies on a broad survey of relevant philosophical, geographical and historical writings as well as on a selection of contemporary publications on issues of circulation and infrastructure, the second part is mainly based on documents from colonial archives in Bhubaneswar, New Delhi and London (many of them so far unused) as well as on official publications, newspaper reports and memoirs. The documentation for the empirical part thus consists predominantly of written evidence preserved in the libraries and archives of the colonial state, whereas largely unrecorded popular memories of infrastructural transformation have not been drawn upon. Moreover, the decision to confine the examination to the regional scale has implied that evidence for local-level processes, even that which is extractable from the colonial archives, could only be used by way of example. This choice of mainly archival meso-level evidence, it should be emphasised, reflects exigencies emerging mainly from the very rudimentary state of research in this field and also from the writer's working conditions. Research for the present study has thus not gone beyond systematic test drillings into the available evidence. The methodological possibilities and sources of information for future social histories of transport remain, therefore, far from exhausted even for the region of Orissa. The present study merely claims to be a stepping stone that might be used for more far-reaching researches relying on a more diverse range of "sources", including oral and literary evidence.

Chapterisation

The first part of this study, entitled "Space–Circulation–Infrastructure", comprises chapters 2 and 3. The former develops the concept of "produced social space" into a theoretical framework consisting of seven working hypotheses. Each of these hypotheses is developed and juxtaposed against ideas prevailing in both colonial and postcolonial writings. Their relevance for the examination of South

Asia's social history of transport is briefly indicated by way of example.

Chapter 3 proceeds to a particular category of spatial practices, that is, circulation. It explores the conceptual field revolving around these practices, and moves on to the problem of (transport) "infrastructure", that is, to the built environments that are generated in response to the exigencies of circulation and at once condition further circulatory practice. The relevant conceptual field is discussed in this context, including the seemingly harmless notion of 'public works'.

The case study of the transformation of Orissa's circulatory regime in the long nineteenth century is organised into the six chapters of Part II. Chapter 4 reconstructs the regional *ancien régime* of circulation, that is, the prevalent modes of transport as well as the spatial and temporal patterns of circulation at the time of Orissa's annexation by the English East India Company in 1803 and during the early decades of colonial rule.

Chapter 5 explores in some detail the various and often conflicting social and political interests with regard to circulation and transport infrastructure in the first half of the nineteenth century. It seeks to explain why no major social actor was intent on major investments in transport infrastructure during these decades.

Chapter 6 takes stock of infrastructural measures effected in Orissa during the first half-century of colonial rule after the annexation in 1803 and examines the historical context from which a more active 'public works' policy emerged in the mid-nineteenth century, assessing in particular the role of the devastating 1866 famine in this policy change.

Chapter 7 turns to the second half of the period under review and discusses the transformation of the circulatory regime in the parts of Orissa under direct British administration in the context of a strong tendency towards economic and social commercialisation. After reconstructing the changes in patterns of commodity circulation since the 1860s and their unevenly distributed social effects, the chapter analyses the colonial regime's 'public works' policy and the controversial debates (involving various social groups) on several infrastructural schemes. A case study of changes in the popular practice of pilgrimage demonstrates that the resulting reorganisation of social space also had unintended effects.

Introduction

Processes of commercialisation also provide the background for chapter 8, which focuses on the transformation of the circulatory regime in the dependent "little kingdoms" of Orissa's interior. It traces the astounding metamorphosis of 'recalcitrant rajas' into 'improving rulers' and the contradictory effects of the ensuing expansion of transport infrastructure. One particularly striking result is examined in detail, namely, the transformation and reinvigoration of *bethi* (forced labour)—the traditional obligation of subordinated classes to unpaid and forced labour.

An appendix of maps will render the arguments of Part II, concerning the reorganisation of Orissa's social space, more easily comprehensible. A concluding chapter sums up the study's results and points at possibilities of further research on the social history of transport under colonialism.

Part 1

SPACE–CIRCULATION–INFRASTRUCTURE

Conceptualising the Social History of Transport in Colonial India

PART I

The development of India's transport infrastructure, scarcely recognised as a significant theme of social history, has so far been approached with a characteristic disregard for conceptual problems. Reflections on terminology have apparently been deemed expendable when dealing with seemingly simple objects and self-explanatory facts like roads or railways. Yet such reflections are indispensable for the development of "concrete abstractions", that is, of workable terms with both explanatory power beyond a particular historical constellation and the potential of being differentiated into conceptual tools that measure up to the distinctiveness of such constellations. Moreover, they must avoid the historiographical pitfall of uncritically accepting and (wittingly or unwittingly) perpetuating colonial modes of representation. For these reasons, chapter 2 delineates and discusses at some length three key terminological fields, that is, groups of concepts, each addressing a problem or phenomenon, which any attempt to write a social history of transportation has to relate to. Both the historical terminology of the period under research and more recent conceptualisations are assessed in order to work out adequate and developable tools of analysis. Much of this examination is directed at the most abstract, fundamental and complex conceptual field: *space* as a dimension of social practice. On this basis, we approach the terminology of *circulation* in the sense of repetitive socio-spatial practices—more specifically, transportation. The chapter concludes with a discussion of concepts referring to the fossilisation of such practises into built environments, of which *infrastructure* is the most common in present parlance.

2
Space–Society–History

The concept of "space" has no doubt emerged in recent years as a pivot of historical debates and the key concept of yet another historiographical 'turn'. Sceptics may suspect, not without foundation, that one obvious and rather uninspiring reason for the accelerating sequence of such "turns" is the debilitating tendency of contemporary academic institutions to adapt scholarly "product life cycles" to the stock exchange culture of "short-terminism". There are, however, reasons for the increased attraction of concepts of "space" meriting more serious theoretical consideration.

It is necessary at this juncture to speak of concepts in the plural as the term "space" is frequently used and sometimes defined in contradictory ways. The most common practice is surely to use space as a *metaphor*. The term is reduced to a metaphor when it is employed for representational purposes as a neutral 'frame' for complex phenomena that are not necessarily regarded as having a spatial dimension in any physical or geographical sense (for example, "public space").[1] This utilisation is inextricably embedded in all levels of language—the spatial metaphor is virtually *irreplaceable*. It is problematic only if it is charged (as is frequently the case) with the implicit assumption that 'space' can be understood as the "unvarying suitcase of the world",[2] that is, as a *receptacle with emptiness and immutability as its*

---

[1] For a critique of metaphorical utilisations of the concept of "social space" by Durkheim and others, see Neil Smith, *Uneven Development: Nature, Capital and the Production of Space* (Oxford/New York: Blackwell Publishing, 1984), 75. Realising that a comprehensive theory of space had become both possible and necessary, Henri Lefebvre conceptualised "social space" as the spatial dimension of social practice in a non-metaphorical, concrete sense. See below.

[2] I am here drawing on Ernst Bloch's inimitably phrased critique of such conceptions: "Derart hat im Raumbild und gerade hier eine alte Eierschale besonders zäh standgehalten, eben die Auffassung des Raums als eines

defining features. This assumption is grounded as much in the philosophical concept of 'absolute space' (based on Euclidean geometry and dominant in its classical formulation by Isaac Newton up to at least the early twentieth century) as in 'common sense' (that is, the synthesis of concepts emerging from quotidian praxis and reflecting the historical limitations of this praxis). We will return to this notion in our discussion of the ideas of space that prevailed in the period under review.

From the mid-nineteenth century onwards, however, against the background of developments in society, culture and science, the assumption of a static and homogenous absoluteness of empty 'space' became less plausible. Relational conceptualisations, that is, conceptualisations negating an existence of space that was independent of matter and time, now prevailed in the sciences and became more influential in the humanities.[3] However, as late as in the 1970s, Ernst Bloch felt that spatial thought had not freed itself altogether from its "old eggshell". There was always the risk of reifying in the process of objectification, that is, the tendency "to render absolute the safety [Geborgenheit] that is seemingly so much more a property of space than of time" and to overlook movement, energy and, finally, production. Yet "elastic space", the notion of *"spaces of the unpacked being of movement"* ("Räume des Unverpacktseins der Bewegung"), claimed Bloch, was valid not only in the realm of modern physics but also with regard to history, geography and aesthetics.[4]

Earlier in the century, however, influential currents of social thought had attempted to overcome the reification of the concept on a different route, namely, by exploding the unity of 'space' and hence by conceptualising it as a *multiple*.[5] One of these proceeded

---

allgemeinen Kofferhaften selber verdinglichter und gleichbleibender Art, als eines erzstabilen Weltkoffers zuletzt, worin die einzelnen Dinge, ob bewegt oder ruhend, eingepackt sind." Ernst Bloch, *Experimentum Mundi: Frage, Kategorien des Herausbringens, Praxis*, Frankfurt a.M.: Surkamp, 1985, 107–8.

[3] David Harvey, *The Condition of Postmodernity: An Enquiry into the Origins of Cultural Change* (Oxford/Cambridge, MA: Basil Blackwell, 1989), 265–83; Martina Löw, *Raumsoziologie* (Frankfurt a.M.: Suhrkamp 2001), 17–34. Also see Lefebvre, *Production of Space*, 25–26; Smith, *Uneven Development*, 66–73; Manfred Stöckler, "Raum und Zeit", in *Enzyklopädie Philosophie*, ed. Hans J. Sandkühler (Hamburg: Meiner, 1999), 1343–46.

[4] Bloch, *Experimentum Mundi*, 108. Also see footnote 2, in this chapter.

[5] Lefebvre pointed out that the intellectual construction of an "infinite multitude of spaces" was an exemplification of the "tendency within present-day

from the uncontroversial observation that 'space' is perceived in very different ways according to the diversity of cultural and social circumstances to the conclusion that there ought to be "as many spaces in reality as there were perspectives on it".[6] Not Bloch's, but this latter subjectivist approach has shaped the agenda of recent research on 'space', by creating an almost exclusive emphasis on *one* (no doubt important) aspect of social spatiality, namely, the perceptions of and discourses on space, while diminishing the interest in the conflictual material structures of social space.[7] On a more theoretical level a spatial dimension is given to the 'postmodernist' refutation of the idea of a unity of human history (which is polemically conflated with normative 'universalism').[8] This involves the

---

society and its mode of production" to subject "intellectual labour, like material labour, ... to endless division." Lefebvre, *Production of Space*, 8–9. Also see Löw, *Raumsoziologie*, 15.

[6] Stephen Kern, *The Culture of Time and Space, 1880–1918* (Cambridge MA: Harvard University Press, 1983), 151 (the quotation recapitulates Ortega y Gasset's position). For a descriptive and sympathetic account of this intellectual development, see Kern, *Culture of Time and Space*, 131–52.

[7] Hence the most influential recent studies on the problematic of colonialism and space are concerned with the "power–knowledge" of geography. See David N Livingstone, *The Geographical Tradition: Episodes in the History of a Contested Enterprise* (Oxford/Cambridge, MA: Blackwell Publishing, 1992); Matthew H. Edney, *Mapping an Empire: The Geographical Construction of India, 1765–1843* (Chicago: University of Chicago Press, 1997). However, the possibility of a shift in the agenda of research towards an inclusion of material dimensions of social spatiality may be signalled by a perceptive and reflective monograph that opens doors for leaving the hermetic world of discourse analysis (though its author appears hesitant to step out fully). See Goswami, *Producing India*.

[8] "Space" is here explicitly used as a "tool to write against assumptions of universal history and ... 'grand narratives'. Iris Schröder and Sabine Höhler, "Welt-Räume: Annäherungen an eine Geschichte der Globalität im 20. Jahrhundert", in *Welt-Räume. Geschichte, Geographie und Globalisierung seit 1900*, ed. Iris Schröder and Sabine Höhler (Frankfurt a.M.: Campus-Verlag, 2004), 19–20 (my translation). This type of rhetorical instrumentalisation of "space" echoes Lyotard's replacement of "meta-narratives" for "local determinism". See Jean-François Lyotard, *The Postmodern Condition: A Report on Knowledge* (Manchester: Manchester University Press, 1993), xxiv, 66. The summary branding of very different theories as "universalist" is, of course, also a main ingredient of many postcolonial writings. See, for instance, Partha Chatterjee, *The Nation and Its Fragments: Colonial and Postcolonial Histories* (Princeton: Princeton University Press, 1993), 13, 32–33, 167–68.

"absolute valorisation of the 'fragment'",[9] that is, the unqualified equation of the 'fragment' (probably one of the most frequent spatial metaphors in recent cultural studies) with resistance against the homogenising pressures of a 'globalising modernity'—an equation that fails to account, however, for the phenomenon that processes of fragmentation are *constitutive* for processes of homogenisation in modern societies such as, for instance, the social and spatial fragmentation of labour processes for the global proliferation of wage labour relations. The celebration of the "fragment" thus tends to replace systematic reconstructions of contradictory, hierarchical but unitary fields of force with a binary, quasi-Manichean juxtaposition of the 'global' and the 'fragment' and, consequently, with kaleidoscopic compositions of disjointed pieces.[10] Closely connected to this intellectual trend is the demand for a "spatialization of the historical narrative", for a "hegemonic shift" away from "historicism" and the "temporal master-narrative"[11]—a problematic demand

---

[9] See Sumit Sarkar, "Postmodernism and the Writing of History", in *Beyond Nationalist Frames: Relocating Postmodernism, Hindutva, History* (Delhi: Permanent Black, 2002), 161; also see 170–71.

[10] Henri Lefebvre explicitly refuted such dualistic conceptions of space: "It is not, therefore, as though one had global (or conceived) space to one side and fragmented (or directly experienced) space on the other—rather as one might have an intact glass here and a broken glass or mirror over there. For space "is" whole and broken, global and fractured, at one and the same time." And elsewhere: "spatial practice consists in a projection onto a (spatial) field of all aspects, elements and moments of social practice. In the process, these are separated from one another, though this does not mean that overall control is relinquished even for a moment". Lefebvre, *Production of Space,* 8, 355–56. See also pp. 365–66; footnote 5 on pp. 20–21 of the present study and Goswami, *Producing India,* 24–25.

[11] Edward W. Soja, *Postmodern Geographies: The Reassertion of Space in Critical Social Theory* (London: Verso, 1989), 1, 11. Soja, it should be said, calls for a new "balance" of space and time in social inquiry and warns his fellow postmodernisers of geography not "to overstate their case, creating the unproductive aura of an anti-history, inflexibly exaggerating the critical privilege of contemporary spatiality in isolation from an increasingly silenced embrace of time" (p. 11, 137). He thus hypothesises that the "materialist interpretation of history and the materialist interpretation of geography are inseparably intertwined and theoretically concomitant, with no inherent prioritization of one over the other" (p. 130). Yet ironically where he lets the pose of the intellectual rebel get the better of him he seems to conform to the hegemonic silencing of questions regarding tendencies of historical change, of processes inhering as well as transcending the present.

insofar as it encourages a prioritisation of space over time and, if pushed to the limit, a drive towards a spatial reductionism that feeds into ideas of *posthistoire*.[12]

The purpose of this discussion cannot possibly be to do justice to the extremely complex debates in philosophy and the social sciences revolving around the problem of "space".[13] Our goal is more limited and specific, namely, to mark out major differences in historiographical uses of the term "space", theoretical choices between opposing and even irreconcilable conceptualisations that

---

Thus he insists that "space and geography may be displacing the primacy of time and history as the distinctive significant dimensions of the contemporary period" and points out as "the insistent premise and promise of postmodern geographies" that "it may be space more than time that hides consequences from us", the "making of geography" more than the "making of history" that provides the most revealing tactical and theoretical world", p. 11, 137, 130, 73, 92–93; also see Soja, "The Postmodernization of Geography: A Review", *Annals of the Association of American Geographers* 77, no. 2, 1987, 289.

[12] Robert Dodgshon argues in a perceptive essay that the notion of a compression or convergence of time and space has induced protagonists of the "spatial turn" to reduce temporality to spatiality. This reduction fails, however, to take account of particularities of social time (such as irreversibility and tendency), and thus feeds into concepts of *posthistoire* by severing the past from the present. Dodgshon shows that elements of this reductionism can be found even in Henri Lefebvre's work. These elements may permit an appropriation of Lefebvre's theory of social space by writers operating within the frame of postmodern life philosophy. Yet I would argue that they may also be considered at variance with the irreducible temporality of the concept of *production* as used and developed by Lefebvre in respect of social space. A systematic analysis of contradictions in Lefebvre's work would no doubt be an important contribution to the further development of concepts of "social space", but is far beyond the scope of this study. Robert A. Dodgshon, "Human Geography at the End of Time? Some Thoughts on the Notion of Time–Space Compression", *Environment and Planning D: Society and Space* 17, no. 5, 1999, 607–20.

[13] The standard account of the history of "space" as a philosophical problem clarifies that no simple conceptual homogeneity can be assumed—neither before nor after Newton. See Alexander Gosztonyi, *Der Raum: Geschichte seiner Probleme in Philosophie und Wissenschaften*, 2 vols. (Freiburg/Munich: Alber, 1976). The range of "absolutistic" and "relativistic" sociological conceptualisations of space is outlined and discussed in Löw, *Raumsoziologie*, 17–68. For a discussion of geographical debates on "space" in their philosophical and sociological context, see Soja, *Postmodern Geographies*, 10–156.

are necessarily (though not always consciously) made as soon as a historian approaches problems of social space. The present study has no use for either the reified (suitcase-like) or the subjectivist concepts of space. Rather it seeks to proceed from a dialectical understanding of space as a dynamic as well as a unitary (yet by no means homogenous) phenomenon. Moreover, the point is not to "spatialise" history by tipping the scales between time and space in favour of the latter, but to appreciate the spatiality of historical processes. In pursuing this objective one can certainly draw on earlier historiographical currents (and particularly on the work of historians associated with the "Annales school").[14] For the purposes of this study, however, it has proved more rewarding to transgress academic boundaries and to engage with the intense debates among philosophers and social geographers on concepts of "space" since the 1970s. The works of Henri Lefebvre and David Harvey, both proceeding from readings of Marx, have been used in particular— 'used' in the sense that they have been quarried freely and most irreverently for conceptual "building blocks" appropriate to the task at hand, without necessarily submitting to the theoretical architecture of these works.[15]

[14] A more influential current in recent European historiography seems content, however, with critically reviewing and reinventing the "geopolitical" approaches on history that were initiated by Mackinder and Ratzel—a current that has little to offer for the objective of this study. For a competent summary of this trend, see Jürgen Osterhammel, "Die Wiederkehr des Raumes: Geopolitik, Geohistorie und historische Geographie", *Neue Politische Literatur* 43, no. 3, 1998, 374–95.

[15] The works found most useful for approaching the conceptual problem of "space" are the following: Lefebvre, *Production of Space*; David Harvey, *The Limits to Capital* (Oxford: Basil Blackwell, 1982); Harvey, *Condition of Postmodernity*; Harvey, *Spaces of Capital: Towards a Critical Geography* (Edinburgh: Edinburgh University Press, 2001). My disclaimer pertains especially to Lefebvre's *Production of Space* which is highly relevant at certain levels of conceptualisation that seem, however, separable from its larger philosophical objective of reconciling Marx with Nietzsche and historical materialism with vitalist philosophy, which is not my concern. Nor does the present study claim to exhaust the possibilities of utilising this iridescent and multilayered intellectual product for historiographical purposes. These possibilities are particularly striking in the field of urban studies as Janaki Nair demonstrates for South Asia in a recent study, Nair, *Promise of the Metropolis*.

As a result, the problem of 'social space' will be approached in this study by way of a conceptual framework that can be resolved into a sequence of *seven hypotheses*. In what follows, these hypotheses will be developed, juxtaposed against common colonial conceptualisations of space in the period under review and discussed according to their relevance for this study.

Hypothesis 1: Production

"Social space" is no neutral container of human society. Rather it is a set of objects and relations produced through social practice and, at the same time, a necessary condition for the realisation of further social practice. "Itself the outcome of past action," wrote Henri Lefebvre, "social space is what permits fresh actions to occur, while suggesting others and prohibiting yet others."[16] Every society generates "a social space to which that society is not identical, and which indeed is its tomb as well as its cradle".[17] These formulations may sound somewhat cryptic, even absurd, as "space" is often imagined to be some*thing* predating and containing all human activities. Natural space after all, predates human society and has no need for it. Yet, as socially organised humans appropriate natural space for purposes of production and reproduction, they create new spatial elements such as pathways and networks, villages and towns, markets and territories. These spatial elements are not simply 'things'—they are *at once* locatable objects and spatial relations. Social spaces are constituted through a complex of such relations—spatial relations that are inseparably integrated with relations between social groups, with property relations in general and relations of land control in particular.[18] In the

---

[16] Lefebvre, *Production of Space*, 73, 77.
[17] Ibid., 34.
[18] Ibid., 77, 81–85, 341–42, 402–3. This conceptualisation has the advantage of pointing out the "dynamic", relational aspect of social spaces without negating their "fixed", absolute aspect, that is, the qualities through which locatable objects acquire distinct identity. It helps to discern tensions that may be lost in the somewhat structuralist notion of a "radically relational production of particular spaces" (see Goswami, *Producing India*, 27) or in attempts to develop "relative, relational and decidedly non-substantialistic concepts of space". Alexander C. T. Geppert, Uffa Jensen and Jörn Weinhold, "Verräumlichung. Kommunikative Praktiken in historischer Perspektive, 1840–1930", in *Ortsgespräche. Raum und Kommunikation im 19. und 20.*

course of historical development less and less unclaimed natural space is available; already 'socialised' spaces must be appropriated again and are thus remoulded and reorganised. Natural space does not disappear but is overlaid by an expanding and increasingly multilayered social space (see hypothesis 3) as each society appropriates this space to its needs.

Social space was, according to Lefebvre, *produced* rather than 'created' or 'worked out' (or, one might add, 'constructed') because the term "production" emphasised the integration of these spatial processes with more general processes of social production and reproduction. Moreover, the notion of a "produced" space captures more of the potential seriality or rigidly scheduled industrial repetitiveness this process took on from the mid-nineteenth century onwards in the context of an increasingly pervasive capitalist economy (see hypothesis 7). While the term "production" thus clearly refers to material dimensions of spatial processes, which the discursive constructivism of the present trend of "spatially turned" historical writing tends to blind out, the concept is not, as Lefebvre argues and demonstrates, to be understood in a narrow economic sense.[19]

If the "production of space" is an abstraction, it is one that is easily rendered concrete when used, for instance, as a methodological vantage point for investigating the history of transport. Roads are thus, as Fernand Braudel observed, no mere ribbons unrolled over land. In other words, neither overland nor sea routes should be understood as lines cutting across empty space, but rather as

---

Jahrhundert, ed. idem (Bielefeld: Transcript-Verlag, 2005), 19. It seems also preferable to Martina Löw's definition of space as a relational alignment ("(An-)Ordnung") of creatures and social goods, which is coupled with the concept of "placement" ("Plazierung" [*sic*]) that suggests external agency rather than internal dynamics. Löw, *Raumsoziologie*, 154 and passim.

[19] Lefebvre, *Production of Space*, 68–77. Also see Roland Boer, *The Sanctuary and the Womb: Henri Lefebvre and the Production of Space*, http://www.cwru.edu/affil/GAIR/papers/2000papers/Boer.html. In Lefebvre's distinction between "work" (oeuvre) and "product" there may also be, as Neil Brenner suggests, echoes of Heidegger's philosophy. Though this line of thought may deserve further exploration (and critique), "production" is here exclusively used as an analytical concept in the sense developed above. Cf. Neil Brenner, "Global, Fragmented, Hierarchical: Henri Lefebvre's Geographies of Globalization", *Public Culture* 10, no. 1, 1997, 158, footnote 39.

networks constituting, conditioning and remoulding social space: they require and imply the interaction of economic, political and cultural institutions in a broad sense—including the social arrangements underlying ports and towns, fairs and markets, pilgrimages and festivals, caravanserais and mail services, toll stations and police posts. Braudel quoted Lucien Febvre's dictum: "la Méditerranée, ce sont des routes", which could be extended by saying that every social space is constituted by its traffic routes, by the circulatory movement on these routes and, more generally, through the totality of its spatial practices.[20]

For the specific purposes of this study, the concept of "social space" is, furthermore, a useful device for a critical evaluation of the ideas of space prevailing in relevant metropolitan, colonial as well as nationalist sources. The rise of railways and steam shipping in the nineteenth century did not only entail what has justly been called a revolution of the transport system, but has also contributed crucially towards the transformation of social space. The (Euro-American bourgeois) experience of this transformation found its standard expression in the emphatic phrase of an "annihilation of space and time"—a phrase that has returned with a vengeance in our own lifetime of electronic telecommunications.[21] "Space", in this understanding, was a void between places that was now being closed, an obstructive emptiness subject to elimination. It had no properties, in this sense except homogenous, unchangeable emptiness, and was thus considered a 'given', a plain fact—not a process.

This understanding of space informed British views of the Indian transport infrastructure in particular ways. Hence G. W. MacGeorge, a former high-ranking official of the colonial Public Works Department (PWD), claimed in 1894 that the British had found a tabula rasa—(consisting of "vast roadless plains, stupendous mountains and

---

[20] Fernand Braudel, *La Méditerranée et le monde méditerranéen à l'époque de Philippe II* (Paris: Colin, 1949), 238–39.

[21] Wolfgang Schivelbusch, *Geschichte der Eisenbahnreise: Zur Industrialisierung von Raum und Zeit im 19. Jahrhundert* (Frankfurt a.M.: Fischer-Taschenbuch-Verlag, 2004 [1st ed. 1977]), 35–42; Duncan S. A. Bell, "Dissolving Distance: Technology, Space, and Empire in British Political Thought, 1770–1900", *Journal of Modern History* 77, 2005, 554–55; Löw, *Raumsoziologie*, 10. For a critical historical assessment of the contemporary discourse, see Rainer Fischbach, *Mythos Netz* (Zürich: Rotpunktverlag, 2005), 22–29, 127–31, 156–65, 206–23. Also see hypothesis 5.

almost impassable rivers")—on which they could engrave a new pattern of circulation at will—constrained only by an as yet untamed nature and lack of funds. He stated explicitly that

> in the whole history of governments—not excluding that of ancient Rome—no alien ruling nation has ever *stamped on the face* [emphasis added] of a country more enduring material monuments of its activity than England has done, and is doing, in her great Indian dependency.[22]

The same sense of spatial blankness was conveyed by William Thornton, a close associate of John Stuart Mill and Secretary to the India Office's PWD, who declared in the early 1870s that the British found India "as trackless as Britain was before the Roman invasion" but "rendered it in most directions as permeable as England was in the early part of the Georgian era".[23] Sir John Strachey, one of the foremost Victorian administrators of *British India*, also held that "[b]efore the establishment of our Government there was hardly a road deserving the name."[24] This official perception of a passive, motionless Indian space, a space abandoning itself as a white canvas or as a surface of soft and even clay to the creative will of the coloniser, had two major implications for colonial spatial practice in South Asia. First, the aim of creating new transport infrastructures was, in this view, "to open up the country"—a phrase repeated with monotonous frequency in colonial documents since at least the

---

[22] MacGeorge, *Ways and Works*, 1, 293. This book is still the most comprehensive historical account of nineteenth-century 'public works' in India. The quoted assertions have been accepted uncritically even by post-colonial Indian authors. For example, see Srivastava, *Transport Development in India*, 242.

[23] William T. Thornton, *The Economic Writings of William Thornton,* ed. Philip Mirowski and Steven Tradewell (London: Pickering & Chatto, 1999), 5: 334. The work is quoted from, William Thomas Thornton, *Indian Public Works, and Cognate Indian Topics* (London, 1875). <http://copac.ac.uk/wzgw?id=08101619bd8f823705b3b6913bca722a84e83e&field=ti&terms=Indian%20Public%20Works,%20and%20Cognate%20Indian%20Topics>

[24] John Strachey, *India: Its Administration and Progress*, 4th ed. (London, 1911 [1st ed. 1888]), rev. by T. W. Holderness, 231. The quoted work, originating from a series of Cambridge lectures, remained on the elementary reading list of aspiring colonial administrators for decades. Also see Strachey and Strachey, *Finances and Public Works of India*, 2; David Arnold, *Science, Technology and Medicine in Colonial India*, New Cambridge History of India III.5 (Cambridge: Cambridge University Press, 2000), 107; Goswami, *Producing India*, 47.

1840s. The task of prising open what was deemed to be a wild and barbarian space external to the space of 'civilisation' was usually couched in the idioms of military logistics, classical political economy and social reform though explicitly religious overtones are also discernible.[25] Apart from contributing to colonial legitimacy, this ideological naturalisation of Indian space also had implications for spatial practices. Earlier social productions of space were often ignored or discounted. In official accounts, precolonial transport facilities were usually dealt with summarily. "Roads in the modern sense", wrote MacGeorge, "were practically unknown in India, until a comparatively very recent period."[26] The second implication of the prevailing colonial conception of an *empty* Indian space was a tendency, especially in the mid-nineteenth century, towards a (sometimes fatal) abstraction from the particularities of natural space in India when new "built environments" (namely roads and canals) were planned. We will return to these points in hypotheses 3 and 4.

[25] These arguments were brought forward with particular force in numerous British publications of the 1840s and 1850s with a view to propagating railway construction in India. See, for instance, the following pamphlets: "H.O.", *Railways in India, Being Four Articles Reprinted from the Railway Register for July, August, September, and November, 1845* (London: Madden & Malcolm, 1845), 3–5; William P. Andrew, *Indian Railways and their Probable Results ..., by an old Indian Postmaster* (London: T. C. Newby, 1848 [1st ed. 1846]), 6–38; Rowland M. Stephenson, *Railways: An Introductory Sketch with Suggestions in Reference to their Extension to British Colonies* (London: John Wale, 1850), 7, 68; John Chapman, *The Cotton and Commerce of India, Considered in Relation to the Interests of Great Britain: with Remarks on Railway Communication in the Bombay Presidency* (London: John Chapman, 1851), 178–79, 211–2; John Chapman, *Principles of Indian Reform: Being Hints together with a Plan for the Improvement of the Constituency of the East India Company, and for the Promotion of Indian Public Works,* 2nd ed. (London, 1853), 10, 19–22. The classical phrasing of the military-cum-economic argument for railways is the famous minute of Lord Dalhousie, former president of the British Board of Trade, then Governor-General of India: Lord Dalhousie, Minute to the Court of Directors of the East India Company, 20 April 1853, reprinted in *Railway Construction in India: Select Documents, 1853–1873,* ed. S. Settar and Bhubanes Misra (New Delhi: Northern Book Centre/Indian Council of Historical Research, 1999), 2: 23–57. Also see Thorner, *Investment in Empire,* 1–12. Various renderings of these arguments in the context of colonial Orissa will be discussed in subsequent chapters.

[26] MacGeorge, *Ways and Works,* 65.

Hypothesis 2: Conflict

Social space is produced, reproduced and transformed through the spatial practices of conflicting social interests. The idea of an immutable space, so long prevalent in European thought, implied an intrinsic, equally immutable order of this space. Ernst Bloch pointed at the stark ideological overtones of such conceptualisations. *Ruhend gesetzter Raum*, "space set to rest", fed into notions of a preordained and unquestionable place for each and all, into the assumption of a fixed social order and, consequently, into apologies of domination.[27] In contrast, our first hypothesis, by stating that space is produced and reproduced (and thus in perpetual movement), implies the existence of identifiable *producers* of social spaces and places. The second hypothesis proceeds from this point and proposes that the totality of social relations must be considered the moving power of social spatiality. In other words, since every act of social practice has a spatial dimension, all social groups contribute in varying proportions (according to their social resources) and in conflicting ways (affected though not mechanically determined by their interests) to the social space of their time. Social space is, therefore, at every point in time bound up with contradictory constellations of social groups; it is resource and product of historical forms of social domination and, at the same time, precondition and result of the limitations of these forms.

Colonial "representations of space",[28] that is, the conceptualisation of space informing the spatial practices of the colonial administration, could not have been more different. Hence the creation of a 'good' transport infrastructure was considered an incontestable boon for an imagined all-embracing 'public'. The following quote is from a pamphlet propagating the construction of railways in India

---

[27] Bloch, *Experimentum Mundi*, 108. Also see David Harvey, "Between Space and Time: Reflections on the Geographical Imagination", *Annals of the Association of American Geographers* 80, no. 3, 1990, 419.

[28] The term "representations of space" (alternatively: "conceived space") is here used as defined by Lefebvre (*Production of Space*, 38–39): "conceptualized space, the space of scientists, planners, urbanists, technocratic subdividers and social engineers, as of a certain type of artist with a scientific bent—all of whom identify what is lived and what is perceived with what is conceived. ... This is the dominant space in any society (or mode of production)."

that was published in London and saw several editions in the late 1840s. It is characteristic of what was asserted until the end of our period by British entrepreneurs and officials both in England and India:

> The state of internal communication of a country then, bears a direct relation to, and is co-equal with, the progress of its people in general[,] improvement, good roads and other means of transit being the infallible signs—because the certain consequences—of civilization—as their absence or imperfection proves the reverse in a greater or less degree. 'Let us travel,' says the Abbé Raynal, 'over all the countries of the earth, and wherever we find no facility of travelling from a city to a town, or from a village to a hamlet, we may pronounce the people to be barbarians.' Sir Henry Parnell, in his admirable 'Treatise on the formation &c., of Roads,' makes the following forcible remark—'The making of roads, in point of fact, is fundamentally essential [sic], to bring about the first change that every rude country must undergo, in emerging from a condition of poverty and barbarism.'[29]

Those who opposed colonial efforts to transform social space by way of constructing roads, railways, canals or other forms of 'built environment' could thus be (and actually were) decried as being "demi-civilized", "uneducated" and "bigoted"—in short, as being irrational.[30] The "general interest" argument found supporters among influential and vocal circles of the Indian middle classes even before the commencement of a more energetic 'public works' policy in the 1850s.[31] Yet by the first decade of the twentieth century

---

[29] Andrew, *Indian Railways and Their Probable Results*, 27–28.

[30] For a typical statement, see Oriental and India Office Collections (henceforth OIOC), Government of Bengal, Public Works Proceedings (henceforth BPWP) December 1862, P/16/59, Com., no. 95, 85 (T. Armstrong, Superintending Engineer (henceforth SE), Cuttack Circle, to Offg. Chief Engineer (henceforth CE) Bengal, 15 November 1862). See also chapters 4, 5 and 8, in this study.

[31] See, for instance, the statements of "Baboo Mutty Loll Seal" and "Baboo Ram Ghopaul Ghose" in Rowland M. Stephenson, *Report upon the Practicability and Advantages of the Introduction of Railways into British India ...*, (London: Kelly & Co., 1845), 35–37. Also see Dipesh Chakrabarty, "The Colonial Context of the Bengal Renaissance: A Note on Early Railway-Thinking in Bengal", *Indian Economic and Social History Review* 11, no. 1, 1974, 92–111; Bipan Chandra, *The Rise and Growth of Economic Nationalism in India: Economic Policies of Indian National Leadership, 1880–1905* (New

the early proponents of an Indian economic nationalism had effectively made their point that British railway policy in India emanated not so much from an improving universalism than from particular British interests. They refuted the claim that the prevailing regime of free trade with its concomitant spatial practices resulted from the "natural laws" of the economy and were, therefore, without alternative.[32] However, they replaced it, as Manu Goswami argues, with the assertion of a territorially bounded and supposedly organic national economy that required a specific economic policy (including 'public works') according to a supposedly unitary "national interest".[33] Economic nationalism aspired to "the nationalization of capital, not its abolition" and, accordingly, the nationalisation, not discontinuation, of state-based development policies (including 'public works') "as there could be no 'going back to barbarism . . . that will not aid national growth'".[34] As Dadabhai Naoroji put it: "We do pray to our British rulers, let us have railways and all other kinds of beneficial public works by all means, but let *us* have their natural benefits, or talk not to a starving man of the pleasures of a fine dinner."[35] Nationalists conceived an equally homogenised and naturalised national space that had no place, either for social conflict over spatial practice within the nation. Many Indian intellectuals, whether tending more to the loyalist or to the nationalist poles of the

---

Delhi: People's Publishing House, 1966), 179–80 (especially footnote 20); Kerr, "Representation and Representations", 302–4.

[32] G. Subramania Iyer thus specifically refuted the assertion that the priority on railway construction was the inescapable consequence of "natural advantages", of "the ordinance of nature . . . that England must export her manufacture to India and India must export her raw materials". G. Subramania Iyer, *Economic Aspects of British Rule in India* (Delhi: Gian Publishing House, 1988), 274–75. For detailed evidence, see Chandra, *Rise and Growth of Economic Nationalism*, 171–216, Goswami, *Producing India*, 104, 212–15.

[33] Goswami, *Producing India,* 220–24, 231–32. Also see Kerr, "Representation and Representations", 304–6.

[34] Goswami, *Producing India*, 273–76, Goswami quotes the Bengali nationalist politician Bipan Chandra Pal; also see Manu Goswami, "From Swadeshi to Swaraj: Nation, Economy, Territory in Colonial South Asia, 1870 to 1907", *Comparative Studies in Society and History* 40, no. 4, 1998, 628.

[35] Dadabhai Naoroji, *Poverty and Un-British Rule in India* (New Delhi: Publications Division, Ministry of Information and Broadcasting, Govt. of India, 1996 [1st ed. 1901]), 172.

ideological continuum, were consequently embarrassed by and suspicious of hostile attitudes among the subordinated classes against colonial spatial practices. Consider, for instance, the irritation among middle-class Oriyas when the construction in the late 1890s, of the East Coast Railway for which they had campaigned for decades, met with widespread popular resentment expressing itself in the elusive (and therefore effective) premodern form of political rumour. An Oriya newspaper thus reported in 1896:

> The construction and progress of rail roads in Orissa have led some mischievous people to invent a rumour to the effect that Government wants a certain number of men and women to be offered up as human sacrifices to the deities that preside over the rivers that are to be bridged over and the mountains that are to be crossed, as those deities can never be propitiated without human blood. The rumour has found such a wide circulation in all the districts of Orissa, that it is noticed by all the native papers of that Province. It has gone so far that the very name of a railway creates a shudder in the mind of the commonest peasant in Orissa. The accidental death of an English Engineer in the Mahanadi and the disappearance of some railway coolies in the Puri district gave rise to the rumour, which was easily swallowed by the credulous, and ingeniously propagated by the mischievously disposed. The District Magistrate of Cuttack and other officers of Government as also the editors of the native papers have taken timely steps to disabuse the mind of the people of this false notion, which is disappearing day by day.[36]

Hostility against spatial practices of the colonial oligarchy and its Indian associates that amounted to expropriation (that is, closing spaces to plebeian use) and disgust at the desecration of social space through industrially built environments (cf. hypothesis 4) were thus generally dismissed as 'mischief', ignorance or irrationality. Specific reasons for such opposition very rarely became a matter of public debate, though they were (as we shall see) extensively recorded in the official correspondence of the engineers overseeing 'public works'. Transport infrastructure, the aspect of spatial practice we are here mainly concerned with, was thus, in its concrete historic form, *result and means of social domination*: it privileged dominant conceptions of space and fortified dominant interests, while discounting and undermining those of the subordinated.

---

[36] Samvadvahika (Baleshwar), 28 May 1896, quoted in *Report on Native Newspapers, Bengal* (henceforth *RNNB*), 18 July 1896, 702.

However, the production of social space cannot be reduced to a simple zero-sum game. Social space can only be brought under control to a certain degree—its structures always contain unresolved contradictions, a multilayered historical inheritance never fully appreciated and exhausted by the forces of the present, tendencies pointing beyond current constellations of social domination.[37] For this reason, it is indispensable but not fully sufficient to identify marks of hierarchy when analysing spatial practice in colonial India.[38] We also need to take notice of elements of ambiguity that are to be found, most visibly, in the *polyvalence* of built environments. This means simply that the same transport infrastructure may be appropriated for various purposes, which may reinforce, deflect or contradict each other. The most obvious (though not yet systematically explored) example for the last case is that the Indian railway and telegraph system achieved its designers' explicit objective of improving military logistics only at the cost of exacerbating the problem they tried to solve in the first place. If colonial control over the subcontinent was increased by the railways and the telegraph, so were the possibilities of transcending earlier geographical limitations of opposing British rule, for example, through the creation of a "national public".[39]

Yet a social history of transport will have to look at the phenomenon of polyvalence not only at the level of national politics, but also at various, interpenetrating regional and local, socioeconomic and cultural levels. The practical importance of this polyvalence of infrastructure is evident even at the level of the quotidian practices

---

[37] See hypotheses 3 and 6.

[38] This is what Manu Goswami's somewhat unidimensional discussion of railways amounts to—they are represented (with good reason) as colonial (and post-colonial) means of producing a homogenous as well as hierarchical social space, while ignoring that they simultaneously provided an infrastructure for spatial practices undermining these hierarchies. Goswami, *Producing India*, 103–31.

[39] The appropriation of the railways and the telegraph for purposes of nationalist or other social movements and the role of railway stations in the "geography of protest" seems evident, but has so far not been explored systematically. See Kerr, Introduction, 60–61. For evidence on the utilisation of the telegraph for mobilising strikes across British India, see Lajpat Jagga, "Colonial Railwaymen and British Rule: A Probe into Railway Labour Agitation in India, 1919–1922", *Studies in History* 3, nos. 1–2, 1981, 121–23.

employed by the labouring poor to secure their subsistence. Such practices were, for instance, recorded when conflicts arose over what could be called 'marginal uses' of transport infrastructure by inhabitants of neighbouring villages. Let us digress for a moment to take a closer look at one particular controversy in Orissa's Mahanadi Delta—the practice of fishing in the roadside drains. In this region, ditches of the main ('trunk') roads had to be deep and capacious as massive road dams were constructed under British supervision to protect such lines of communication from regularly occurring inundations. When the waters of the Mahanadi drained off after swamping large parts of the extensive delta region, rich stocks of fish were left behind in these ditches. Villagers rendered this unplanned side-effect of 'scientific road construction' into a source of subsistence. Catching fish with the help of *bunds* (flood embankments) had been a traditional practice in which local magnates partook by levying a *jalkar* (fishing tax). In order to facilitate fishing and with the backing of *zamindars* (various types of local rulers) villagers 'cut' road drains accordingly, that is, divided them into sections, thereby impeding the drainage of the road and damaging its embankment.[40]

The point here is not merely that the spatial practice of constructing raised and metalled roads created numerous conflicting possibilities for their appropriation and myriads of struggles over the use-right of what was, from different points of view, state land, a source of revenue for local magnates or, a commons. An

---

[40] Orissa State Archives, Bhubaneswar (henceforth OSA), Cuttack Division, Board of Revenue Loose Records (henceforth BoRLR) 26, 943 ("injury inflicted on the road by zamindars and others on account of fisheries", 1856); ebd., 26,945 ("correspondence regarding fisheries on the drain on the Jagannath Road", 1856); ebd., 26,946 ("measures for suppressing the practice of bunding and fishing in the road khalls", 1856); OIOC, BPWP December 1870, P/432/60, Com., nos. 21–3, 26–28. For bund fishing and the imposition of local taxes upon fishing, see William W. Hunter, *The Annals of Rural Bengal: Orissa* (London: Smith, Elder & Co., 1872), 3: 233–34; ibid., Appendix, 4, 36, 119–20; Biswamoy Pati, *Resisting Domination: Peasants, Tribals and the National Movement in Orissa, 1920–50* (Delhi: Manohar, 1993), 5; Rohan D'Souza, "Colonialism, Capitalism and Nature: Debating the Origins of Mahanadi Delta's Hydraulic Crisis (1803–1928)", *Economic and Political Weekly* 37, no. 13, 2002, 1261–72; Rohan D'Souza, "Canal Irrigation and the Conundrum of Flood Protection: The Failure of the Orissa Scheme of 1863 in Eastern India", *Studies in History* 19, no. 1, 2003, 52. For further cases in point see chapters 5–7.

understanding of the very concrete issues of conflict over social space—the utilisation of road drains no less than the distribution of newspapers—and of the field of force resulting from the totality of these conflicts is required to avoid the conflation of dominant spatial norms with socio-spatial practice.

Hypothesis 3: Historicity

Social space cannot, in its entirety, be eradicated and newly invented according to the will of even the most powerful social forces. The space of the present is interlaced with spaces of the past, the latter are thus overlaid, reorganised, transformed. The historicity of social space manifests itself, therefore, in its increasingly complex and multilayered structure. In Lefebvre's graphic words, the structure of social space was "far more reminiscent of a flaky mille-feuille pastry than of the homogenous and isotropic space of classical (Euclidean/Cartesian) mathematics."[41] Earlier spatial structures were dominated, partly destroyed, partly enhanced, in any case re-contextualised and thereby charged with new social content. Yet "[n]o space ever vanishes utterly, leaving no trace"—the creation of closed, historically unconditioned spatial systems was thus precluded.[42]

One important implication of this is that the numerous *scales*, on which spatial practice came to realise itself over long historical periods (for eample, the local, the regional, the supraregional), were suspended neither by the emergence of that new type of territorial scale, the colonial state, nor by that increasingly global scale of social practice called the 'world market'. Earlier scales were rather remoulded, reorganised and interwoven into a dynamic hierarchy of spatial scales. "No space," wrote Lefebvre, "disappears in the course of growth and development: the *worldwide does not abolish the local*."[43] And he developed this supposition as follows:

> the *places* of social space are very different from that of natural space in that they are not simply juxtaposed: They may be intercalated, combined, superimposed—they may even sometimes collide. Consequently the local (or 'punctual', in the sense of 'determined by a particular

[41] Lefebvre, *Production of Space*, 86.
[42] Ibid., 164–65, 229.
[43] Ibid., 86, emphasis in the original.

'point') does not disappear, for it is never absorbed by the regional, national or even worldwide level. The national and regional levels take in innumerable 'places'; national space embraces the regions; and world space does not merely subsume national spaces, but even (for the time being at least) precipitates the formation of new national spaces through a remarkable process of fission.[44]

The heuristic potential of these observations for the study of modern Indian history is demonstrated by recent research.[45] The persistence of the *local* is, for instance, pointed out by Neeladri Bhattacharya in his fine micro-historical study of the peddling trade when he states "that the world market could not simply have established its domination from above, that it could not have incorporated rural areas into a network of international exchange by eliminating all 'traditional' structures and institutions."[46] Manu Goswami takes Lefebvre's hint at the "remarkable process of fission" as a point of departure when she argues that the "production of India" as a modern territorial entity was grounded in a dialectical process comprised of two interdependent and complementary tendencies—the "deterritorialising", homogenising drive towards world market expansion and the "reterritorialising", fracturing pressures towards a bounded colonial and subsequently national "state space".[47] Moreover, the dialectics of spatial scales were also perpetually articulated and rearticulated *within* the subcontinent's social space in numerous ways that merit closer examination: the transformation of networks of subregional, regional and interregional circulation, the ensuing redefinition of subregions and regions resulting in the reorganisation of spatial hierarchies.[48] Burton Stein's sophisticated *longue durée* analysis of the historical generation and transformation of the subregional spatial units (or scales) of the

[44] Lefebvre, *Production of Space*, 88, see also 90, 101.
[45] For a brilliant summary and discussion of Lefebvre's writings on scalar hierarchies in social space and their relevance for the study of modern societies, see Brenner, "Global, Fragmented, Hierarchical", 135–67.
[46] Neeladri Bhattacharya, "Predicaments of Mobility: Peddlers and Itinerants in Nineteenth-Century Northwestern India", in *Society and Circulation: Mobile People and Itinerant Cultures in South Asia, 1750–1950*, ed. Claude Markovits, Jacques Pouchepadass and Sanjay Subrahmanyam (Delhi: Permanent Black, 2003), 163.
[47] Goswami, *Producing India*, 14–17, 35–39, 66–72 and *passim*.
[48] Cf. Lefebvre, *Production of Space,* 112.

Tamil country *(nadu, periyanadu, mandalam)* demonstrated the explanatory scope of such approaches almost thirty years ago (without, unfortunately, inspiring much research on similar lines).[49] More recently, several empirical studies have indicated that these are core issues for social historians of colonial India, too, and the present study contributes to this corpus by investigating the effects of colonial infrastructure policies for the spatial realignment and reorganisation of the region of Orissa.[50]

While multilayered complexity thus provided concrete possibilities and means of structuring social space, it also set limits to the efforts of institutionalised social interests—even of the far-reaching institutions of the modern state—to shape it in their own image. It defined, in other words, the *measure* in which social space was subject to control and generated what Lefebvre called "differential space": space emerging from the contradictions of the structures of "social space", but exceeding these structures, bearing possibilities of future transformation.[51] The contradictions of these dominant structures of social space emerged both from their internal and external determinations. Since the nineteenth century, for instance, such contradictions have hence been generated—first, according to the dynamics of the social relationships embodied in capital (namely, their inherent tendency of creating 'spatial chaos' and "uneven development"; see hypothesis 6) and, secondly, from the irreducible historical particularities of the various scales of social space on which the trend towards the generalisation of these relationships acquired concrete shape. Turning to this latter aspect, we find that the multilayered temporal structure of a social space, the tensions between these 'layers' or, the specific synchrony of the non-synchronous in this space, delimit the scope for its control.

This observation is particularly relevant for our purposes. It directs our attention to the extreme unevenness in the transformation of transport infrastructure and, by implication, of social space in

---

[49] Burton Stein, "Circulation and the Historical Geography of Tamil Country", *Journal of Asian Studies* 37, no. 1, 1977, 7–26. There is no discernible direct connection between Stein's and Lefebvre's work. Related concerns led them apparently towards similar theorisations of socio-spatial practice.

[50] See especially Varady, "Rail and Road Transport", Ian D. Derbyshire, "Economic Change and the Railways in North India", *Modern Asian Studies* 21, no. 3, 1987, 521–45; Yang, *Bazaar India*.

[51] Lefebvre, *Production of Space*, 52, 62–63.

nineteenth- and early twentieth-century India. For this transformation was dramatic and incisive at some levels, no doubt, but gradual or even imperceptible at others and slow in its totality. The "transport revolution" of the age of railways and steamships, it is argued, rather superimposed itself upon older patterns of land and water transport than superseding them altogether.[52] This corresponds to Fernand Braudel's observation that events in the political foreground should not be exaggerated while studying the history of roads.[53] Yet it runs counter to most colonial accounts of India's transport history, which dismissed precolonial infrastructures as negligible and ascribed to foundational documents penned by charismatic colonial administrators (such as Dalhousie's "Minute on Railways" of 1853 or, in the case of Orissa, the report of the Parliamentary Commission on the 1866 famine) a quasi-magical capacity of making transport history.[54] This observation also points at a drawback of most studies of India's modern transport history, including recent ones: even historians who set out to critique self-congratulating colonial representations have almost always restricted themselves to the most recent 'layer', the 'surface' of Indian social space. *The Cambridge Economic History of India* is quite representative in this respect: railways are discussed in a substantial chapter as if they were a self-contained system or the single important element of the subcontinent's transport infrastructure, while other forms of overland traffic and the waterways are only referred to in passing.[55]

[52] This is particularly evident in the case of India's maritime shipping. While British concerns almost exclusively controlled the steamship sector up to the end of the colonial period, Indian owners of "traditional" sailing vessels succeeded in securing a (no doubt subordinated and less profitable) place for themselves in the shipping market and even expanded their businesses during the world wars. There is evidence that more seamen were recruited on India's western coast for such sailing vessels than for steamships as late as in the early 1940s. See Ahuja, "Lateinsegel und Dampfturbinen", 207–25.

[53] Fernand Braudel, *Sozialgeschichte des 15.-18. Jahrhunderts* (Munich: Kindler, 1990 [1st French ed.: *Civilisation matérielle, économie et capitalisme, XVe-XVIIIe siècle*, Paris: Colin, 1979]), 1: 456.

[54] For a critique of the assumed importance of the Orissa famine report for infrastructural policies in that region, see chapters 6 and 7. Lord Dalhousie, Minute to the Court of Directors of the East India Company, 20 April 1853, 2: 23–57.

[55] Kumar, *The Cambridge Economic History of India* (especially chapter VIII.2), Hurd, "Irrigation and Railways: Railways", 2: 737–61. Other modes of

Yet even in Bengal, a focus of Indian railway construction since the 1850s, precolonial modes of transport and most prominently the so-called 'country-boats' were not simply sunk in the region's extensive system of rivers when the first locomotive made its appearance. As late as in 1900, railways carried less than two-thirds of the total tonnage of Calcutta's trade and interestingly only about one-third of the tonnage of its grain trade.[56]

By disregarding such synchronies of the non-synchronous, social space is 'emptied out' and bereft of its history, sanitized of the accumulated accretions of a continuous process of human practice. Indian space as *conceived* by colonial administrators and engineers is confounded with spatial practice as a whole. Our task, then, is to unearth the multilayered structure of spatial practice revolving around the problem of transport and to reduce the steam technologies of transport from a *deus ex machina* to a historical phenomenon, which acquires and develops its concrete, differentiated and contradictory forms only in specific socio-spatial contexts.

Hypothesis 4: Relativity

While the "socialisation" of natural space is at once precondition and result of all historical forms of social practice, a tendency towards "relative" (or "abstract") space acquires predominance only after the advent of industrial capitalism. In early forms of human society, it is suggested, natural and social space coincide: society has no conceptual or practical

---

transport are, in fact, relegated to the chapters on regional economies up to 1857, of which Sabyasachi Bhattacharya, "Regional Economy (1757–1857): Eastern India" stands out by giving some attention to issues of transportation (271–73). After the advent of the railway, however, non-motorised modes of transport and their infrastructures do not seem to have had much impact on the development or underdevelopment of the 'modern economy' in India's history—according to the second volume of the *Cambridge Economic History of India*. For a more elaborate critique, see also this chapter's section on 'public works', later.

[56] Mukul Mukherjee, "Railways and Their Impact on Bengal's Economy, 1870–1920", *Indian Economic and Social History Review* 17, no. 2, 1980, 201–2. Even the author who provides these interesting figures is, however, exclusively interested in the transformative effects of the railways and treats traditional river transport as a mere residue, an inert background, without asking for the causes of its remarkable resilience.

autonomy from its particular location in nature; natural space is "absolute"[57] (or "concrete") in the sense that it is a heterogeneous aggregation of places (such as, for instance, hills, rivers and caves) imbued with religious and political meaning or, in other words, invested with absolute and concrete social qualities. Lefebvre argues that the emergence of the town–country split, of commodity production and circulation as well as of the state account for a *tendency* towards abstraction from these qualities of space and thus towards relationality (though the old absolute space was never totally annihilated, but rather superimposed upon; see hypothesis 3). This tendency derived from an increasing though always relative autonomy of spatial practice from natural location (the creation by society of a 'second nature', for example, the town) and, moreover, from a growing practical preponderance of *relations* between locations (centre–periphery, distance, travelling time, etc.) over absolute (natural or social) qualities of these locations. Harvey illustrates this idea by pointing at the transformation of European cartography since the fifteenth century, where abstraction from the sensual perception of particular places and their specific qualities permitted the conceptualisation of space as a neutral grid of parallels and meridians for measuring quantitative relations between places. The measurement and representation of spatial relations acquired new significance and was realised in various forms in the age of the formation of the early modern state and merchant capital—not solely in Europe, but also, for instance, in precolonial South Asia.[58] While

---

[57] It should be noted that "absoluteness" indicates, in this context, not the Newtonian idea of an ontological independence of space but rather a determination of space through absolute, concrete qualities. See below.

[58] Harvey, *Condition of Postmodernity*, 243–54. South Asian precolonial modes of spatial measurement and cartography are a difficult and still under-researched field. Yet the present state of research suggests that (a) localities on maps were mostly arranged according to "importance" (that is, absolute, qualitative properties) and almost never according to scale (that is, relative, quantitative properties); (b) there are, however, road maps for military uses giving distances; (c) there are also cadastral and village maps systematically representing social relations within space; (d) European cartographic techniques were appropriated by Indian rulers since the seventeenth century. See Susan Gole, *Indian Maps and Plans from Earliest Times to the Advent of European Surveys* (New Delhi: Manohar, 1989), 13–15, 29–46; Joseph E. Schwartzberg, "South Asian Cartography", in *The History of Cartography*

abstract or relative space assumed even greater importance with the emergence of colonial empires, it rose to *dominance*, it is argued, only when merchant capitalism was replaced by industrial capitalism, that is, when capital came to control production directly. For the rise of abstract space was connected to the rise of abstract labour (that is, labour irrespective of its concrete qualities, reduced to a quantifiable, exchangeable commodity). Neil Smith explains this as follows:

> Insofar as we are concerned with the concrete labour process, our conception of space is essentially absolute. The particularity of labour implies the particularity of its spatial attributes. With abstract labour, however, the situation is different. The realization of abstract labour as value implies a spatially integrated system of commodity exchange, money relations, credit facilities, even the mobility of labour. This requires the construction of specific transportation and communication links between individual places of concrete production, and demands that we are able to conceive of space in relative as well as absolute terms. The integration of an erstwhile isolated place of production into a national or international economy, for example, does not alter its absolute location, but in the process of altering its relative location, this act of spatial integration also enhances the realization of abstract labour as value.[59]

As labour was separated from the soil and transformed into abstract labour, as the use-value of artefacts was rendered secondary to their exchange-value as commodities, as circulation became integrated with production, relative space, the homogenising space of the expanding markets, came to enfold and dominate absolute space and its heterogeneous structure of qualitatively defined places— absolute spaces became the "raw material for the production of relative space."[60] Relative (or abstract) space was thus, as it were, the spatial dimension of commodification and monetisation, of a process reducing all natural and social phenomena to quantifiable and exchangeable units. As an editorial in *The Times* on Indian railways

---

Cartography in the Traditional Islamic and South Asian Societies, vol. II, book 1, ed. J. B. Harley and David Woodward (Chicago/London: University of Chicago Press, 1992), 295–509, especially 400–9, 435–49; 507–8; Kapil Raj, "Circulation and the Emergence of Modern Mapping: Great Britain and Early Colonial India, 1764–1820", in *Society and Circulation*, ed. Markovits et al., 32–35, 43–45, 51–52.
[59] Smith, *Uneven Development*, 82.
[60] Ibid. 83.

put it in 1847, "[i]n the present dialect of mechanics, [geomorphic and climatic] difficulty means cost".[61] This process of conversion abstracted from use-value or material qualities, but also fed on them. The 'dominance' of abstract space thus did not imply the annihilation of concrete spaces with their particular qualities but rather that the impact of absolute spaces became increasingly dependent on their relative position in the matrix of abstract space. The generation of networks and infrastructures of transport is a concrete expression of the emergence of this matrix, a process Lucien Febvre seems to have sensed when he asked evocatively: "For, without routes and communications, how could men succeed in reconstructing, out of the debris of the natural units they have broken into pieces, homogenous ensembles to suit their convenience?"[62]

These theoretical considerations provide important clues for explaining why the transformation of South Asian social space was no immediate result of British rule in India, no necessary concomitant of the colonial state—based on a British coalition of merchant capitalists and aristocrats—that took shape in the second half of the eighteenth century. In fact, there is sufficient evidence to suggest that a qualitative change in the patterns and infrastructures of circulation characterising eighteenth-century India occurred decades later—in the case of Bengal, only after a century of British rule. Under the regime of the East India Company a negligible fraction of the government revenue was spent on infrastructure, existing roads were badly maintained and new projects were often political or military *ad hoc* measures that were soon abandoned.[63] While

---

[61] Editorial, *The Times,* 9 April 1847.
[62] Lucien Febvre, *A Geographical Introduction to History: An Introduction to Human Geography* (London et al.: Kegan Paul, 2003), 316.
[63] MacGeorge, *Ways and Works,* 80. A director of the East India Company admitted that even the so-called "New Road" that had been built in the late eighteenth century on the essential line of communication between Calcutta and Benares fell into disrepair after twenty-five years, while its more recent extension to Allahabad was likewise "very much neglected". Henry St. G. Tucker, *Memorials on Indian Government,* ed. John William Kaye (London: Bentley, 1853), 425–26. As late as in the early 1870s, a critic of the 'public works' policy in India could claim: "I never yet saw a road really properly kept up in India. They are made and too often allowed to go to ruin before anything is done." Frederick Tyrell, *Public Works Reform in India* (London: Edward Bumpus, 1873), 42. Also see Yang, *Bazaar India,* 33–43;

high-ranking colonial officials felt that roads were unnecessary and had already been made in Bengal at a "vast and disproportionate expense",[64] Lord Bentinck, the utilitarian Governor-General (1828–1835), remarked: "I really believe that there is not one middle-sized county in England, in which there is not more laid out on general improvement per year, than all the three Presidencies put together."[65] Yet even after the reforms implemented under his governorship in 1834 less than £1.5 million were spent on 'public works' in the course of fourteen years—slightly more than 0.5 percent of the revenue.[66] In 1858, a member of the Institution of Civil Engineers was quoted with the following blunt statement:

---

chapters 5 and 6 of the present study and, for details of 'public works' expenditure, footnote 66 in this chapter.

[64] Tucker, *Memorials on Indian Government*, 427 (quoting the opinion of Metcalfe and Blunt).

[65] Letter to Edward L. Ellenborough, President of the Board of Control, 5 November 1829, quoted in S. Ambirajan, *Classical Political Economy and British Policy in India* (Cambridge: Cambridge University Press, 1978), 249.

[66] Leland H. Jenks, *The Migration of British Capital to 1875* (London: Jonathan Cape, 1938 [1st ed. 1927]), 208. The precise figures given by Jenks are the following: £1,434,000 between 1834 and 1848 out of an average *annual* revenue of twenty million pounds. These figures seem to be based on examinations of the parliamentary Cotton Committee of 1848; also see "Parliamentary Intelligence, House of Commons" (23 June 1857), *The Times*, 24 June 1857 (speech by J. B. Smith). Lord Wharncliffe stated in 1851 that during the preceding twenty years the greatest annual expenditure on 'public works' had been £238,000 out of an annual revenue of sixteen [sic] million pounds: "Parliamentary Intelligence, House of Lords" (2 June 1851), *The Times*, 3 June 1851. Also see "Parliamentary Intelligence, House of Lords" (2 May 1853), *The Times*, 3 May 1853 (speech by the Earl of Aldemarle who stated that on average £266,751 had been spent in the course of the preceding thirteen years); Strachey and Strachey, *Finances and Public Work of India*, 86. For the Bengal Presidency, it was reported by a correspondent with *The Times* in 1841, that about 1 per cent of the revenue of the preceding twenty years had been spent on 'public works', while corresponding investments in the other presidencies were held to be considerably less. The "home government", that is, the authorities in Britain, were identified as the "grand opposer of all improvement in roads, canals and other great public works": See "China and India", *The Times*, 5 November 1841. As for the proportion of the Government of India's *expenditure* allocated to 'public works', it has been stated that it was "seldom more than two per cent" in the first half of the nineteenth century. Ambirajan, *Classical Political Economy*, 254.

On the subject of public works generally, all persons must agree with the Author in his regret that while 'money to any amount was always procurable for the purposes of war, and might have been as readily obtained for objects of public improvement' so little had been done during the last century. The one Grand Trunk Road, the Ganges Canal, and the Jumna [Jamuna] Canal were the only public works of importance, for the improvement and development of the resources of the country, which had been constructed during the British rule. In the matter of district roads, practically nothing had been done. In the district with which he was most familiar, the roads were actually in a worse condition than during the period of native rule; and relatively, comparing roads in Bengal with roads in England a hundred years ago and now, they were then much superior.[67]

Corresponding opinions were frequently voiced in the British public.[68] It was only after India came more comprehensively into the orbit of expanding capital and commodity markets that the transformation of its transport infrastructure turned from a discursive colonial practice into a material force, that a radical "reorganisation of space" (as David Sopher put it) was not only conceived of by the powerful few, but lived and experienced by the many.[69]

Yet the idea that the constitution of space was increasingly relational can also serve as an analytical tool for discerning and

[67] George B. Tremenhere, *On Public Works in the Bengal Presidency (with an Abstract of the Discussion upon the Paper)*, Excerpt Minutes of Proceedings of the Institution of Civil Engineers, vol. XVII, session 1857–58 (London: William Clowes & Sons, 1858), 45– 46. The quote is from the comment of one Mr Sibley who had been an East India Company engineer in Bengal. For a similar statement, see "China and India", *The Times*, 5 November 1841.

[68] "India: Private Correspondence", *The Times*, 5 November 1841; Speeches by Lord Wharncliffe and the Earl of Harrowey in the House of Lords, 2 June 1851, *The Times*, 3 June 1851 (Parliamentary Intelligence); Editorial, *The Times*, 4 May 1853; Speech by Lord Stanley in the House of Commons, 23 June 1857, *The Times*, 24 June, 1857. Also see L. S. S. O'Malley, "Mechanism and Transport", in *Modern India and the West: A Study of the Interaction of Their Civilizations*, ed. L. S. S. O'Malley (London: Oxford University Press, 1941), 235; Deloche, *Transport and Communication*, 1: 197.

[69] David Sopher, "The Geographic Patterning of Culture in India", in *An Exploration of India: Geographical Perspectives on Society and Culture*, ed. David Sopher (New York: Cornell University Press, 1980), 317–19; Also see B. R. Tomlinson, *The Economy of Modern India, 1860–1970*, New Cambridge History of India III.3 (Cambridge: Cambridge University Press, 1993), 55–56.

explaining the more particular phenomena we are concerned with in this study. The proliferation of relative space was not restricted to the colonial metropolises—Calcutta, Bombay, Madras—and to their immediate peripheries, but extended even, as we shall see, to the 'remotest' areas of the subcontinent such as the 'little kingdoms' in the mountainous interior of Orissa. This general process realised itself, however, in particular, divergent, even contradictory ways as relative space was superimposed on absolute spaces differing widely in their natural as well as social qualities and as the integration of these spaces into a wider relative space created a complex, heterogeneous and asymmetric structure. The theoretical exposition of a *systematic* link between abstract labour and abstract space does not, for instance, permit the mechanical conclusion that the proliferation of relations of wage labour and the development of transport infrastructure were synchronous *historical* processes across South Asia. In fact, the history of road construction in Orissa's princely states during the late nineteenth and early twentieth centuries suggests the opposite: the implementation of colonial 'public works' policies, in this region, paradoxically reinforced pre-capitalist coercive labour relations—particularly the recourse to *bethi* (corvée) labour (see chapter 8). The expansion of abstract space, thus needs to be studied historically for each concrete space not merely to satisfy the historians' predilection for complex and multi-shaded pictures but, more importantly, to disclose the concrete spatial disparities that were produced in the very process of spatial abstraction and homogenisation (see hypothesis 6).

The idea that abstract or relative space was superimposed on accumulated layers of natural and social space is also useful for explaining concrete attitudes of various social actors towards the new spatial practices of the age of industrial capitalism—attitudes that may otherwise be simply dismissed with the "enormous condescension of posterity".[70] Hence rumours of human sacrifices on railway construction sites, virulent not only in Orissa but also in other regions,[71] may be interpreted as an expression of the shock

---

[70] Edward P. Thompson, *The Making of the English Working Class* (London: Penguin, 1991 [1st ed. 1963]), 12.

[71] For Orissa, see hypothesis 2. A similar rumour was reported from the North Cachar Hills of Assam, where it was alleged by the local population, when

and disgust caused by 'abstracting' (or homogenising) spatial practices that sought to separate places from gods, denude space of its sacro-political meaning and erase all its accumulated qualities to place it like unstained graph paper on the drawing board of colonial engineering.

Conversely, the hypothesis of a tendency towards spatial abstraction helps to explain a colonial attitude that was particularly widespread in the early decades of the infrastructural transformation. This was the notion that spatial practice could more or less ignore particular natural or social configurations of the spaces concerned. If bureaucrats and engineers condemned the alignment of traditional roads along meandering rivers and watersheds by insisting on the exclusive rationality of the straight line,[72] if they felt that "[a]ll Deltas require essentially the same treatment" and that the delta of the Mahanadi was, therefore, to be subjected to a standardised scheme of irrigation works and commodified water management,[73] this attitude and its results reflected both the ongoing superimposition of abstract or relative space and its inextricable interdependence with its concrete or absolute underpinnings. Expanding capital and commodity markets made it both necessary and possible to apply

---

the Bengal–Assam Railway was constructed in the late 1890s, that Pashtun workers abducted toddlers to sacrifice them on the construction sites of tunnels or bridges. Arup K. Dutta, *Indian Railways, the Final Frontier: Genesis and Growth of the North-East Frontier Railway* (Guwahati: Northeast Frontier Railway, 2002), 144.

[72] MacGeorge, *Ways and Works*, 66–68; Deloche, *Transport and Communication*, 1: 115–16. Also see chapter 5 of the present study.

[73] Sir Arthur Cotton on the Mahanadi in 1858, quoted in: Christopher V. Hill, "Ideology and Public Works: 'Managing' the Mahanadi River in Colonial North India", *Capitalism, Nature, Socialism* 6, no. 4, 1995, 51, see also 52, 63–64; Rohan D'Souza, *Flood, Embankments and Canals: The Colonial Experience in Orissa, 1803–1928*, Nehru Memorial Museum and Library, Research-in-Progress Papers "History and Society", 3rd ser. no. 6 (Delhi: Centre for Contemporary Studies, 1996), 7–9, 13; D'Souza, "Colonialism, Capitalism and Nature", 1261–72; D'Souza, "Canal Irrigation and Conundrum of Flood Protection", 41–68; chapter 7 of the present study. For conceptual issues of colonial hydraulic engineering, also see David Gilmartin, "Models of Hydraulic Environment: Colonial Irrigation, State Power and Community in the Indus Basin", in *Nature, Culture, Imperialism: Essays on the Environmental History of South Asia*, ed. David Arnold and Ramachandra Guha (Delhi: Oxford University Press, 1996), 211–13.

greater resources and new technologies to the construction of transport (and irrigation) infrastructure and gain, thereby, greater practical autonomy from absolute qualities of natural space—for instance, from the alignment of watersheds. Yet road embankments washed away during the monsoon or the disastrous ecological and financial results of the Orissa Canal Scheme were very concrete reminders of the fact that though absolute space was conceptualised and acted upon as a tabula rasa, it could not actually be transformed into one. Moreover, as Rohan d'Souza argues, the case of the failed commodification of the Mahanadi delta's hydrology shows that the "production of nature in the image of capital" could be even less efficient in achieving a greater degree of freedom from nature than earlier non-commodified modes of water management.[74] "The notion of the instrumental homogeneity of space," noted Lefebvre, "is illusory—though empirical descriptions of space reinforce the illusion—because it uncritically takes the instrumental as a given." In other words: "Abstract space *is not* homogenous; it simply *has* homogeneity as its goal, its orientation, its 'lens.'"[75]

Hypothesis 5: Compression

The emergence of capitalist world markets and centralising territorial states implied a qualitative change in social time-space relations. One aspect of this change was what could be experienced as "time-space compression": a radical reconfiguration of social space by way of a transformation of the relative distances between its locations. We have already seen (in hypothesis 1) that the radical reconstitution of social space in the nineteenth century was typically verbalised by contemporary Anglo-American intellectuals as an "annihilation of space *and* time" (see ch 2, fn 21). Harvey and Smith have pointed out that Karl Marx preferred to pronounce an "annihilation of space *by* time" ("Vernichtung des Raums durch die Zeit")[76]—a phrase that was, it should be pointed

---

[74] D'Souza, "Canal Irrigation and Conundrum of Flood Protection", 66–67. Also see chapter 7, in this study.
[75] Lefebvre, *Production of Space*, 285, 287.
[76] Karl Marx, *Grundrisse: Foundations of the Political Economy (Rough Draft)*, trans. Martin Nicolaus (London: Penguin Books, 1973), 539; Karl Marx and Friedrich Engels, *Werke* (henceforth MEW), vol. 42, Karl Marx, Ökonomische Manuskripte 1857/1858 (Berlin: Dietz, 1983), 430. Also see Smith, *Uneven Development*, 93–95; Harvey, *Spaces of Capital*, 244–49.

out, more widely used in a German intellectual context, where dialectical figures of thought were more easily understood and accepted than elsewhere.[77] This latter phrase has the advantage of avoiding the eschatological tinge of the former, drawing attention instead to the interdependence of (social) space and time, to concrete changes in their relation, to the transformation of this 'timespace' *as history*, rather than *end* of history.[78] While social practice cannot change the absolute, physical distance between two locations, its spatial dimension also consists in reducing the 'energy input' required to cover physical distance. In other words, spatial practice creates differentials between absolute distance (measurable in length) and relative distance (measurable in transportation time and cost). Hence if we drew two maps of the same historical space, one displaying distances measured in length and the other showing distances measured in transportation time, the two maps would be disproportional for any historical constellation, not merely because of uneven geomorphic and climatic conditions but also due to social practices like the application of transport technologies or the construction of infrastructure. These disproportions changed but slowly over long historical periods (for reasons discussed in the following section on 'circulation') in both Europe and India, but were already heightened in the former region and especially in Britain by the infrastructural improvements of the second half of the eighteenth century.[79]

---

[77] Koselleck quotes, for instance, a corresponding paragraph from a German encyclopaedia published in 1838 (Brockhaus Conversations-Lexikon der Gegenwart). Reinhart Koselleck, *Zeitschichten Studien zur Historik* (Frankfurt a.M.: Suhrkamp, 2003 [1st ed. 2000]), 198. Heinrich Heine made a similar claim on occasion of the opening of the first French railway line in 1843: *Durch die Eisenbahnen wird der Raum getödtet, und es bleibt uns nur noch die Zeit übrig* ("Space is killed by the railways and only time remains with us", my translation); quoted in Geppert et al., "Verräumlichung", 31. Also see Nigel Thrift, "Transport and Communication, 1730–1914", in *An Historical Geography of England and Wales*, ed. Robert A. Dodgshon and R. A. Butlin (London: Academic 1990, 474, 484 (note 124).

[78] Cf. footnote 12 on page 23 of the present study.

[79] Thrift, "Transport and Communication", 454–60, 473–74; Philip S. Bagwell, *The Transport Revolution* (London: Routledge, 1988 [1st ed. 1974]), 1–20, 26–48; Simon P. Ville, *Transport and the Development of the European Economy, 1750–1918* (Houndmills/London: Macmillan, 1990), 14–29; Koselleck, *Zeitschichten*, 93–94.

Yet these disproportions were swiftly increased and thrown into sharp relief in the age of expanding world markets and centralising territorial states, with the enormous acceleration of communications and transport, with the concomitant dwindling of distances measured in transport time and also in cost. This process was (and still is) experienced, in Harvey's suggestive formulation, as "time–space compression".[80] On this experiential level, these changes were embodied in and, therefore, appeared to result from technology. The locomotive, the steamship and the telegraph, it was often said, annihilated distance—"brought together" "the ends of the world".[81] Correspondingly, much of the contemporary as well as historical literature deals with the process of spatial reconfiguration in heavily technicistic terms.[82] A different, more analytical perspective was provided by Marx who perceived these changes as rooted in the exigencies of capital accumulation: "the velocity of circulation, the *time* in which it is accomplished, is a determinant of ... how often capital can be realized in a given period of time, how often it can *reproduce* and *multiply* its value." The incessant drive towards accelerating turnover times of capital thus gave a much stronger incentive than earlier social relations to reduce distance to time: "the important thing ... is not the market's distance in space, but the speed—the amount of time—with which it can be reached." The ensuing acceleration was even more dramatic as it was coupled with a tendency towards spatial expansion:

> Thus, while capital must on one side strive to tear down every spatial barrier to intercourse, that is, to exchange, and conquer the whole world for its market, it strives on the other side to annihilate this space with time, that is, to reduce to a minimum the spent time in motion from one

---

[80] Harvey, *Condition of Postmodernity*, 239 and passim.

[81] The quote is from a speech by Lord J. Russell, quoted in Stephenson, *Railways: An Introductory Sketch*, 68.

[82] Ronald E. Robinson argues, for instance, that railway technology should be considered, in addition to political expansionism and the economics of capitalism, as the third quasi-autonomous driving power of imperialism: "the railroad was not only the servant but also the principal generator of informal empire; in this sense imperialism was a function of a railroad." Ronald E. Robinson, "Introduction: Railway Imperialism", in *Railway Imperialism*, ed. Clarence B. Davis and Kenneth E. Wilburn (New York et al.: Greenwood Press, 1991), 2.

place to another. The more developed capital, therefore, the more extensive the market over which it circulates, which forms the spatial orbit of its circulation, the more does it strive simultaneously for an even greater extension of the market and for greater annihilation of space by time.[83]

The ensuing process of "time-space compression" (see p. 50, fn 80) affected (in uneven proportions and contradictory ways) all spheres of social life and also all scales of social space, not only metropolitan locations of industrial enterprise and factory production. Regions like the cotton-growing districts of central India, where industrial capital was virtually non-existent in the mid-nineteenth century, were thus linked up with Britain's industrial cities via fast-growing railway junction towns and the booming colonial metropolises of Calcutta, Bombay and Madras, all of them on or near the subcontinent's coastline. The intensification of communication and transport between these nodal points is well researched and does not require lengthy repetition. A few indicators will, therefore, suffice: technology (motorised shipping) and infrastructure (especially the Suez Canal) facilitated the reduction of travelling time between London and Calcutta from somewhere between five and eight months in the early nineteenth century to two weeks before World War I.[84] In 1900, 65 per cent of the railways of Asia (excluding Russia) were located in India—almost 39,000 route kilometres. Meanwhile, the world's fourth largest railway network employed 380,000 people, carried nearly 183 million passengers and 43 million tons of goods, often at a speed of 650 kilometres per day.[85] The reduction of freight rates extended "time–space" compression to the sphere of bulk trade: "By 1930–31 freight prices by rail per ton kilometre were 94 per cent less than prices per ton kilometre for pack-bullocks in 1800–40 and 88 per cent less than charges per ton

---

[83] Marx, *Grundrisse*, 538–39. For a systematic theoretical exposition and discussion of Marx's observations on the spatiality of capital, see Harvey, *Spaces of Capital*, 237–66.
[84] Robert Kubicek, "British Expansion, Empire, and Technological Change", in *The Oxford History of the British Empire: The Nineteenth Century*, ed. Andrew Porter (Oxford: Oxford University Press, 1999), 3: 255; Daniel R. Headrick, *The Tentacles of Progress: Technology Transfer in the Age of Imperialism, 1850–1940* (New York/Oxford: Oxford University Press, 1988), 20.
[85] Kerr, Introduction, 1–4; Hurd, "Railways", 745; Tomlinson, *Economy of Modern India*, 55; MacGeorge, *Ways and Works*, 422.

kilometre for bullock-carts in 1840–60".[86] These were not merely changes in quantity. Time–space compression permitted the circulation of commodities, capital and labour over long distances at a qualitatively new level of intensity and thus facilitated the emergence of integrated world markets. It implied a thorough reorganisation of social space according to the dynamics of a colonial economy that provided Britain with Indian foodstuffs (such as wheat or tea) and raw materials for her industry (such as cotton), turning India simultaneously into the largest export market for British textiles and a captive market for other manufactures.[87] Yet time–space compression was fuelled as much by the dynamics of violence and state power as by those of the commodity and 'the market'. As the Governor-Generals Hardinge and Dalhousie had pointed out in the 1840s, the construction of railways created new levels of military efficiency by accelerating the circulation of troops along "interstitial corridors of power" between strategic locations.[88] Railway construction acquired, after all, a strong impetus after the large-scale insurrection of 1857 had raised questions regarding the military backbone of colonial domination with particular urgency.[89]

---

[86] Hurd, "Railways", 740.

[87] Ibid., 745; Tomlinson, *Economy of Modern India*, 51–56; Dietmar Rothermund, *An Economic History of India: From Precolonial Times to 1991*, 2nd ed. (London/New York: Routledge, 2000), 37–42; Amiya K. Bagchi, *The Political Economy of Underdevelopment* (Cambridge: Cambridge University Press, 1982), 86. Also see Harvey, *Spaces of Capital*, 249–53.

[88] Minute by Lord Hardinge, Governor-General, 28 July 1846, British Parliamentary Papers 1847 (68.) (151.) xli.233.257, Railway Reports from India; Lord Dalhousie, Minute to the Court of Directors, 20 April 1853, item 174, 2: 24–25. Also see "H.O.", *Railways in India*, 2–6; Thorner, *Investment in Empire*, 63, 86–87, 92–93. The quoted phrase is borrowed from: Kerr, Introduction, 31.

[89] "The occurrences of 1857, while they for a time tended to suspend all progress, gave such manifest proof of the enormous utility of improved communications, that the systematic extension of roads in connection with the main lines of railway ..., was among the measures most earnestly taken up when the financial pressure caused by the Mutiny had subsided." Strachey and Strachey, *Finances and Public Works of India*, 87. Also see Ian J. Kerr, *Building the Railways of the Raj, 1850–1900* (Delhi el al.: Oxford University Press, 1997), 37–38.

Hypothesis 6: Disparity

The very process of world market integration paradoxically heightened differences and disparities between states, regions and localities. The transformation of social "time-space" was thus a double-edged and uneven process: compression was accompanied by dispersion, openings entailed closures, centralisation produced peripheries. The concept of "time-space compression", as introduced in the previous hypothesis, is useful insofar as it points at processes of acceleration and "annihilation of space by time" that have been—no more and no less—the *dominant aspect* of the transformation of social space ever since the mid-nineteenth century. This dominance should not be underrated in its practical consequences: the reduction of regional fluctuations (together with a general rise) of grain prices was, for instance, only too real a process throughout the subcontinent.[90] The concept stood to lose its critical potential, however, if what is only *one* (even though the dominant) "side" of a contradictory complex was rendered absolute.[91] Assuming a homogeneous universality of 'compression' thus amounts to confounding once more the dominant spatial schemes ("conceived space") with the totality of spatial practices, to taking hegemonic conceptualisations of a shrinking world of continuous, all-encompassing, ever quickening "flows" at face value.[92]

At an abstract level, the unevenness of social space emerges from the division of labour in hierarchical societies: "We know that the *technical division of labour* introduces *complementarities* (rationally

---

[90] Hurd, "Railways", 745–46; Rothermund, *Economic History of India*, 33–34. Also see Michelle Burge McAlpin, "Railroads, Prices, and Peasant Rationality: India, 1860–1900'. *Journal of Economic History* 34, no. 3, 1974, 662–84.

[91] Even David Harvey sometimes appears to overemphasise the moment of compression and visualises this overemphasis in a "shrinking map of the world through innovations in transport which "annihilate space through time". Harvey, *Condition of Postmodernity*, 240–42. Elsewhere, however, Harvey, *Spaces of Capital*, 246–47, has pointed out the contradictions of this process more clearly. For critical assessments, see Dodgshon, "Human Geography"; Fischbach, *Mythos Netz*, 27–29.

[92] For a critique of such "globalising" discourses, see Frederick Cooper, "What is the Concept of Globalization Good for? An African Historian's Perspective", *African Affairs* 100, 2001, 193 and *passim*. Also see Brigitte Reinwald, *Routen, Koordinaten und Konturen einer seascape. Überlegungen zur Historiographie des modernen Indischen Ozeans* (unpublished manuscript).

linked operations), whereas its *social division* generates disparities, distortions and conflicts in a supposedly 'irrational' manner."[93] Though Lefebvre refers in this observation to the uneven development of spaces of capital (for example. the world market), its relevance extends logically to the spaces of all societies doubly characterised by a technical as well as social division of labour. Hence all social hierarchies and disparities have a spatial dimension, articulating themselves in spatial hierarchies and disparities at every scale—though in a plurality of concrete forms that are shaped in their respective historical contexts. Socio-spatial disparities thus did not require the prevalence of the social relationships embedded in capital. In the Indian context, it has been observed accordingly (but not yet explained in concrete terms) that the political and economic dynamics of the seventeenth and eighteenth centuries articulated themselves in space in highly differentiated ways.[94] While the focus of recent research has mainly been on North India, Bengal and the Tamil and Maratha regions where interlinked processes of commercialisation and state formation were remarkably dynamic,[95] it is also clear that other regional spaces moved in the opposite direction. This is particularly pertinent to the region of Orissa where all available evidence suggests that the eighteenth century—especially its latter half (the period of Maratha dominance)—saw a sharp decline in circulation, commercial production and urban settlement, a process of spatial marginalisation that continued and deepened in the half-century following the British annexation of coastal Orissa in 1803 (see chapter 4).

Yet the phenomenon of worldwide as well as regional uneven development acquired a new sharpness and urgency in both social practice and perception as the nineteenth century drew towards its close. In India, this experience gave rise to a powerful "economic

[93] Lefebvre, *Production of Space*, 404.
[94] Christopher A. Bayly, *Indian Society and the Making of the British Empire*, New Cambridge History of India II.1 (Cambridge: Cambridge University Press, 1988), 4, 33–37; Christopher A. Bayly, *Rulers, Townsmen and Bazaars: North Indian Society in the Age of British Expansion, 1770–1870* (Delhi: Oxford University Press, 1992), 495 (epilogue to the Indian edition).
[95] For an overview of the rich corpus of regional studies for the eighteenth century, see Seema Alavi, Introduction to *The Eighteenth Century in India*, ed. Seema Alavi (Delhi: Oxford University Press, 2002), 7–21.

nationalism" and a "territorial nativism".[96] In Europe, "uneven development" was also an issue of Marxist debates on imperialism (and Lenin's contribution in particular), while the emerging non-Marxist social sciences, too, discovered "aerial differentiation" as an important problem.[97] The age of capital unleashed the homogenising forces of commodification and spatial abstraction only to exacerbate, as we shall see, spatial differentiation and contradictions between and within the various spatial scales—a double-edged process that needs to be examined on its own terms. Lefebvre saw a fundamental cause for the "spatial chaos engendered by capitalism" and "experienced at the most parochial level just as on a worldwide scale" in the contradictory combination of "very strong political hegemony, a surge in the forces of production, and an inadequate control of markets", in the incoherence of commodity and capital markets and, more particularly, in the failure to "establish control over the capital market itself".[98] Harvey has developed this idea more concretely and argues that the disparities of social landscapes are reproduced in cycles of disruption and realignment resulting from efforts to solve crises of over-accumulation by way of a "spatial fix". In order to prevent a rapid devaluation of capital, its massive export from the crisis-affected spatial scale may appear to be a solution. There is, however, the danger that the destination of the capital exports emerges in due course as a strong competitor in the commodity markets. The very crisis that was to be averted thus returns with a vengeance. The spectacular case in point being the USA, whose economy flourished on becoming the premier destination of British capital exports in the nineteenth century only to replace Britain as the leading industrial power. The expansion of a world market for capital thus reconstituted economic disparities rather than evening them out.[99] Contemporary British observers were well aware of this phenomenon and advocates of a redirection of capital exports from the USA and continental Europe to India and other parts of the Empire built their arguments on it.[100] Colonial

[96] Goswami, *Producing India*, 270–71 and passim.
[97] For a brief discussion of that moment, see Soja, *Postmodern Geographies*, 32–33.
[98] Lefebvre, *Production of Space*, 62–63, 404.
[99] Harvey, *Spaces of Capital*, 302–3, 337–39.
[100] See for example, Holt S. Hallett, *New Markets and Extension of Railways in India and Burmah* (London: P. S. King & Son, 1887), 3–5.

capital exports seemed to offer a way out: while British investment in Indian railways (£150 or 200 million according to different calculations) was "the single largest investment within the nineteenth-century British empire",[101] state power made it possible to render India into a "captive market" for British industrial products, to neutralise most of the industrialising "linkage effects" railway construction had in non-colonial contexts and, consequently, to slow down the emergence of a new industrial competitor.[102] However, these schemes also delimited the scope for profitable British capital exports to India in crises of overaccumulation and could, therefore, complement but not replace "investments outside empire". "Thus India," writes Harvey, "under British domination from the start, mounted no competitive challenge to British industry but by the same token it was less significant as a field for the absorption of surpluses than, for example, the US."[103]

The resulting colonial division of labour reduced India to the position of an importer of industrial commodities and an exporter of raw materials, implying not merely the creation of a sharp disparity on the global scale of social space but also a reconfiguration of spatial scales *within* South Asia. I have already referred to the rise of new towns at railway junctions and the phenomenal growth of colonial metropolises on or near the coastline—processes that were coupled, however, with the decline of earlier urban centres in the interior and, consequently with a low general level of urbanisation. These changes in the patterns of settlement were connected, as Sunil Kumar Munsi has argued for Eastern India, with colonial

---

[101] Kerr, *Building the Railways of the Raj*, 4. According to Thorner (*Investment in Empire*, viii) investment in Indian railways was even "the largest single unit of international investment in the nineteenth century". Also see Damien Bailey and John McGuire, "Railways, Exchange Banks and the World Economy: Capitalist Development in India, 1850–1873", in *27 Down: New Departures in Indian Railway Studies,* ed. Ian J. Kerr, 101–88 (Delhi: Orient Longman, 2007).

[102] Frederick Lehmann, "Great Britain and the Supply of Railway Locomotives of India: A Case Study of 'Economic Imperialism'", *Indian Economic and Social History Review* 2, no. 4, 1965, 297–306; Hurd, "Railways", 749–50. Also see Bailey and McGuire, "Railways, Exchange Banks and World Economy", 142–43; Goswami, *Producing India*, 42–45.

[103] Harvey, *Spaces of Capital*, 337, see also 302–3, 338–39.

infrastructure policies that prioritised radial mainlines directed towards Calcutta and the world market over cellular networks of inland communication, that is, over a honeycomb-pattern of differentiated routes connecting local and regional markets.[104] Even official statements admitted that "[a]ll the railways of the province are primarily designed to feed the great port of Calcutta".[105] This general trend was shot through, however, with a movement towards higher levels of spatial integration in the most commercialised regions of the subcontinent[106] though it has been questioned whether these developments extended, even in these regions, much beyond the railtracks before the turn of the century.[107] The general tendency towards radial mainlines was further exacerbated by a structure of freight rates that rendered it cheaper to transport commodities to or from port cities than between places in the interior.[108] Though "spatial divergence alongside spatial convergence" was also experienced in Britain,[109] India's overall development was clearly distinct from that of the metropolis where the construction of a dense network of macadamised roads and canals had preceded

[104] Sunil K. Munsi, "Railway Network and Nodes in Eastern India: The First Fifty Years of Interaction", *International Geography* 6 (1976; 23rd International Geographical Congress, Moscow, section 6: General Economic Geography), 235–36. For a summary of the larger debate on uneven development in colonial India, see Goswami, *Producing India*, 59–63.
[105] Government of Bihar and Orissa, *Bihar and Orissa in 1927–28* (Patna: Superintendent of Government Printing, Bihar and Orissa, 1929), 108.
[106] See especially Douglas E. Haynes, "Market Formation in Khandesh, c. 1820–1930", *Indian Economic and Social History Review* 36, no. 3, 1999, 275–302. Also see Yang, *Bazaar India*, 46–52 (for Gangetic Bihar); Derbyshire, "Economic Change and the Railways", 523–33 (for the western Doab). Significantly, all of these regions are located in those parts of India (mainly the Ganges plains between Delhi and Bengal as well as parts of western India) where, according to Hurd, railways were not subsidised by the Government of India between 1879 and 1900, that is, where they earned an annual profit of at least 5, often more than 8 per cent. For the whole of India, however, railway earnings began to exceed the subsidies only by the latter date. Hurd, "Railways", 742–43.
[107] McAlpin, "Railroads, Prices, and Peasant Rationality, 680–84.
[108] Hurd, "Railways", 757–58.
[109] Michael J. Freeman, Introduction to *Transport in Victorian Britain*, ed. Michael J. Freeman and Derek H. Aldcroft (Manchester: Manchester University Press, 1988), 50–52.

and created an unplanned but effective underpinning for a much denser railway network criss-crossing the country. India's and Britain's trajectories of spatial practice were clearly heading in different directions (see map 1).[110]

It is at this point that the problem of uneven time–space transformation can be stated more systematically with respect to transport infrastructure. The outline of a given "time-space" (as the totality of distances between the locations of a space measured in time) would only be proportional to the outline of the corresponding physical space (as the totality of geometrical distances between the locations of a space) if the speed of transport and communication was identical on all routes and even then only if all of these routes were aligned as the crow flies. This is obviously impossible. Even if we could imagine a space without any transport or communications infrastructure, the proportion would be distorted due to its geomorphic structure and climatic conditions. More to the point, every decision to build a road between two locations while leaving two others unconnected, to improve one road while leaving another unchanged, to construct a railway link here, but a navigable canal there, is bound to transform and even increase these distortions: Space *is* annihilated by time on *certain* routes but never to the same extent on *all* routes. Relative distance between well-connected nodal points of circulation shrinks, while other locations that are closer in terms of geometrical measurement almost vanish into a hazy distance as they are rendered comparatively less accessible in terms of transport time (or cost). Centralisation creates peripheries; "time–space compression" entails "time-space dispersal".

While this "technical" cause for uneven patterns of circulation can be assumed valid under all social conditions, spatial unevenness became a striking feature of a period when world market expansion was coupled with transport revolution[111] and assumed a particular severity in the context of colonial capitalism—as discussed above.[112]

---

[110] Thrift, "Transport and Communication", 457–68; Bagwell, *The Transport Revolution*, 1–20, 26–48.

[111] The importance of such differentials for the circulation of capital was pointed out by Karl Marx, MEW, vol. 24, *Das Kapital*, vol. II (Berlin: Dietz, 1963), 252–54. Also see Harvey, *Spaces of Capital*, 246; Smith, *Uneven Development*, 145.

[112] Cf. Bagchi, *Political Economy of Underdevelopment*, 34; also see Hurd, "Railways", 757.

The reduction of relative distances between the nodal points of colonial world market integration implied, for instance, the marginalisation of regions like Orissa that were more or less by-passed by the new transport and communications networks. We have already seen that by the late nineteenth century an Indian railway accelerated the transport of goods and passengers to nearly 650 km per day, while the almost 2,000 km between Bombay and Calcutta could even be traversed in about forty hours as opposed to ten days in 1840. Yet the average travel speed on the largely unsurfaced roads of rural regions like Orissa was still the same as a century earlier: it was reckoned that usually a rate of 20 km per day was attainable by both pedestrians and bullock carts.[113] Even a eulogist of colonial 'public works' like G. W. MacGeorge admitted that "there still exists throughout the country, a large number of railway stations which are absolutely inaccessible to a loaded cart for five months in the year." This phrase was borrowed verbatim from an 1858 publication but was apparently still to the point after more than three decades of extensive (and expensive) railway construction.[114] The oft-quoted assertion of the same author that "[r]ailways in India have reduced the effective size of that continent to less than one-twentieth of its former dimensions" is, thus, rather misleading.[115] The assertion of a quantifiable 'annihilation of space' obscures the enormous differentials in transport speed, the widening gap between geometrical and relative distances between the new colonial main lines (especially the

---

[113] Stephenson, *Report upon the Practicability*, 61; MacGeorge, *Ways and Works*, 422, 427; Headrick, *Tentacles of Progress*, 88; OIOC, BPWP, August 1882, P/1831, Railway, no. 4, 3–4: "An Appeal for a Light Passenger Railroad from Ranigunge to Pooree through Bankoora, Midnapore, Balasore, Cuttack, and Khorda'; Mukherjee, "Railways and their Impact", 196; Deloche, *Transport and Communication*, 1: 284–86. Even "*dak* runners", that is, postal foot couriers, usually reached a rate of about a hundred km per day on unsurfaced roads and of about 200 km on the best maintained lines of communication in the early half of the nineteenth century. See Deloche, *Transport and Communication*, 1: 283; Ivie G. J. Hamilton, *An Outline of Postal History and Practice with a History of the Post Office of India* (Calcutta: Thacker, Spink & Co., 1910), 152.

[114] MacGeorge did not indicate a source, but see Tremenhere, *On Public Works in Bengal Presidency*, 47: "There were stations on the East Indian Railway which, for five months of the year, were inaccessible to a loaded cart" (from the comment of one Mr Sibley).

[115] MacGeorge, *Ways and Works*, 16, 221.

railways) on the one hand and a largely unchanged or even decaying infrastructure of rural "mud roads" on the other.[116] Yet we do not even have to look out for villages in mountainous interior regions in order to perceive these differentials. Consider, for instance, the seat of Orissa's colonial administration, which was in the last quarter of the nineteenth century connected to Calcutta at least by a macadamised 'trunk road' and (parts of the route) by a navigable canal. According to geometric measurement, Bombay is four times as distant from Calcutta as Cuttack, but measured in time the distance between the two metropolises was less than half of that between Calcutta and Cuttack in the last quarter of the nineteenth century.[117] Moreover, far from effecting a uniform reduction of distance, these differentials *severed* earlier intra- and inter-regional patterns of circulation—fragmenting social space, heighting regional disparities and the non-synchrony of the synchronous.[118] Areas like Orissa were thus 'put in their place' as 'backward' outer peripheries of Calcutta and other centres of colonial extraction (see chapters 5–8).

The bias of most relevant historical studies on railways implies, therefore, an inadequate limitation of research to the regions on which colonial infrastructure programmes concentrated and, often even more narrowly, on the urban centres of these regions.[119] It also implies that the colonial decision to impose a pattern of outward-oriented main routes upon South Asia's social space is taken for granted, while the development of a cellular and differentiated network of routes is rarely perceived as a forgone historical alternative. A more comprehensive approach is required to appreciate the dialectic of compression and dispersal in its concrete forms of articulation.

---

[116] See the section on "infrastructure" in chapter 3.

[117] While the fastest Calcutta train reached Bombay within forty hours, passengers still needed four to eight days to reach Cuttack on the fastest route, that is, the East Coast Canal. *Utkal Dipika*, 4 May 1889, quoted in *RNNB*, 25 May 1889, 437.

[118] These differentials were already pointed out in Dhananjay R. Gadgil, *The Industrial Evolution of India in Recent Times, 1860–1939*, 5th ed. (Delhi: Oxford University Press, 1972 [1st ed. 1924]), 145, 147–48. The divergent effects of railway development on different regions are also reflected in a corpus of more recent regional studies. For a brief but excellent summary of this current of research, see Kerr, Introduction, 34–38.

[119] Cf. Kerr, Introduction, 13–14.

Hypothesis 7: Rhythm

The transformation of social "time-space" in the age of capital involved not only the reconfiguration of relative distances but also changes in the rhythms of social life, the superimposition of "serial spaces" over older "cyclical spaces". "Everywhere where there is interaction between a place, a time and an expenditure of energy, there is rhythm", wrote Lefebvre in skilful simplicity.[120] Spatial practice had, in this sense, been rhythmic throughout human history: structured in its temporality by the cyclical and locally specific rhythms of nature. Periods of circulation were defined—as much in Orissa as in other regions of the subcontinent[121]—in a most fundamental way by the seasons, the rhythm of the monsoons, the periodic inundations of the fluvial plains. Human societies had superimposed their own rhythms on this basis: cycles of agricultural and non-agricultural production, calendars of festivals and fairs, pilgrimage seasons, etc. These were rhythms that were always mediated with and correlated to the rhythms of nature and earlier social formations without being fully absorbed by them (cf. hypothesis 3). For even spatial practices like the construction of irrigation ponds or bridges already implied polyrhythmic effects, that is, a (however limited) deviation and the achievement of a degree of freedom from the cyclical rhythms of nature.[122]

After the mid-nineteenth century, the productive and reproductive rhythms of capital were superimposed upon the older rhythmic configurations not only of the industrialising metropolitan spaces, but to some extent also of the largely non-industrial social spaces of what emerged as a colonial periphery. These superimposed rhythms were less constrained by the rhythms of nature than those of earlier societies: the railway and the steamship rendered, for instance, traffic

---

[120] Henri Lefebvre, *Rhythmanalysis: Space, Time and Everyday Life,* trans. Stuart Elden and Gerald Moore (London/New York: Continuum, 2004 [1st French ed. 1992]), 15.

[121] Cf. Deloche, *Transport and Communication,* 1: 274–80.

[122] See chapter 3 of the present study. For a distinction between a "season of production" and a "season of circulation" in Indian agrarian society, see David Ludden, *An Agrarian History of South Asia,* New Cambridge History of India IV.4 (Cambridge: Cambridge University Press, 1999), 19–31. For a short but perceptive discussion of seasonal trade patterns and corresponding notions of time, see Bhattacharya, "Predicaments of Mobility", 213–14.

rhythms considerably more independent of weather and season. This was in fact a major, sometimes even crucial, advantage of steam technologies of transport. Thus it took several decades before steamships could undercut the freight rates of clippers in the Euro-Asian transoceanic trade. If the first steamship link between Suez and Bombay was established as early as in 1830, it was not for purposes of bulk transport but rather to provide a means of regular and speedy postal exchange and to facilitate the transfer of high-ranking functionaries between Britain and India.[123] Moreover, while travel speed on India's waterways or largely unsurfaced roads varied widely according to direction of river flow, weather and season, the rhythm of railway transport could be regularised and codified in timetables—spatial distances could now be converted into units of homogeneous, abstract, that is, "denaturalised" time with considerable precision.[124] A rhythm of production and circulation based mainly on the cycle of seasons was now overlaid with the accelerating human-made beat of capital turnover. Rigidly scheduled short-term cycles permeated the repetitiveness of social practices, a tendency that may be conceptualised as the production of "serial spaces".[125] Spatial relations resulted, as it were, more often from

[123] A regular mail service via the Suez was established in 1837 and the transfer time of mail from London to Calcutta was reduced from about 20 weeks to 41 days by 1844. John K. Sidebottom, *The Overland Mail to India: A Postal Historical Study of the Mail Route to India* (London: Allen and Unwin Ltd, 1948), 144–45; Hamilton, *Outline of Postal History*, 148–50; Headrick, *Tentacles of Progress*, 20, 23–25. Similar observations can be made for river transport where steamboats, far from replacing the so-called "country boats", could compete only in certain market segments. Cf. Henry T. Bernstein, *Steamboats on the Ganges: An Exploration in the History of India's Modernization through Science and Technology* (Bombay: Orient Longman, 1960), 100; Mukherjee, "Railways and Their Impact", 200–1; Arnold, *Science, Technology and Medicine*, 104–5.

[124] On the rhythms of road and river transport in Orissa, see chapter 3. Also see Yang, *Bazaar India*, 27–31; Mukherjee, "Railways and Their Impact", 198–99. For related but earlier changes in Britain, connected to the spread of turnpike roads and stage coaches in the latter half of the eighteenth century, see Thrift, "Transport and Communication", 473–74.

[125] This is a modification of Lefebvre's term "repetitive spaces"—a modification that has, in my view, the advantage of distinguishing between repetition (which is a modality of social practice in all societies) and seriality (which is a specifically industrial mode of repetition). Lefebvre, *Production of Space*, 75; also see the section on "circulation" in chapter 3 of the present study.

"serial production" of consistent quality and within standardised time-spans. This observation is not confined in its relevance to the "economic sphere" or even more narrowly to industrialised economies. The beat of these transformed rhythms could be felt even in the most 'de-industrialised' peripheries of South Asia and in various spheres of social and political life.

New rhythms and circuits of labour migration are a case in point. This has been demonstrated, for the case of coastal Andhra—a region of southeast India where the massive import of British textiles (made possible by the revolution in transport) entailed particularly severe levels of deprivation in the late nineteenth century. In this region, many of the labouring poor had seasonally shifted between agricultural labour and the weaving of low-quality fabric—a subsistence strategy that now ceased to be feasible. Yet the new 'serial spaces' created by steam shipping, namely, the regular, fast and cheap steamer link between Andhra and Southeast Asia (chiefly Burma and Malaya), permitted the evolution of a new seasonal rhythm: when the demand for agricultural labour dropped in their home villages, thousands and thousands set out to work in the port of Rangoon or on rubber plantations across the Bay of Bengal only to return as soon as the harvest season started. The accelerating repetitiveness of industrial rhythm thus did not simply replace the slower historic rhythms of seasonal cyclicity and rural social life. Rather, a new polyrhythmic beat emerged from the interpenetration of these rhythms. In the writings of colonial authors, this eminently historical configuration was, however, given a semblance of naturalness as the new transregional migrants were often referred to as "birds of passage".[126]

Consider also briefly the transformation of the circulatory practice of pilgrimage. The steam technologies of transport were a disappointment to the missionaries of 'civilisation' insofar as they had hoped that 'opening up the country' would dispel 'irrational' practices such as (non-Christian) pilgrimage. Far from it, Indian railways and Indian Ocean steam shipping induced a considerable increase of both Hindu and Muslim pilgrimage and extended this prestigious

---

[126] Adapa Satyanarayana, "'Birds of Passage': Migration of South Indian Laborers to Southeast Asia", *Critical Asian Studies* 34, no. 1, 2002, 89–115. For similar migratory patterns within the subcontinent, namely, between Orissa and Calcutta, also see chapter 7 of the present study.

socio-spatial practice to social groups that earlier would not have been able to cover the costs or leave their fields for as long as a pilgrimage took. Not only the average duration but also the routes, the ritual form, the organisation and the experience of a pilgrimage were transformed[127]—a complex dialectic between technological change and social (and, therefore, spatial) practice that is so far, as David Arnold has pointed out, not well understood by those historians who tend to think in unidirectional models of technological diffusion.[128] All these changes also had implications for the rhythm of the spatial practice itself. The *rath yatra* (car festival), the prime event in Puri's festival calendar, attracted many more pilgrims in the early 1900s than before the opening of the East Coast Railway, while the stream of Jagannath's worshippers outside the traditional pilgrimage seasons grew larger and more continuous at the same time (see chapter 7). Once again, an existing social 'time-space' with its particular rhythmic qualities was superimposed upon rather than annihilated.

Before we turn to the next conceptual field, let us briefly sum up the sequence of hypotheses:

(1) Social space is not the empty and unchanging container of society but historically produced and reproduced: it is at once a product of and a precondition for social practice.

[127] Cf. Kerr, "Reworking a Popular Religious Practice", 304–27. For a discussion of transportation and pilgrimage to the important Jagannath temple in Puri, also see Ravi Ahuja, "'The Bridge-Builders': Some Notes on Railways, Pilgrimage and the British 'Civilizing Mission' in Colonial India", in *Colonialism as Civilizing Mission: The Case of British India*, ed. Harald Fischer-Tiné and Michael Mann (London: Anthem, 2004), 195–216, and chapter 7 of the present study. Effects of steam technologies of transportation on the *hajj* (pilgrimage to Mecca) of South Asian Muslims are even less explored than those on Hindu *yatras* (pilgrimages) though source material (mainly relating to issues of 'public health') abound. See Kenneth McPherson, Frank Broeze, Joan Wardrop and Peter Reeves, "The Social Expansion of the Maritime World of the Indian Ocean, Passenger Traffic and Community Building, 1815–1939", in *Maritime Aspects of Migration*, ed. Klaus Friedland (Cologne/Vienna: Böhlau, 1998), 427–40; Mark Harrison, *Public Health in British India: Anglo-Indian Preventive Medicine, 1859–1914* (Cambridge: Cambridge University Press, 1994), 117–38.

[128] Arnold, *Science, Technology and Medicine*, 92; Also see David Arnold, "Europe, Technology and Colonialism in the Twentieth Century", *History and Technology* 21, no. 1, 2005, 85–106.

(2) Social space is produced not in the image of the dominant social groups, but in a hierarchical and dynamic field of force of conflicting social interests.
(3) Social space cannot be reinvented in its entirety, cut off from its history. Synchrony of the non-synchronous permeates its complex, multilayered structure.
(4) With the rise of capitalism (and most forcefully since the nineteenth century) a marked tendency towards spatial abstraction is observable. Relations between spaces and places thus assume preponderance over their absolute qualities.

This last tendency implies a thorough transformation of the relationship between social time and social space or, the emergence of a new 'time–space'. This development has three main aspects:

(5) An enormous acceleration of the circulation of commodities, capital, persons and information occurs, which is bound up with a drive towards social homogenisation and may be experienced as "time-space compression".
(6) Yet this is no even development: spatial disparities are heightened as relative distance is "annihilated" between certain places at the cost of others. Fragmentation, peripheralisation and exclusion travel in the train of homogenisation, centralisation and integration.
(7) The 'beat' of social life (including the rhythms of circulation) assumes greater autonomy from the cycles of nature. Human-made, rigidly scheduled and short-term elements are thus superimposed in differentiated degrees and forms upon older rhythms, increasing the polyrhythmic complexity and unevenness of 'time-space'.

These hypotheses, extracted from the vast and abstract conceptual field of 'social space', can be used as stepping stones for scaling the next higher level of concretisation—the conceptualisation of circulation and infrastructure as specific spatial practices.

3

Circulation and Infrastructure

This chapter begins with an exploration of the conceptual field referring to spatial practices of circulation, that is, to repeatable forms of movement in space. In the second section, the discussion moves on to what may be called the accretions of such circulatory practices: to the conceptual field relating to what is presently called 'infrastructure', and to the built environments that are socially produced for purposes of circulation.

Circulation, Communication and Transport

This is a study of roads, rails and waterways, of their construction and utilisation. The spatial practice we are looking at, therefore, is 'transport'. From the perspective of our times, this phrase seems commonsensical in its drabness—beyond any need of historical contextualisation and almost without alternative. Yet in the period under review, British officials were much more likely to use another term. The heading in 'public works' records relating to issues of overland traffic or waterways thus reads "communications" and within this category we find numerous references to "works of communication", "navigable communication", "road communication", "railway communication" and so on. The word "transport" (or, alternatively, "transit") was not used with regard to infrastructures of mobility but merely to describe the actual movement of goods. This preference is significant as it indicates a semantic shift that has occurred since the nineteenth century—a shift reflecting important changes in the relation of information transfer to the movement of goods and persons.[1] Hence the material infrastructures of transport and

---

[1] Cf. *Oxford English Dictionary,* 2nd ed. (Oxford: Clarendon Press, 1989): "communication": "Now rare of things material". Simon P. Ville, "British Transport History: Shifting Perspectives and New Agendas", in *Studies in Economic*

communication became progressively disentangled in the course of the twentieth century—a process embodied by the large-scale diffusion of the telephone and greatly accelerated by the emergence of new information technologies. Meanwhile, 'communication' has assumed an almost ethereal, disembodied appearance as the social visibility of its material underpinnings fades away, while the obvious materiality of 'transport' seems to belong to a different, somewhat cruder sphere of social practice.[2] Projecting the prejudices of the present onto the past, however, merely generates anachronism. As our period of review drew to a close, a sharp conceptual separation between transport and communication was still implausible, even irrelevant. As Nigel Thrift puts it, "each relie[d] upon the other" in many and very direct ways:

> the development of newspapers is tied up with the history of the Post Office, the railways and the telegraph, the development of the Post Office is tied up with the history of the railways and the telegraph, the development of the railways would have been hindered without the invention of telegraphy and the telegraph's development would have been slower without the railways.[3]

If the telegraph wire was a ubiquitous adjunct of the railway line, the integration of transport and communication can be said to have been even closer before the emergence of a worldwide telegraph network. Administrative correspondence, military intelligence reports, private letters, bills of exchange and other media of information had to be moved, after all, upon the same waterways or roads

---

and Social History: Essays in Honour of Derek J. Aldcroft, ed. Michael J. Oliver, (Aldershot: Ashgate, 2002), 6: "Transport carries people, goods and information, while communications is particular about the transfer and dissemination of information. In spite of the similarities between the two concepts they are rarely analysed together in the historical literature.'"

[2] The authors of a recent theoretical essay on the problem of "space and communication" appear, for instance, somewhat puzzled by the "extremely broad" conceptualisation of communication by historians associated with the *Annales* "school" (and particularly by Lucien Febvre in the interwar period). Reconstructing the semantic history of this concept may not only explain why Febvre understood "communication" like he did but also permit a more critical reflection on seemingly nonideological contemporary uses. Geppert et al., "Verräumlichung", 23.

[3] Thrift, "Transport and Communication", 453.

that were used for the shipment of goods or as routes of travel. The point is that transport needs to be understood historically as an elementary aspect of communication and not as a related but essentially separate phenomenon. This is most apparent in the 'infrastructural policy' of the early colonial regime. Before the establishment of a 'Public Works Department' in 1854, road construction was undertaken, if at all, by the Military Board of the East India Company's administration.[4] The administrative logic of this arrangement was rather obvious since the construction or improvement of overland routes was predominantly motivated by two objectives well into the 1840s: first, the speedy deployment of troops (for which temporary and, therefore, relatively inexpensive arrangements were often considered sufficient) and, second, the transfer of political and military intelligence. Regularly maintained roads were therefore, as we shall see, often so-called *dak* roads (mail roads) that were not necessarily amenable for the transport of goods by bullock cart but were perfectly adequate for purposes of information transfer. The objective was to guarantee the safe transmission of letters by 'dak runners' at the comparatively fast rate of often more than a hundred km per day along a chain of post stations. The famous Grand Trunk Road from Calcutta to Delhi, celebrated in Rudyard Kipling's novel *Kim*, was the exception to the rule in that it established a cartable long-distance connection as early as in 1855. However, several decades passed, writes Yang, before it was "finally usable year-round for all kinds of transport".[5] As late as in 1860–61, more than 84 per cent of the total mileage of postal lines consisted of 'runners' lines' and waterways, 13 per cent of cartable roads and the remaining 3 percent of railways.[6] The administrative head 'communications' thus does not merely indicate the close correlation between the need for a speedy transfer of information (and treasure) on the one hand and for a cheap transportation of goods on the other—it even reflects the *priority* of the former over the latter in the policies of the early colonial regime.

---

[4] Strachey and Strachey, *Finances and Public Works*, 87; Elizabeth Whitcombe, "Irrigation and Railways: Irrigation", in *The Cambridge Economic History of India*, 2: 690–91.
[5] MacGeorge, *Ways and Works*, 72–73, 80–85; Deloche, *Transport and Communication*, 1: 280–83; Yang, *Bazaar India*, 34–36; also see chapters 5 and 6 of the present study.
[6] Cf. Hamilton, *Outline of Postal History*, 210.

Yet another term from this conceptual field proves even more useful for the purposes of this study: *circulation*. Organicistic metaphors of sanguineous circulation within the body politic, it has been pointed out, were extensively used in pre- and early modern political writings in both Europe and India as well as in eighteenth-century economic theory and especially by the French Physiocrats.[7] In nineteenth- and twentieth-century European writings the related analogy of the 'artery' was frequently employed for main channels of transportation and communication. Thus we read of "arterial or trunk roads", of "the arteries of trade", of railways as "arterial sources of wealth and prosperity" and of "great arterial communications which connect one province with another".[8] Even more explicitly, roads and bridges were designated "the veins and arteries of a country ... as indispensable to a State as those parts of the system were to the human frame".[9] In the age of "high imperialism", metaphors of the body were moreover frequently applied to the new modes of communication in order to dispel doubts regarding the sustainability of the British Empire.[10] The Cambridge historian J. R. Seeley thus argued in the 1880s that "science has given the political organism a new circulation, which is steam, and a new nervous system, which is electricity."[11] Such organicist conceptualisations of social phenomena have the effect of legitimating contradictory social phenomena by naturalising them.

---

[7] Claude Markovits, Jacques Pouchepadas and Sanjay Subrahmanyam, "Introduction: Circulation and Society under Colonial Rule", in *Society and Circulation: Mobile People and Itinerant Cultures in South Asia*, ed. Claude Markovits, Jacques Pouchepadas and Sanjay Subrahmanyam, 3.

[8] Stephenson, *Railways: An Introductory Sketch*, 95; *Report of the Commissioners Appointed to Enquire into the Famine in Bengal and Orissa in 1866*, Report etc. (Calcutta: Office Superintendent Government Printing, 1867), 1: 161; Hunter, *The Annals of Rural Bengal*, 3: 102; K. G. Mitchell and L. H. Kirkness, *Report on the Present State of Road and Railway Competition and the Possibilities of their Future Co-ordination and Development, and Cognate Matters, in Governor's Provinces* (Calcutta: Government of India Central Publication Branch, 1933), 2. For the prevalence of arterial metaphors beyond Britain, also see Dirk van Laak, "Infra-Strukturgeschichte", *Geschichte und Gesellschaft* 27, no. 3, 2001, 386.

[9] "Parliamentary Intelligence, House of Lords" (2 May 1853), *The Times*, 3 May 1853 (speech by the Earl of Aldemarle).

[10] Cf. Bell, "Dissolving Distance", 553–57.

[11] J. R. Seeley, *The Expansion of England: Two Courses of Lectures* (London: Macmillan, 1885 [1st ed. 1883]), 74.

The term 'circulation', if used in this way, thus conceals the friction between the diverse practices it encompasses by postulating a seemingly natural balance. If the ballast of organicist connotations is jettisoned, however, the concept offers considerable explanatory potential. The geographer David Sopher and the medievalist Burton Stein thus used 'circulation' as early as in the 1960s and 1970s as a short-hand for repetitive cultural and social practices ("circulatory flows" such as pilgrimage or temple endowments) that generated what they called "behaviour regions", "functional regions" or, more adequately for a historiography of social praxis, "circulatory regions".[12] Stein's 'circulatory' approach towards medieval history, in particular, was clearly at variance with the hegemonic historical narrative of the static and self-sufficient Indian village community. In the meantime, however, numerous studies have perforated this mythical construct from a variety of vantage points: mobility in early modern South Asia, it has been demonstrated, was not merely an attribute of the lives of rulers in camp, military commanders and scribes in search of employment, of wandering saints, hungry scholars and merchants trading in luxury goods. Banjara traders in salt and grain circulated with caravans comprising tens of thousands of pack-oxen as much as other pastoralists, peddlers, itinerant artisans, well-diggers, dak-bearers and peasant-soldiers. Communities of weavers crossed the whole length of the subcontinent to resettle in an alien linguistic environment where they found better living conditions. Even peasants routinely threatened to leave the country and actually did so in many cases and regions when rulers tried to increase tributes beyond the limits that seemed legitimate under the prevailing conditions of land plenty.[13] "You are the head of one country, we have a thousand countries to go to" wrote Bengali

---

[12] Stein, "Circulation and Historical Geography", 9, 11 and *passim*; Sopher, "Geographic Patterning of Culture", 289–91.

[13] For a general discussion, see David Ludden, "History Outside Civilization and the Mobility of South Asia", *South Asia* 17, no. 1, 1994, especially 13–18; also see David Washbrook, "Progress and Problems: South Asian Economic and Social History c. 1720– 1860", *Modern Asian Studies* 22, no. 1, 1988, 66–68; Markovits, Pouchepadass, Subrahmanyam, "Introduction", 4–8. For Banjara traders, see Irfan Habib, "Merchant Communities in Precolonial India", in *The Rise of Merchant Empires: Long-distance Trade in the Early Modern World, 1350–1750*, ed. James D. Tracy (Cambridge: Cambridge University Press, 1990), 371–79; Robert G. Varady, "North Indian Banjaras: Their Evolution as Transporters", *South Asia* 2, nos. 1–2, 1979, 1–18; also see

raiyats (peasants) in a time-tested idiom of protest to the East India Company's district officer during the "Rangpur *dhing*", a peasant rebellion in 1783.[14] The repression of established forms of circulation that seemed detrimental or even subversive to British administrators was, it has been shown, a permanent feature of the policies that consolidated colonial rule in the following decades.[15] The editors of a recent collection of essays, aptly dedcated to the memory of Burton Stein, have in some respects developed the concept further against this historiographical background:

> Circulation is different from simple mobility, inasmuch as it implies a double movement of going forth and coming back, which can be

---

chapter 4 of the present study. For migrations of weavers, see Douglas E. Haynes and Tirthankar Roy, "Conceiving Mobility: Weavers' Migrations in Precolonial and Colonial India", *Indian Economic and Social History Review* 36, no. 1, 1999, 35–67. For seasonally soldiering peasants, see Dirk Kolff, *Naukar, Rajput and Sepoy: The Ethnohistory of the Military Labour Market in Hindustan, 1450–1850* (Cambridge: Cambridge University Press, 1990); Stewart Gordon, *Marathas, Marauders, and State Formation in Eighteenth-Century India* (Delhi/Oxford: Oxford University Press, 1994), 182–208; Jos Gommans, *Mughal Warfare: Indian Frontiers and High Roads to Empire, 1500–1700* (London/New York: Routledge, 2002), 67–97. For peasant mobility, see Ludden, *Agrarian History of South Asia*, 39–41, 137–39; Aditee Nag Chowdhury-Zilly, *The Vagrant Peasant: Agrarian Distress and Desertion in Bengal, 1770–1830* (Wiesbaden: Franz Steiner, 1982). For problems of mobility and resistance, also see Ravi Ahuja, "Labour Unsettled: Mobility and Protest in the Madras Region, 1750–1800", *Indian Economic and Social History Review*, 35, no. 4, 1998, 381–404.

[14] "Petition of Ryots of Cargeehat, Futtypore &ca.", quoted in Jon E. Wilson, "'A Thousand Countries to Go to': Peasants and Rulers in Late Eighteenth-Century Bengal", *Past and Present* 189, 2005, 84.

[15] Bayly, *Indian Society and Making of British Empire*, 138–50. For specific aspects of the suppression of circulation see, for instance, Eugene F. Irschick, *Dialogue and History, Constructing South-India, 1795–1895* (Delhi/Oxford: Oxford University Press, 1994); Seema Alavi, *The Sepoys and the Company: Tradition and Transition in Northern India, 1770–1830* (Delhi: Oxford University Press, 1998); Laxman D. Satya, "Colonial Sedentarisation and Subjugation: The Case of the Banjaras of Berar, 1850–1900", *Journal of Peasant Studies* 24, no. 4, 1997, 314–36; Meena Radhakrishna, *Dishonoured by History: Criminal Tribes and British Colonial Policy* (New Delhi: Orient Longman, 2001); Arnaud Sauli, "Circulation and Authority: Police, Public Space and Territorial Control in Punjab, 1861–1920", in *Society and Circulation*, 215–239; Michael H. Fisher, "The East India Company's 'Suppression of the Native Dak'", *Indian Economic and Social History Review* 31, no. 3, 1994, 311–48.

repeated indefinitely. In circulating, things, men and notions often transform themselves. Circulation is therefore a value-loaded term which implies an incremental aspect and not the simple reproduction across space of already formed structures and notions. The totality of circulations occurring in a given society and their outcomes could be viewed as defining a 'circulatory regime', susceptible of change over time. This 'circulatory regime' in its turn tends to shape society, which can be seen as an ensemble of crisscrossing circulatory flows. Rather than a specialised area of expertise, circulation has to be treated as a fairly general framework within which to look at Indian society and the transformations it underwent in the modern period, that is at least from the eighteenth century, if not from an even earlier period.[16]

This conceptualisation misses out on the important aspect of Stein's notion of 'circulation' as a modality of social practice that is capable of generating (or, to use Lefebvre's terminology, producing) nested and overlapping, interdependent and dynamic sets of spatial scales (regions, subregions, etc.).[17] It also appears to overstate the moment of fluidity (thereby understating the moment of structural solidification) by *equating* society with "crisscrossing circulatory flows".[18] Two elements of this conceptualisation are, however, eminently useful for the purposes of this study. First, the appreciation of an "incremental aspect"[19] of circulation permits to think in terms of a processual cyclicity rather than of a two-dimensional circularity: A round of circulation is concluded at its place of origin, which is, however, not quite the same place as it has been changed in the meantime (or, 'covered by a new layer') through social practice including that very round of circulation (cf. hypothesis 3 in chapter 2). Secondly, the notion of "circulatory regimes" can be used as a conceptual tool of periodisation, that is, for the identification of discontinuities in the forms and contents of circulation. Distinguishing circulatory regimes enables us to acknowledge a long history of circulation in South Asia without glossing over the changing contexts and divergent articulations of this modality of socio-spatial practice.

[16] Markovits, Pouchepadass, Subrahmanyam, "Introduction", 2–3.
[17] See pp. 37–38.
[18] This equation, pushed to its limits, suggests a spatial reductionism that postulates fluidity without tendency and thus bereaves social analysis of temporal depth. This seems, however, incoherent with the authors' emphasis on "incremental aspects" of circulation and is thus presumably not their intention; see below.
[19] Markovits, Pouchepadass, Subramanyam, "Introduction", 3.

There is, for instance, no necessary link between the prevalence of circulatory practices and the existence of capital—both mercantile and industrial. Circulation had occurred already in early societies as a cultural appropriation of the cycles of climatic seasons, it could emerge (in Stein's view) from the dynamics of a "segmentary state" or served (according to Pouchepadass) as a "modality of the exercise of power" by the itinerant kings of medieval and early modern states in general.[20] Yet the growth of mercantile capital, commercial manufacture and a more general trend towards the monetisation of social relations during the seventeenth and eighteenth centuries certainly implied considerable intensification and social re-contextualisation of circulatory practices—in other words, a transformation of the circulatory regime. The decline in the export of artisan manufactures, the heavy taxation on agriculture, the demilitarisation of society and the attrition of urban centres of consumption broke this tendency during the early decades of British rule in India setting the stage—as we have already seen—for the imposition of new patterns of circulation upon the subcontinent's social spaces from the 1840s onwards.[21] This latter process was deeply entangled with the emergence of a novel circulatory regime in Britain, which implied not merely quantitative changes (that is, spatial expansion, intensification and acceleration of circulation) but also a new role for circulation in the organisation of production and in society in general.

In the middle of the nineteenth century, when the transport revolution threw the problem of circulation into sharp relief, Karl Marx reflected on these qualitative implications. He argued that the circulation of money and goods (which could imply circulation in space) had seemed to be a process *beside* or *beyond* production in earlier social formations but that it became *integrated into* the production process itself under industrial capitalism, with the universalisation of the commodity form.[22] Hence when products are

---

[20] Stein, "Circulation and the Historical Geography", 17 and passim; Jacques Pouchepadass, "Itinerant Kings and Touring Officials: Circulation as a Modality of Power in India, 1700– 1947", in *Society and Circulation*, ed. Claude Markovits, Jacques Pouchepadass and Sanjay Subrahmanyam, 246–49, 273.
[21] See hypothesis 5 and footnote 15 on page 71 of the present study.
[22] Marx, *Grundrisse*, 514, 517 or MEW, vol. 42, 421, 424. Also see MEW, vol. 24, 150.

turned into commodities, "the spatial condition, the bringing of the product to the market, belongs to the production process itself. The product is really finished only when it is on the market."[23] Such observations appear to have been in the air of the mid-nineteenth century and were not confined to radical critics of capitalism. A hard-headed French engineer, Jules Dupuit, while looking for a method to measure the "utility of public works" thus arrived at a strikingly similar conclusion in an essay of 1844 that became a "classic" of mainstream economic writing: what determined the "utility" of improving transport infrastructure was not the reduction of the costs of transport (or circulation), but of the costs of production as a whole, that is of what it costs to render an article consumable.[24]

With regard to Asia, Marx was prejudiced by the culturalistic outpourings of the relevant British 'experts' of his time, and believed that the circulation of commodities had been insignificant and roads, therefore, had been absent in a precolonial India of supposedly self-sufficient village communities. While this assertion is clearly untenable (as subsequent research has shown), Marx's more general argument does help to understand the transformation of South Asia's circulatory regime in the course of the nineteenth century: As only surpluses, a limited proportion of produced goods were circulated in supralocal space in pre- and early colonial India, the generation of circulatory patterns and infrastructures—such as the establishment of fairs and the construction of roads—no doubt *contributed* to conditioning social production and reproduction without, however, turning into a *sine qua non* of their continuation as a whole.[25] The 'improvement' of means of transport and

---

[23] Marx, *Grundrisse*, 533–534 or MEW, vol. 42, 440. Also see Harvey, *Spaces of Capital*, 242–45.

[24] "Ainsi, le but final d'une voie de communication doit être non pas de diminuer les frais de transport, mais de diminuer les frais du production," a sentence he explains as follows: "Par frais de production nous entendons ce qu'il en coûte pour rendre un objet propre à la consommation." Dupuit's argument was that the total cost of production, to which manufacturing and transport costs contributed in varying proportions, determined whether a commodity could be profitably sold in a market and, consequently, provided the measure of the utility of transporting it to that market. Jules Dupuit, "De la mesure de l'utilité des travaux publics", in *De l'utilité et de sa mesure,* ed. Mario de Bernardi (Torini: La Riforma sociale, 1934 [1st publ. 1844]), 46.

[25] Cf. Marx, *Grundrisse*, 514, 517, 524–25 or MEW, vol. 42, 421, 424, 430–31.

communication was, therefore, rarely a priority concern even for the dominant social groups of early modern South Asia (see chapter 5). For the construction of a line of communication was—in both the precolonial and the early colonial periods—more often a diminution of the productive resources than a contribution to their economic exploitation or development; it amounted to an irregular tribute on the surplus product that rulers imposed on their subjects merely out of political exigency.

This constellation began to change, unevenly and contradictorily, from the 1840s onwards. It was then that the integration of industrial production with circulation within Britain began to have implications for South Asia. Apprehensions of a 'cotton famine' afflicting Lancashire's textile mills, the need for growing markets for British commodities and, most instrumentally, the search by various financial interests for profitable and secure outlets for overabundant British capital created conditions for a change in the patterns of colonial exploitation and for the peculiarly lopsided transformation of South Asia's circulatory regime.[26] The production of Lancashire textile mills now relied, to some extent, on heavy investment in Indian railways and was "really finished only" when its manufactures reached Indian bazaars. This is not to say that 'Manchester' (in other words, Britain's industrial bourgeoisie) was the most important social agent in the transformation of South Asia's transportation system and regime of circulation (nor that the findings of the proponents of the "gentlemanly capitalism" thesis can be ignored).[27] The point is merely that the 'logistical policies' implemented in India since the 1840s were conditioned by the new industrial context of circulation in the British economy—by the increasing

[26] See hypothesis 6. For a recent critical appraisal of the debates on colonial investment and exploitation, see Amiya K. Bagchi, "The Other Side of Foreign Investment by Imperial Powers: Transfer of Surplus from Colonies", *Economic and Political Weekly* 37, no. 23, 8 June 2002, 2229–38. For the implications of apprehensions of a "cotton famine" for 'public works' policy in India, see chapter 6.

[27] Hence Cain's and Hopkins' contention that the "Lancashire lobby" was "far less powerful than Marx supposed" and that its successes in influencing policy in India "were achieved largely because its aims were congruent with those of Indian rulers" appears to be based on sound evidence and is not contradicted here. Cf. P.J. Cain and A. G. Hopkins, *British Imperialism, 1688–2000*, 2nd ed. (Harlow: Longman, 2002), 167–74, 276–302.

integration of circulation with production.[28] For the universalisation of the commodity form implied ever more extensive hierarchical networks of production-cum-circulation and, consequently, a permanent redefinition of the scales of social space.

Yet any attempt to separate the 'spheres' of economy and polity in order to provide a narrowly economic (or political) explanation of British 'logistical policies' in colonial India would be fallacious for the formation of markets and the development of territorial, imperial and international institutions were inextricably intertwined. The tendency towards global market expansion was, as has been argued already, doubled by the tendency towards territorially homogenous and centralised states (both national and colonial).[29] The synchrony and mutual reinforcement of these tendencies pooled and enhanced the impact of the dominant circulatory practices, giving them a coherent direction, although specific objectives and contents of the logistical policies of state agencies and joint-stock companies differed, of course, in often contradictory ways. By the time the insurrection of 1857 had been crushed, British state functionaries and business leaders thus concurred in principle on the necessity of massive expenditure on Indian communications infrastructure—even if the concrete allocation of investment remained highly contested between and within the dominant groups and the balance sheet of individual projects could sum up very differently, according to the parameters set. Some major projects— namely, the Grand Trunk Road or the "trunk" railways—were, of

---

[28] Damien Bailey and John McGuire have developed this argument convincingly: "Certainly, there is little doubt that Marx did assume that the industrial complex in Britain had more influence than in fact it did have, and that the service and financing sector were less powerful than they were. Yet it is also important to emphasise that it was the industrialisation that was occurring globally that provided the means for the massive overseas investment by the financial and service sector in the City, London, a process which crossed national and colonial boundaries, and which, in the case of Britain and India, could be seen in the investment in the railway system. In short, the rise of financial capital and services in the City in the second half of the nineteenth century cannot be understood outside the context of the rise of industrial capital globally and its drive to impose a logic on all other forms of capital." Bailey and McGuire, "Railways, Exchange Banks and World Economy", 161.

[29] See p. 37.

course, 'lifelines' of colonial state and society in more than one sense. Yet the railway to the North-West Frontier served military rather than economic purposes. So-called "preventive" ot "protective lines"[30] were justified as measures against famine and thus primarily of political importance, while the navigable Buckingham Canal in the South had little military relevance.

At the end of the day, however, the production of a homogeneous territory by way of imposing a bureaucratic administration and a state monopoly on the use of force depended as much as the equalisation of commodity prices in territorial markets on an intensification of circulatory flows. On the cognitive level, Newton's Second Law of Motion (with its categories: 'mass', 'acceleration' and 'force') thus seems to have prefigured the logistical equations of nineteenth-century economists and military strategists alike. Hyde Clarke, a leading railway economist of the time, thus argued that in the Indian context, the "saving of time" afforded by railways "resolves itself into four heads—1) Saving of interest. 2) Saving of market. 3) Saving of quality. 4) Saving of stock."[31] An acceleration of capital turnover by improved means of circulation in space thus reduced the "mass" or volume of capital required to achieve a particular annual rate of profit (in other words, of economic efficiency or "force").[32] Moreover, the military benefits of an improved transport and communications infrastructure were calculated in exactly the same terms. Hence, in 1847, when the commercial viability of Indian railways was still a matter of debate in the British public, the East India Company's governor-general in India, Lord Hardinge, advocated their construction on the basis of the following reckoning:

> In a military point of view, I should estimate the value of moving troops and stores with great rapidity would be equal to the services of four

[30] Report from the Select Committee on East India Railway Communication, British Parliamentary Papers 1884 (284) xi.1, v–ix, 34. Also see footnote 87 in this chapter.
[31] Hyde Clarke, *Practical and Theoretical Considerations on the Management of Railways in India* (n.p., [1847?]), 7–10.
[32] The intellectual origin of such calculations was pointed out by Marx, when he observed that a "law of the substitution of velocity for mass, and mass for velocity" was to be encountered in the circulation of both money and capital, a law that "holds in production just as in mechanics". Marx, *Grundrisse*, 519, or MEW, vol. 42, 425–26.

regiments of infantry. The reduction of military establishment would be a saving of £50,000 a year, on the lowest scale.

... In this country, where no man can tell one week what the next may produce, the facility of a rapid concentration of infantry and artillery and stores may be the cheap prevention of an insurrection, the speedy termination of a war, or the safety of the empire.

... on military considerations alone, the grant of one million sterling, or an annual contribution of five lacs [500,000] of rupees, may be contributed to the great line, when completed from Calcutta to Delhi, and a pecuniary saving be effected by a diminution of military establishments, arising out of the facility with which troops would be moved from one point to the other.[33]

Military manpower (mass) was thus conceived substitutable by improved lines of communication (acceleration) in achieving the same level of military efficiency (force) at reduced cost. These calculations resonated with the writings of military theoreticians of the Enlightenment,[34] and can be interpreted as operationalisations of the tendency towards abstract space discussed above—of the increasing prevalence of spatial relations over concrete, absolute spatial properties. If abstract space was a new matrix for concrete spaces (rather than their demise), logistical calculations informed the politics of circulation pursued by the dominant social forces rather than circulatory praxis as a whole. For circulatory praxis was superimposed upon a complex, historically produced infrastructure—

---

[33] Minute by Lord Hardinge, Governor-General, 28 July 1846, in British Parliamentary Papers 1847 (68.) (151.) xli.233.257, Railway Reports from India, 23–24. Hardinge's arguments regarding the political and administrative advantages of the railway are phrased in a similar vein. Also see Memorandum from Major J. P. Kennedy to the Court of Directors, 14 September 1852, in *Railway Construction in India: Select Document, 1832–1852*, ed. S. Settar and Bhubanes Misra, item 161, 1: 507–12; Lord Dalhousie, Minute to the Court of Directors, 20 April 1853, item 174, 2: 25, 27; Speech by Sir James W. Hogg, MP and Director of the East India Company, in the House of Commons, 18 April 1856, *The Times*, "House of Commons", 19 April 1856.

[34] Adam von Bülow, Henry Lloyd and, most influentially, Antoine-Henri Jomini had theorised spatial aspects of strategy such as the deployment of troops and organisation of supply lines by applying concepts borrowed from geometry and mechanics, including Newton's Second Law of Motion. Cf. Azar Gat, *A History of Military Thought: From the Enlightenment to the Cold War* (Oxford: Oxford University Press, 2001), 72–73, 84–85, 118–19.

taking us to the next conceptual field, a field we have severally touched upon.

Infrastructure, 'Public Works' and 'Productivity'

Circulatory practices produce their own institutions and material environment by way of repetition. Circulation beats, in other words, its own tracks: It generates more or less permanent channels of communication and transport as well as the social arrangements for their upkeep and 'fossilises', finally, into built environments—consisting, for instance, of wells, rest houses, bridges or railway tracks. The 'circulatory regime' of a specific historical constellation and, more particularly, the scope for the regularisation and acceleration of rhythms of circulation and for the intensification and expansion of circulatory practices are, conversely, delimited (though not fully determined) by the built environment of that time. The built environment is itself a multilayered spatial manifestation of social relations of power; it reflects the sequence of dominant conceptions of social space and the succession of constellations of control over social resources.

Institutions and facilities for circulatory practices have come to be subsumed under the head 'infrastructure' in the course of the twentieth century. Dirk van Laak has recently traced the development of this concept: The neologism *infrastructure* seems to have originated from late nineteenth-century France where its first known utilisation (1875) referred to the "permanent way", to embankments and other permanent installations for railway traffic. In an age of industrial warfare with increased logistic requirements, the term soon acquired strong military connotations. However, its semantic range was widened in the mid-twentieth century when it came to include various institutional arrangements and state investments with regard to transport, energy and water supply, education and research, health services and other areas of social reproduction.[35]

---

[35] Dirk van Laak, "Der Begriff "Infrastruktur" und was er vor seiner Erfindung besagte", *Archiv für Begriffsgeschichte* 41, 1999, 280–99; Van Laak, "Infra-Strukturgeschichte", 370–86; Dirk Van Laak, *Imperiale Infrastruktur: Deutsche Planungen für eine Erschließung Afrikas 1880 bis 1960* (Paderborn et al.: Schöningh, 2004), 17–34. Also see René L. Frey, *Infrastruktur: Grundlagen der Planung öffentlicher Investitionen* (Tübingen/Zurich: Mohr et al., 1970), 1–10.

The successful dissemination of the phrase 'infrastructure' seems due to a great extent (though not exclusively), to the twentieth-century neo-positivistic tendency of framing the social in the language of engineering: of equating rational social praxis with "piecemeal technology" and of representing conflict-ridden institutions as socially neutral, quasi-technical installations derivable from inescapable cybernetic or systemic laws.[36] Today, the term 'infrastructure' seems almost unavoidable if one chooses to use a comprehensible language while discussing problems of transport. Turning it into a tool of critique rather than of legitimation requires, however, the grinding off of the accretions of that technicist discourse.

The ascendancy of the concept of infrastructure also reflects the growing complexity and resource intensity of social arrangements for transport and communications—a process that commenced, as we have already seen, long before this neologism was coined. In the period under review, English sources generally referred to transport facilities as 'works of public utility' or, even more frequently, as 'public works'. The semantic history of the latter phrase still awaits a thorough exploration,[37] but we may assume that it was attained by direct translation from the Latin "opera publica".[38] By the seventeenth century it was used in English writings as a loose term for a range of related social practices: first of all, for state buildings in ancient Rome (often referring to their erection by means of slave or penal labour); second, for contemporary facilities for 'public use'

---

[36] The idea of the engineer as the impersonation of improvement in a broader sense certainly emerged from the context of nineteenth-century industrialisation. However, Karl Popper's elaborations on "social engineering" and "piecemeal technologies" in his critique of "historicism", published first in 1960, just at the time when the concept of infrastructure gained wider currency, was surely a foundational text for respective ideologies of the twentieth century. Karl Popper, *Das Elend des Historizismus*, 6th rev. ed. (Tübingen: Mohr, 1987), 51–57.

[37] A historical exploration of the phrase 'public works' in the English language would be extremely useful for our purposes, but is to the knowledge of this writer not available as yet. Its inconspicuous appearance seems to have prevented it even from being included as an entry in the monumental Oxford English Dictionary.

[38] See, for instance, Livy, *The Romane Historie Written by T. Livius of Padua. Also, the Breviaries of L. Florus: with a Chronologie to the Whole Historie: and the Topographie of Rome in Old Time. Translated out of Latine into English, by Philemon Holland* (London: A. Islip, 1600), 520, 858, 1165.

erected by the state or by municipalities (not necessarily associated with involuntary service); third, in a wider sense with a distinct religious connotation, that is, as "publick Works of Piety".[39] In the eighteenth century, the phrase still carried with it connotations of forced labour—partly due to the historical context of classical antiquity in which it was frequently used[40]—though one should also note that many English roads were maintained by means of compelled unpaid village labour up to the early nineteenth century.[41] However, the phrase was increasingly imbued with "gentlemanly", bourgeois-aristocratic ethical notions of "improvement" and reworked

---

[39] This rough outline is based on a random sample of seventeenth-century publications. For the first meaning, see for example, Eusebius of Caesarea, *The History of the Church from our Lords Incarnation, to the Twelfth Year of the Emperour Maricius Tiberius, or the Year of Christ 594 ... also, The Life of Constantine in Four Books* ... (Cambridge: Printed by John Hayes... for Han. Sawbridge, 1683), 434, 558, 561. For the second, see for example, Walter Blith, *The English Improver Improved* ... (London: John Wright, 1653), 163; William Dugdale, *The History of Imbanking and Drayning of Divers Fenns and Marshes, both in Forein Parts and in this Kingdom, and of the Improvements thereby* ... (London: Alice Warren, 1662), 423; Gilbert Burnet, *Three Letters Concerning the Present State of Italy* (n.p., 1688), 168, 170, 187. For the third see, for instance, Edward Reynolds, *The Rich Man's Charge Delivered in a Sermon at the Spittle* ... (London: G. Thomason, 1658), 38, 42. "Publick works of piety" are here defined as follows: "publick works are building and endowing of Schools, of Churches, of Lecturers, of Work-houses, of Hospitals, of Manufactures, furnishing of Libraries, maintaining of publick Professors, Legacies to the poor, repairing Ways and Bridges, Loans to set up poor Tradesmen, and other the like Benefactions which have a common and publick influence."

[40] This is tentatively indicated by a search for the keyword "travaux publics" in Diderot's and Alembert's "Encyclopedie" (where the term is used 26 times and ten times alone in the article on "corvée"), but also for 'public works' in a 1798 edition of the *Encyclopedia Britannica* (where the term is used more diversely, but still often with references to forced labour in ancient Rome, early modern Italy or "oriental despotisms" (especially China). This keyword search has been conducted in recently digitalised versions of these encyclopedias: *Encyclopaedia; or, A Dictionary of Arts, Sciences, and Miscellaneous Literature* ..., 18 vols. (Philadelphia: Dobson, 1798 [1st American ed.]), Thomson Gale Databases, "Eighteenth Century Collections Online"; Denis Diderot, and Jean Le Rond d'Alembert, *L" Encyclopédie ou Dictionnaire raisonné des sciences, des arts et des metiers,* 17 vols. (Paris, 1751–1772), http://portail.atilf.fr/encyclopedie/.

[41] Bagwell, *The Transport Revolution*, 24–25.

as a concept of the emerging discourse of "political economy".[42] In the nineteenth century, 'public works' were accordingly understood not only as the result of the improving dynamics of private property aided by the state, but also as the property of a nation,[43] as facilities "for the use ... not of particular individuals but of any of the whole mass of individuals composing the nation who may be in a position to take advantage of them."[44] Moreover, the phrase was turned into an institutional branch of the nation state; the École Centrale des Travaux Publics was founded in revolutionary France, for instance, in 1794.[45] The notion of 'public works' was thus

[42] For its ethical content, see for example, Richard Savage, "Of Public Spirit in Regard to Public Works: An Epistle", in *The Works of Richard Savage .... With an Account of the Life and Writings of the Author, by Samuel Johnson* (London: T. Evans, 1775), 2: 131–43 ("Thus Public Spirit, liberty, and peace, /Carve, build, and plant, and give the land increase; /From peasant hands imperial works arise, /And British hence with Roman grandeur vies; /Not grandeur in pompous whim appears, /That levels hills, that vales to mountains rears; /.../Tho' no vast wall extends from coast to coast, /No pyramid aspires sublimely lost; /Yet safe road thro' rocks shall winding tend, /And the firm causeway o'er the clays ascend.' Ibid., 134). For the formation of "improvement" as a concept intimately connected to the notion of private property, see Ellen Meiksins Wood and Neal Wood, *A Trumpet of Sedition: Political Theory and the Rise of Capitalism, 1509–1688* (London/New York: Pluto Press, 1997), 131–34. For the conceptualisation of 'public works' in the new discipline of political economy, see Adam Smith, *The Wealth of Nations,* Books IV–V, edited and with an introduction by Andrew Skinner (London: Penguin Books Ltd, 1999), 310–48.

[43] See, for instance, the influential work by the mathematician, engineer and politician Baron Charles Dupin (the French original was published in 1824, of which English and German translations were available in the following year) that was not only a survey of 'public works' in Britain but also a comparative study of 'public works' policies and legislations in Britain and France with the explicit objective to strengthen the latter nation state by emulating the former. Charles Dupin, *The Commercial Power of Great Britain Exhibiting a Complete View of the Public Works of this Country* ... (London: Knight, 1825). Also see Charles Dupin, *Du commerce et de ses travaux publics en Angleterre et en France: discours prononcé le 2 juin 1823* (Paris: n.p., 1823).

[44] Thornton, *Economic Writings,* 5: 313.

[45] Janis Langins, *La République avait besoin de savants: Les débuts de l'École polytechnique: l'École centrale des travaux publics et les cours révolutionnaires de l'an III* (Paris: Belin, 1987), 24. The curricula of this institution reveal a very wide notion of "travaux publics", though transport infrastructure was also among the subjects. Ibid., 44–45.

remoulded into a conceptual tool for the production of national (as well as colonial) space. The persistent use of a term associated with imperial Rome at once placed the infrastructural policies of the modern state (both in the metropolis and in the colonies) in a prestigious line of historical continuity.[46]

Be that as it may, it is clear that the phrase 'public works' enriched modern idioms of political legitimacy in at least three ways. First of all, it concealed—as effectively as the later expression 'infrastructure'—the contradictory social interests involved in the production of built environments for purposes of transport by asserting their 'naturalness', general utility and contribution to an assumed 'common good'. Hence Malapert ascribed the origin of *travaux publics* to *nos instincts naturels*—an instinct shared by humanity as a whole that was hardly dissimilar from the urge of rabbits and bees to have burrows and hives.[47]

Second, ample evidence could be quoted from India as well as from other regions of a more direct utilisation of 'public works' as sources of 'basic' political legitimacy.[48] Queen Victoria's famous proclamation of 1858, published and read out in India after the suppression of the 'mutiny', may serve us here as a typical specimen of such ideological constructs. In this announcement of the assumption of direct government over the possessions of the East India Company the promotion of 'public works' was given pride of place as a desideratum of future policy and, with admirable clarity,

[46] The most systematic contemporary attempt to construct such a line of continuity was possibly Malapert's voluminous monograph on the legal history of 'public works' in France since the Roman period: M. F. Malapert, *Histoire de la législation des travaux publics* (Paris: Ducher et ci, 1880).
[47] Malapert, *Histoire de la législation*, v, vi.
[48] Trutz von Trotha has argued for the West African context that the colonial state derived "basic legitimacy" ("Basislegitimität") from 'public works' as expressions of an awe-inspiring "organisational efficiency". Trutz von Trotha "Über den Erfolg und die Brüchigkeit der Utopie staatlicher Herrschaft. Herrschaftssoziologische Beobachtungen über den kolonialen und nachkolonialen Staat in Westafrika" in *Verstaatlichung der Welt? Europäische Staatsmodelle und außereuropäische Machtprozesse*, ed. Wolfgang Reinhard (Munich: Oldenbourg, 1999), 235–37. For a penetrating analysis of the ideological utilisation of technological aspects of 'public works', see Michael Adas, *Machines as the Measure of Men: Science, Technology, and Ideologies of Western Dominance* (Ithaca/London: Cornell University Press, 1989), chapters 3–5. Also see Ahuja, "'The Bridge-Builders'".

as a means of manufacturing consent among her majesty's Indian subjects:

> When, by the blessing of Providence, internal tranquillity shall be restored, it is our earnest desire to stimulate the peaceful industry of India, to promote works of public utility and improvement, and to administer its government for the benefit of all our subjects resident therein. In their prosperity will be our strength, in their contentment our security, and in their gratitude our best reward.[49]

The urgency of this task was well appreciated in colonial circles. "[I]t is a serious truth," an anonymous contributor to the influential *Calcutta Review* pointed out in 1870, "in India, upon finance, upon the land question, and upon Public Works pre-eminently, *the governing classes are on their trial*."[50] Conversely, the potential of built environments to generate "basic legitimacy" was pointed out by Juland Danvers, the "Government Director of the Indian Railway Companies" in 1877. Railways, in his view,

> bring home ... to the native observer, whether he resides within or without our territory, the wonderful energy, power, and resources of the governing race. Nothing, perhaps, shows the effect of our rule upon India more than the railways. It is visible, tangible, and felt by all.[51]

Third, the notion of 'public works' owed much of its effectiveness to its convenient ambivalence: it left considerable leeway for the interpretation of the actual composition of the 'public' (as the proper agency of conceiving these built environments). Mid-nineteenth-century British interventions with regard to 'public works' policy in India thus explicitly excluded the 'native population' from the forces whose opinion had to be considered. John Chapman, one of the most effective early lobbyists for railways in India, reasoned, for instance:

> The public opinion which rules a country is commonly native to it; but that of India, as far as the sentiment of the people can be learned,

---

[49] *The Times*, 6 December 1858 (India: Proclamation of the Queen).
[50] "The Organization of the Public Works Department", *The Calcutta Review* L, 1870, 72 (emphasis in the original). *The Calcutta Review*, at this time, was a quarterly mainly reflecting the views of the colonial establishment.
[51] Juland Danvers, *Indian Railways: Their Past History, Present Condition, and Future Prospects* (London: Effingham Wilson, 1877), 30.

delegates its own task to the public opinion of England. ... The public opinion in England rules India chiefly through two means of action. First, through the fact, or ever impending possibility, of the actual proceedings of our Indian governments and officers being reviewed in England .... Second, through the English sentiments of those actually employed in the Government of India.[52]

Lord Stanley, soon to become Secretary of State for India, made the same point in the House of Commons with less subtlety and greater authority by squarely *equating* the Indian public with the colonial oligarchy, with the gentlemanly British residing in the subcontinent: "The public in India consist[s] of civilians and the military".[53] In the later decades of the period under study, official opinion held that Indian participation should be confined to deliberations of "non-political" financial and administrative aspects by "persons of local knowledge, weight, and intelligence" and especially to the local level.[54]

Social practices of producing built environments for purposes of circulation are, of course, much older than their ideologically charged denominations in nineteenth- and twentieth-century Europe. Nor were they geographically confined to that western appendage of the Asian landmass. Suffice it to hint at a few of the practices in medieval and early modern South Asia: The construction of numerous masonry bridges and causeways;[55] the erection and maintenance of *sattirams, dharamsalas, sarais* and other rest houses along pilgrim and trading routes by the mighty and the rich;[56] the

[52] Chapman, *Principles of Indian Reform*, 15.
[53] The term "civilian" denoted a member of the colonial "Indian Civil Service". Speech by Lord Stanley in the House of Commons, 23 June 1857, *The Times*, 24 June 1857.
[54] Strachey and Strachey, *Finances and Public Works of India*, 425–27; also see p. 108 of this chapter.
[55] Jean Deloche, *The Ancient Bridges of India,* 1st Engl. ed. (New Delhi: Sitaram Bhartia Institute of Scientific Research, 1984); also see Bejoy Kumar Sarkar, *Inland Transport and Communication in Mediaeval India* (Calcutta: Calcutta University Press, 1925), 36–41; Abul Khair M. Farooque, *Roads and Communications in Mughal India* (Delhi: Idarah-i Adabiyat-i Delli, 1977), 40–54; Catherine B. Asher, *Architecture of Mughal India*, New Cambridge History of India I: 4 (Cambridge: Cambridge University Press, 1992), 87.
[56] Sarkar, *Inland Transport and Communication*, 41–48, 74–75; Deloche, *Transport and Communication*, 1: 160–83; Farooque, *Roads and Communications*, 96–104;

establishment by Indian rulers (and especially by Sher Shah Suri [r. 1539–1545] and his Mughal successors) of convex and raised though almost always unsurfaced 'highways' lined with shade trees and punctuated with wells, and *kos minars* (one *kos* equals two statute miles; *minar*-tower) that served as resting places and *dak chaukis* (relay stations for the imperial mail);[57] even more intensive measures of road construction by certain early modern regional polities such as the Ahom dynasty of Assam and the eighteenth-century sultans of Mysore.[58]

Monuments like palaces, forts or mosques may well have absorbed the larger part of the social energies early modern states and dominant interests had transformed into buildings—not merely because of their primarily military, administrative and religious

---

Tapan Raychaudhuri, "Inland Trade", in *The Cambridge Economic History of India, c. 1200–c. 1750*, ed. Tapan Raychaudhuri and Irfan Habib (Cambridge: Cambridge University Press, 1982), 1: 354–55; for a local case outside the core area of the Mughal empire, also see Ravi Ahuja, *Die Erzeugung kolonialer Staatlichkeit und das Problem der Arbeit. Eine Studie zur Sozialgeschichte der Stadt Madras und ihres Hinterlandes zwischen 1750 und 1800* (Stuttgart: Steiner, 1999), 28–30. Indian notables continued to endow dharamsalas or sarais during the British period; for examples from Orissa, see George Toynbee, *A Sketch of the History of Orissa from 1803 to 1828* (Calcutta: Bengal Secretariat Press, 1873), 83; OIOC, BPWP July 1861, P/16/52, Com., no. 31, 39 (Report by F. Bond . . . submitted in accordance with the Offg. Superintending Engineer's Circular Memorandum, 15 April 1861). Yang (*Bazaar India*, 46, footnote 59) states that a monastery near Gaya "provided free food and a place to stay for weary and poor travellers for three consecutive days" and covered the expenses by holdings in several villages.

[57] Sarkar, *Inland Transport and Communication*, 30–34; Deloche, *Transport and Communication*, 1: 32–34, 105, 120–21, 147–49, 153–59, 167–82; Farooque, *Roads and Communications*, 29–33, 125–45; Irfan Habib, "The Technology and Economy of Mughal India", *Indian Economic and Social History Review* 17, no. 1, 1980, 11–13; Raychaudhuri, "Inland Trade", 353– 54; Asher, *Architecture of Mughal India*, 111, 230.

[58] Sarkar, *Inland Transport and Communication*, 32–33; Deloche, *Transport and Communication*, 1: 110–12, 118, 121. On the remains of the partly bridged and occasionally paved "sultan salai" ("sultan's road") in Mysore, see Jean Deloche "Études sur la circulation en Inde. VIII. De la trouée de Palghat et du plateau de Maisur a la pédipleine Tamoule: Liaisons routières anciennes et vestiges de chemins", *Bulletin de l'École Française d'Extrême-Orient* LXXVIII, 1991, 59– 61, 66, 78–83.

functions. They were also *landmarks* that generated absolute spaces imbued with political and social meaning (see hypothesis 4), and radiated status and legitimacy. However, it is likely that the existing accounts of South Asia's early modern built environment, mainly written by art historians, have tended to neglect the often more inconspicuous and less durable everyday architecture of roads and irrigation works.[59] Yet it has been demonstrated that irrigation works were a crucial feature of India's precolonial built environment—an indispensable means of securing the subsistence and raising the productivity of a largely non-commodified and predominantly agrarian society.[60] As for transport infrastructure, both Muslim and Hindu notables considered the endowment of various types of rest houses a pious work that would be a means of preserving the benefactor's memory and of enhancing his social status as well as of gaining from trade, displaying power and incurring the favour of the Mughal emperor. This is particularly significant since such rest houses were probably the most important infrastructural precondition for premodern long-distance traffic providing to merchants and other travellers food, accommodation and protection of life and property as well as forage for their beasts of burden. Moreover, they served as nodal points for the exchange of information, commodities and ideas and hence as 'workshops' for the generation of social space. Some of these buildings were large enough to give shelter to several thousand travellers at one time.[61] Moreover, roads were

[59] Even more recent textbooks of Mughal architecture do, for instance, provide some information on the more spectacular structures of the sarais but have little to say about bridges and roadworks. See, for example, Asher, *Architecture of Mughal India*; Ebba Koch, *Mughal Architecture: An Outline of Its History and Development, 1526–1858* (Munich: Prestel, 1991) (for page references with regard to "sarais", see footnote 61, below).

[60] For a survey of precolonial irrigation infrastructure, see Anil Agarwal and Sunita Narain, *Dying Wisdom: Rise, Fall and Potential of India's Traditional Water Harvesting Systems* (New Delhi: Centre for Science and Environment, 1997).

[61] Most historical writings on pre-colonial rest houses focus on endowments and architecture, while their social history is little explored. The erection of such structures appears to have been particularly frequent during the reign of Jahangir (r. 1605–1627), who had ordered the construction of sarais and religious buildings on his accession to the throne. Wayne E. Begley, "Four Mughal Caravanserais Built During the Reigns of Jahangir and Shah Jahan",

important enough to induce rulers from Akbar (r. 1556–1605) to Aurangzeb (r. 1658–1707) to maintain institutional arrangements for their construction and upkeep. While *jagirdars* (who held the right to the revenues of a territory), *mukaddams* (village headmen), *kotwals* (town magistrates) or *faujdars* (military commanders) were held responsible for the security of travellers and the maintenance of rest houses in Mughal India, zamindars had to keep important roads in repair—chiefly it is said by means of forced labour. A high-ranking official, the *Diwan-i-Bayutat*, was in charge of an advance party of hundreds of stonecutters, earthworkers and other artisans who cleared and repaired the roads for the frequently travelling Mughal Court—an arrangement that has sometimes been called, somewhat anachronistically, a "department" or "engineer corps".[62] This confirms, once again, the observation that circulatory practices were a common feature of social life in early modern South Asia.[63] However, this point should not be pushed too far. From the present state of research, it seems safe to conclude that the social need for an expensive built environment for purposes of circulation was limited and confined to vital strategic links and certain pilgrimage roads.[64]

---

in *Muqarnas: An Annual on the Visual Culture of the Islamic World*, 1, 1983, 167–79; Asher, *Architecture of Mughal India*, 128, 137–39, 143, 156, 227, 280; Koch, *Mughal Architecture*, 66–68, 90–92, 123–24, 131. For a seventeenth century description of a sarai on the "Jagannath Road" near Jaleshwar by a European traveller, see Sebastien Manrique, *Travels of Fray Sebastien Manrique, 1629–1643*, Hakluyt Society, 2nd series, vol. 61; introduced and annotated by C. Eckford Luard (Oxford: Hakluyt Society, 1927), 20: 99–101. Also see footnote 56, pp. 85–86.

[62] Local arrangements for the protection and accommodation of travellers are dealt with in the available literature in rather general terms and merit further research. Sarkar, *Inland Transport and Communication*, 60–71; Farooque, *Roads and Communications*, 21–26; Deloche, *Transport and Communication*, 1: 120; also see Asher, *Architecture of Mughal India*, 261.

[63] See the section "circulation" in this chapter.

[64] For the priority of strategic links, see Deloche, *Transport and Communication*, 1: 90–92, 122–23. The road from Bengal to the Jagannath temple in Puri, which will be dealt with at length in the second part of this study, is the most striking example of a pilgrim road of minor strategic importance that was exceptionally well provided with masonry bridges from the medieval period. Ibid., 1: 140.

Circulation and Infrastructure

This takes us back to Marx' observation that circulation remained external to the production process as long as only the "excess product is exchanged", and as long as the primary (though not sole!) objective of production was to afford the subsistence of the producer (the realisation of the use value) and not the accumulation of capital (the realisation of the exchange value).[65] Relating to pre-industrial modes of circulation in space, Marx observed that the waterway (*Wasserweg*) "as the route which moves and is transformed under its own impetus, is that of the trading peoples par excellence."[66] Hence merchant capital in marketing a society's "excess product" rather followed the course of natural lines of communication than creating its own. This can also be shown for South Asia where rivers and the Indian Ocean provided the lines that required the least energy input,[67] though there were also modes of overland traffic involving little long-term investment and offering freight rates that permitted trade in low-value bulk articles like grain and salt: The desert, like the ocean, did not demand or permit infrastructures beyond a network of support bases (ports or oases),[68] and the Banjaras provided an extremely cheap mode of overland bulk transport by letting their sizeable bullock caravans graze their way along shifting tracks through pasture lands across the subcontinent at a travel speed of no more than eight or ten kilometres

---

[65] Marx, *Grundrisse*, 524 or MEW, vol. 42, 430. Also see p. 73, above.

[66] Marx, *Grundrisse*, 525 or MEW, vol. 42, 431. Martin Nicolaus" translation of "Wasserweg" as "sea route" instead of the literal "waterway" is inadequate, since the generic phrase "Wasserweg" includes navigable rivers (the importance of which as premodern channels of transportation the Rhinelander Marx was unlikely to overlook).

[67] For the importance of river transport in precolonial India, see Jean Deloche, *Transport and Communication in India Prior to Steam Locomotion: Water Transport*, 2: 5–39, 129–77; Irfan Habib, *The Agrarian System of Mughal India, 1556–1707*, 2nd rev. ed. (Delhi: Oxford University Press, 1999), 70–71. For the lower Ganges, see Yang, *Bazaar India*, 27–32. For eastern India, see especially Munsi, *Geography of Transportation in Eastern India*, 16–22; Bhattacharya, "Regional Economy (1757–1857): Eastern India", 2: 271–73, and chapter 4 of the present study.

[68] For a perceptive reference to the similarity of the sea and the desert as ecological underpinnings for circulatory practices, see Kirti N. Chaudhuri, *Asia before Europe: Economy and Civilisation of the Indian Ocean from the Rise of Islam to 1750* (Cambridge: Cambridge University Press, 1990), 140–42.

per day.[69] As for "highways" or built roads, Marx wrote that they "originally fall to the community, later for a long period to the governments, as pure deductions from production, deducted from the common surplus product of the country, but do not constitute a source of its wealth, that is, do not cover their production costs."[70]

"That the erection and maintenance of the public works which facilitate the commerce of any country, such as good roads, bridges, navigable canals, harbours, etc., must require very different degrees of expense in the different periods of society" had already been noticed by Adam Smith in whose lifetime the stunning growth of the British turnpike road network provided ample proof of a society's changing needs for transport infrastructure.[71] With the expansion of commodity production the existing material underpinnings of circulation proved inadequate and were transformed. Goods could only be produced as commodities, if they could be carried to the market. The expansion, acceleration and reduction of the costs of transport became a precondition for the growth of commodity production and the extension of accumulation. Transport charges were consequently integrated with production costs. Though raised and gravelled roads, canals and railways required much larger investments than the earlier "natural" lines of communication, the massively increased volume of commodity transport permitted a secular decline of freight rates that increased the profitability and the further spatial expansion of commodity exchange. Conversely, the construction of transport infrastructure turned from a mere consumption of surplus labour into an area of capital investment when the growth in the volume of commercial traffic made sure "that the road pays for itself, that is, that the price demanded for the use of the road *is worth* that much exchange value for the producers, or supplies a productive force for which they can pay that much."[72] The desirability of a built line of communication was hence, from the perspective of political economists and administrators, increasingly determined by its ability

---

[69] Habib, "Merchant Communities in Precolonial India", 373–75; Habib, *Agrarian System of Mughal India,* 69–70; Clarke, *Practical and Theoretical Considerations,* 38, 42. Also see chapter 4 of the present study.
[70] Marx, *Grundrisse,* 525 or MEW, vol. 42, 431.
[71] Smith, *Wealth of Nations,* Books IV–V, 311. For the "turnpike system", see Bagwell, *The Transport Revolution,* 26–29.
[72] Marx, *Grundrisse,* 530 or MEW, vol. 42, 436. Also see Smith, *Wealth of Nations,* Books IV–V, 312.

to "pay for itself", to offer a profitable investment opportunity or to meet at least the cost of its construction and maintenance.

Yet investment in transport infrastructure had its own particularities. The capital requirements for establishment, operation and maintenance (especially with regard to railways and steam shipping) were massive, the proportion of fixed capital unusually high and the turnover speed exceedingly low. All this implied that such works were usually taken in hand not by individual entrepreneurs but rather by joint stock companies that were often subsidised by the state or even that the state undertook them directly. Moreover, while comprehensive networks of communication were soon conceived of as a social necessity, not all of the lines constituting these networks could be profitable to the same extent. This created tensions between the interests of individual investors and the requirements of expanding markets that often entailed further state involvement.[73] Even the high priest of the "invisible hand" opined that it was the duty of the "sovereign or commonwealth" to erect and maintain "those public works, which, though they may be to the highest degree advantageous to a great society, are, however, of such a nature that the profit could never repay the expense to any individual or small number of individuals".[74]

This new political economy of 'public works' underwent, however, serious modifications when it was applied by the agencies of colonialism to the conditions of nineteenth-century India—modifications whose general features will be briefly outlined in the remainder of this chapter. To put the argument in a nutshell, while 'public works' were likewise turned into an area of massive capital investment after the 1840s there were two major differences: First, built lines of communication did not have to "pay for themselves"[75] in the same way as in Britain and second, the state pursued a much more active and coercive policy.

In discussing this modified political economy of 'public works' under colonialism we may begin with the observation that utilitarian fervour of colonial administrators and "the Victorian conception of civilisation and improvement" were, contrary to what Cain

---

[73] Cf. Marx, *Grundrisse*, 530–33 or MEW, vol. 42, 437–40; Harvey, *Spaces of Capital*, 243, 246–48.
[74] Smith, *Wealth of Nations*, Books IV–V, 310.
[75] See footnote 72 in this chapter.

and Hopkins assert, no sufficient preconditions for the transformation of India's transport infrastructure.[76] For all the dramatic effect of placing "steamboats on the Ganges"[77] the utilitarian radicalism of a Governor-General Bentinck (1828–1835) hardly made a ripple as far as India's overall communications infrastructure was concerned. The most revolutionary changes occurred paradoxically around and after the great insurrection of 1857 when more conservative attitudes to Indian society were blended with a particularly authoritarian strand of the "utilitarian legacy".[78] The attribute 'revolutionary' seems particularly adequate in this context as the changes were fundamental in both qualitative and quantitative terms. It has been mentioned before that not even 1 per cent of the revenue the British extracted from their Indian possessions was spent on infrastructure until the late 1840s,[79] which meant—if John Bright got his figures right in the House of Commons—that "the single city of Manchester, in the supply of its inhabitants with the single article of water, has spent a larger sum of money than the East India Company has spent in the fourteen years from 1834 to 1848 in public works of every kind throughout the whole of its vast dominions".[80] Even a Chairman of the "Honourable Company" would admit in this period that "if we were to retire from India in four or five years there would be hardly anything left to present a trace of our having

[76] "Manchester did indeed press for 'public works', but these were already part of the Government of India's development plans, and had been since at least the 1820s. Governments did not need to be persuaded of the importance of railways in 'opening up' the country because they were an integral feature of the Victorian conception of civilisation and improvement." Cain and Hopkins, *British Imperialism, 291.*
[77] Cf. Bernstein, *Steamboats on the Ganges*—an account of these events written in the early 1960s in the then prevailing vein of a modernising triumphalism.
[78] Cf. Eric Stokes, *The English Utilitarians and India* (Delhi: Oxford University Press, 1989 [1st ed. 1955]), 234–322; Thomas R. Metcalf, *Ideologies of the Raj*, New Cambridge History of India III. 4 (Cambridge: Cambridge University Press, 1994), 43–65.
[79] See footnote 66 on page 44 of the present study.
[80] John Bright, Speech in the House of Commons, 24 June 1858, in *Speeches on Questions of Public Policy by John Bright, M. P.,* ed. by James E. T. Rogers, 2nd ed. (London: Macmillan, 1869), 1: 42. Decades later, Sir John Strachey commented that he did "not doubt that Mr. Bright's statement was substantially not far from correct." Strachey, *India,* 233.

been there."[81] The lofty "Victorian conception of civilisation and improvement" had to coincide with powerful economic and political needs for an extended transport infrastructure in India before it could turn into a material force. But when it did, the picture changed dramatically in less than two decades: by 1869–70 almost 20 per cent of the gross revenue of "British India" was spent under the head of "public works"[82] and about 7,000 km of railway were open for traffic.[83] This was the very year when Viceroy Lord Mayo (1869–72) asserted grandly that "we are determined as long as the sun shines in heaven to hold India"—an objective less interesting for our present argument than the grounds adduced for its urgency: "Our national character, our commerce, demand it; and we have, one way or another, two hundred and fifty millions of English capital fixed in the country."[84]

While a thorough infrastructural transformation became perceivable in many Indian regions only after the insurrection of 1857 and the dissolution of the East India Company in the following year, this process was rather reinforced than caused by these events: the emergence of a momentous 'public works' policy along aggressive strategic orientations clearly commenced in the early half of the 1850s, when the expenditure on 'public works' rose from a miserly average of £250,000 to the more considerable tune of 2 million (increasing further to about 5 million in the following decade).[85] More importantly, it was at this juncture that the pillars of a 'public works' policy were erected that proved on the whole sustainable throughout the period under review. For 'public works' in India served at once three potentially conflicting interests within the British ruling block: (a) they increased and even created new sources

---

[81] Quoted by the Earl of Ellenborough who said he remembered this statement from the time when he had been Chairman of the Board of Control (which he was from 1828 to 1830, in 1834–35 and again in 1841). "Parliamentary Intelligence, House of Lords", 2 May 1853, *The Times*, 3 May 1853.

[82] This included "productive works" and the respective service of debt as well as "ordinary public works", see below. Strachey and Strachey, *Finances and Public Works of India*, 432–33, 444–45.

[83] Kerr, *Building the Railways*, 211.

[84] Mayo to Sir A. Buchanan, 26 September 1869, quoted in Sarvepalli Gopal, *British Policy in India, 1858–1905* (Cambridge: Cambridge University Press, 1965), 120–21.

[85] Strachey and Strachey, *Finances and Public Works of India*, 86–87.

of revenue for the colonial state and the oligarchy attached to it; (b) they offered attractive interest rates for British finance and private investors; (c) they generated markets where British industrialists could buy raw materials (especially cotton) cheap and sell their products profitably. All three interests converged in a fourth objective of colonial 'public works' policy considered to be of utmost urgency after the insurrection of 1857—namely that these works were to guarantee the security of these revenues, investments and markets (as well as of other benefits of colonial rule) by reinforcing the political and military hold over the subcontinent.

On a conceptual level, the keystone of this 'public works' policy was the distinction (first introduced by Dalhousie in 1853) between, "ordinary works" on the one hand and, on the other, works "of permanent utility" that yielded (directly or indirectly) enough revenue to "pay for themselves" at the least. The latter were, therefore, accounted for at different junctures as "remunerative", "reproductive", "extra-ordinary" or "productive public works". On the most general level, the former "ordinary" category comprised infrastructural projects that were held to be a necessary but "unproductive" consumption of revenue, while the latter was believed to consist of "productive" investments. "Productivity" was defined, however, differently at various stages: it could imply that these works bore annual interest at a rate acceptable to private or public investors, but also that they contributed to "developing the resources of the country" and were, therefore, expected to increase the revenues of the colonial state in the medium term. In 1858, a "Committee ... on the Classification of Public Works Expenditure" thus drew a distinction between (a) non-remunerative "State Works"—comprising mainly official buildings, and (b) "Works of Internal Improvement"—"being profitable in a pecuniary point of view ... to the entire body politic of the State (both government and community, as partners)"— which included all works of irrigation and communication.[86] However, the actual classification of expenditure on 'public works' in the government accounts of subsequent decades digressed significantly from this categorisation. On the one hand, "ordinary" (that is, unproductive) works included not only the various types of official buildings but also "minor" irrigation works and, more importantly for

---

[86] Quoted in, Whitcombe, "Irrigation", 692.

our discussion, the construction and maintenance of all roads. The head of "extra-ordinary" works subsumed, on the other hand, large (and partly navigable) irrigation works and most railways. These were considered to be either "productive", that is, to bear annual interest for the state and/or private investors, or to be "preventive"—a term introduced in the 1870s for projects that were expected to reduce the need for costly famine relief programmes rather than to "pay for themselves" directly. While "ordinary works" were exclusively funded from state revenue, the "extra-ordinary works" were opened for British capital in various forms ranging from direct investment to government bonds.[87]

This categorisation clearly relied on Adam Smith's economic conceptualisation of 'public works' of transport as means of "facilitating commerce"—"defraying", in their greater part and wherever possible, "their own expense".[88] Yet the distinction between "ordinary" and "productive public works" implied a particular a priori ranking of the economic viability and desirability of the various types of transport infrastructure and entailed, consequently, important political choices and a particular economy of space. By the end of the Company regime the emphasis was thus squarely shifted to *large* infrastructural projects requiring heavy investment—to projects of a type, which could be undertaken, handled and "turned to account" most efficiently by a highly centralised colonial state and joint stock companies based in faraway London.[89] It is true that a spurt in the construction of roads can be made out for a period starting in the 1840s and extending well into the 1860s. This spurt

---

[87] For this paragraph, see Edwin Arnold, *The Marquis of Dalhousie's Administration of British India* (London: Otley and Co., 1865), 2: 234–35; Strachey and Strachey, *Finances and Public Works of India*, 95–112; Report from Select Committee on East India Railway Communication, iii–ix; Ambirajan, *Classical Political Economy*, 247, 255–57; Whitcombe, "Irrigation", 692–700; Arun Banerji, *Finances in the Early Raj: Investments and the External Sector* (New Delhi: Sage Publications, 1995), 54–58, 77–79, 86–87, 207–11, 214. Also see chapters 5–7 of the present study.
[88] Smith, *Wealth of Nations*, Books IV–V, 311.
[89] This shift in priorities may be an answer to the question Tirthankar Roy raises with his observation that "government for some reason did not seriously explore the possibility of involving private enterprise in constructing a network of tolled roads." Tirthankar Roy, *The Economic History of India, 1857–1947* (New Delhi/Oxford: Oxford University Press, 2000), 266.

was connected to the aggressive policy of expansionism followed prior to the insurrection of 1857, to ensuing colonial security needs, and to some extent also to the rising British demand for Indian raw cotton and other agricultural produce.[90] Yet this was also the period when crucial policy decisions permanently shifted the priority to railways and, to a less extent, to large irrigation works. One discursive consequence of this new emphasis was that a very large proportion of the official records and publications on subsequent 'public works' is focused on these two heads.[91] William Thornton, high-ranking India Office bureaucrat in the relevant department, hardly mentioned roads when expanding on "Indian Public Works" at considerable length in the early 1870s.[92] Subsequently, most historians of infrastructure seem to have been led by the structure of the available material to confine their studies to irrigation and, even more often, to railways.[93]

This bias reflected the priorities in the allocation of funds: in the 1870s, railways and irrigation accounted for about half of the Government of India's expenditures on 'public works' (a head including heavy administrative charges in addition to various types of building projects).[94] While the expenditure of all levels of government on roads was estimated at about £1.5 million per year during the

[90] MacGeorge, *Ways and Works*, 80–85, 104. For the region of Awadh, which was a focus of such activities, see Varady, "Rail and Road Transport", 34–47. For an elaborate scheme of "imperial roads" ordered by Governor-General Canning just before the commencement of the "mutiny", see OSA: BoRLR 27,539 (W. E. Baker, Secry to GoI, PWD, to A. R. Young, Secry. to GoB, 17 April 1857). Also see Munsi, *Geography of Transportation in Eastern India*, 27, and chapters 5–6 of the present study.

[91] MacGeorge, who had the most privileged access to the relevant records when he wrote his official history of colonial 'public works', could not but remark: "Very little statistical data or information appears to be available in connection with road construction generally in India." *Ways and Works*, 104.

[92] Thornton, *Public Works in India*.

[93] Both Romesh Chunder Dutt's classic of economic nationalism, *The Economic History of India in the Victorian Age: From the Accession of Queen Victoria in 1837 to the Commencement of the Twentieth Century*, 7th ed. (London: Routledge and Kegan Paul, 1950 [1st ed. 1903], and the "revisionist" second volume of the *Cambridge Economic History of India* (1982) thus implicitly equate infrastructure with irrigation and railways.

[94] Strachey and Strachey, *Finances and Public Works of India*, 432–33, 444–45. Also see Banerji, *Finances in Early Raj*, 216–17.

Circulation and Infrastructure

three decades before 1889,[95] the capital expenditure on railways amounted to an annual average of almost £4 million between 1849–50 and 1878–79.[96] According to Banerji's annual estimates for the period between 1880–81 and 1897–98, "private" and "public" investment in railways amounted in that period to Rs 1,925 million as opposed to Rs 988 million in "roads and building"—the latter category obviously comprising, to a large extent, facilities for purposes other than circulation.[97] In the following three decades, "public investment" in Indian railways regularly dwarfed the combined expenditure of the central, provincial and local governments on "roads and buildings".[98] The long-term and overall effect of this financial prioritisation on the structure of transportation facilities was summed up as follows by the Indian Road Development Committee in 1928:

> it is inevitable in a country so vast as India that the network of railways should have a very wide mesh. The intervals should be filled by roads, and it would appear that the development of railways has outstripped the development of roads. It is stated in the Railway Board memorandum that "railways in India have always felt the lack of roads to feed them". It is indeed somewhat incongruous that there should be nearly 40,000 miles of railway in India, while the total mileage of surfaced roads in British India is only 59,000.[99]

The uneven development of transport infrastructure and, consequently, of social space[100] was further exacerbated by the fact that many of these surfaced main roads ran parallel to railway lines. Therefore, they rather competed with than functioned as "feeders" for the railways while their construction and maintenance consumed much of the available road funds.[101] Road policy (and even,

---

[95] MacGeorge, *Ways and Works*, 104.
[96] Calculated from the figures given in Bailey and McGuire, "Railways, Exchange Banks and World Economy", 131.
[97] Banerji, *Finances in Early Raj*, 218–19.
[98] 1898/99: 75:56; 1901/02: 88:67; 1919–20: 256:198; 1927–28: 434:245 (million Rs.). Dharma Kumar, "The Fiscal System", in *The Cambridge Economic History of India*, 2: 936.
[99] *Report of the Indian Road Development Committee, 1927–28* (Calcutta: Government of India Press, 1928), 1: 20.
[100] See hypothesis 6 in chapter 2 of the present study.
[101] "nearly one-half of the total milage [sic] of railway in British India has a metalled road parallel and within ten miles of it." Mitchell and Kirkness,

in the case of Orissa, the alignment of navigable canals)[102] thus intensified rather than counterbalanced the reorientation of India's patterns of circulation along radial mainlines of railway instead of developing cellular networks on the basis of precolonial patterns of circulation. In Sunil Kumar Munsi's view, the British Government in India "never seriously concerned itself with the development of the rural road system . . . as a part of a self-sustaining rural economy centering around local, sub-regional and regional marts."[103] This conclusion appears rather safe on the basis of the available evidence for "British India" as a whole though the dynamics of uneven development generated considerable regional disparities in this respect, too.[104]

When motorised road traffic expanded from the 1920s onwards, the contradictions of this 'public works' policy reached an intensity that turned it into an impediment—even for practices of circulation the colonial regime conceived of as desirable. These contradictions were then, as we have just seen, more openly admitted even in official statements. Yet numerous objections had already been raised since the middle of the preceding century by British and, later Indian nationalist critics against the priorities of the imperial 'public works' policy on the subcontinent.[105] They had also propounded, time and again, the feasibility of alternative scenarios.

Report on the Present State of Road and Railway Competition, 1–2, 7. Also see Munsi, *Geography of Transportation in Eastern India*, 37–38. This problem seems to have been especially grave in Orissa—the region our case study is concerned with. Cf. E. Satyanarayana Sarma, *Report on Road Development for the Orissa Province* (Cuttack: Government Press Orissa, 1942), 16–17.

[102] See chapters 6 and 7 of the present study.

[103] Munsi, *Geography of Transportation in Eastern India*, 27–29; see also pp. 44–46, 131.

[104] See, for instance, Anand Yang's contention that railway construction actually boosted road development in Gangetic Bihar. Yang, *Bazaar India*, 50–52. Also see Derbyshire, "Economic Change and the Railways", 523–33, where it is held that in North India railway development was accompanied by a shift from pack bullock to bullock carts and a considerable rise in the number of the latter. However, Derbyshire also points at subregional disparities when he remarks that the eastern Doab, formerly the region's focus of commercial production, "suffered in many ways" from the introduction of railways and turned into an area of labour emigration. Ibid., 536.

[105] For the arguments of early nationalists, see Chandra, *Rise and Growth of Economic Nationalism in India*, 207–14.

One of the earliest and most articulate of these critics was Sir Arthur Cotton who entered the East India Company's service in 1819 and acquired a high reputation as a senior engineer in the 1850s for designing revenue-raising irrigation schemes in South India. He remained an assiduous campaigner for large-scale irrigation works in other regions of the subcontinent for many decades, which all but cost him his reputation in British government circles,[106] while Romesh Chunder Dutt used his statements as key evidence for the case of Indian economic nationalism.[107] Cotton had insisted in his influential book *Public Works in India* (1854) that there was scope for choice not only between railways and irrigation but also between railways and "cheaper" (that is, less capital-intensive) transportation facilities and that the latter alternative was preferable in each case.[108] This triggered off a major public debate in Britain and *The Times*, a powerful promoter of railway construction in India, recapitulated and discussed Cotton's arguments in an elaborate review article stretching over three issues.[109] The reviewer quoted Cotton's calculation that "the same money and time required to make one mile of high speed-railway, will make 100 miles of good river navigation, 24 of first-class steam canal, 12 of very good low speed railway, 20 of an inferior kind, 40 of perfect common road with timber bridges, or 24 with masonry works."[110] Cotton had argued that

> in a rich country already provided with a complete system of *cheap transit, high speed of transit* is the grand object to be sought; but that in a very poor country, paralyzed by utter want of means in transit at a moderate cost, *speed in forming a general system of cheap transit*, is the great desideratum to which everything else should give way.[111]

---

[106] A. J. Arbuthnot, "Cotton, Sir Arthur Thomas (1803–1899)," rev. by Peter L. Schmitthenner, in *Oxford Dictionary of National Biography*, ed. H. C. G. Matthew and Brian Harrison (Oxford et al.: Oxford University Press, 2004).
[107] Dutt, *Economic History of India in the Victorian Age*, 360–70, 545–46.
[108] Arthur Cotton, *Public Works in India, their Importance; with Suggestions for their Extension and Improvement* (London: Richardson Brothers, 1854).
[109] *The Times*, 28 and 29 December 1853, 3 January 1854 ("Public Works in India").
[110] *The Times*, 3 January 1854 ("Public Works in India"); Cotton, *Public Works in India*, 282.
[111] Cotton, *Public Works in India*, 283, see also 8–9 (emphasis in the original).

The point was thus "not to make the most perfect communication possible on some few hundred miles" but "to adopt a system of communications, by which the principal part of the cost of transit will be saved, to be executed throughout the whole country, in the shortest possible time" and that this task required the "improvement" of rivers by means of embankments etc., the construction of "steam canals", tramways and "common roads" rather than the prioritisation of "high-cost railways".[112] On the influential pages of *The Times* the reviewer conceded that "if India were obliged to take her choice between the two, it would be far better to provide a moderate speed over her whole surface than to travel with great velocity of a few hundred miles, and be reduced to travel by dawk [dak] over the remainder of the country. But," he argued,

> we deny that there is any such alternative. There is no reason why India should not have both. There is no reason why English companies should not be employed in providing India with complete railways at the same time that the Government occupies itself with those cheaper and less ambitious works.[113]

While the subsequent decades established as a fact that "India" did not get either, the colonial administration seemed little concerned to find the reasons for the unevenness its policy generated, merely paid lip service to the desirability of a dense network of local transportation, and continued to give preference to the railways. Hence Thornton admonished "circles betraying a tendency to railway mania . . . that common roads are not so much the proper supplements of railways as railways are of common roads" without, however, giving roads or waterways any weight in his own discussion of "communications".[114]

Both approaches to infrastructure, that of the 'railway maniacs' (or advocates of a capital-intensive transport infrastructure) as much as that of the proponents of irrigation and 'cheap communications',

---

[112] Ibid., 277.
[113] *The Times*, 3 January 1854 ("Public Works in India"). Similarly, the *Economist* also admitted that under Indian conditions "fewer and cheaper railways, and more numerous roads and canals" would have been better investments but emphasised the superior "civilising influence" of the former. *The Economist*, 25 July 1857, 810, quoted in Jenks, *Migration of British Capital*, 216.
[114] Thornton, *Public Works in India*, 337.

were based on the same preconception of South Asian natural and social space as a tabula rasa to be engraved upon at will. Both rested on the same notion of 'public works' as a means and indicator of universal progress serving the 'community at large'—a progress to be achieved, depending on the political point of view, either by way of an authoritarian British 'civilising' crusade against the inertia of 'native' society (an opinion preached with particular violence by the evangelist and colonial engineer Arthur Cotton)[115] or in the process of the Indian nation's coming into its own (which required, in the view of liberal nationalists like R. C. Dutt, an increased representation of the "Indian people" in the "Executive Government").[116] Both ideas were also based on Adam Smith's general assumptions of a political economy of 'public works', that is, that financial return should be the measure of roads and that 'public works' should be private undertakings as far as possible.[117] Yet these

---

[115] Cotton thus blamed the state of 'public works' to a failure of imposing English virtues and science upon India: "The system of imbibing erroneous ideas from the Natives instead of teaching them, pervades every branch of the Indian service, and is at the bottom of all our blunders. . . . Every European in the country has learnt in England the essential importance of communications and other public works; but yet he acts exactly as if he knew nothing about it. If intelligent Natives went to England, they would be astonished beyond measure when seeing the inconceivable effect of cheap transit, that the English in their country should have been content to throw away all their own ideas on the subject, and adopt the ignorant narrow ideas of their subjects and that instead of bringing their western knowledge, energy, activity, and common sense to bear, they should have adopted the views of a people without books or science. When the English begin to think for themselves, and bring their own Anglo-Saxon notions fairly to bear upon India, there will be a wonderful change. A Native is by nature a very intelligent being, but he is utterly without our advantages. Imagine what a nation of Anglo-Saxons would be, who had not a single book worth reading in their language; and who had learnt nothing from the books but drivellings such as are found in the Hindoo religious writings, which they themselves could see to be utter nonsense. And yet, such are the people we are content to learn from, instead of teaching them." Cotton, *Public Works in India*, 11. The assertions that "not a single book worth reading" existed in Indian languages echoed, of course, Macaulay's famous "Minute on Education" of 1835. Cf. Adas, *Machines as the Measure of Men*, 275–84; Metcalf, *Ideologies of the Raj*, 34.

[116] Dutt, *Economic History of India in Victorian Age*, 174, 177–78, 553–54. Also see Goswami, *Producing India*, 222.

[117] Smith, *Wealth of Nations*, Book, IV–V, 310–19.

assumptions were open to conflicting interpretations even within the context of colonial India.[118] The promoters of irrigation and 'cheap communications' envisioned a broad-based enhancement of agricultural production combined with the development of a dense network of local markets, an augmentation of state revenue (either by increasing the taxation of land or by taxing the use of water) and also an increase of profits for British capital (through investing in joint stock irrigation companies or availing itself of the more abundant and cheap Indian produce). The railway lobby sought to link up certain agricultural regions and centres of consumption in India with the chains of production and the spaces of circulation of British industrial capital, so as to create a profitable foreign investment option for British finance and a new source of government income—for instance, in the form of railway returns.[119] The resulting colonial policy was a combination of both approaches to 'public works' with a clear preponderance of the latter and an emphasis on large-scale projects attracting British capital.

Yet this policy remained riven with contradictions—namely, between the objectives of increasing the state revenues and safeguarding the profits of British investors. This accounts for various policy changes in the second half of the nineteenth century—for instance, with regard to the so-called "guarantee system". In 1849, the British railway lobby succeeded in securing an undertaking of the East India Company to guarantee the shareholders of Indian railway companies (who were, in fact, British joint stock companies "centred in London and oriented to British needs")[120] an annual 'interest' of 5 per cent, irrespective of the actual profits of the railways. If profits remained below the stipulated rate (as they actually did in most cases until the turn of the century), the Government thus had to cover the balance from state revenues. This decision, arrived at after long negotiations,[121] was due to the characteristic trait of transport infrastructure to generate profits only after large investments and comparatively very long periods of operation, but implied at

[118] Cf. Ambirajan, *Classical Political Economy*, 265–66.
[119] Ibid., 251–53.
[120] Daniel Thorner, "The Pattern of Railway Development in India" (1st published in 1955), reprinted in Kerr, *Railways in Modern India*, 94.
[121] For a detailed narrative of the origins of the "guarantee system", see Thorner, *Investment in Empire*, 119–67.

Circulation and Infrastructure

the same time that the shares of British–Indian railway companies bore interest even if the respective railroad did not yield profit or "pay for itself"[122]—which applied to 70 per cent of the total track length in 1900. Hence, between 1849 and 1900, Rs 568 million was paid out to railway company shareholders from Indian revenues.[123] Daniel Thorner has famously summed up this policy as amounting to "private enterprise at public risk",[124] though Bailey's and McGuire's recent characterisation seems preferable as it is more specific with regard to the social character of this arrangement. According to them, the shareholders of British–Indian railway companies "held a title to a share of the surplus produced by Indian raiyats and workers, a surplus that was appropriated by the Government of India as revenue":[125] Capital was here accumulated not so much by way of profit (or, the realisation of surplus value) as through the appropriation of a part of the revenue the colonial state derived, in the main, from siphoning off large proportions of the surpluses.

Another crucial implication of rendering the dividend independent of profit was that all breaks on railway expenditure were released: the cost of construction of a mile of Indian railway now more than doubled the original estimate in the 1850s and 1860s.[126] British standards of railway construction were transposed to the

---

[122] See footnote 72 in this chapter.

[123] Hurd ("Railways", 741–43) argues that this sum was small in proportion to the national income and more than offset by savings in transport cost, but agrees with the critics of colonial 'public works' policy that "the capital expended on much of the railway system would have yielded higher social rates of return had it been spent on other projects."

[124] Thorner, *Investment in Empire*, 168.

[125] Bailey and McGuire, "Railways, Exchange Banks and World Economy", 141.

[126] Thorner, "Pattern of Railway Development in India", 85. The cost of railway construction in India had been estimated by Dalhousie at £8,000 per mile but actually reached £18,000 in the 1850s and 1860s exclusive of the payments on account of the "guarantee". Jenks, *Migration of British Capital*, 222; Kerr, Introduction, 27–28. This amounted to about half of the average cost per route-mile in Britain despite large differentials in various expense factors and particularly with regard to land acquisition. Construction costs in Britain were considered excessive by contemporaries and appear to have been eight times higher per route-mile in 1844 than in the United States (and still four times higher in 1884). Bagwell, *The Transport Revolution*, 87–88; T. R. Gourvish, "Railways, 1830–1870: The Formative Years", in Freeman and Aldcroft, *Transport in Victorian Britain*, 62–63.

subcontinent although it was admitted in official circles that cheaper modes of construction like the ones simultaneously practiced in the United States were "far more suitable for India".[127] As W. N. Massey, a former Finance Member of the Government of India, put it in 1872:

> All the money came from English capitalists and so long as he was guaranteed 5 per cent. on the revenues of India, it was immaterial to him whether the funds that he lent were thrown into the Hooghly or converted into brick and mortar.[128]

However, this ingenious investment scheme also created mounting pressure on the revenue base of the colonial state and generated conflicts between the various political and economic interests on whose alliance the Indian railway boom rested. The colonial regime implemented a shift of policy in 1869, when no new guarantees were given to railway companies. Thereafter, the state assumed direct control of the construction of new railways, which were then financed to a large extent by means of government loans. The conflict simmered on, however, resulting in another reversal of policy in the early 1880s, when state construction was drastically reduced and guarantees for private railway investment were re-introduced at rates of up to 4 per cent.[129]

---

[127] "In England before a single mile of railway was laid down we had a most complete system of canal communication, which practically sufficed for the carriage of heavy goods. The railways came in to supplement the canals, not to supersede them. In India, on the other hand, the case was rather that which existed a few years ago in the United States, where the railway did not supersede the canal, but was the first and only communication introduced. It was therefore clearly the policy of those who planned the railways in the United States to execute them at the lowest possible cost, and to treat with comparative indifference the question of speed, but to press forward the completion of the works with the utmost despatch, even though they should be finished in a somewhat rough and clumsy manner. Thus they would be opened for a slow and heavy traffic at the earliest practicable period." Speech by Lord Stanley in the House of Commons, 23 June 1857, *The Times*, 24 June 1857.

[128] Report on East Indian Finance 1872, question 8867, quoted in Dutt, *Economic History of India in Victorian Age*, 356. Also see Jenks, *Migration of British Capital*, 221–22.

[129] Thorner, "Pattern of Railway Development in India", 86–87. Also see Kerr, Introduction, 26–27; Ambirajan, *Classical Political Economy*, 260–65.

The contradictions of 'public works' policy expressed themselves in various other ways: in the inconclusive debate on the relative effectiveness of large-scale irrigation works and railways as means of famine protection and their respective financial costs and benefits;[130] in the emergence of a complicated pattern of railway ownership and management that combined the agency of the colonial government and of dependent Indian states with that of British joint stock companies in various ways;[131] in the so-called "battle of the gauges", where the conflict between the advocates (mainly the military establishment) of a uniform "broad gauge" of 5 feet 6 inches that permitted greater load and those (mainly in the "civil administration") who proposed to build new railways with a narrower "metre gauge" of 3 ft 3⅜ inches in order to reduce construction costs, resulted in the coexistence of several incompatible systems of railway track.[132]

Despite all these conflicts, colonial 'public works' policies in India were consistent in that they favoured the interests and the involvement of British finance and industry, but also in that they relied to a much higher extent on coercion and on centralised state power than in Britain itself. The 'public works' policy of the Government of India certainly went beyond Adam Smith's allowance for state involvement, which required—in a period of free trade rhetoric—considerable legitimatory effort. It was the achievement of John Stuart Mill to provide key arguments for limiting the validity of laissez-faire principles with regard to colonial public works. These arguments, formulated in his *Principles of Political Economy* (first edition 1848) while in the service of the East India Company, had, as we shall see below, considerable political weight, which may justify quoting them at some length:[133]

[130] Cf. Ambirajan, *Classical Political Economy*, 251–53.
[131] Cf. Hurd, "Railways", 739; Kerr, Introduction, 27.
[132] MacGeorge, *Ways and Works*, 412–14, 417–18 (MacGeorge admitted that the "metre gauge" reduced construction costs by almost 60 per cent but argued that this difference partly resulted from the fact that the broad gauge had been used for trunk lines, where embankments had generally been built for double lines with a view to future developments and where more expensive engineering works such as bridges over large rivers could not be avoided); Thorner, "Pattern of Railway Development in India", 88–89.
[133] On J. S. Mill's attitudes towards India, also see Stokes, *English Utilitarians and India*, 49–50, 298; Metcalf, *Ideologies of the Raj*, 31–33.

the intervention of government cannot always practically stop short at the limit which defines the cases intrinsically suitable for it. In the particular circumstances of a given age or nation, there is scarcely anything really important to the general interest, which it may not be desirable, or even necessary, that the government should take upon itself, not because private individuals cannot effectually perform it, but because they will not. At some times and places, there will be no roads, docks, harbours, canals, works of irrigation, hospitals, schools, colleges, printing-presses, unless the government establishes them; the public being either too poor to command the necessary resources, or too little advanced in intelligence to appreciate the ends, or not sufficiently practiced in joint action to be capable of the means. This is true, more or less, of all countries inured to despotism, and particularly of those in which there is a very wide distance in civilization between the people and the government: as in those which have been conquered and are retained in subjection by a more energetic and more cultivated people. In many parts of the world, the people can do nothing for themselves which requires large means and combined action: all such things are left undone, unless done by the state.[134]

This paragraph contains a historical perspective on 'public works' that is rather different from Adam Smith's already quoted observation that infrastructures for purposes of commerce "must require very different degrees of expense in the different periods of society".[135] Mill's argument rested instead on the implicit assumption that while the *need* for 'public works' was a given, the *capability* of achieving them was subject to historical variation and also unevenly distributed among the 'nations'. In those parts of the world where 'the people' were insufficiently enlightened, prosperous or organised to advance 'public works' themselves, it was thus the responsibility of the state to take the initiative. Mill was careful to point out himself that this was particularly the case with colonies that were historically "inured in despotism" and where the "distance in civilization" between rulers and subjects was considerable. Contemporary European readers were likely to immediately associate 'despotism' with the 'Oriental', and the reference to India would not have been lost on them. As the Stracheys pointed out: "It is

[134] John Stuart Mill, *Principles of Political Economy with Some of Their Applications to Social Philosophy*, Books III–V, introd. by V. W. Bladen, textual ed. J. M. Robson (Toronto: University of Toronto Press, 1968), 956–57 (Book V, chapter xi, § 12).
[135] See page 90, above.

obvious that these opinions were specially directed to the actual condition of India, with the administration of which Mr. Mill had been connected for a great part of his life."[136] The authoritarian implications of the argument were equally clear: those "retained in subjection" could do "nothing for themselves"—that had to be done by their "more energetic and more cultivated" (that is, British) rulers. This authoritarian edge was only seemingly softened in the subsequent sentences:

> In these cases, the mode in which the government can most surely demonstrate the sincerity with which it intends the greatest good of its subjects, is by doing the things which are made incumbent on it by the helplessness of the public, in such a manner as shall tend not to increase and perpetuate, but to correct, that helplessness. A good government will give all its aid in such a shape, as to encourage and nurture any rudiments it may find of a spirit of individual exertion. It will be assiduous in removing obstacles and discouragements to voluntary enterprise, and in giving whatever facilities and whatever direction and guidance may be necessary: its pecuniary means will be applied, when practicable, in aid of private effort rather than in supersession of them, and it will call into play its machinery of rewards and honours to elicit such efforts.[137]

The notions of laissez faire were thus, according to Mill, not to be the guiding principles of the colonial 'public works' policy of the present but rather an educational goal for the future. This intellectual operation achieved for the problem of infrastructure what was worked out for other areas of policy, too:[138] the legitimate objective of the colonial state was to be the daily teacher of the benighted rather than the nightwatchman of the enlightened. This ostensibly benign imagery provided a convenient and authoritative ideological justification for those who asserted a close and centralised state control over social space, circulatory practices and 'public works' in India and strove to restrict to a minimum the participation of 'natives' in related processes of decision-making. The brothers John

[136] Strachey and Strachey, *Finances and Public Works of India*, 409.
[137] Mill, *Principles of Political Economy*, 957 (Book V, chapter xi, § 12).
[138] This was, of course, a basic component of "civilising" ideologies of European dominance. For an overview, see Adas, *Machines as the Measure of Men* and, for the adaptation of such ideologies to the Indian context, Harald Fischer-Tiné and Michael Mann, eds., *Colonialism as Civilizing Mission: Cultural Ideology in British India* (London: Anthem, 2004); Metcalf, *Ideologies of the Raj*, especially chapters 2–4.

and Richard Strachey, for decades among the most powerful figures in the colonial administration of India and its 'public works' policy, after extensively quoting the above passages, thus argued that the

> full acceptance of Mr. Mill's principles, when applied to the case of India, leads immediately to the conclusion that progress should be sought by the application of the superior knowledge and resources of the State, but in such a manner as gradually to accustom the people to manage their own affairs, and to entrust them with such management as soon and as far as it is practicable.[139]

They also specified the limits and forms of entrustment they considered practicable: "It is one of the present inevitable conditions of Indian administration that it should be almost entirely free from the immediate control of what is commonly described as public opinion." This they considered unfortunate since any "expression of public opinion, even if it were not always intelligent ... would not only be beneficial to the local government, but valuable as steps in political education."[140] However, they left no doubt that Indian participation had for all practical purposes to remain strictly within narrowly defined limits:

> Nothing could be more foolish than to attempt to create assemblies having plenary power over the public income and expenditure. India is not a country for such experiments. What is really to be desired is not to weaken the action of authority, but to take a step towards the formation of a public opinion which shall assist the responsible Government for the advancement of provincial and local objects. Checks, which under different social and political conditions are useful and necessary, would be wholly out of place, and the object in view could probably be safely obtained by creating local consultative bodies. ... Such a body should contain the chief executive officers of the local government, together with non-official persons of local knowledge, weight, and intelligence. Political discussion should under no circumstances be permitted.[141]

Moreover, in their controversies with the adversaries of state property in railways the Stracheys used Mill's reasoning also to defend the necessity of restraints on the ability of British capital to

---

[139] Strachey and Strachey, *Finances and Public Works of India*, 409.
[140] Ibid., 425–26.
[141] Ibid., 425–27. Also see Stokes, *English Utilitarians and India*, 283–85.

determine the policy and implementation of 'public works'.[142] "The intervention of great companies of foreign capitalists, having their seat of business out of the country," they argued, "differs little ... from the establishment of a strong foreign despotism." Hence while admitting the necessity of employing British capital, they asserted that it was the "duty of the State" to take care of the "true interest of India" and

> to provide the means of eventually replacing it [that is, the agency of British companies] by a truly local and national system, without undue cost to the public; and to secure at the same time for India the greatest practicable share of the profits, the whole of which are ultimately derived from the industry of the people of India and the natural resources of their country.[143]

The "true interest of India" was thereby reduced to the imposition of a stricter state control of the costs of railway construction and to cutting down government expenditure on interest payments to British investors. The policy of the 1870s, that is, state construction of railways instead of engaging railway companies on the basis of guaranteed interest, was seen as consistent with this "duty of the State". So much for the theory of colonial infrastructure policy.

In practice, the colonial state determined the priorities as well as the particular elements of 'public works' policy—irrespective of whether railway investors were guaranteed an annual interest or the railways were directly constructed and managed by the government. And it did so, the "true interests of India" notwithstanding, with an eye on the exigencies of Empire and the demands of British industry and finance. As opposed to England's, the Indian railway network was organised according to a master plan, roughly outlined in 1845 by the railway lobbyist R. M. Stephenson (see map 2), and formulated as a "general system of railways connecting the several Presidencies, and constituting the grand trunk lines within them" by Governor-General Dalhousie in 1853.[144] The structure of the

---

[142] For the arguments of their opponents, see Ambirajan, *Classical Political Economy*, 256–57, 260–64.

[143] Strachey and Strachey, *Finances and Public Works of India*, 409–10; also see 411–13.

[144] Stephenson's design for an Indian railway network was elaborated and also presented in the form of a map in his *Report upon the Practicability* (1845). Its

emerging railway network was closely controlled by the colonial government, as the placement of every line had to be sanctioned.[145] After 1869, the construction, management and ownership of railways was time and again shifted, redistributed and rearranged between various joint stock companies and government agencies with a long-term tendency towards state ownership and management—a tendency that was, however, far from linear. Only by the end of British rule had all Indian mainlines been turned into state property.[146] The construction of a network of "imperial trunk roads" or of waterways suitable for inland navigation (such as the Orissa Coastal Canal) were likewise highly centralised efforts on the part of the colonial state to conceive, plan and develop social space and patterns of circulation in South Asia.[147] Moreover, by declaring itself the proprietor of Indian soil and by establishing comparatively high levels of coercion the colonial state had effective means to override the numerous claims of common or personal rights to the land required for 'public works'. "Land acquisition", a major but sorely underresearched aspect of 'public works' and, more generally, of the production and reorganisation of social space, was therefore considerably cheaper and more difficult to resist under colonial conditions.[148] Furthermore, the colonial state could resort openly or by

---

best summary and discussion is still: Thorner, *Investment in Empire*, 44–68; Dalhousie's plan, which was accepted by the East India Company, is developed in Lord Dalhousie, Minute to the Court of Directors, 20 April 1853, item 174, 2: 23–57.

[145] MacGeorge, *Ways and Works*, 319–22; Hurd, "Railways", 741–43.

[146] G. S. Khosla, *A History of Indian Railways* (New Delhi: Ministry of Railways (Railway Board), Govt. of India, 1988), 174–75; Hurd, "Railways", 739. Also see Vera Anstey, *The Economic Development of India* (London et al.: Longmans, Green and Co., 1929), 134–39.

[147] For roads, see MacGeorge, *Ways and Works,* 73–74, 80–81, 85–86; also see footnote 90 on page 96, above. For canal construction and irrigation policy in general, see Whitcombe, "Irrigation". For the Orissa Coastal Canal, see chapter 7 of the present study.

[148] This is a complex issue requiring in-depth research. For our present purposes the general observations may suffice, however, that land was granted free to the railway companies by the colonial government who regulated the acquisition of land for "public purposes" in various Acts since the 1850s. Crucially, compensation claims were unilaterally settled by official arbitrators or the district collector *after* possession had been taken of the land. Hena Mukherjee, *The Early History of the East Indian Railway, 1845–*

underhand means to various forms of forced labour (such as prison labour, "famine protection works" or forms of corvée labour like *begar* and *bethi*) on the pretext of 'public works' more freely than non-colonial governments—practices that assumed considerable proportions and continued right to the end of the colonial period.[149] Finally, the exclusion of almost the whole population from formal political participation, the absence of any "frivolous opposition" (as a British commentator put it)[150] and of any accountability of the

---

1879 (Calcutta: KLM, 1994), 89 100; Amit Mukerji and R. C. Sharma, "Acquisition of Land for Railway Construction in the Agra District", in *Proceedings of the Indian History Congress*, 51st Session, Calcutta (Delhi: Indian History Congress, 1991), 420–22; Henry Campbell, *The Law of Land Acquisition in British India: Being a Full Commentary on the Land Acquisition Act, Act No. I of 1894* (Bombay: N. M. Tripathi & Co., 1911), 2, 44, 47–49. Also see Goswami, *Producing India*, 52–53.

[149] Henry St George Tucker was thus satisfied in 1832 that "the labour of convicts" was being turned "to good account by a vigorous discipline" on road works. Tucker, *Memorials on Indian Government*, 428. MacGeorge *Ways and Works*, 84 wrote with hindsight that "a large proportion of the earlier work" on the famous Grand Trunk Road was "done by convicts, or by famine relief labour." Convict labour was employed on roads especially under the East India Company though the practice continued well into the twentieth century. For a detailed discussion among colonial officials on the benefits and drawbacks of convict road labour, occasioned by the Report of the Prison Discipline Commission (1838), see National Archives of India, Military Board Proceedings (henceforth NAI, MBP), 8 December 1840, 7585–661. This phenomenon has only recently caught the interest of one of India's finest labour historians: Chitra Joshi, "Working the Roads: Convicts, Runaways in Nineteenth-Century India" (unpublished paper for the 4th International Conference of the Association of Indian Labour Historians, 18–20 March 2004, Noida). For references to the employment of "impressed" or corvée labour on railway embankments, see Kerr, *Building the Railways of the Raj*, 92–94. On the forced character of "famine relief labour", see Sanjay Sharma, *Famine, Philanthropy and the Colonial State: North India in the Early Nineteenth Century* (Delhi/Oxford: Oxford University Press, 2001), 143–71; David Arnold, "Famine in Peasant Consciousness and Peasant Action: Madras, 1876–8", in *Subaltern Studies III*, ed. Ranajit Guha (New Delhi: Oxford University Press India, 1984), 103–9. For detailed evidence from Orissa for convict, corvée and "famine relief" labour on roads and other 'public works', see also chs 5 and 7 of the present study.

[150] Edward Davidson, *The Railways of India: With an Account of their Rise, Progress, and Construction* (London: E. & F. N. Spon, 1868), 96, quoted in *Another Reason: Science and the Imagination of Modern India*, by Gyan Prakash (Delhi: Oxford University Press, 2000), 165.

Government to its subjects permitted a centralisation of resources and agency for 'public works' to a much higher extent than, for instance, in Britain, where the parliament exerted control, and the parishes, the famous "turnpike trusts" and the municipalities were important agencies of infrastructure policy.[151] Though the care for "local roads" was delegated in the second half of the century to ferry fund committees, to road cess committees and finally to district and local boards, the institutional and financial weakness of these administrative bodies turned this measure into an affirmation of the centralisation of power and the corresponding priority of radial axes directed at the colonial metropolises over local networks of circulation rather than a counterweight against these.[152] This centralisation constituted a problematic institutional and socio-spatial inheritance, which the postcolonial Indian state accepted together with its inbuilt contradictions and imbalances.[153]

This study has so far attempted to conceptualise South Asia's social history of transport, which required a critical assessment of dominant concepts of space, circulation and infrastructure prevalent in both the period under review and the present. This critical assessment had to remain, however, highly aggregated as a result of the systematic, bird's-eye view we had assumed. For the same reason, these concepts could be located in their specific historical context only up to a certain degree of concreteness, which could be

---

[151] Cf. Stokes, *English Utilitarians and India*, 250–51; Bagwell, *The Transport Revolution*, 23–48.

[152] This problem was noticed by perceptive nationalist observers already in the 1890s: "Before railways were constructed, Government had to construct good roads and keep them in repair for the transport of troops. Since the construction of railways, roads have received less attention, but not so large public buildings. Roads and many public buildings have been made over to the District boards, which have to keep them in proper order out of the funds granted to them from the road and public works cesses, of which the best portion is retained by Government itself." *Bangavasi* (Bangla), 5 May 1894, in *RNNB* 12 May 1894, 362. From the late 1920s onwards, a causal connection between bad road conditions and maintenance through financially starved district boards was also admitted in official reports; see for example, Mitchell and Kirkness, *Report on the Present State of Road and Railway Competition*, 8, and (for Orissa), Sarma, *Report on Road Development*, 27 and 316–21. Also see MacGeorge, *Ways and Works*, 104; Munsi, *Geography of Transportation in Eastern India*, 34–35, 44–46, 48–50.

[153] Cf. Munsi, *Geography of Transportation in Eastern India*, 40–43.

transgressed only by way of example. Moreover, while this examination of the practices and structures of transportation through the looking-glass of concepts has been a necessary preliminary, it would be heavily biased if it stood alone. For following the dominant concepts leads inevitably to what Lefebvre called "conceptualized space": "the space of scientists, planners, urbanists, technocratic subdividers and social engineers, as of a certain type of artist with a scientific bent." This is "the dominant space in any society" as is clearly demonstrated by the above analysis of political and economic debates on 'public works', where the multiple and conflicting spatial practices of the various Indian social groups seem to vanish in the haze. This dominance also consists in the assertion that social space—in our case, circulation and infrastructure—is actually lived and perceived by the many just as it is conceived by the few or, in other words, that social space is identical with conceived space.[154] The conflation of dominant spatial norms with sociospatial practice as a whole has been refuted—mainly on theoretical grounds already delineated in hypothesis 2 of chapter 2. The point is now to test the hypotheses and conceptualisations so far developed in this study by applying them to specific social spaces. Their worth as tools of historical analysis can only be established by using them in an attempt to comprehend more concretely the rich social histories of circulation and infrastructure. This calls for a change, even for a reversal of perspective. If we have so far pursued systematic analysis, it is now necessary to move on to sequential reconstruction. From macro-levels of history we need to shift methodologically to meso- and, as the occasion arises, even to micro-levels. From conceptualisations of 'social space' we proceed to an examination of a concrete geographical space of circulatory practice in a specific period: to Orissa in the long nineteenth century.

---

[154] Lefebvre, *Production of Space*, 38–39.

Part II

CIRCULATORY REGIMES AND 'PUBLIC WORKS'

The Case of Colonial Orissa in the Long Nineteenth Century

Part II of this book examines circulatory practices and infrastructure policies between the final decades of the eighteenth century and World War I. It focuses on a geographical area that has come to epitomise infrastructural underdevelopment in eastern India: on the region that is roughly congruent with the present State of Orissa. Politically, this region consisted

(a) of the "Cuttack Division" of the East India Company's "Bengal Presidency" (that is, the "Mughalbandi" coastal districts of Balasore, Cuttack and Puri, annexed in 1803),
(b) of the coastal district of Ganjam (ceded to the "Madras Presidency" in 1765) and
(c) of numerous "little kingdoms" in the interior, most of which were allowed to keep a semblance of independence until the end of British rule and were variously designated in official documents as "Garhjats" or "Khond Mehals", as "Tributary" or "Feudatory States".

In order to comprehend the transformation of the region's circulatory regime, the sequence of processes and events needs to be reconstructed. The argument is, therefore, developed in chronological order. Chapter 4 sketches the natural constraints, the social underpinnings as well as the spatial and temporal patterns of circulation in *ancien régime* Orissa. Chapter 5 examines the objectives of British communications policies in Orissa from the annexation of the coastal plains in 1803 to the mid-nineteenth century and discusses why and how these policies were supported, endured or resisted by various social groups. After assessing the infrastructural "achievements" under colonial rule up to the mid-century, chapter 6 turns to the emergence of new political, social and economic compulsions and schemes for remoulding Orissa's circulatory regime in the 1850s and 1860s. Each of the remaining two chapters covers the subsequent period up to about World War I. Chapter 7 discusses conflicts over colonial infrastructure policy in the commercialising and directly ruled coastal plains of Orissa and the purposeful appropriation of steamships and railways by large sections of Indian society. Chapter 8 traces how the dynamics of colonial capitalism affected practices of circulation, 'public works' policies and conflicts around them in Orissa's "little kingdoms".

4
Patterns of Circulation and Modes of Transport in Ancien Régime Orissa

If a precolonial history of circulation is frequently denied to South Asia in general such assumptions are even more prevalent in the case of the region of Orissa. Since colonial times, most historical accounts suggest that the only line of communication in that part of eastern India predating the mid-nineteenth century and worth mentioning was the new Jagannath Road—the pilgrim road from Bengal to Cuttack and Puri—which was improved and partly realigned after 1812.[1] On the whole, however, we are told that "modern" (that is, "scientifically constructed") channels of circulation came into being only in consequence of the official report on the severe Bengal and Orissa famine of 1866. Colonial officials celebrated themselves as the Promethean demigods of an age of improvement who had carried famine protection lines (rather than fire) to the unenlightened human populace of Orissa.[2] In this narrative, as in most legends, the suggested causality and sequence of events are rather loosely connected to documented historical processes.[3] The story has, however, been retold time and again even by postcolonial authors and thereby has established itself as indisputable common knowledge.[4] As for

---

[1] For a discussion of the construction of this road, see later in this chapter.
[2] The ostensible juncture of 1866 was, for instance, disseminated in 1906 by a colonial gazetteer which has since been used extensively and rather uncritically by many historians: L. S. S. O'Malley, *Bengal District Gazetteers: Cuttack* (Calcutta: Bengal Secretariat Book Depot, 1906), 146. For an almost verbatim repetition of O'Malley's statement, see for example, Sudhira C. Bhola, *British Economic Policy in Orissa* (New Delhi: Discovery Publishing House, 1990), 123–24.
[3] See section 4, later.
[4] This common knowledge is not merely spread by repetitive textbooks on Orissa's colonial history that rely mainly and uncritically on colonial gazetteers but has even sneaked into otherwise well-researched historical and

the state of transport infrastructure at the onset of colonial rule, almost *every* relevant historical work has dealt with it summarily by quoting the following sentences from an official history of early colonial Orissa published in 1873 and authored by George Toynbee, at one time Commissioner (that is, head of administration) of the Bengal Presidency's Cuttack Division:

> When we took the province in 1803 there was not a road, in the modern sense of the word, in existence. What were then called roads were mere fair-weather cart-tracks, without bridges and without proper ferry arrangements for crossing the numerous water-courses which they intercepted.[5]

This statement has been reiterated uncritically over and over again, though remains of ancient bridges might have suggested to historians a rather more complicated story. Archaeological evidence as well as several European travel accounts from the eighteenth century thus indicate that not less than twelve masonry bridges (one of them at least reaching a length of 120 metres and a width of 10 metres), were constructed across minor (and more easily bridgeable) rivers of the Orissa plains along the pilgrimage roads to Puri. According to a painstaking survey of precolonial bridges, most of Orissa's peculiarly shaped masonry bridges were constructed between the eleventh and fourteenth centuries, though the region's post-Mughal administration of the early eighteenth century also engaged in bridge-building. From a subcontinental perspective, Deloche observes that "the main road of Orissa ... seems to have been the best provided in this regard".[6] Alexander Hamilton, who travelled to Puri in 1708, noticed "many Bridges of Stone over those little Rivers",[7]

---

geographical studies. For recent examples of the former type, see J. K. Samal, *Economic History of Orissa, 1866–1912* (New Delhi: Mittal, 1990), 125–27. For the latter category, see Nayak, *Development of Transport and Communication*, 3–4, 13–64; B. N. Sinha, *Geography of Orissa,* 3rd rev. ed. (New Delhi: National Book Trust, 1999), 252.

[5] Toynbee, *A Sketch of the History of Orissa*, 81.

[6] Deloche, *Ancient Bridges of India*, 10–11, 29–31; Deloche, *Transport and Communication*, 1: 136–40. Also see K. N. Mahapatra, *Ancient Pilgrims' Routes of Orissa* (Bhubaneswar, 1972; xeroxed MS., Orissa Archive, South Asia Institute, Heidelberg, 265 mss 16/146), 39–43.

[7] Alexander Hamilton, *A New Account of the East Indies,* ed. William Foster (London: Argonaut Press, 1930 [1st ed. 1727]), 1: 214.

while Andrew Stirling, writing half a century before Toynbee, commended the bridges of Orissa as "the most creditable ... monuments of its indigenous princes" and mentioned five principal ones which he had seen personally.[8] In 1860, one British engineer, when commenting on one of these medieval monuments, admitted "that the adjacent Bridge which is an extension and represents the present Government is still more faulty than the old structure".[9] Fergusson made a similar observation somewhat later with regard to the *Athara-nala* (that is, eighteen-channel) Bridge at Puri: "It may be unscientific but many of these old bridges are standing and in use while many of those we have constructed out of the ruins of the temples and palaces have been swept away as if a curse were upon them."[10]

Toynbee thus glossed over built environments "representing" governments other than his own, over facts that would have qualified, but certainly not staved off the general thrust of his argument. For, twelve large brick constructions hardly suffice to prove the existence of a comprehensive built environment for transport purposes in precolonial Orissa. Seventeenth- and eighteenth-century travellers reported, after all, that journeys across the fluvial plains of that region were experienced as being particularly cumbersome as a result of road conditions considered "bad" by the standards of the time and of the numerous watercourses that had to be crossed by ferry and often even without.[11] The available evidence, moreover, leaves little doubt that circulation created denser networks and

[8] "Many of these works are to be found in different parts of the province, still in excellent state of preservation. The principal bridges which I have seen are that between Simleh and Soro, of fourteen nálehs or channels; the Atháreh or eighteen náleh bridge, at Púri; the Chár náleh, in the same neighbourhood; the bridge at Delang, and another over the Dya, between Khúrda and Pipley." Andrew Stirling, "An Account, Geographical, Statistical and Historical of Orissa Proper, or Cuttack", *Asiatic Researches* XV, 1825, 336– 37.

[9] This referred to a bridge (allegedly built around 1300) over the Kansbansa River. OIOC, BPWP 25 May 1860, P/16/41, Com., no. 87, 420 (J. P. Beadle, SE, Lower Provinces, to Offg. Engineer, Lower Provinces, 20 January 1860). Note the remarkable formulation that the new bridge "*represents* the present Government".

[10] James Fergusson, *History of Indian and Eastern Architecture* (London: John Murray, 1910 [1st ed. 1876]), 2: 112–13.

[11] See, for example, Manrique, *Travels of Fray Sebastien Manrique*, 98–99.

infrastructures in other regions of the subcontinent during the three centuries preceding colonial annexation and possibly over an even longer period. Hence, whoever has read from Toynbee's statement that the precolonial rulers of Orissa spent comparatively little on transport infrastructure appears to be in accord with documented history. Indeed, the rub of this statement is neither the contention that there were (in "premodern" times) no roads "in the modern sense" (which is as unexciting as it is tautological), nor mere factual inaccuracy. Far more problematic are Toynbee's implicit premises whose inadvertent or conscious acceptance has induced postcolonial historians to disconnect the "modern" (or colonial) history of circulation as sharply as the official imperial chroniclers from that of the "premodern" (or precolonial) era. If patterns and infrastructures of circulation predating the establishment of colonial rule were dubbed "premodern", the inference was always that they were *irrelevant* for any analysis of "modern" Orissa's transport system and required, therefore, no detailed examination.

However, if official writings continuously denounced an *inordinate* deficiency of Orissa's transport infrastructure as a major economic impediment and social risk over 150 years, the question then is how had a circulatory regime emerged that could be perceived by contemporaries as comparatively underdeveloped? To what extent was relative underdevelopment due to geomorphic conditions, the outcome of long-term social processes and the result of colonial domination? As has been argued earlier in chapter 2, every stage in the production of social space necessarily preconditions the possibilities and constraints for subsequent spatial practices that are thus superimposed upon an increasingly multilayered structure. A historical evaluation of the impact of colonialism on the pace and direction of infrastructural development must, therefore, commence with a more serious review of Orissa's *ancien régime* of circulation, that is, the patterns and modes of circulation at the onset of colonial rule. This "circulatory regime" can be traced back to the seventeenth century at least and underwent fundamental transformations (as will be shown in this and the following chapter) only when colonial interventions into regional society had acquired some depth and permanence. The *immediate* effects of colonial rule should hence not be exaggerated. As for the loosely controlled mountainous *Garhjat* region,[12] colonial officials had not even a clear perception of the existing patterns of circulation before the 1860s (see map 4). Though the pace of road construction in coastal as well as inland Orissa gained some speed somewhat earlier, the available evidence suggests that colonial policies did not alter the *ancien régime* of circulation significantly before the dissolution of the East India Company.

Furthermore, we need to examine precolonial, colonial as well as postcolonial patterns and modes of circulation *in their own historical context*. "Adequate" or "good" means of transport have meant different things at different times. At the time of writing, major as well as controversial investments in Orissa's road and railway infrastructure are being undertaken by the Indian and the Orissa State Government, by the transnational steel giant POSCO and the World Bank in order to link iron ore mines of the interior with new steel plants and ports located near the coast. Against this backdrop, present conceivers of space affirm that "Orissa has not undertaken any significant public investments nor adequately maintained its infrastructure",[13] though there is indisputable quantitative evidence for very considerable changes since independence.[14] When the demand

[12] The term garhjat, a Persian plural form of "garh" (fort), was used to denominate the hill and forest tracts of inland Orissa where a large number of petty princes ruled their estates from simple "mud forts". Henry Yule and A. C. Burnell, *Hobson-Jobson: A Glossary of Colloquial Anglo-Indian Words* (New Delhi: Munshiram Manoharlal, 1984), 404; Horace H. Wilson, *A Glossary of Judicial and Revenue Terms*, reprint of 1855 ed. (New Delhi: Munshiram Manoharlal, 1997), 168.

[13] Orissa has recently become a major target of foreign direct investment as well as domestic investment in manufacture as several steel plants and apposite infrastructural programmes are being projected. "Memorandum of Understanding between the Government of Orissa and M/s POSCO for Establishment of an Integrated Steel Plant at Paradeep," 22 June 2005, http://orissagov.nic.in/posco/ POSCO-MoU.htm; Prafulla Das, "Mines of Conflict", *Frontline* 22, no. 24, 5–18 November 2005; "Centre Paves Way for Reforms in Infrastructure Development", *The Economic Times*, 21 December 2005. The quotation is from: World Bank, *Project Information Document: India Orissa State Roads Project*, 24 October 2005, http://www-wds.worldbank.org.

[14] Orissa's total road mileage increased from 3,200 on the eve of the First (Five-year) Plan (1951–56) to 178,453 miles in 1993–94 (of which over 150,000 miles were accounted for by village and forest roads). Sinha, *Geography of Orissa*, 252–54. However, these figures merely give an idea of the general development—it is likely that the figure for 1951–56 is too low.

for motorable roads rose significantly from the mid-1920s, the existing network of routes was judged to be far off the mark, too.[15] Yet the engineers in charge of communications development in the late nineteenth century had taken pride in their achievements and "scientific" standards and, in turn, ridiculed the "free-and-easy manner" of their predecessors' "*mofussil* engineering".[16] Toynbee, writing at the end of this period of "mofussil engineering" had, as we have seen, nonetheless celebrated the "modernity" of the lines of communication the colonial administration had so far conceived and established. What constitutes a "good road" has thus been continuously redefined in accordance with the current circulatory needs of the dominant forces of society even within the "modern age". If the infrastructure of the colonial period cannot be measured by the yardsticks of the present, it is equally inappropriate to list a few ancient roads and harbours in order to judge them according to the standards of later periods—a procedure most "modernist" historians have chosen, if they have cared at all to mention the channels of *ancien régime* circulation.[17] What is required, instead, is a historical reconstruction of ecological and socio-economic constraints working on the spatial and temporal patterns of circulation and on the modes of transport in Orissa from the seventeenth century until about 1860. This is the purpose of the following sections.

A reconstruction of the complex "system" of circulation in pre-colonial Orissa discloses a basic spatial pattern. Physical geography has structured the emergence and development of long-distance lines of communication in the Orissa region along *two major axes*: one ran parallel to the coastline, almost exactly from northeast to southwest, being cut across by the other, which was aligned roughly from west to east-southeast (see map 3).

---

[15] Mitchell and Kirkness, *Report on Present State of Road and Railway Competition*, 7–9.
[16] "Mofussil" (Hindustani from Arabic *mufassal*, that is, separate, particular): provincial, rural. "The Cuttack–Midnapur–Calcutta Railway", *The Indian Engineer: An Illustrated Weekly Journal for Engineers in India and the East* 20/365, 7 April 1894.
[17] For a most comprehensive "list" of this type, mainly drawing on reports of early modern European travellers, see Bhabani C. Ray, *Orissa under Marathas, 1751–1803* (Allahabad: Kitab Mahal, 1960), 149–59.

Along the Coast, Across the Plains and Uplands: The NE-SW Axis

Physiographically, Orissa has been "divided into three broad regions: the coastal plains; the middle mountainous country; the plateaus and rolling uplands."[18] The coastal plains, extending from the Subarnarekha River in the northeast beyond the Chilka Lake to the Rushikulya River in the southwest, can again be divided into three parallel zones: the salt belt, five to ten miles narrow, along the shoreline; the broader rice plains in the middle and the submontane tract blending into the mountainous Garhjat country.

The NE-SW axis followed the general direction of these parallel zones and fully determined the alignment of two *major channels of circulation* in pre- and early colonial Orissa while at least partly coinciding with the position of a third one.

(1) The first of these channels of circulation was the coastal traffic route along a dense chain of petty ports and trading posts which were frequently located on or near the mouth of a river.[19] Though most of these village 'portlets' were not suitable for larger European ships and were chronically suffering from silting up, they were used by numerous smaller coastal vessels.[20] They served as outlets for inland produce and hence considerable quantities of salt, food

---

[18] Sinha, *Geography of Orissa*, 11.

[19] The following places of anchorage have been identified by Deloche (from SW to NE): Gopalpur, Ganjam at the mouth of the Rushikulya River, Manikpatna at the mouth of Chilka Lake, Puri, Machhagan (Machgaon) on the Debi River, Dhamara (Dhamra) at the mouth of the river with the same name, Chudamana (Churaman) on the Gamai River, Laichampur on the Kansbansa River, Baleshwar on the Burhabalang River, Pancapada (Panchpara) and Pipili on the Subarnarekha River. Deloche, *Transport and Communication* 2: 110–17. For Baleshwar District, even more minor ports are identified in William W. Hunter, *A Statistical Account of Bengal* (Delhi: Concept Publishing Company, 1976 [1st ed. 1877]), 18: 252–62. Also see W. A. Inglis, *The Canals and Flood Banks of Bengal* (Calcutta: Bengal Secretariat Press, 1909), 431–32; Purna C. Das, *The Economic History of Orissa in the Nineteenth Century* (New Delhi: Commonwealth Publishers, 1989), 248–58; Nayak, *Development of Transport*, 126–27.

[20] Stirling, "An Account ... of Orissa", 191–92; Deloche, *Transport and Communication*, 2: 112–17. Quantitative evidence on coastal shipping is scarce but Hunter reported that about 200 black salt-sloops lay rotting in the side-channels of the Burhabalang River after the demise of the Balasore salt trade. Hunter, *The Annals of Rural Bengal*, appendix, 3: 41–42.

grains, textiles and other products were exported from coastal Orissa to various ports in the Bay of Bengal and beyond from about the sixteenth well into the nineteenth century.[21] Integrated with this line of coastal communications was Chilka Lake on which extensive commodity and passenger traffic was conducted by boat.[22]

(2) The second major channel of circulation along this axis was surely Jagannath Road, the pilgrimage route from Bengal via Baleshwar (Balasore), Bhadrak, Jajpur, Cuttack and Pipili to Puri. At this famous centre of the Jagannath cult, the road converged with another pilgrim route from South India which, after touching Ganjam, followed the narrow sandy strip that separated the Chilka Lake from the Bay of Bengal. As has been mentioned before, some rivers and *nalas* (smaller watercourses) on this route had been bridged, though not the major streams where ferry services were often supplied. The pilgrims' road was integrated into the surrounding society in many ways—wells and tanks, *dharamsalas* and *sarais* (rest houses), *chaukis* (toll stations) and *garhs* (minor forts), numerous weekly *haats* (markets), some regular bazaars and several market towns had emerged and conferred on it not merely religio-cultural but also political and economic importance.[23]

---

[21] Binod S. Das, *Studies in the Economic History of Orissa from Ancient Times to 1833* (Calcutta: KLM, 1978), 228–33. In the late eighteenth century, Orissa emerged as one of the major export regions of rice to the Tamil region: Sinnappah Arasaratnam, *Maritime Commerce and English Power: Southeast India, 1750–1800* (New Delhi: Sterling Publications, 1996), 257–58, 314. Up to the early nineteenth century, Orissa's demand for cowries ensured that ships from the Maldives called at Balasore every sailing season. Hamilton, *A New Account of the East Indies*, 218; Stirling, "An Account ... of Orissa", 194.

[22] OIOC, BPWP August 1866, P/432/41, Com., no. 8, 13–14 (J. Ouchterlony, Acting Deputy CE, Northern Circle, to W. H. Horsley, Secry. to Govt. of Madras, PWD, 1 March 1862); and no. 16 (J. G. Ryves, SE, 1st Division, to C. A. Orr, Secry. to Govt. of Madras, PWD, 16 November 1864). Also see below.

[23] For reports from the Maratha period, see Thomas Motte, "A Narrative of a Journey to the Diamond Mines at Sumbhulpoor", reprint of a 1766 diary, *Orissa Historical Research Journal* 1, no. 3, 1952, appendix, 1–16; Daniel R. Leckie, *Journal of a Route to Nagpore by the Way of Cuttae [sic], Burrosumber, and the Southern Bunjare Ghautin the Year 1790: With an Account of Nagpore and a Journal from that Place to Benares by the Sohagee Pass* (London: John Stockdale, 1800), 3–13. Also see Ray, *Orissa under Marathas*, 154–57.

(3) The third major channel of circulation that corresponded to this axis (though only very roughly and with considerable deviations) was a trading route across the uplands of Central India, which connected the Berar "cotton country" via central India's "rice bowl" Chhattisgarh with western Orissa. Two roads, both directed towards the Mahanadi, branched off from this route at Arang, some 35 km west of Raipur. One of them headed towards Sonepur, the other to Sambalpur. From this latter place, an important road turned away in northerly direction to Ranchi in Chota Nagpur.[24] There is evidence, moreover, for further roads that extended the axis to the northeast by connecting Sambalpur with the Mayurbhanj kingdom of northern Orissa.[25] In line with this axis were also two or three narrow colonial "Mail Roads" between Midnapur and Sambalpur, which were successively cleared out, maintained for some time and given up again since the 1820s[26] and, several decades later, the Bengal–Nagpur Railway (see chapter 7).

Following the Rivers: The W-ESE Axis

The geomorphic feature that determined the W-ESE axis was the course of the numerous rivers of Orissa, the six most important of which are (from north to south) the Subarnarekha, the Burhabalang, the Baitarani, the Brahmani, the Mahanadi and the Rushikulya.

---

[24] Deloche, *Transport and Communication*, 1: 86–87, and map opposite page 88. Also see Ray, *Orissa under Marathas*, 150–51.

[25] Markham Kittoe, "Account of a Journey from Calcutta via Cuttack and Pooree to Sumbulpúr, and from thence to Mednipúr through the Forests of Orissa", *Journal of the Asiatic Society of Bengal* VIII, 1839, 675–76; excerpt from: "A New Map of Hindostan" by J. and C. Cary, 1824, in *A Historical Atlas of South Asia*, ed. Joseph E. Schwartzberg, 2nd ed. (New York/Oxford: Oxford University Press, 1992), 58.

[26] OIOC, Board of Control, Board's Collection, F/4/925, no. 25921, 52–53 (report on tour by W. R. Gilbert through the hill country of Singhbhum, Cuttack, Sambalpur, 1823); OIOC, Board's Collection, F/4/1196, no. 30905/29, 6–8 (W. R. Gilbert, Agent to Governor-General in Sumbhulpore and South Behar, to Secry. Swinton, 22 June 1825, extract from Bengal Political Consultations, 15 July 1825); and 37–39 (W. R. Gilbert, Agent to Governor-General, South West Frontier, to Secry. Swinton, 29 May 1827, extract from Bengal Political Consultations, 17 August 1827). Also see sections 3 and 4, in this chapter.

Some of these rivers had carved out deep valleys through the barrier of the "middle mountainous" or Garhjat country and branched off into numerous minor streams once they had entered the coastal plains—most spectacularly, the Mahanadi with its vast delta of 7,526 km².

These watercourses were the most important channels of inland communication and many of them were navigable.[27] Eighteenth-century British travellers observed cargo and passenger boats on the Mahanadi "with flat sides and bottom, ... long in proportion to their breadth, and many of them neatly finished".[28] According to these early reports, these boats carried loads of up to eight tons, while nineteenth-century colonial officials referred to considerably larger vessels.[29] Most rivers could only be shipped during the rainy season over longer distances though the Mahanadi remained precariously navigable, at least for small cargo boats, throughout the year up to Binika, about 25 kms to the north of Sonepur, that is, over a length of about 240 kms above Cuttack. During the highwaters of the rainy season, navigation was possible up to Arang, a locality about 35 km east of Raipur, though it was reported that

[27] For rivers other than the Mahanadi, see Sinha, *Geography of Orissa*, 269–70; Prabhat Mukherjee, *Irrigation, Inland Navigation and Flood Problems in North Orissa during the British Rule* (n.p., n.d.), 31–32.

[28] James Davidson, "Journal of a Route from Cuttack to Nagpore", 1790, folio 101, British Library, Additional Manuscripts (henceforth Add., MSS).

[29] Motte ("A Narrative of a Journey", 19) reported in 1766 that the boats he had seen on the Mahanadi could carry from sixty to one-hundred "maunds" (if he referred to Bengal "bazaar maunds": from 2.2 to 3.7 tons). An unidentified British traveller observed that after he left Benares, he first saw boats in Binika near Sonepur. These vessels could carry about 50 "maunds" while those he encountered further down the river near Barmul carried four times that weight (200 "Bengal maunds" were then about 7.9 tons). "Journey from Nagpoor to Cuttack in Jan. & Feb. 1782", folios 110–11, British Library, Add. MSS. 13588. Temple observed eight decades later that Mahanadi boats carried loads between four and fourteen tons. Richard Temple, "Report on the Mahanuddy and its Tributaries; the Resources and Trade of the Adjacent Countries and the Proposed Works for the Improvement of Navigation and Irrigation", in *Selections from the Records of the Government of India, in the Public Works Department*, vol. XLIII (Calcutta: John G. Hirons, PWD Press, 1864), 22. Hunter (*A Statistical Account of Bengal* vol. XIX, 200) even mentioned "flat-bottomed boats of about twenty-five tons burden" on the Mahanadi.

boats were usually laden at Nandghat on the Sheonath River.[30] This river's importance as a channel of inter-regional commodity circulation with Central India was noticed by colonial officials immediately after the annexation of Orissa.[31] Another important use of the rivers for purposes of transport was the floating of timber from the hill regions to the plains, for instance from Angul to Cuttack on the Mahanadi and from the Mayurbhanj hills to Baleshwar on the Burhabalang.[32]

While a thorough survey of oral and literary traditions is beyond the scope of this monograph, future studies of Orissa's popular culture are likely to enrich our understanding of rivers as channels of economic, social and cultural circulation in the precolonial period. There is, for example, a legend of a temple on an island in the Mahanadi River near the village of Kandarapur. According to this the founder and benefactor of the temple was a "rich merchant... coming down from the western provinces in a large vessel".[33] The clearest indication of the importance of rivers as lines of social integration emerges, however, from the region's urban geography: "All but a few towns of Orissa"—centres of trade as well as of administration—"have sprung up by the side of rivers" who served in precolonial times simultaneously as means of circulation and as natural defences.[34]

Practically all of Orissa's rivers ceased, however, to be navigable in their higher reaches during the dry season of the year. Even on the upper Mahanadi only few boats of the smallest variety were then laboriously dragged downstream at a speed of two miles per hour

---

[30] Temple, "Report on the Mahanuddy", 21–22; Deloche, *Transport and Communication*, 2: 32; Sinha, *Geography of Orissa*, 269. Also see Stirling, "An Account ... of Orissa", 185.

[31] Mukherjee, *Irrigation, Inland Navigation and Flood Problems*, 29.

[32] OIOC, Board's Collection, F/4/505, no. 12139, 24 (John Richardson on province of Cuttack, extract from Bengal Revenue Consultations, 18 May 1815); [Lieutenant] Righy, "Memorandum on the Usual Building Materials of the District of Cuttack...", *Journal of the Asiatic Society of Bengal* XI, no. 129, 1842, 837–38.

[33] The legend was narrated to Lieutenant Kittoe in the 1830s: Markham Kittoe, "Extracts from the Journal of Lieut. Markham Kittoe, submitted to the Asiatic Society at the Meeting of the 6th Oct. 1836." [sic 1837?], *Journal of the Asiatic Society of Bengal* VII, 1838, 662.

[34] Sinha, *Geography of Orissa*, 184. Also see list of precolonial ports in footnote 19, in this chapter.

(as compared to five or six miles per hour during the monsoon).[35] The boat journey from Sambalpur to Cuttack took twelve to fifteen days in April and May instead of four days during the rains.[36] Hence, long-distance overland routes, several of which were also aligned along the W-ESE axis, supplemented and competed with the lines of river navigation. The most important precolonial road seems to have been along the right bank of the Mahanadi from Raipur to Cuttack via Arang, Binika, Sonepur and Kantilo (see map 4). This road served as a pilgrim route since medieval times and was provided with temples and water tanks.[37] In the late eighteenth century, its condition was in many sections "good", according to the standards of contemporary British travellers.[38] This may indicate that repair works were undertaken, possibly by local rulers who habitually demanded *bethi* service (corvée) for construction purposes from their subjects.[39]

Points of Intersection and the Network of Circulation

In order to perceive the spatial pattern of circulation in pre- and early colonial Orissa, we need to keep in mind that the two axes crossed each other: Long-distance lines of communication intersected

[35] Temple, "Report on the Mahanuddy", 22.
[36] K. K. Basu, "Tour-Diary of J. R. Ouseley" [1840], *Orissa Historical Research Journal* 5, no. 3, 1956, 171. Correspondingly, another contemporary report reckoned three days for a boat journey from Sonepur to Cuttack during the monsoon season. Davidson, "Journal of a Route from Cuttack to Nagpore", 1790, folio 101, British Library, Add. MSS. 13588.
[37] Mahapatra, *Ancient Pilgrims' Routes*, 23–24.
[38] Leckie, "Journal of a Route to Nagpore", 18, 21–23, 25, 31, 33; "Journey from Nagpoor to Cuttack in Jan. & Feb. 1782", folios 109–110, British Library, Add. MSS. 13588.
[39] The Commissioner and Superintendent of the Orissa "Tributary Mehals" (Garhjat states) thus reported in 1830: "All the work of the Zemindars whether repairing his residence or building a fort is done by forced labour, so many days labour being apportioned to each village, from which people come with provisions calculated to last the period of their being occupied. I imagine there will be very little variation from this system which has prevailed for ages". OSA, BoRLR 18,167 Commissioner of Cuttack Division (henceforth CoCD) to H. Shakespear, Secry. to GoB, Judicial Dpt., 19 July 1830). However, the present writer has not been able to find any positive evidence for *roadworks* undertaken by Garhjat princes prior to the second half of the nineteenth century.

at several points and consequently generated a loosely integrated regional space through an irregular network—a network, whose alignment and pattern was structured according to the two axes.

An important nodal point of precolonial circulation was surely the royal town of Khurda where, according to a British map of 1804, five roads converged. Each of these connected Khurda to a town or village adjacent to a waterway: (1) to Aska on the Rushikulya River, (2) to the trading and temple town of Kantilo on the Mahanadi river, (3) to the urban centre of Cuttack at the apex of the Mahanadi delta, (4) to Balianta on the deltaic Kuakhai river and the Jagannath Road and (5) to the pilgrimage town of Puri on the shores of the Bay of Bengal (see "Koordha" on map 5). This latter road has been described as "the backbone of the Khurda kingdom" that connected its political and religious centres. The importance of consolidating this axis was reflected by the establishment of five Brahmin *sasana* villages along the road by Khurda's most energetic raja Ramachandra in the late sixteenth century.[40]

In the early nineteenth century, however, the most conspicuous point of intersection was the old fortified capital of Cuttack, Orissa's largest urban settlement with about 40,000 inhabitants.[41] It was strategically located not only at the apex of the Mahanadi delta but also at the very point where the east-west river and overland routes of the Mahanadi valley met the NE-SW axis: the Jagannath Road to Puri (see "Kuttack" and "Jaggernauth" on map 5).

Further northeast on that old pilgrimage road from Bengal, the river crossing at Jajpur constituted another important intersection of these axes. The Baitarani was navigable up to Anandpur. An annual fair was held at the river's source, which was connected to the religious and commercial centre of Jajpur by a long chain of places of worship, each of them about ten to twelve miles (or a day's journey) at a distance. The same small town was also a destination of pack-bullock convoys from Central India through the

---

[40] Hermann Kulke, "The Struggle between the Rajas of Khurda and the Muslim Subahdars of Cuttack for the Dominance of the Jagannatha Temple", in *The Cult of Jagannath and the Regional Tradition of Orissa*, South Asian Studies no. 8, ed. Anncharlott Eschmann, Hermann Kulke and Gaya C. Tripati (Delhi: Manohar, 1986), 328.

[41] Stirling, "An Account . . . of Orissa", 191.

Kendujhar (Keonjhar) tract.[42] Jajpur had decayed as an administrative centre in the period of Maratha rule over Orissa (1751–1803), but still sustained a community of merchants before the British realigned Jagannath Road.[43]

Baleshwar—lastingly corrupted into "Balasore" by the British[44]—was likewise located at a point where the pilgrimage route crossed a navigable river, the Burhabalang. It also was connected by a road from the northwest passing through the kingdom of Mayurbhanj via its pre-1804 capital Hariharpur (see map 6). Baleshwar's sizeable mercantile community exported salt to the Garhjats, Bihar and, being one of eastern India's premier early modern ports, along the coast to Bengal. The salt trade became even more important when Baleshwar ceased to be one of the centres of Indian Ocean trade in the Bay of Bengal in the course of the eighteenth century and its overseas exports of fine cotton fabrics and food grains declined.[45] The father and uncle of Fakirmohan Senapati (1843–

---

[42] For the places of worship along the Baitarani, see Kittoe, "Account of a Journey", 614. For references to pack-bullock traffic from Sambalpur to Jajpur, can see OSA, BoRLR 26,977 (R. N. Shore, Magistrate of Cuttack, to E. A. Samuells, CoCD, 23 May 1856). There is also evidence for a track from Chaibassa to Anandpur, the town up to which the Baitarani was navigable: OIOC, BPWP August 1864, P/16/68, Com., No. 36, 20 (extract from a report on the administration of the Tributary Mehals for 1863–64, no. 38, 21 June 1864).

[43] As late as 1766, "a great number" of muslin weavers lived in the Jajpur area. Motte, "A Narrative of a Journey", 11–12. In the mid-1830s Jajpur's Brahmins complained that the new road had diverted much of the former pilgrim traffic. Kittoe, "Extracts from the Journal", 56. In the 1850s, pack-bullock traffic to Jajpur from Sambalpur was still substantial, but colonial officials stated that the pilgrim traffic had declined and were surprised not to see a single "hackery" (bullock cart) in what they considered a "large city". OSA, BoRLR 26,977 (R. N. Shore, Magistrate of Cuttack, to E. A. Samuells, CoCD, 23 May 1856); OSA, BoRLR 27,525 (T. Armstrong, EE Jagannath Road, to E. L. Ommanney, SE, Lower Provinces, 21 April 1857). Also see Leckie, "Journal of a Route to Nagpore", 7.

[44] Throughout the sources on which this study is based, the anglicised form "Balasore" has been used. It has been the predominant transcription even up to the time of writing like many other corrupted place names (such as Cuttack, Baroda or Benares). For reasons of convenience the town will consistently be called Balasore in subsequent chapters.

[45] Hamilton, *A New Account of East Indies*, 217–18; James Rennell, *A Bengal Atlas Containing Maps of the Theatre of War and Commerce on that Side of*

1918), a founder of modern Oriya literature, were major contractors for sail in that port. Having worked in his uncle's business as a young man, Senapati recalled that between five and six hundred ships had still been in commission in Baleshwar in his boyhood: "Three quarters of them were salt-carriers and the rest transported commercial goods to Madras, Colombo and islands in the Bay of Bengal".[46] Even though Senapati's absolute figures may well have been exaggerated in memory, his recollections reflect a prosperity, which this traditional port had lost almost totally after six decades of British rule.[47]

If the pilgrimage route to Puri was one line where the two axes intersected, the Orissa coast was another. Here, as mentioned earlier, several minor ports were located at river mouths in addition to the more considerable port of Baleshwar. They constituted a chain of nodal points—places where inland produce was brought to on watercourses or bullock trails to be exchanged for products imported from other coastal trading posts. Ganjam, for instance, remained the destination of large Banjara *tandas* (pack-bullock convoys of itinerant traders in salt and other bulk commodities) from Raipur till the end of the nineteenth century.[48]

Hindoostan. Compiled from the Original Surveys; and published by Order of the Honourable the Court of Directors for the Affairs of the East India Company ([London]: n.p., 1781), table 7; Motte, "A Narrative of a Journey", 4–5; Leckie, "Journal of a Route to Nagpore", 3; Stirling, "An Account . . . of Orissa", 191–92; Das, *Studies in Economic History of Orissa*, 231–35, 246–49, 261–62, 274–75; Om Prakash, *Bullion for Goods: European and Indian Merchants in the Indian Ocean Trade, 1500–1800* (Delhi: Manohar, 2004), 209–18, 242–51, 256–57.

[46] Phakirmohan Senapati, *My Times and I (Atma-Jivana-Carita)*, trans. John Boulton (Bhubaneswar: Orissa Sahitya Academy, 1985), 13.

[47] Hence the British Master Attendant of Balasore reported in 1867 that the number of seagoing vessels in that port had declined from 246 in 1831/32 to 22 during the recent famine, which reflected, he believed, a more general tendency towards decline: "The district has certainly gone back . . ." *Report of the Commissioners . . . Famine in Bengal and Orissa in 1866*, 1: cli-clii (statement by Captain A. Bond, Master Attendant and Assistant Salt Agent, Balasore, 8 February 1867). Also see chapter 6.

[48] T. J. Maltby, *The Ganjam District Manual*, ed. by G. D. Leman (Madras: Government Press, 1918 [1st ed. 1882]), 232; Temple, "Report on the Mahanuddy", 20–21, 29–30. For precolonial evidence, see Deloche, *Transport and Communication*, 1: 88–89, footnote 30.

Sonepur on the Mahanadi and on the main overland route to Raipur was probably the foremost urban settlement in precolonial western Orissa, and was described in the 1780s as a "big scattered Town with a large Mud and Bamboo Fort and very large Topes" (orchards).[49] Yet, Sambalpur was even then an important traffic junction: located further up the Mahanadi it was the starting point of another road towards Raipur in the west, of a Banjara track to Gumsur in the south via Baudh and of at least two routes towards Chota Nagpur in the northeast.[50] In 1838, Kittoe observed that merchants from Cuttack, Bhadrak, Nagpur, Bhopal, Chhattisgarh and Sirguja assembled in Sambalpur to conduct their business though the volume of trade appeared to him surprisingly small.[51] Investigating Sambalpur's trade patterns in the early 1860s, colonial officials remarked that a number of merchants and "Mohajun's agents" (commercial brokers) resided in this town and that traders from Cuttack, Jajpur and Baleshwar arrived regularly in October to buy Sambalpur cotton.[52]

Rhythms of Circulation

A more dynamic perspective on the *ancien régime* of circulation is required, however, than that permitted by an exclusively geographical reconstruction of lines, points of intersection and networks. Most importantly, we need to look at the circulatory needs of a specific precolonial society, of the region's socio-economic structure before the transformations of colonial capitalism acquired ground-level efficacy. The intensity of commodity production and circulation was certainly considerably lower here than in other regions of

---

[49] "Journey from Nagpoor to Cuttack in Jan. & Feb. 1782", folio 110, British Library, Add. MSS. 13588.
[50] See the extract from Rennell's map of 1788 in Motte, "A Narrative of a Journey", opp. p. 1; for the Gumsur–Baudh link, see Samuel C. MacPherson, *Report upon the Khonds of the Districts of Ganjam and Cuttack* (Calcutta: n.p., 1842), 92.
[51] Kittoe, "Account of a Journey", 375.
[52] OIOC, BPWP July 1861, P/16/52, Com., no. 22, 18–25 (Rivers Thompson, Offg. Secry. to BoR, to Secry. to GoB, 10 May 1861); OIOC, BPWP April 1862, P/16/57, Com., no. 281, 193 (T. Armstrong, SE Cuttack Circle, to Offg. CE, Bengal, 7 April 1862).

India at the onset of colonial rule.[53] Trade had probably declined in the course of the eighteenth century.[54] Stirling thought in 1825 that the "Manufactures and Trade of Orissa Proper are very inconsiderable and unimportant".[55] Nevertheless, "village communities" of the region cannot be assumed to have rested in a primordial state of self-sufficiency and hence detached from processes of circulation altogether.[56] While society apparently did not create a pressing demand for channels of circulation that could be used throughout the year, *seasonal* patterns of communication and exchange are clearly perceptible. These patterns were to a large extent determined by the cycles of rural production in coastal Orissa[57] which, in turn, depended on the cycle of seasons.

The division of the agricultural year into a "season of [crop] production" and a "season of circulation"[58] and the corresponding temporal pattern or rhythm of *ancien régime* circulation is represented schematically in the following table.

---

[53] Alexander I. Tchitcherov, *India: Changing Economic Structure in the Sixteenth to Eighteenth Centuries; Outline History of Crafts and Trade*, 2nd ed. (New Delhi: Manohar, 1998), 259.

[54] Das, *Studies in Economic History of Orissa*, 8–10.

[55] Stirling, "An Account ... of Orissa", 194.

[56] The image of the "self-sufficient" village is still alive even though most authors acknowledge the wide-spread use of cowry currency on the village level, the existence of rural money-lending, regular haats and *melas* (fairs) as well as considerable grain and salt exports from the region. Cf.: Nabin K. Jit, *The Agrarian Life and Economy of Orissa—A Survey, 1833–1897* (Calcutta: Punthi Pustak, 1984), 81–82; Das, *The Economic History of Orissa*, 262–63. For cowry currency in the early nineteenth century, see S. C. De, "Cowry Currency in Orissa", *Orissa Historical Research Journal* 1, no. 2, 1952, 10–21. The image of isolated village republics is also disturbed by evidence for a rather high intensity of peasant migration in the eighteenth century. See Das, *Studies in Economic History of Orissa*, 119–21.

[57] It would certainly be more precise to take into account not only the coastal production cycles but also those of the Garhjats, Chhattisgarh, Berar etc. The present author's justification for confining the reconstruction of seasonal patterns to coastal Orissa is merely that this simplification renders the argument more comprehensible without distorting the more general patterns of seasonality in the period under review.

[58] Cf.: Ludden, *Agrarian History of South Asia*, 19–31 (for the quoted phrase, pp. 24, 26).

TABLE 1: Seasons of climate, production and circulation in Orissa, c. 1800[59]

	Jan	Feb	Mar	Apr	May	Jun	Jul	Aug	Sept	Oct	Nov	Dec
Climate	cold season		hot season			rainy season (SW monsoon)					Cold season	
Production												
1. agriculture (plains)	rabi crops		slack season			kharif crops (rice cultivation)						
2. salt manufacture			peak season									
Communication												
1. river trade: Mahanadi	↔ Coastal Orissa (off-season)					Chhattisgarh ↔ Coastal Orissa (peak)					Sonepur ↔	
2. overland trade	...cart traffic on various roads					roads impassable					bullock and...	
3. coastal shipping	sailing season			Difficult sailing conditions					sailing off-season			
4. chief pilgrim festivals			Dola			Snan, Rath						

Source: Data for this model have been drawn from various sources—many of them refer to later periods but concern phenomena that had also existed in the precolonial period and were unlikely to have undergone major changes since. *Climate*: Sinha, *Geography of Orissa*, 60–64; Hunter, *A Statistical Account of Bengal*, vol. XVIII, 234, 366. *Agriculture*: Stirling, 'An Account ... of Orissa', 171–72; O'Malley, *Bengal District Gazetteers: Cuttack*, 77–87; Sinha, *Geography of Orissa*, 60–64. *Salt Manufacture*: Sadananda Choudhury, *Economic History of Colonialism: A Study of British Salt Policy in Orissa* (Delhi: Inter-India Publications, 1979), 1–9, 25–31, 180; Bhaskar Das, *Social and Economic Life of Southern Orissa: A Glimpse into Nineteenth Century*, Orissa Studies Project 23 (Calcutta: Punthi Pustak, 1985), 208, 216.

[59] For references concerning the cycles of circulation, see the following paragraphs.

Patterns of Circulation and Modes of Transport in Ancien Régime Orissa

The two chief productive activities of eighteenth-century coastal Orissa were agriculture (with rice as the staple crop) and salt manufacture. Earlier, in the seventeenth century, commercial textile manufacture had been specialised, spatially concentrated and considerable in extent but it had already declined when the British came to power.[60] Since both agricultural produce and salt were to some extent produced as commodities, the annual peaks of circulatory activity corresponded to the periods when these products 'entered the market'. The principal rice crop of the plains (locally called *saradh*) was sown in May and June and reaped from mid-November to mid-January, which coincided with the main harvest season in agriculture as a whole. Salt manufacture—in both the more expensive *panga* (boiling) and the cheaper *karkatch* (solar evaporation) methods of production—depended at least partly on the energy of the sun and was mainly conducted during four to six months of the dry season. Accordingly, the necessity of distributing agricultural produce and salt within the region and of exporting these goods arose in a period of the year which largely coincided with the "dry season" from the cold months of December and January (when the main rice crops had just been harvested) until the beginning of the southwest monsoon in about mid-June (when salt manufacture came to a stop). Roads, transformed into bands of sticky mud during the rains, became passable again from November.[61] A few of these roads were even cartable, though often only

[60] William Bruton reported in 1632 that a town called Hariharpur (today part of Jagatsinghpur) in the Mahanadi delta alone supported many merchants and at least "3000 Weavers that are house keepers, besides all other that doe worke, being bound or hired." P. Thankappan Nair, ed., *Bruton's Visit to Lord Jagannatha 350 Years Ago: British Beginnings in Orissa* (Calcutta: Minerva Associates, 1985), 66, 87 (footnote 87). B. S. Das has shown that there were several other weaving centres in the sixteenth and seventeenth centuries, that the demise of the industry began in the eighteenth century when numerous Orissa weavers migrated to south-western Bengal and cotton cultivation in the "Garhjat states" declined, that by the end of the 1820s commercial textile production had become insignificant in Orissa. Das, *Studies in Economic History of Orissa*, 19–21, 228–50. Also see Motte, "A Narrative of a Journey", 4, 12, 16; Leckie, "Journal of a Route to Nagpore", 3, 6; Stirling, "An Account ... of Orissa", 192, 194.

[61] Ricketts described this pattern in his report on the state of the Cuttack Trunk (or "Jagannath") Road, which, according to him, had not changed

with especially high-wheeled "Cuttack hackeries".[62] Several rivers remained navigable throughout the dry season for cargo boats in their lower, tidal reaches.[63] Moreover, by the end of December the winds became more favourable in the Bay of Bengal and for numerous coastal vessels the sailing season started again.[64] It was through this network constituted by simple trails and roads, river channels and the shoreline that coastal Orissa was to some extent integrated by way of circulation and connected to other coastal regions in the Bay of Bengal and even in western India from December to June.

Yet it was also in this peak season of circulation that overland traffic became feasible along numerous unsurfaced but now dried-up tracks from the Orissa plains to the Garhjats, to neighbouring coastal regions and to the inland tracts of Chota Nagpur, Chhattisgarh and Berar. There were several levels at which this overland traffic occurred. To begin with, there is evidence from the early decades of

---

since his first visit in the 1830s. This road was not metalled and hence quite comparable to precolonial fair-weather tracks as far as seasonal impassability was concerned. Henry Ricketts, *Reports on the Districts of Midnapore (Including Hijelee) and Cuttack* (Calcutta: John Gray, 1858), 83.

[62] One Sahu Gopal Das travelled in 1785 from Benares to Puri accompanied by 200 men, 15 palanquins and 16 bullock carts. See Prabhat Mukherjee, *History of the Jagannath Temple in the Nineteenth Century* (Calcutta: KLM, 1977), 20. The East India Company's troops who snatched Orissa from the Marathas in 1803 were followed by a train of "eight hundred bullock-carts of grain". Hunter, *The Annals of Rural Bengal*, 3: 55. Moreover, we learn that "Bullock Carts are very scarce thróout the [Baleshwar] District but more plentiful in Cuttack [District]." OSA, BoRLR 26,542 (Offg. Collector of Balasore to CoCD, 18 September 1855). There is also evidence for some "country cart tracks" in the Garhjats. In 1859 it was reported that "there is a very good Cart track, though of course a fair-weather one only, and natural, not one Rupee having ever been expended on its construction or repairs" between Sonepur and Sambalpur for about 50 miles. OIOC, BPWP 25 May 1860, P/16/41, Com., no. 102, 442–44 (E. H. Harington, Acting District Engineer, Ganjam, to CE, PWD, 17 June 1859). A similar report for 1836 is quoted in *Papers on the Settlement of Cuttack and the State of the Tributary Mehals*, in Selections from the Records of Government III (Calcutta: W. Palmer, Military Orphan Press, 1851), 75. The "Cuttack hackeries" are referred to in Ricketts, *Reports on Districts of Midnapore . . . and Cuttack*, 38.

[63] Mukherjee, *Irrigation, Inland Navigation and Flood Problems*, 31–32; Sinha, *Geography of Orissa*, 269–70.

[64] Deloche, *Transport and Communication*, 2: 214–16.

colonial rule that despite the non-existence of made roads itinerant traders from the Orissa plains ventured into the hills to barter for the highly demanded agricultural and forest produce of the Garhjats (for example, cotton, rice, timber, bamboo, turmeric and shellac).[65] The following concise description of such transactions was penned down much later but the modalities of these practices had probably not undergone major changes since the early nineteenth century:

> The system is for traders to push on into the hill tracts, inaccessible for cart traffic, early in the year: they settle down with their pack-bullocks or ponies and scour the country side, bringing in head-loads of grain by means of cooly transport: in due course these supplies are transferred to the pack-bullocks and ponies, which either carry them to the places where the carts are waiting for them, or transport them direct [sic] to their destination.[66]

Even for the remote Khond Mahals of southern Orissa it was reported that villagers took their produce to regular markets and fairs themselves even in the second quarter of the nineteenth century and that the "head man of each village usually acts as a chief merchant".[67] Moreover, the various Garhjat localities became

---

[65] John Campbell, *A Personal Narrative of Thirteen Years Service amongst the Wild Tribes of Khondistan for the Supression of Human Sacrifice* (n.p., 1864), 121: "Several of the most inaccessible tribes have never acknowledged the authority of the Rajah, and generally the sacrificing Khonds of Chinna Kimedy do not visit the plains to attend the fairs, as do those of Goomsoor and Boad, but dispose of their turmeric, their sole article of barter, for salt, cloth, or brass vessels, to traders from the plains, who are also very frequently professed kidnappers [of Meriahs]." For more references to itinerant traders in the Khond Mahals, see *History of the Rise and Progress of the Operations for the Suppression of Human Sacrifice and Female Infanticide in the Hill Tracts of Orissa*, Selections from the Records of the Government of India [Home Department] No. V (Calcutta: Bengal Military Orphan Press, 1854), 33, 128. For Kendujhar, see OIOC, BPWP March 1888, P/3170, Railway, no. 46, app. B, 47 (J. M. Luff, Temporary Engineer, on Keonjhar Division of 1884–85).

[66] L. E. B. Cobden-Ramsay, *Feudatory States of Orissa*, Bengal Gazetteers, vol. XXI (Calcutta: Bengal Secretariat Book Depot, 1910), 82. Also see *Report on the Administration of the Tributary Mahals of Orissa* [hereafter *RATMO* followed by year] 1893–94 (Calcutta: Bengal Secretariat Press, 1894), 29.

[67] Campbell, *A Personal Narrative*, 15.

destinations for pilgrimages of local importance during the dry season, probably acquiring some commercial significance, too, on these occasions.[68]

Apart from these local and regional patterns of circulation, inter-regional road traffic was also mainly conducted during the dry season. There were, of course, the large trains of pilgrims for Jagannath, mainly from Bengal and northern India. The largest pilgrim festivals were the *Dola, Snan* and *Rath* Yatras.[69] The participants in the former were, according to W. W. Hunter, predominantly north Indians who returned during the dry season while the latter two festivals (taking place when the southwest monsoon was approaching) were mainly attended by Bengalis.[70] The main pilgrimage route through Orissa led from northeast to southwest via the toll station of Khunta Ghat in the Mayurbhanj kingdom across the coastal plains to Puri.[71] Yet, the same route also served as a major channel for labour migration from the Orissa plains to Calcutta as early as in the eighteenth century—most of the well-organised so-called "Balasore bearers" who carried palanquins in the streets of the colonial metropolis originated, in fact, from the area around Bhadrak.[72]

---

[68] When Kittoe visited Deogan in Kendujhar in 1838 he noted the tradition of an annual "large fair" to which pilgrims flocked "from all parts of Orissa". Markham Kittoe, "Mr. Kittoe's Journal of his Tour in the Province of Orissa", *Journal of the Asiatic Society of Bengal* VII, 1838, 685. In the early 1880s, when the patterns of circulation had scarcely changed in this area, it was observed that Deogan's *mela* attracted 10,000 or 20,000 pilgrims as well as some "petty traders" from Cuttack and Baleshwar annually in March. OIOC, BPWP March 1888, P/3170, Railway, no. 46, app. B, 47 (J. M. Luff, Temporary Engineer, on Keonjhar Division of 1884–85). Also see Cobden-Ramsay, *Feudatory States of Orissa*, 83.

[69] Cf.: David Smith, *Report on Pilgrimage to Juggernauth, in 1868,* part II (Calcutta: E. M. Lewis, Calcutta Central Press, 1868), 15–16.

[70] Hunter, *The Annals of Rural Bengal* (London: Smith, Elder & Co., 1872), 2: 156; Hunter, *A Statistical Account of Bengal*, 19: 70.

[71] OSA, Cuttack District Records, Board of Revenue (henceforth BoR) Proceedings 1805, no. 2c (C. Groeme, Collector, to Thomas Fortescue, Secry. to CoCD, 10 June 1805); OIOC, Board's Collection F/4/315, no. 7220, 25–30 (J. Melvill to George Dowdeswell, Secry. to GoB, Revenue Dpt., extract from Bengal Revenue Consultations, 28 May 1807).

[72] Motte, "A Narrative of a Journey", 9–10.

Interregional overland traffic had, however, also developed along the W-ESE axis. The main travellers seem to have been the Banjaras or Lambadas, itinerant traders from Berar and Chhattisgarh whose main business was to exchange cotton, wheat, hides and oil-seeds from Central India for coconuts, brass utensils and, above all, salt from the Orissa coast.[73] They travelled, as mentioned before, with hundreds and sometimes even thousands of pack-bullocks in so-called tandas or convoys.[74] One British engineer reported in 1864 that he had counted 7,000 pack bullocks in one day moving up the Kalinga Ghat on their way from Ganjam to Raipur.[75] They seem to have driven their cattle from Central India to the coast between December and February at a speed not exceeding five miles per day usually and spent the months of April, May and June on the return journey.[76] Banjara tandas marched along various routes to all parts of coastal Orissa—south as well as north of the Mahanadi.[77] They

---

[73] OIOC, BPWP 25 May 1860, P/16/41, Com., no. 95 (G. F. Cockburn, CoCD, to F. Bond, EE, 15 July 1859); Temple, "Report on the Mahanuddy", 27– 30. The findings of the following paragraph are corroborated by studies on Banjara history in other regions of the subcontinent; see Varady, "North Indian Banjaras", 1–18; Habib, "Merchant Communities in Precolonial India", 372–79; Satya, "Colonial Sedentarisation and Subjugation", 314–36.

[74] Temple, "Report on the Mahanuddy", 20–21; OIOC, BPWP April 1862, P/16/57, Com., no. 281, 194 (T. Armstrong, SE, Cuttack Circle, to Offg. CE, Bengal, 7 April 1862).

[75] OIOC, BPWP May 1864, P/16/67, Com., no. 38, 35 (C. T. Phillips, Executive Engineer (henceforth EE) of Ganjam, to R. N. Shore, CoCD, 9 April 1864). Another former official even asserted that these bullock trains could comprise as many as 200,000 animals—an exaggeration indicating that contemporary observers were staggered by the volume of Banjara operations. George T. Haly, *Appeal for the Sufferers by the Present Famine in Orissa* (London: Smith, Elder & Co., 1866), 9.

[76] Maltby, *Ganjam District Manual*, 232. Other accounts of Banjara trade mention a speed of six to seven miles per day and state that twelve miles per day were the maximum speed. See Deloche, *Transport and Communication*, 1: 251, footnote 134.

[77] Evidence is more abundant for Banjara tandas moving between Raipur and the Ganjam coast (see below). Yet Kittoe, for instance, also mentioned intensive Banjara traffic along a route from Cuttack to Dhenkanalgarh, onwards to Mangalpur and Kharagprasad (both on the Brahmani River) and terminating at Baudh on the Mahanadi river. Markham Kittoe, "Report on

had only limited use for permanent roads. In order to find sufficient fodder for their cattle, the Banjaras in fact required alternating routes. They needed a choice between several tracks towards the same destination and to find one which had not been used by another convoy too recently.[78] Though it appears that Banjaras regularly passed through certain hill *ghats* (passes) and landmarks to which they ascribed sacred meaning,[79] the present author has not been able to ascertain the route many tandas chose in the nineteenth century for the long journey from Raipur via Khariyar, Patna and Kalahandi to the salt pans on the Ganjam coast. However, a majority of the Banjaras took to travelling along the Mahanadi valley down to Sonepur, Baudh or Kantilo from where they turned south towards Ganjam through the Khond Mahals.[80]

The Mahanadi route at that time was even more crucial for another type of interregional overland trade—the business conducted by *mahajans* (merchants, moneylenders) and their agents. Significantly, Oriya traders seem to have refrained from establishing direct dealings with central India's commodity markets in the eighteenth and early nineteenth centuries while Central Indian merchants

---

the Coal and Iron Mines of Tálcheer and Ungool...", *Journal of the Asiatic Society of Bengal* VIII, 1839, 140. He also referred to a "Bunjara halting place" near Deogarh and a "Brinjarah's Tank" in Bisoi (northern Mayurbhanj District). Kittoe, "Account of a Journey", 475, 675.

[78] OIOC, BPWP, March 1865, P/16/71, Com., no. 30, 18 (A. G. Crommelin, Secry. to the Chief Commissioner, Central Provinces, PWD, 4 March 1865).

[79] On his journey in 1790, James Davidson referred, for instance, to a certain mountain pass as "the little Benjarrie Ghaut" and made the following interesting note in his diary: "some scattered Trees, one of which the Benjarie Carriers rendered conspicuous, by the numerous Relicks which they have placed around its trunk, and on the Branches as thanks giving of preservation from Danger in their long and frequent Journeys. Their offerings are well adapted to express this Relief, being the ablest of their Tent Pins, Mallets, and Oxen Bells." Davidson, "Journal of a Route from Cuttack to Nagpore", 1790, folios 101, 105, Brisith Library, Add. MSS. 13588. Also see Leckie, "Journal of a Route to Nagpore", 43–44; footnote 77, above.

[80] MacPherson, *Report upon the Khonds*, 92; Temple, "Report on the Mahanuddy", 20; Deloche, *Transport and Communication*, 1: 88–89, footnote 30; OIOC, BPWP May 1864, P/16/67, Com., no. 38, 35 (C. T. Phillips, EE of Ganjam, to R. N. Shore, CoCD, 9 April 1864).

generally kept away from Orissa's main area of cultivation and salt manufacture. Hence, merchants rarely undertook commercial operations covering the whole distance between Central India and the Orissa plains. The regions were thus integrated by separate, but intersecting circuits of exchange. Points of intersection were, for instance, several small entrepôt towns that had sprung up on the Mahanadi, where commodities from both these regions were exchanged, more often by barter than by means of monetary transactions. In the early nineteenth century, Kantilo in the little kingdom of Khandpara seems to have been one of the most flourishing of these emporia. This town possessed an important medieval Nilamadhaba temple and had emerged as the location of a seasonal fair, and could therefore retain some commercial importance throughout the nineteenth century. According to Davidson, cotton and cloth from Central India were exchanged in Kantilo for various goods from Orissa including copper, salt, betel and coconuts in the late 1700s. While this little river town seems to have hibernated more or less during the rains, it was soon revitalised when the dry season set in. From January to April Kantilo housed numerous merchants from the Mahanadi delta, Ganjam and Central India; a bustling market emerged and even the road was deemed "very good" by Leckie in 1790.[81] The Commissioner of Cuttack, G. F. Cockburn, noted as late as in 1846 that he had met a party of merchants from the Raipur region who had travelled to Kantilo with 400 pack oxen to sell cotton and buy coconuts and salt. The return journey, they reckoned, would take them six weeks.[82]

[81] Davidson, "Journal of a Route from Cuttack to Nagpore", 1790, folio 99, Brisith Library, Add. MSS. 13588. Motte, "A Narrative of a Journey", 22–23, 48; Leckie, "Journal of a Route to Nagpore", 18–19. In 1862, it was stated that even without colonial road construction schemes a cartable road connected Kantilo via Nayagarh and Ranpur with Tangi on the Chilka Lake. OIOC, BPWP July 1862, P/16/58, Com., nos. 113–16, 65–68. In the early 1870s, Hunter mentioned Baideswar and Padmabati as further Mahanadi trading towns but emphasised that Kantilo was one of the two towns over 1,000 houses in the nineteen states then constituting the Orissa Tributary Mehals. See Hunter, *The Annals of Rural Bengal*, 3: 103. Also see Cobden-Ramsay, *Feudatory States of Orissa*, 234. For Kantilo's temples, see Mahapatra, *Ancient Pilgrims' Routes*, 23–24.

[82] Commissioner G. F. Cockburn's Diaries of his Tours in Cuttack Province, 1846 and 1847, 49. OIOC, Eur. MSS B 266.

In precolonial Orissa, communications did not come to a total standstill even when the monsoon rendered most roads impassable. River navigation could replace road transport during the rains and the Mahanadi became navigable almost up to Raipur. Coastal shipping also continued after the monsoon had set in, though in a very limited way. Sailing conditions remained hazardous until December—most "native craft" were drawn up the shore for the stormy last quarter of the year all along the coast of the Bay of Bengal.[83]

The Intensity of Circulation

No quantitative data are presently known regarding the intensity of circulation along these routes for the precolonial period. The controversial pilgrim tax, which *yatris* (pilgrims) to Jagannath had to pay to the East India Company, gave occasion to the first counts of transregional traffic. Colonial officials thus reported about 89,000 pilgrims reached Puri annually via precolonial roads an average between 1816 and 1824.[84] More detailed information is only available after 1850. A report on the traffic along that section of the NE-SW axis between the District of Ganjam and the Province of Cuttack (both parts of the Orissa region but belonging to different British Presidencies) for the year 1863–64 seems to confirm the suspicion that pilgrim estimates tended to err on the low side. About 90,000 travellers were said to have trekked along or traversed the Chilka Lake in that year, of whom 65,000 were said to be pilgrims on their way to Puri from distant places in South India.[85] This

---

[83] Deloche, *Transport and Communication*, 2: 112–17, 214–16.
[84] Smith, *Report on Pilgrimage*, part II, 10.
[85] OIOC, BPWP August 1866, P/432/41, Com., no. 8, 16 (J. G. Ryves, SE, 1st Division, to C. A. Orr, Secry. to Govt. of Madras, PWD, 16 November 1864). Also see nos., 13–14 (J. Ouchterlony, Acting Deputy CE, Northern Circle, to W. H. Horsley, Secry. to Govt. of Madras, PWD, 1 March 1862). For the accuracy of early counts of pilgrims in Puri, Hunter (*The Annals of Rural Bengal*, 2: 150) felt that they "notoriously fell below the truth". Richardson estimated the number only of the *solvent* pilgrims reaching Puri every year at about 100,000. OIOC, Board's Collection, F/4/505, no. 12139, 70 (John Richardson on province of Cuttack, extract from Bengal Revenue Consultations, 18 May 1815).

indicates a large six-figure number of travellers along the NE-SW axis per annum considering that contemporary accounts suggest that only the smaller part of the pilgrims reached Puri from the South, while many more wandered the Jagannath Road from Bengal and North India.[86] This was indeed very remarkable for pre-railway nineteenth-century India when even the Grand Trunk Road between Benares and Calcutta—perhaps the most heavily beaten track across one of the most densely populated parts of the subcontinent—was used by 470,000 and 700,000 travellers annually according to estimates from the 1840s.[87]

The same report estimated the trade volume between the District of Ganjam and the Cuttack Division on this route, that is, the goods transported along or across the Chilka Lake, at 110,000 tons consisting mainly of rice and oil-seeds with a value of about Rs 2,500,000.[88] These were no negligible figures either, though the intensity of intraregional commodity transport was far higher in areas of Bengal and the north Indian plains at that period.[89]

Of considerable interest, furthermore, is a quantitative assessment of the trade patterns of the neighbouring Chhattisgarh region in Central India that had been prepared for Sir Richard Temple's "Report on the Mahanuddy and its Tributaries" of 1863. This trade estimate gives a rough idea of the intensity of interregional commodity exchange along the other, the W-ESE axis of Orissa's regime of circulation (see map 7, tables 2 and 3).[90]

---

[86] See p. 140, above.
[87] G. Ashburner to R. M. Stephenson, 2 September 1844, in Stephenson, *Report upon the Practicability*, 25; Andrew, *Indian Railways and their Probable Results*, 35; Yang, *Bazaar India*, 44–45.
[88] See footnote 85, in this chapter.
[89] For a count of the traffic volume between Bardhaman (Burdwan) and Calcutta, both in western Bengal, in the early 1840s, see Stephenson, *Report upon the Practicability*, 65–67, 70–71, see also 56–57, 60–61; for traffic from the region of Awadh in 1858 and 1860, see Varady, *Rail and Road Transport*, 84–92 (though his annual figures, derived at by simple multiplication of data for shorter time spans in the dry season, appear doubtful).
[90] The following tables and, unless referenced otherwise, all figures presented in the subsequent paragraphs of this section are computed from data in Temple, "Report on the Mahanuddy", 25–31.

TABLE 2: Interregional trade of Chhattisgarh in Central India: Routes and estimated volume, 1862

Trade Routes	Exports			Imports		
	Bulk, long tons	Bulk, percent	Value, Rs.	Bulk, long tons	Bulk, percent	Value, Rs.
Chhattisgarh to Mirzapur (North India, on the Ganges)	3,028	6	443,896	139	2	88,081
Chhattisgarh to Nagpur (Central India)	28,245	58	3,242,582	742	9	1,132,596
Chhattisgarh to Jabalpur (Central India, on the Narmada)	3,152	6	223,280	205	3	17,200
Chhattisgarh to Sironcha (South India, on the Godavari)	unknown		unknown	unknown		unknown
Subtotal non-Orissa routes	*34,425*	*70*	*3,909,758*	*1,086*	*14*	*1,237,877*
Chhattisgarh to Sambalpur and Binika	2,651	5	495,026	2,676	33	356,238
Sheonarayan[91] to Cuttack (land route along the Mahanadi)	1,194	2	163,886	537	7	39,046
Sheonarayan to Cuttack (river route on the Mahanadi)	1,864	4	152,541	939	12	77,187
Chhattisgarh to Ganjam	9,231	19	251,967	2,687	34	292,710
Subtotal Orissa routes	*14,940*	*30*	*1,063,420*	*6,839*	*86*	*765,181*
Total	49,365	100	4,973,178	7,925	100	2,003,058

[91] Sheonarayan designates a location in the Chhattisgarh region at the confluence of three rivers: Sheonath, Jonk and Mahanadi.

TABLE 3: Interregional trade of Chhattisgarh in Central India: regional distribution of the estimated total trade volume, 1862 (exports and imports)

	Bulk, long tons	Value, Rs.
Total	57,290	6,976,236
Various regions in North, Central and South India	35,511	5,147,635
Orissa	21,779	1,828,601
Percentage Orissa	38	26

Some caution is in order with regard to these figures: the colonial state's ability to "know" circulation in this region was still limited;[92] the bulk of trade was conveyed on the backs of pack oxen who required, as mentioned before, alternating tracks rather than fixed roads and could, therefore, more easily evade counts;[93] the salt policy of the colonial government, as we shall see soon, forced Banjaras and other trading groups either out of business or into clandestine practices.[94] Even if Sir Richard Temple, who submitted this report, thought that "the great bulk of the traffic may be said to be pretty fairly represented",[95] the figures appear to be estimates rather than counts, while no data could be supplied for the trade between Chhattisgarh and the Godavari River basin in the South, which he believed to be considerable.

Despite all limitations, this survey is significant for our purposes insofar as it permits a glimpse of a decaying pattern of *ancien régime* circulation along the W-ESE axis, which was based on an economic

---

[92] A senior 'public works' official wrote, for instance, as late as in 1862 that "[t]hese 'Guijats' [Garhjat] Districts are sealed books, as things are, to the European traveller". OIOC, BPWP April 1862, P/16/57, Com., no. 281, 195 (T. Armstrong, SE, Cuttack Circle, to Offg. CE, Bengal, 7 April 1862).

[93] Hence Temple ("Report on the Mahanuddy", 18) himself remarked with regard to the Chhattisgarh–Ganjam line, the route with the largest intensity of traffic: "the registry return for this route is incomplete, and that much traffic has escaped registry. This is very probable from the habit of the Bunjarra carriers to travel away from the most direct routes in view to securing forage and water for their large herds of cattle."

[94] Das, *Studies in Economic History of Orissa*, 258, 272–73.

[95] Temple, "Report on the Mahanuddy", 25.

complementarity of the two neighbouring regions: Chhattisgarh had not only exported part of its grain surplus to Orissa, but was also the closest of the cotton growing districts of Central India and accounted for a large proportion of the raw material required by Oriya weavers. Orissa supplied the adjacent inland region, in turn, with the product of its coastal salt pans—exports that became even more important when commercial textile manufacture declined in the eighteenth century.[96] This pattern was still clearly discernible as food grains accounted for 68 per cent and raw cotton for 9 per cent of the bulk transported from Chhattisgarh to Orissa, while salt made up for 61 per cent of the total tonnage conveyed in the reverse direction.

However, it is equally evident that considerable shifts had occurred since the commencement of British rule. What Stirling had called in 1825 the "great road leading along the Mahánadi to Sembelpur and Berar"[97] was far from being a major trade route in 1862 according to Temple's estimates: the tonnage shifted along the Mahanadi road amounted to about 15,000 bullock loads; 200 boats left Nandghat on the Sheonath River annually for Cuttack, while further 1,000 vessels were available for hire in Sonepur, Binika and Sambalpur; the total volume of the Mahanadi trade between Chhattisgarh and Cuttack (including both the river and the land route) was estimated at about Rs 230,000 and less than 3,000 tons.[98] In comparison, 10,000 tons of salt were believed to be shipped annually from Agra to Bengal in the early 1600s; 30,000 boatmen were held to be in *constant* employ in lower Bengal in 1780 and the trade between Calcutta and Benares (or places further upstream) amounted to about 180,000 tons on the river route and an additional 20,000 tons on the Grand Trunk Road in the 1840s.[99]

---

[96] Choudhury, *Economic History of Colonialism*, 83–86; Das, *Studies in the Economic History of Orissa*, 261–62.

[97] Stirling, "An Account ... of Orissa", 194.

[98] These figures exclude, of course, all intra-regional utilisations of the Mahanadi for purposes of circulation. They reflect neither the local and intra-regional river traffic nor the practice of floating timber from the hill regions to the plains.

[99] Sarkar, *Inland Transport and Communication*, 12–13, 16; Bhattacharya, "Regional Economy (1757–1857): Eastern India", 271; G. Ashburner to R. M. Stephenson, 2 September 1844, in Stephenson, *Report upon the Practicability,*

The smallness of the Mahanadi trade was clearly not exclusively due to lower levels of production and population, nor to the Mahanadi's rocky bed and correspondingly increased navigational risks since freight charges were apparently not necessarily higher than on the Ganges.[100] What is particularly striking about the 1862 figures is that Stirling's "great road", the waterway of the Mahanadi and the land route along its bank, together accounted for merely 21 per cent of the total tonnage of the Chhattisgarh–Orissa trade, while 55 per cent or more than 80,000 bullock loads were conveyed on obscure tracks to Ganjam, which Temple described as "one of the wildest and most unhealthy routes in all India".[101] This distribution seems even more eccentric if we take into account that transport costs of pack-bullocks in Orissa per ton and mile were reckoned to be at that time between four and five times higher than those of the Mahanadi boats.[102]

The solution to this mystery lies in the policy of the East India Company which had imposed a monopoly on the manufacture and sale of salt immediately after the annexation of the "Cuttack Province". This monopoly, followed by a sequence of further legislations, was aimed at protecting the very considerable government revenues from the salt monopoly in Bengal against cheap imports from Orissa. Considerable taxes were thus also imposed upon salt produced in the coastal districts of Puri, Cuttack and Balasore. Export to Bengal expanded to such an extent that salt became scarce in Orissa itself until cheap English salt, shipped to India as ballast without charge, swept the market of Bengal and Orissa from the mid-century and marginalised what had been a mainstay of the latter region's commodity production in the precolonial period. For

---

25, 71; Andrew, *Indian Railways and their Probable Results*, 34; Yang, *Bazaar India*, 44–45.

[100] Temple ("Report on the Mahanuddy", 32) calculated that transport costs on the Mahanadi did not exceed one Anna (the sixteenth part of a Rupee) per mile and ton, while similar computations for the Ganges arrived at a figure about 30 per cent above that rate even for the mid-1840s. Yang, (*Bazaar India*, 31) however, gives somewhat lower rates between one half and three quarters of an Anna for Bihar in the 1860s. G. Ashburner to R. M. Stephenson, 2 September 1844, Stephenson, *Report upon the Practicability*, 25.

[101] Temple, "Report on the Mahanuddy", 20.

[102] Ibid., 31–32.

itinerant traders from Central India who calculated with small margins, the salt pans of the northern and central coastal districts of Orissa ceased to be a lucrative destination soon after its annexation. The southern Ganjam District, however, was part of the Madras Presidency where a somewhat less prohibitive salt policy was pursued. It is documented that a considerable part of the trade in coastal salt to both Chhattisgarh and interior Orissa shifted towards Ganjam, while a reduction of the overall volume of interregional trade along the W-ESE axis appears likely.[103] Stirling had remarked as early as in 1825 that legal salt exports of the "Cuttack Province" to various regions of Central India and Bihar had dropped from more than 11,000 tons to about 730 tons.[104] In 1862, the export of salt from the three districts of that Province to Chhattisgarh amounted, according to Temple's report, to less than 1,600 tons, that from Ganjam to additional 2,500 tons. A decade later, Sir William Wilson Hunter, colonial administrator and official statistician of the Raj, observed that it

> is as if we had thrown a wall across one of the finest trade routes in the world. Our Orissa Salt Duty practically blockades the Mahánadí just as effectually as if we had filled it up with rocks.[105]

These are indications for destructive aspects of a production of social space, for a historical process of *spatial disarticulation*. References to decayed towns, deserted villages and emigrated weavers in various European accounts suggest that a decline in the intensity of circulation may have commenced already in the eighteenth century, especially in the period of Maratha rule.[106] But the early nineteenth century was clearly a period of continued attrition of earlier

---

[103] Choudhury, *Economic History of Colonialism*, 34–58, 88–93; OIOC, BPWP February 1873, P/200, Com., nos. 22–26, 11–13. Also see OIOC, BPWP August 1860, P/16/44, Com., no. 5, 6–7 (G. F. Cockburn, CoCD, to Secry. to GoB, PWD, 19 June 1860). For the salt monopoly imposed by the Government of Madras on Ganjam, see R. C. Misro and L. K. Patnaik, "Salt Monopoly in South Orissa under the British Raj", *Quarterly Review of Historical Studies* (Calcutta), 39, nos. 1–2 1999, 36–45.

[104] Stirling, "An Account . . . of Orissa", 194.

[105] Hunter, *The Annals of Rural Bengal*, 3: 162.

[106] Das, *Studies in Economic History of Orissa*, 8–10 and passim. Also see Davidson, "Journal of a Route from Cuttack to Nagpore", 1790, folio 102, British Library, Add. MSS. 13588.

channels of circulation and contemporaries appear to have experienced their lifetime as a period of decaying trade. Inhabitants of Kantilo, formerly a vibrant entrepôt town and still one of the largest settlements of the "Garhjat" region, thus pointed out to a British official in 1847 that the number of houses had declined from 1,200 to 900, while cloth had disappeared from the market.[107]

An Ancien Régime of Circulation

A study of the available evidence thus indicates an *ancien régime* of circulation more complex than that suggested by the general colonial accounts on which historiography has so far mainly relied. The frequently quoted assertions of the 1866 Famine Commission that Orissa was "geographically isolated to an excessive degree", that Jagannath Road was "the only ordinary mode of communication with the outside world" and that travelling conditions had not much changed since the "days of Asoka"[108] need some qualification.[109] The partial commercialisation of textile, salt and agricultural production, cultural practices like pilgrimage as well as processes of state formation had created and repeatedly remoulded patterns and modes of circulation in the Orissa region and had generated a rich socio-spatial inheritance. All agencies of society, including the colonial regime, had to relate to this inheritance in their spatial practice irrespective of whether or not they chose to acknowledge it.

One aspect of this inheritance was that intra- as well as inter-regional practices of circulation had assumed a particular *geographical pattern*. The proposed "two axes model" is, of course, no more than a schematic, simplified representation of a far more complicated pattern—a pattern that was, moreover, in all likeliness far from stable during the two or three centuries before 1860. Yet the model can serve as a tool for the synthesis of the complex processes of growth and decline in the intensity of circulation, of compression

---

[107] Commissioner G. F. Cockburn's Diaries of his Tours in Cuttack Province, 1846 and 1847, 49, OIOC, Eur. MSS B 266. Also see various similar observations on Baleshwar, Jajpur, Cuttack and Sambalpur quoted earlier in this chapter.
[108] The Maurya ruler Ashoka established supremacy over large parts of the subcontinent between 268 and 231 BCA.
[109] *Report of Commissioners . . . Famine in Bengal and Orissa in 1866*, 1: 8–9.

and dispersal, of articulation and disarticulation, of the spatial reorganisation of Orissa under the colonial regime. To anticipate the hypothesis that will be developed in detail in this case study: one major colonial contribution to the transformation of the region's transport infrastructure consisted in consolidating the NE-SW axis and simultaneously destabilising the W-ESE axis. The Orissa coastal region's links with the colonial capital of Calcutta (and to a less extent with the southern metropolis of Madras) were thus reinforced while those with Central India and even its own "Garhjat" hinterland lost much of their *relative* significance, though there can be little doubt that the *absolute* volume of traffic increased considerably on most lines of communication on both axes in the course of the long nineteenth century.[110]

Another inheritance that cannot be ignored was that circulatory practices followed a particular *temporal pattern* in accordance with climatic, productive and cultural seasons. This seasonality was an indication of a comparatively low level of autonomy of social practice from natural location or, in other words, of an as yet rather weak tendency towards abstract space.[111] The extended scope for river transport during the monsoon months could only partly compensate for the impassibility of most roads and the inaccessibility of most ports in that season. The overall rhythm of circulation thus slowed down considerably. This was felt most dramatically during the 1866 famine: when rice was at last sent down the coast from Bengal and Burma after the onset of the rains it could not be landed for weeks in some instances.[112] Land routes, moreover, were generally not chosen and constructed to establish the shortest possible link between two locations. Instead, they were rather adapted to the natural contours of the surrounding landscape as they had to be serviceable under conditions when the social need for commodity circulation was not urgent enough to warrant large investments in the removal of natural constraints: roads followed watersheds and elevations of the countryside and avoided places prone to inundation and with adverse soil conditions. Hence colonial officials found these routes to be circuitous and condemned them as being

---

[110] For an elaboration of this argument, see chapters 6, 7 and 8 of the present study.
[111] See hypothesis 4 in chapter 2 of the present study.
[112] Mukherjee, *Irrigation, Inland Navigation and Flood Problems*, 30–31.

indicative of the "complete apathy" and "neglect of all considerations of convenience and economy" of Indians.[113] However, they also experienced that their own straight and "scientifically" constructed roads could be defended against the forces of nature only with difficulty and at high maintenance costs while the old winding tracks reflected the villagers' age-old experience of their environment. One engineer admitted ruefully "that he would never again desert the track of the Villagers in making a fair-weather Road. The route, he said, might be somewhat circuitous, but there was always some good reason for its selection."[114] Low investment in roads thus did not imply their non-existence, but rather that none of these old roads was surfaced and while the majority was almost or fully impassable during the rains only few would permit cart traffic even during the dry season. This entailed that travelling speed was very low, that there was little scope for changes of transport technology and that the pack bullock survived as the most important mode of overland transport well into the nineteenth century. Costs of animal porterage were, however, in this region reckoned to exceed those of conveyance by cart by about 60 per cent.[115] This set, in turn, firm limits to the intensity of circulation as trade in many commodities remained only marginally profitable if at all.

Finally, both the intensity of circulation and the density of the region's transport network should not be exaggerated—both were certainly low according to contemporary Indian standards. This was, as has been suggested already, not merely due to particular geomorphic conditions but even more crucially to a specific constellation of socioeconomic and political interests with regard to the problem of circulation. This constellation had been shaped in the eighteenth century and persisted, in modified form, throughout the early colonial period—a phenomenon to be discussed in the following chapter.

---

[113] MacGeorge, *Ways and Works*, 66–68.
[114] OIOC, BPWP May 1861, P/16/52, Com., no. 89, 63 (E. T. Trevor, CoCD, to Secry. to GoB, no. 73, 15 March 1861).
[115] "[C]arriage by carts cost 2 ½ or 3 annas per ton per mile, and 4 or 5 annas per mile by pack-bullocks". Temple, "Report on the Mahanuddy", 31.

5

Who Needs a Road? Circulation, Society and the East India Company

Infrastructures of circulation cannot *per se* be assumed to be in the "general interest" nor is their non-development necessarily a result of "neglect". While those who have so far written on Orissa's transport history appear to have assumed an implicit consensus of all social forces with regard to the desirability of "good communications", it has already been argued in this study that transport infrastructure was (a) a result and means of social domination and (b) a polyvalent social product that could be appropriated for conflicting purposes by various social agencies (chapter 2, hypothesis 2). More concretely, a road was not just a road: it was only serviceable as a means of circulation if integrated with a "logistic infrastructure", if linked to a number of economic, political and cultural institutions that afforded provisions, protection, shelter, medical care and other services (see chapter 2, hypothesis 1). Such institutions—be it a market, a fort, a pilgrims' rest house or a ferry and toll *ghat*—were places where contradictory social interests confronted and related to each other: they were sites of social conflict and integration. On accepting these premises, we face the task of exploring, which of the major social forces were interested in intensifying circulation in early colonial Orissa and to what extent? This is the purpose of the present chapter.

British writings on circulation in British India were generally filled with the familiar rhetoric of "improvement" (see chapter 3). This can also be shown for the case of Orissa, where the colonisers' commitment to the task of "opening up the country" was piously recited like a mantra. The declared objectives of colonial rule were to establish law and order, to overcome the "barbarous" superstitions and customs of the "natives", to create circumstances under which they would be "driven to work at high pressure"[1], to promote commercial exchange, in short, to bring the boons of "civilisation" to the people of Orissa. The following two quotes from writings of high-ranking colonial operatives with regard to infrastructure in the interior Garhjat area of Orissa are fairly representative samples of standard formulations found in many documents. An official letter, addressed in the mid-nineteenth century to the Government of Bengal, gave, for instance, particular emphasis to the commercial dimensions of the process of "civilisation" through infrastructure:

> Along this road would be conveyed the produce of many of the Tributary Mehals ... these extensive tracts of wild country would be greatly benefited & the people would be induced to clear their jungles and bring more land under cultivation when this means of exporting the produce was available—while being enriched and coming more into contact with the people of the plains they would acquire more civilized tastes & habits than they possess at present.[2]

An official report, written by the Commissioner of Cuttack in the early 1840s, reveals more clearly the contradictions of this process by blending the lyric of civilisation with the "prose of counterinsurgency"[3]:

> I consider the opening of roads through uncivilized and jungly countries as the greatest auxiliary of civilization, and the most efficient instrument in putting down rebellion; it should go hand in hand with education, that handmaid of good Government, to the diffusion of which we must mainly look for improving the state of the Tributary Mehals.[4]

The violent undertones of colonial improvement discourse were not lost on perceptive contemporary commentators. The concept of the "spread of civilisation" as a nineteenth-century Bangla journal

---

[1] Temple, "Report on the Mahanuddy", 41.
[2] OSA, BoRLR 26,979 (CoCD to Secry. to GoB, Judicial Dpt., 25 October 1856).
[3] The quoted phrase is, of course, borrowed from Ranajit Guha's famous essay "The Prose of Counterinsurgency", in *Subaltern Studies II: Writings on South Asian History and Society*, ed. Ranajit Guha (New Delhi: Oxford University Press, 1983), 1–42.
[4] A. J. Moffat Mill's report on the Tributary Mehals, in *Papers on the Settlement of Cuttack*, 67.

cogently observed, was synonymous with "extension of Empire".[5] Its affirmative use-value was then as apparent as it is today. Yet, if we move away from the exclusively discursive or narrowly textual approaches of present-day hegemonic academics, more interesting tensions between the ideological claims and the quotidian, dusty, even material realities of circulation come into view. For, in the case of early nineteenth-century Orissa, official fantasies of "opening up the country" were rather inadequate representations of the prevailing politics of social space.

Colonial Priorities: Securing Communications and Quelling Insurgency

What has to be accounted for is that the colonial regime's priority of developing transport infrastructure, despite all proclamations to the contrary, was in fact rather low in the first four or five decades after 1803 when the Company had wrested the control of Orissa from the Bhonsles—a Maratha lineage that had established itself as the ruling dynasty in the central Indian region of Berar since 1719.[6] The crucial point seems to be that the colonial government was not so much interested in making a way *into* Orissa than in *getting past it* without hindrance. Before 1803, British expansionists did not primarily seek to get access to the region's economic resources in order to exploit them. More important were political and military considerations of obtaining a missing strategic link, a secure "life line" between the colonial core regions of Bengal and South India.[7] In the latter half of the eighteenth century, the Company had tried to secure safe and rapid communications between the two presidencies and had established by 1764 a chain of regular dak stations

---

[5] *Navavibhakar*, 14 March 1881, quoted in *RNNB* for the Week Ending 26 March 1881, 2.

[6] C. U. Wills, *British Relations with the Nagpur State in the Eighteenth Century: An Account, Mainly Based on Contemporary English Records*, Nagpur, 1926, 5–21.

[7] Clive enquired in 1766 whether the Marathas could not be persuaded to "cede the province of Orissa, for an annual tribute, and thereby give a contiguity to the British dominions in India, which would strengthen them greatly". Motte, "A Narrative of a Journey", 2. Wellesley planned Orissa's annexation in order to "unite the Northern Circars by a continued line of sea coast with Bengal". Quoted in, Ray, *Orissa under Marathas*, 106–7.

on the "old Jagannath Road" in Bhonsle-ruled Orissa, under the supervision of three British postmasters.[8] The Governor-in-Council, moreover, obtained the permission to march Bengal troops to South India through the Orissa coastal plains in 1781 as enforcements in the Second Anglo-Mysore War (1780–1784).[9] However, the absence of direct control over this important thoroughfare was a constant matter of concern throughout the latter half of the eighteenth century.[10] Hence the costs of conquest were considered. James Rennell contributed to this debate when he pointed out in his famous *Memoir* that the Bhonsle's dominions were "too widely extended, in proportion to their value, to form a powerful state" as Cuttack was no less than 770 km from the kingdom's capital Nagpur.[11] This analysis proved correct in 1803 when the Company's troops met with little resistance when they annexed the Orissa plains.[12] Strategic considerations remained central even after the capture of Orissa and the fall of the Mysore sultanate. An 1815 report on the province of Cuttack, for instance, pointed out that the

> importance of this Territory to the British Government consists chiefly in its geographical situation, the possession of which connects the two Presidencies of Fort William and Fort St George[,] secures an uninterrupted intercourse between the two Governments of Bengal & Madras and places the whole range of Coast on this side of the Bay under the immediate eye and control of the British Government.[13]

Like their Mughal and Maratha predecessors, the British did not initially try to extend direct control beyond the plains of the "Mughalbandi" coastal area—the region constituting the missing link between the Bengal and Madras Presidencies, which was also

---

[8] Ray, *Orissa under Marathas*, 156; Munsi, *Geography of Transportation in Eastern India*, 21.

[9] Ray, *Orissa under Marathas*, 101–2, 152; Das, *Studies in Economic History of Orissa*, 103–4.

[10] Ray, *Orissa under Marathas*, 87–105.

[11] James Rennell, *Memoir of a Map of Hindostan or the Mogul Empire*, 3rd ed. (London: G. Nicol, 1793), cxxx.

[12] Ray, *Orissa under Marathas*, 106–26; Prabhat Mukherjee, *History of Orissa in the Nineteenth Century* (Cuttack: Utkal University 1964), 13–22.

[13] OIOC, Board's Collection, F/4/505, no. 12139, 7 (John Richardson on province of Cuttack, extract from Bengal Revenue Consultations, 18 May 1815).

the part of Orissa where expectations for revenue from ground rent, salt manufacture and transit duties were highest.[14] The only major project of road construction in the period under review—the "new Jagannath" or Orissa Trunk Road answered precisely these strategic and revenue considerations.[15]

As for the Garhjat area, it largely continued to be governed—not just formally but also for most practical purposes—by numerous Oriya and "tribal" chiefs.[16] Until 1818 even the Maratha rulers of Berar were allowed by the British to retain control over part of this region, namely the so-called "Sambalpur group" of little kingdoms that was formally ceded only in 1826.[17] The degree of colonial intervention into the numerous Garhjat principalities—in practical terms of administrative control, economic utilisation or even information retrieval—thus remained rather low before the middle of the century.[18] A loose control over these petty principalities that could hardly pose a serious threat to British strategic interests was deemed fully sufficient by the East India Company's authorities even though the emergence of a more interventionist policy can be discerned from the 1840s.[19] Correspondingly, the need to link up the Orissa highlands more closely by way of major infrastructural schemes continued to be very limited throughout the pre-railway and pre-industrial period of colonial rule, when the rich timber and mineral resources of this area attracted but little attention. During the period under review, no considerable land revenue or other returns were expected from these "distant and unproductive districts" and investment in their direct administration (or infrastructure) seemed, therefore, unremunerative.[20]

---

[14] Stirling, "An Account ... of Orissa", 167–68.
[15] See section 4, below.
[16] Cobden-Ramsay, *Feudatory States of Orissa*, 24–29.
[17] Ibid., 27; Mukherjee, *History of Orissa*, 26–33, 43–46, 260–62.
[18] Significant exceptions, as yet insufficiently analysed by historians, were, however, the prolonged campaigns against "Meriah" human sacrifices in the "Khond Mahals" on the part of the Madras Government. See especially, *History of the Rise and Progress*; Campbell, *A Personal Narrative*.
[19] Mukherjee, *History of Orissa*, 23–53, 220–62.
[20] OIOC, Board's Collection, F/4/505, no. 12139, 62 (John Richardson on province of Cuttack, extract from Bengal Revenue Consultations, 18 May 1815).

However, even in the directly controlled coastal plains administration was run on a low budget and annexation did not entail any considerable investment in 'public works' for several decades. Village-based textile manufacture had already declined before the onset of colonial rule. Except for a brief period of recovery, weaving as well as cotton cultivation deteriorated further from the 1820s.[21] One of the main objectives of the "conquerors" had been to stop illicit salt imports to Bengal. By 1863, large-scale manufacture and trade of salt in the "Cuttack Province" had been stifled by the Company's policies and imports of cheap Liverpool salt increased.[22] We have already seen that these developments implied an attrition of the region's overland trade links with Central India, but it also entailed a decline in shipbuilding and coastal shipping in general and of the port of Baleshwar in particular.[23] As for agriculture, the colonial state's demands for land revenue were inordinately heavy in comparison to other regions of eastern India[24] leaving little scope for productive investment, while state expenditure on infrastructure remained on a modest scale before the 1860s.[25] Even a contemporary colonial Commissioner of Orissa felt that the directly administered estates were treated "as a milch cow from which the last drop may justifiably be squeezed rather than as a property to be attended to and managed for the joint benefit of landlord & tenantry."[26]

---

[21] Das, *Studies in Economic History of Orissa*, 247–50; Jit, *The Agrarian Life*, 140–43.

[22] This aspect of Orissa's economic history is well researched. See especially, Choudhury, *Economic History of Colonialism*.

[23] Ibid., 113–15. Also see chapter 4 of the present study.

[24] Binay Chaudhuri, "Agrarian Relations: Eastern India", in *The Cambridge Economic History of India*, ed. Dharma Kumar, 2: 133–34; Jit, *The Agrarian Life*, 192–224.

[25] The first major irrigation (and inland navigation) projects in Orissa were executed only after 1862 and originally by a private shareholder company, the East India Irrigation and Canal Company. The uncompleted works were bought up by the colonial state in 1869: H. W. Gulliver, Offg. CE of Bengal, Irrigation Branch, 19 February 1875, in *Papers Relating to the Orissa Canals: 1869 to 1877 and 1881 to 1883* (Calcutta: Bengal Secretariat Press, 1884), 91. For early colonial investments in transport infrastructure, see chapter 6.

[26] OSA, BoRLR 28,024 (G. F. Cockburn, CoCD, to Secry. to GoB, 17 February 1858).

Occasionally the practice of colonialism appears to have disturbed the preferred self-image of its operatives as torchbearers of improvement.

While colonial economic interest thus did not create strong incentives for investment in infrastructure in the early colonial period, military considerations probably did so to some extent.[27] Roads were—in the words of Moffat Mills, the Commissioner of Cuttack of the early 1840s—the "death-blow to rebellion", a precondition of efficient counter-insurgency operations. He felt that the suppression of the Khurda uprising of 1818 would have taken three months rather than three years and would have been much cheaper if the present Orissa Trunk Road had existed at the time.[28] Such arguments convinced, at times, even the East India Company's Court of Directors who advised their subordinates in 1838 that the

> protracted campaign in Goomsur which caused so great an expenditure of blood and treasure, were mainly owing to our ignorance of the localities, and the want of practical roads on which to move our troops to the required points. Even in a financial point of view, therefore, the formation of ready means of communication is of paramount importance[.][29]

Thirty-five years later, when imperial domination had been established more firmly in the Garhjat region, T. E. Ravenshaw, then Commissioner of Orissa, still found reason to warn his superiors of impending security dangers in case of neglect of road repairs:

> The Tributary States are all very quiet now, and may very probably remain so, but a little fire would make a great blaze, and then, in case of

---

[27] Munsi, *Geography of Transportation in Eastern India*, 24.
[28] Letter by A. J. Moffat Mills, CoCD, 1 June 1844, in *History of the Rise and Progress*, 85. Also see Moffat Mill's report on the Tributary Mehals, in *Papers on the Settlement of Cuttack*, 67. The same view of the utility of Ganjam Road was already expressed in the 1830s: OSA, BoRLR 19,253 (W. Wilkinson, Collector, to J. Master, Offg. CoCD, 6 February 1835). For similar arguments, see OSA, BoRLR 27,528 (letter to Secry. to GoB, Judicial Dpt., 24 July 1857); OIOC, BPWP April 1862, P/16/57, Com., no. 281, 195 (T. Armstrong, SE, Cuttack Circle, to Offg. CE, Bengal, 7 April 1862); OIOC, BPWP July 1862 P/16/58, Com., no. 113, 65 (R. N. Shore, Offg. CoCD, to Secry. to GoB, 15 May 1862).
[29] Despatch of Court of Directors to Madras Government, 24 October 1838, in *History of the Rise and Progress*, 16. For a later case, in which the Keonjhar Raja was forced to construct roads after the frequent uprisings in his state, see *RATMO* 1896–97, 26–27.

need, I think, Government would be very sorry to have lost command of the country by the roads being allowed to go to ruin.[30]

Ravenshaw's statement points to the fact that even military interest had hitherto not necessarily entailed a continuous policy of infrastructural development. It has already been pointed out that important military roads—not to speak of minor thoroughfares—were rarely kept in regular repair by the colonial administration but were rather brought into a passable condition when actually required.[31] In 1852, for instance, a bullock track between Ganjam and Sonepur via Kalinga Ghat and Shankarakol was "opened out". It was partly bridged by a detachment of the Madras Army commanded by one Lieutenant Wyld. Traders, who trekked the difficult and increasingly important salt routes between Central India and Ganjam, immediately took to this improved channel of circulation. It was said that about 20,000 pack bullocks trod along this road in the first year of its existence. Yet, this achievement "came to nothing after the very first season for want of necessary annual repairs, so that the route soon became almost as impracticable as before." Even then "Detachments of Troops, unaccompanied, however, by Carts," marched up and down in this area, "but this was more a making of way across Country, I apprehend, than travelling in the ordinary style of comfort and ease."[32]

Thus far it has been argued that the early colonial regime's interest in an active 'public works' policy in Orissa was rather limited—

---

[30] OIOC, BPWP February 1873, P/200, Com., nos. 22–26, 12 (T. E. Ravenshaw, report on Cuttack–Sambalpur roads).

[31] "Fair-weather roads were constructed by, and for the use of, armies on the march, but these were neglected almost as soon as they had fulfilled their immediate purpose, and those absolutely necessary for the control of newly acquired territories were only kept open by constant reconstruction." MacGeorge, *Ways and Works*, 80.

[32] OIOC, BPWP August 1860, P/16/44, Com., no. 5, 5–7 (G. F. Cockburn, CoCD, to Secry. to GoB, PWD, 19 June 1860). Also see OIOC, BPWP 25 May 1860, P/16/41, Com., no. 95, 433 (G. F. Cockburn, CoCD, to F. Bond, EE, Cuttack and Sumbulpore Road, 15 July 1859); OIOC, BPWP 25 May 1860, P/16/41, Com., No. 102, 443 (E.H. Harington, Acting District Engineer, Ganjam, to CE, PWD, 17 June 1859). In another case, a road was (re-)opened after the Mayurbhanj rebellion of 1866 but overgrown again soon after; see Bhagabana Sahu, *Princely States of Orissa under the British Crown, 1858–1905* (Cuttack: Vidyapuri, 1993), 84.

whether looked at from an economic or political-military point of view. However, other social actors, for instance, the precolonial local authorities, the zamindars of coastal Orissa and the "little kings" of the Garhjats had their own perspectives on problems of circulation.

Exigencies of Local Power: The Uses and Dangers of Roads

Various levels of local rulers had derived considerable revenue and other benefits from the control of traffic routes in the precolonial period and many Garhjat kings continued to do so even after the emergence of British power. In the Orissa plains, numerous *chaukis* (toll stations) had been established along the old Jagannath Road where various charges on travellers and goods were exacted. Leckie believed in 1790 that in Maratha-ruled Orissa

> the greatest branches of the revenue are the customs, and tax upon pilgrims going to Jugurnaut. A bullock-load of silk is taxed at six rupees; and so on in proportion to the bulk and value of the load. Pilgrims from the Decan pay six rupees; those from Bengal, who are generally richer, ten rupees. They however are not severe in the exaction when they think the party really poor; and they make up their loss occasioned by this lenity when they find out a wealthy subject in disguise, which is frequently the case.[33]

As many as twelve toll stations were said to have been established on the short road section between "Raj Ghat" on the Subarnarekha River and the town of Baleshwar where pilgrims and traders were thus fleeced after about every three kilometres of journey.[34] Earlier in the century, in 1708, an English merchant who travelled the road from Puri to Baleshwar noted that tolls had been due after about every 20 km. The customs collected at seven or eight stations along the 165 km of road between Cuttack and Baleshwar had been equal to 80 per cent of the wholesale price of cotton fabric in the former area and had amounted to 32 per cent of their market value in the latter town. Tolls in the Ganjam area and on river routes were said to be even higher.[35] Chaukis were often located at river crossings, and

---

[33] Leckie, "Journal of a Route to Nagpore", 13.
[34] Motte, "A Narrative of a Journey", 4.
[35] Hamilton, *A New Account of the East Indies*, 215–217; also see Hunter, *The Annals of Rural Bengal*, 3: 44–45.

the zamindars had rented out these "ferry ghats" to mahjis (owner of ferryboat) who were free to extract as much profit from this concession as they could.[36] The ferry collections along the Orissa Trunk Road and its branch to Puri were reported to yield Rs 12,386 per annum when they were appropriated by the colonial administration in 1857.[37]

The Raja of Nilgiri, a minor chief in northern Orissa, had allegedly annexed a tract to the immediate west of Baleshwar in about the 1730s with the sole purpose of gaining control over a section of the old road to Jagannath.[38] This enabled him to participate in the gains other zamindars and their overlords already made by levying pilgrim tax and customs duties at various toll stations between Khunta Ghat in the kingdom of Mayurbhanj and Athara-Nala Bridge in Puri.[39] In fact, most of his revenues seem to have originated from this source during the Maratha period.[40] Less permanent was the fortune of the family of Asadullah Khan who controlled the fortified town of Garhpada near the Subarnarekha River, about 40 km to the northeast on the same road. This local magnate was a dependent of the Mayurbhanj Raja in the early half

---

[36] OSA, BoRLR 25,947 (Collector of Cuttack to E. A. Samuells, CoCD, 25 September 1854). Wilson (*Glossary of Judicial and Revenue Terms*, 329) translates the term *majhi* as "steersman of a boat". They were probably the owners of the ferry boats as well.

[37] OSA, 27,528 (CoCD [?] to Secry. to GoB, Judicial Department, 24 July 1857); OSA, 27,530 (R. N. Shore, Magistrate of Cuttack, to G. F. Cockburn, CoCD, 10 June 1857).

[38] "The Road from Balasore to the Southward ran about 80 Years ago through Sheirghur in the Mogulbundee about 2 Miles to the Westward of Actiarpore but from the thickness of the Jungle infested by Tygers and from the attacks and depredations committed by the Inhabitants on the Travellers, and by the Inhabitants of the adjacent Villages, this Road was by degree deserted and Travellers took the road by Actiarpore, the Rajah on this seized on the Ghaut at Actiarpore and from that period it has been claimed as part of the Territories of Neelghur." OIOC, Board's Collection, F/4/315, no. 7220, 39 (extract from Bengal Revenue Consultations, 4 August 1809, George Webb, Collector, to Thomas Graham, Acting President).

[39] OSA, CBRP 1805, no. 2c (C. Groeme, Collector, to T. Fortescue, Secry. to CoCD, 10 June 1805); Toynbee, *A Sketch of the History of Orissa*, 59–60.

[40] OIOC, Board's Collection, F/4/505, no. 12139, 31–32 (John Richardson on province of Cuttack, extract from Bengal Revenue Consultations, 18 May 1815).

of the eighteenth century, when the *nawabs* (governors of province in Mughal India) of Bengal controlled coastal Orissa. In this context, he "apostatized from Hinduism and became a Mussulman. Like most other apostates", opined a British traveller in 1766, "he became a zealot to his new profession, and collected extravagant sums from persons who passed these towns on their pilgrimage to Jaggernaut." After extending their dominions to coastal Orissa in 1751, the Maratha rulers of Berar destroyed Asadullah's fortifications, however, and established their own chauki in nearby Basta even without the impetus of "apostasy" to Islam.[41] The ruler of the neighbouring kingdom of Mayurbhanj, Rani Sumitra Bhanja (r. 1796–1810), declared that she was deprived of a major part of her revenues when her new British overlords prohibited the imposition of all local taxes including the *sayer* (transit duties) on pilgrims and merchants at Khunta Ghat and other toll stations under her authority. Previously, under Maratha rule, the Mayurbhanj rajas had surrendered ten out of sixteen of such collections to their overlords and retained the balance which, after deducting the annual collection charges, was believed to have been between Rs 8,000 and 10,000. Sumitra Devi raised a claim for an annual compensation to Rs 11,251, which was rejected. Her successor, however, achieved to get the State's annual tribute permanently fixed to a comparatively small sum of Rs 1,001 in 1812, when he offered to forego all claims on pilgrim tax.[42]

The East India Company claimed exclusive right to taxation and prohibited, accordingly, all local cesses in the "Mughalbandi" districts one year after their annexation in 1803, replacing them with a unitary internal transit duty that was hesitantly abolished (like all

---

[41] Motte, "A Narrative of a Journey", 3.

[42] OIOC, Board's Collection, F/4/315, no. 7220, 26–27, 30 (J. Melvill, former CoCD, to George Dowdeswell, Secry. to GoB, Revenue Dpt., extract from Bengal Revenue Consultations, 28 May 1807); OIOC, Board's Collection, F/4/505, no. 12139, 23–26 (John Richardson on province of Cuttack, extract from Bengal Revenue Consultations, 18 May 1815); *Notes on the History of Mayurbhanj* (n.l., n.d.), 27–29 (This printed study bears the annotation "for private use only" on its title page. It may have been written for the Mayurbhanj court in about the 1930s). For a brief description of the relevant negotiations, see Debendra M. Praharaj, *Tribal Movements and Political History in India—A Case Study from Orissa, 1803–1949* (New Delhi, 1988), 67–69.

such duties in the Bengal Presidency) in 1836.[43] The pilgrim tax, another source of early colonial revenue, fell in 1840 after considerable evangelical pressure when the management of the Jagannath Temple and its lands was transferred to the Khurda Raja.[44] However, not all transit duties ceased to exist under British rule: the ferries at the numerous river crossings of the Jagannath Road were leased up to the end of the century at least to private contractors, who were entitled to impose tolls on passengers and goods.[45]

Pilgrims, traders and other travellers, however, were not only taxed on the road from Bengal to Puri across Orissa's coastal plains, but also on other routes. In the Garhjat region, for instance, the practice of levying customs was equally widespread. Thomas Motte described this practice in the 1760s as follows: "The merchants who travel in these parts apply to the Rajah of the country they are passing through, and making him a present, get a guard, who convey them into the territories of the next Rajah".[46] There is evidence that the overland road connecting Cuttack with Central India along the southern banks of the Mahanadi was a considerable source of revenue for various rulers. Trade suffered, complained Hamilton in the early eighteenth century, as numerous rajas loaded "the Trade with so many Taxes and Impositions".[47]

---

[43] For the abolition of internal transit duties in Bengal and British India in general, see Ambirajan, *Classical Political Economy*, 184–86, and Romesh C. Dutt, *The Economic History of India: Under Early British Rule, 1757–1837* (Delhi: Publications Division, Ministry of Information and Broadcasting, Govt. of India, 1970 [1st ed. 1903]), 210–14.

[44] Nancy Gardner Cassels, *Religion and Pilgrim Tax under the Company Raj*, (Delhi: Manohar, 1988). For the pilgrim tax and internal transit duties in Orissa, also see Das, *Studies in Economic History of Orissa*, 142–51.

[45] S. L. Maddox, *Final Report on the Settlement of the Province of Orissa (Temporary Settled Areas), 1890–1900* (n.l., n.d.), 1: 27. The "extortions" which "tyrannical ferrymen" imposed upon pilgrims were frequently complained of in the latter part of the nineteenth century. See, for example, *Utkal Dipika*, 7 July 1883, quoted in, *RNNB* for the Week Ending 21 July 1883; *Utkal Dipika*, 28 June 1884, quoted in, *RNNB* for the Week Ending 19 July 1884; Senapati, *My Times and I*, 18; Mukherjee, *History of the Jagannath Temple*, 426–27.

[46] Motte, "A Narrative of a Journey", 28–29, see also 38. Very similar practices were described almost a century later in Moffat Mill's report on the Tributary Mehals, in *Papers on the Settlement of Cuttack*, 67.

[47] Hamilton, *A New Account of the East Indies*, 216.

One of the bottlenecks of the Mahanadi route, where taxes could be imposed easily on traders and other travellers was the strategically crucial Barmul (Baramu) Pass, a narrow defile that Leckie described in 1790 as the "Western gate of the country dependant on Cuttae". Barmul Pass and the areas towards the east were controlled by the Raja of Daspalla, the adjacent western tracts by the Raja of Baudh in alliance with several Khond chiefs. In the late eighteenth century, the Maratha overlords had exempted both rajas from the payment of tribute in order to secure free passage to their officials and troopers. The Raja of Daspalla maintained a chauki at Bailparra (Belparapatna), where travellers had to pay a toll, while a "bamboo fort" or palisaded village was located at Barmul for the defence of the pass and to enforce payment. There was a natural water reservoir called "Puddam Talow" (*padmatola*, that is, "lotus tank") on the summit itself, which belonged in 1780 to the Raja of Baudh who had also established a chauki on his side of the defile.[48] The importance these revenues had had for the latter raja during the Maratha period was emphasised by S. C. Macpherson in his report of 1842:

> the geographical position of Boad, so long as the Domain included both banks of the Mahanuddee, became in a great measure through the exclusive relations of its Chiefs with the Khonds, an unfailing source of consequence and of wealth. Productive tolls levied on merchandize, pilgrims, travellers, and cattle, at the passes of the Valley, and upon the river, supplied a fund for the maintenance of a small mercenary force which rendered the Zemindar formidable to rival Chiefs, while complete exemption from State imposts was readily conceded by the Sovereigns of Berar, until the fall of the Mahratta Empire, as the price of secure communication betwixt their Eastern and Western provinces.[49]

A few miles to the northwest, in the little kingdom of Angul, the town of Tikerpara controlled another important thoroughfare. Here the Mahanadi was less than 200 yards wide thus enabling the raja as late as in the 1840s to collect taxes amounting to several

---

[48] Davidson, "Journal of a Route from Cuttack to Nagpore", 1790, folios 100–101; Add. MSS 13588. "Journey from Nagpoor to Cuttack in Jan. & Feb. 1782", folio 110, British Library, Add. MSS 13588; Motte, "A Narrative of a Journey", 23–26; Leckie, "Journal of a Route to Nagpore", 19–22.
[49] MacPherson, *Report upon the Khonds*, 24.

thousands of rupees per annum from boats passing by.[50] Customs were also imposed on floated timber.[51]

With regard to the comparatively extensive kingdom of Sambalpur, Motte noted in 1766 that "duties on merchants and others passing through the country" were "not settled, but depend on the conscience of the Raja",[52] whereas J. R. Ouseley pointed out in 1840 that transit duties were "light, but so many different jagirdars had assumed the authority of stopping merchants that it very much checked trade."[53]

All the profits Orissa's petty rulers derived from the existing channels of circulation could not, however, make them forget one fundamental experience that had shaped regional politics for generations, namely, that inaccessibility was a "little king's" best protection against overbearing overlords. Thus when Alivardi Khan, the powerful ruler of Bengal (r. 1740–1756), marched a large army into Mayurbhanj in the first year of his reign, the raja of this extensive kingdom "with his effects, followers and dependents, fled to the top of a hill, and hid himself in a secret fastness".[54] The surroundings of his capital Hariharpur were surrounded with dense *sal* (north Indian hardwood) forests and the Simlipal range provided an even more impregnable cover. Hence, when Alivardi's army was withdrawn for another engagement and Mayurbhanj's occupation ended, Raja Raghunath Bhanja (r. 1728–1751) returned to Hariharpur unscathed.[55] In the backdrop of such experiences, the headquarters of Garhjat chiefs were often located not near the major traffic routes but in remote, densely wooded parts of their dominions. They consisted of unpretentious mud forts or palisaded villages. Hunter observed that the

---

[50] *Papers on Settlement of Cuttack*, 66–67. An 1815 report mentions that the Angul Raja received annually Rs 10,000 "from a Tax levied at Pergurparah Ghaut on all goods and Merchandize passing". The name of the locality may have been "Tickerparah Ghaut" in the original report and was probably misspelled by the copyist. Cf.: OIOC, Board's Collection, F/4/505, no. 12139, 35–36 (John Richardson on province of Cuttack, extract from Bengal Revenue Consultations, 18 May 1815).

[51] Hunter, *The Annals of Rural Bengal*, 3: 44–45.

[52] Motte, "A Narrative of a Journey", 38.

[53] Basu, "Tour-Diary of J. R. Ouseley", 170.

[54] *Notes on the History of Mayurbhanj*, 7.

[55] Ibid., 7–8.

few landholders who had houses worth burning, belted them round with dense thickets of bamboos. A winding narrow passage afforded the sole means of approach, and these jungles formed secure fortifications against invaders who would only fight on horseback. Such greenwood defences survive to this day. Once in the Tributary [State of Athgarh] being struck by the close overgrown site of a chieftain's fort, an old man explained to me that the jungle had been planted to keep off the Mahrattá Horse.

This practice may be interpreted as an element of a historically contingent "infrastructure policy". It prevailed, contrary to Hunter's assertion, not only during the period of Maratha rule but was consciously continued for several decades after the British annexation of Orissa.[56] Hence the Raja of Angul—as we have seen a great beneficiary of transit duties—"deeming his former residence insufficiently protected, abandoned it soon after he was threatened with a visit [sic] by Mr. Ricketts [the Commissioner of Cuttack Division] in 1837, and constructed his present abode in the most inaccessible part of his country."[57] Ricketts' own report on the headquarters of another Tributary Mahal, Nayagarh, shows that such a policy was indeed a cheap and efficient deterrent against potential annexation plans. After meticulously describing the difficult approach on a narrow pass through "bamboo jungle" and forest which in some places had room for only one to walk and was easily defensible from several breastworks he concluded that

> an attack upon the place should never be attempted without Pioneers and Artillery; it would be necessary to fill in the roads as you passed along to get them up; all this time the force would be suffering from people in the jungle, well defended; a great many lives would be lost; the Ghur itself is commanded by hills on both sides covered with jungle. On no account should force ever be employed against this Rajah without it is absolutely unavoidable, there is nothing to be gained. I believe to take it would cost more than the country would yield in 10 years, could it be managed at no expense.[58]

[56] Hunter, *The Annals of Rural Bengal*, 3: 34.
[57] Moffat Mill's report on the Tributary Mehals, in *Papers on the Settlement of Cuttack*, 86–87.
[58] Henry Ricketts' report on his visit in Nayagarh in 1836, quoted in: ibid., 74–75. Similar observations as for the inadvisability of military expeditions into "wild and unproductive" hill areas and the advantages of ruling them

Even three decades later one British engineer observed that the rajas "still seem to think that their security and peace lie in encouraging the growth of jungle, particularly near the road."[59]

Moreover, as in other regions of India,[60] the very existence of roads was often considered a security risk by local rulers. In order to protect their villages from Maratha incursions the zamindars of the Bahmangatti area in the north of the kingdom of Mayurbhanj had thus, according to one account, blocked a road to Sambalpur that had earlier been heavily frequented.[61] Under Company rule rajas often opposed the construction of new roads in their dominions for similar reasons.[62] They were particularly against any lines of communication built near their headquarters.[63] There is very detailed evidence for the persistent attempts on the part of the rajas and zamindars of Mayurbhanj, Kendujhar, Pal Lahera, Bonai, Bamra and Sambalpur to withhold information, distract, bribe, boycott and even intimidate Lieutenant Markham Kittoe who was in charge of the survey and construction of the "Raipur Mail Road" from 1838 to 1841.[64] Not only were they totally opposed to roadworks themselves but even the attempt to gather any geographical information whatsoever was strongly resisted. Guides deliberately led British officers away from better roads and prosperous villages, and trees were felled across pathways as a warning not to proceed any further.

---

indirectly through local power holders were also made by officials of the Madras Presidency at that time. See David Arnold, "Rebellious Hillmen: The Gudem-Rampa Risings, 1839–1924", in *Subaltern Studies I*, ed. Ranajit Guha (Delhi: Oxford University Press, 1982), 104.

[59] OIOC, BPWP June 1868, P/432/50, Com., no. 60, 61 (remarks on "Angul Road" by Frederick Bond, EE Cuttack Division).

[60] Verghese, *Development and Significance of Transport*, 166–67.

[61] Kittoe, "Account of a Journey", 676.

[62] Ricketts, *Reports on the Districts of Midnapore . . . and Cuttack*, 94.

[63] Kittoe, "Account of a Journey", 476–77.

[64] Ibid., 377, 616–18; OSA, BoRLP 20,868 (M. Kittoe, Surveyor of Raipur Mail Road, to T. Prinsep, Secry. to GoB, General Dpt., 19 February 1839); NAI, MBP 16 April 1841, 12977–78 (M. Kittoe to J. A. Crommelin, Offg. SE, S.E. Division, 24 February 1841); NAI, MBP 20 August 1841, 3840–51 (M. Kittoe's journal on Raipur Mail Road, May 1841). For a detailed account, see Ravi Ahuja, "'Captain Kittoe's Road': Early Colonialism and the Politics of Road Construction in Nineteenth-century Peripheral Orissa", in *Periphery and Centre in Orissa: Groups, Categories, Values*, ed. Georg Pfeffer (New Delhi: Manohar, in press).

Kittoe met with a similar experience as Motte seven decades before him, who had recorded his impression that he was intentionally led along almost impassable "bye-roads" and away from the better ones by the emissary of the Baudh Raja. Kittoe raged that villagers generally refused to give any information having "the old ooreya story ready of 'what do I jungle manush know'[,] I live far away[,] ask the Rajah[']s Mooktar". He believed that a *raiyat* (subject) who disclosed details of a state's geography or economy to outsiders put his life at risk.[65] It was, however, possible to obtain some information from a raja on the chiefdoms of his neighbours and rivals, though never on his own.[66] Until the last three decades of the nineteenth century, colonial records contain frequent complaints against the "demi-civilised Native Rulers" who were "unfortunately a class entirely opposed to roads being constructed through their lands" and thereby led to be "obstructive and passively unassisting".[67] "It is most difficult, almost disheartening, to carry on Public Works in the lands of these Independent Rajahs," wrote the Superintending Engineer of Cuttack in 1862:

> When the Commissioner and Superintendent of Tributary Mehals requests their assistance and co-operation for the works of the Government, even then they assist in the most indirect, disagreeable, and uncertain way, and all these Native Chiefs appear to dislike any opening of their country by roads, they imagine evidently that some ulterior views or objects are contemplated, which will not result to their benefit, and they cannot understand demi-civilized and uneducated, and I may say

---

[65] Motte, "A Narrative of a Journey", 30; Kittoe, "Report on the Coal and Iron Mines", 140; idem, "Account of a Journey", 379–80, 382, 678. For the quoted phrase, see NAI, MBP 20 August 1841, 3825 (Kittoe's journal on Raipur Mail Road, May 1841). A *mukhtar* was an agent or representative: Wilson, *Glossary of Judicial and Revenue Terms*, 353.

[66] NAI, MBP 20 August 1841, 3829–30 (M. Kittoe's journal on Raipur Mail Road, May 1841).

[67] OIOC, BPWP April 1862, P/16/57, Com., no. 33, 19 (T. Armstrong, SE Cuttack Circle, to Offg. CE Bengal). The rajas' policy changed in the late nineteenth century. However, the following opinion was uttered as late as 1899: "The Chiefs of Gurjat States do not, as a rule, view with favour the opening out of their States by means of roads. They fear that to render their States accessible means to diminish their authority, and this contingency they regard as a far greater evil than the retarding of the development of their States." *RATMO 1898–99*, 16 (G. Stevenson, SI of Tributary Mahals, to Chief Secry. to GoB, 17 July 1899).

bigoted, as they are, [of] what very great imperial and local importance a road ... must be ...[68]

This "passive resistance" that was "so hard to meet and overcome" took various forms including the obstruction of labour recruitment, the overcharging of foodstuffs and outright refusal to supply any victuals. In one case, an engineer down with malarial fever had neither been able to obtain a cup of milk nor palanquin bearers in the market town Kantilo without a *parwana* (written Government order).[69] Colonial interpretations attributed this attitude to the "demi-civilised" character of the rajas, their addiction to "sensuality"[70] and lack of interest in the "improvement" of their states.

From the same accounts some information can, however, be gleaned as to the specific interests of rajas, zamindars and village headmen that clashed with colonial road projects. The intention seems to have been not only to prevent direct military intervention in periods of crisis and, in the worst case, the annexation of the state by the colonial overlords. Road construction and the institution of intra- and inter-regional routes, moreover, undercut and eroded the authority of local rulers even under non-crisis conditions. The mere presence of construction parties, dak stations or road police posts in their territories—all of them protected by armed men beyond their command—was an open challenge to their authority. Civil or military detachments moving up and down the roads were entitled to demand *rasad* (here: forage and victuals) from the localities they passed—a service which often assumed the form of forced contributions though colonial regulations required some kind of payment. Hence the rajas of the Tributary Mahals frequently stated "their unwillingness, if not inability, in bad seasons to supply this

---

[68] OIOC, BPWP December 1862, P/16/59, Com., no. 95, 85 (T. Armstrong, SE Cuttack Circle, to Offg. CE Bengal, 15 November 1862).

[69] *Report Showing the Progress Made ... in Imperial Public Works under the Bengal Government for 1862–63* (Calcutta: Calcutta Gazetteer Office, 1863), 100–1 (T. Armstrong, SE, Report on Cuttack Circle, 26 May 1863). The phrase "passive resistance" is a verbatim quotation from this text. For a similar case in the Khond Mahals, see Kittoe, "Account of a Journey", 381–82. For a very detailed account of such a conflict in Mayurbhanj, see footnote 76, in this chapter.

[70] Ricketts, *Reports on the Districts of Midnapore ... and Cuttack*, 94.

Russud."[71] In 1840, there was a "universal complaint" in Kendujhar and other states "of the extortion of the Ramgurh Light Infantry that was employed to take away money to pay the Post Office establishments. These men pressed the people as *begaries* (unpaid labourers), took all they wanted without making any payment and committed extortions of every shape of enormity."[72] On such occasions, village authorities were, for instance, frequently pressurised to give *salami* (gifts) to officials passing by.[73]

Petty rulers and their office bearers, no doubt, profited from arrangements according to which they received money from the colonial state for supplying coolies. These were usually forced to perform *begar* or *bethi*, that is, corvée labour without or with unremunerative pay—a practice often condoned by the colonial authorities. In 1830, the Commissioner of Cuttack reasoned thus:

> The design of this Govt. in giving a sum of money to the Zemindars is that it may be paid to the labourers by whom the work is actually done. There is reason however to apprehend that it would be perverted to other purposes and would either remain with the Zemindar or find its way into the pocket of his managing agent. All the work of the Zemindars whether repairing his residence or building a fort is done by forced labour, so many days labour being apportioned to each village, from which people come with provisions calculated to last the period of their being occupied. I imagine there will be very little variation from

---

[71] The quote refers to conflicts emerging after the improvement of the road following the south bank of the Mahanadi since Madras troops were "now continually moving along" this route from Cuttack to Sambalpur. OIOC, BPWP February 1865, P/16/71, Com., no. 49, 30 (F. B. Simson, Offg. SI, Tributary Mehals, to Secry. to GoB, PWD, 10 February 1865). Also see NAI, MBP 16 April 1841, 12988–89 (M. Kittoe's report on Raipur Mail Road, 24 February 1841); *Report Showing the Progress Made ... in Public Works under the Bengal Government, 1861–62* (Calcutta: Savielle & Cranenburgh, 1862), 107 (T. Armstrong, SE, Report on Cuttack Circle, 15 May 1862). In another case, a zamindar was detained by a British officer to enforce the supply of victuals; see Kittoe, "Account of a Journey", 373. For rasad as a colonial term, see Yule and Burnell, *Hobson-Jobson*, 776.

[72] Basu, "Tour-Diary of J. R. Ouseley", 167. This report is corroborated by Kittoe, "Account of a Journey", 618. Also see NAI, MBP 19 February 1841, 10574 (M. Kittoe, SI Raipur Mail Road, to J. A. Crommelin, Offg. SE, S.E. Division, 7 February 1841).

[73] Kittoe, "Account of a Journey", 476. Kittoe asserted that such gifts were regularly extorted by "native servants of political establishments", especially those from Cuttack.

this system which has prevailed for ages, even thó the public money was given to the Zemindar and therefore conceived that such money would in fact be thrown away. Were it probable that the labourers would be paid, of which there is but little prospect unless the distribution were entrusted to some servant of this Govt., I would not suggest any expedient which may aid in perpetuating as well as in sanctioning a system so abhorrent as that of forced labour from the already poor and indigent. But, believing that equal compulsion would be used whether an expense be or be not incurred I am desirous that it should [be] saved.[74]

A. J. Moffat Mills, who held the commissioner's post a decade later, stated freely that the labour on the Raipur Mail Road "has this season been entirely compulsory" and argued in less ambiguous terms:

> The Rajah of a Country like Mohurbunge exercising, as he does almost unlimited control of his subjects will not forego his right to a portion of the Coolies labour—objectionable as the system is, it must be endured and Captain Kittoe would do well not to look into matters such as these, but to settle with the Rajah . . .[75]

Though bethi was useful in the recruitment of a workforce, it was a comparatively inefficient form of organising the labour process and forcibly enlisted coolies tended to abscond at the first opportunity. British engineers, moreover, were keen to take their road coolies along with them across the 'borders' of Garhjat states. They were accordingly interested in paying wages directly to road labourers and removing the local authorities from these social relationships. Consequently, they were (unwittingly or not) undermining the latter's control over the village population. The rajas' resistance against such attempts generally proved successful during the period under review, and road coolies often had to be 'imported' to the Garhjats from the district of Cuttack or from Chota Nagpur.[76]

---

[74] OSA, BoRLR 18,167 (CoCD, to H. Shakespear, Secry. to GoB, Judicial Dpt., 19 July 1830).
[75] NAI, MBP 5 January 1841, 8562–63 (A. J. Moffat Mills, CoCD, to GoI, General Dpt., 23 October 1840). Also see ibid., 8560 (A. J. Moffat Mills to Secry. to Military Board, 11 December 1840); NAI, MBP 26 March 1841, 12374 (M. Kittoe's report on Raipur Mail Road, February 1841).
[76] A relevant report states that labourers "are paid daily by myself and supplied from my bazar, but scantily, as the Rajahs people object to it, for they fear that if once we establish a system of payment and protection to the lower

Similar clashes of interest would emerge over the control of bazaars or the sale of victuals in general. While engineers were interested in commanding the supply of provisions to their construction parties as directly as possible, the increased demand for foodstuffs and other items also afforded opportunities of gain to local rulers or their officials. Once again, Kittoe recorded a conflict of this type in great detail, when he charged the *mukhtars* (attorneys) of the Raja of Mayurbhanj of using political clout for forcibly acquiring provisions from the villagers by way of "begging, bouncing and plundering" and making enormous gains by selling them dearly in the camp bazaar. "[A]ll of these worthies," fumed Kittoe, "are of the Mahuntie or writer Caste and either directly related to the head functionaries of the Raja's Court or Caste brothers to whom they pay a share of their ill gotten gain."[77]

Finally, the presence of an external military and economic force in their zone of influence could also create problems for "little kings" in Orissa's Garhjat country by enabling subordinate zamindars or village headmen to gain some independence from their overlords. In 1841, for instance, the following complaints of Raja Jadunath Bhanj of Mayurbhanj (r. 1828–1863) were recorded:

---

classes they will rebel against their own system of slave labour whenever they may chance to call for it". NAI, MBP 26 March 1841, 12374 (M. Kittoe's report on Raipur Mail Road for February 1841). Also see OIOC, BPWP April 1862, P/16/57, Com., no. 33, 19 (T. Armstrong, SE Cuttack Circle, to Offg. CE, Bengal, 26 March 1862); *Report Showing Progress Made ... in Public Works under Bengal Government, 1861–62*, 107–8 (Armstrong, Report on Cuttack Circle, 15 May 1862); OIOC, BPWP December 1862, P/16/59, Com., no. 95, 84–85 (T. Armstrong to Offg. CE Bengal, 15 November 1862); OIOC, BPWP March 1863, P/16/61, Com., no. 44, 28 (T. Armstrong to GoB); *Report Showing Progress Made ... in Imperial Public Works under Bengal Government for 1862–63*, 100–1 (Armstrong, Report on Cuttack Circle, 26 May 1863).

[77] NAI, MBP 16 April 1841, 12985 (M. Kittoe's "Special report on the conduct of the Servants of the Raja of Mohurbunj"). This conflict is extraordinarily well documented. Also see ibid., 12981–88; and 12967–968 (translated excerpts from an Oriya petition of the Raja of Mayurbhanj to the CoCD); and 12974–76 (M. Kittoe to J. A. Crommelin, Offg. SE, S.E. Division, 24 February 1841); NAI, MBP 5 January 1841, 8561 (A. J. Moffat Mills, CoCD, to GoI, General Dpt., 23 October 1840); NAI, MBP 5 March 1841, 10996–1005 (journal of M. Kittoe on Raipur Mail Road, January 1841).

It appears that Captain Kittoe wishes to take grain directly from the subordinate Zemindar or Surberakar of Jaseepoor, and the Rajah asserts that Captain Kittoe has made it a point to encourage this person by promises and kindness to such a degree that he now disregards the Rajahs authority and is aiming to become an independent zemindar. He asserts that the grain collected in Bumunghattee is sent to Jaseepoor and that he is kept in ignorance of the quantity ... by the zemindar, who on the plea of having furnished supplies and sustained loss thereby, has refused to pay him any revenue for the last two years.[78]

From the point of view of Raja Jadunath, the problem was not merely a loss of revenue and reduced profits from grain sales but a loss of authority. His own words were translated as follows:

It is always customary throughout my Raj that my dependents shall furnish supplies through my appointed Mooktears [that is, representatives,] if the Sahib breaks through the old established usage my dependents will rebel against my authority, and my country will be ruined.[79]

Summing up the foregoing paragraphs, we may state that road construction and infrastructural policies in general affected various social and political arrangements of "little kingdoms", *zamindaries* and localities. Such measures entailed the transformation of their social spaces according to colonial conceptions and exigencies. 'Public works' therefore, emerged necessarily as a hotbed of social and political conflict in the region's mountainous interior.

Plebeian Perspectives: Circulation and Coercion

In the coastal plains of Orissa, where most of the few early colonial projects of road construction were located, the zamindars and other precolonial authorities had not been able to retain influence to the same degree as in the Garhjats. Some of them profited from the sale of road construction materials, land and ferry rights,[80] remonstrated

---

[78] NAI, MBP 16 April 1841, 12963 (A. J. Moffat Mills, CoCD, to G. A. Bushby, Secry. to GoI, General Dpt., 12 February 1841)

[79] Ibid., 12969–70 (translated excerpts from an Oriya petition of the Raja of Mayurbhanj to the CoCD).

[80] OSA, BoRLR 17,629 (T. Pakenham, Collector of Cuttack, to W. Blunt, CoCD, 10 June 1823); OSA, BoRLR 17,719 (E. R. Broughton, Superintendent

against the alignment of a certain road,[81] pleaded for the improvement of another[82] or contributed to planting trees along the Jagannath Road for the convenience of pilgrims and other travellers.[83] Late in the century, moreover, a colonial official recalled protests in Baleshwar against road embankments obstructing the drainage of flood water in earlier times: "When the Grand Trunk Road was constructed zamindars and raiyats alike were up in arms and I believe their complaints were substantial."[84] Yet when the British administration considered the setting up of a "Road and Improvement Committee" in 1832, which was to include some zamindars or other notables of that region, the collectors of Balasore, Cuttack, and Khurda concurrently reported that no eligible resident of sufficient means and influence could be found.[85]

(henceforth SI) of New Jagannath Road, to R. Stevenson, Quarter Master General, 11 September 1825); ibid. (J. Craigie, Secry. to Military Board, to Secry. to GoB, Territorial Dpt., 22 November 1825); OSA, BoRLR 17,805 (J. Cheape, SI Public Works, Province of Cuttack, to J. Craigie, Secry. to Military Board, 23 February 1827); OSA, BoRLR 17,824 (G. Becher, SI of Cuttack Division of Jagannath Road, to J. Cheape, SI Public Works, Province of Cuttack, 10 March 1827); OSA, BoRLR 25,947 (Collector of Cuttack to E. A. Samuells, CoCD, 25 September 1854); *Report Showing the Progress Made ... in Imperial Public Works under the Bengal Government for 1862–63*, 114–19 (T. Armstrong, SE, Report on Cuttack Circle, 26 May 1863); Toynbee, *A Sketch of the History of Orissa*, 82–83.

[81] OIOC, BPWP May 1861, P/16/52, Com., no. 89, 63 (extract from letter of E. T. Trevor, CoCD, to Secry. to GoB, 15 March 1861).

[82] For "Petition presented by the Zemindars and Merchants of Balasore" concerning, among other problems, the metalling of Jagannath Road and the construction of a fair-weather road, see Henry Ricketts, "Reports on the Districts of Pooree and Balasore", in *Selections from the Records of the Bengal Government*, Vol. XXX (Calcutta: John Gray, 1859), 69.

[83] OSA, BoRLR 17,765 (Thomas Pakenham, Offg. CoCD, to C. Molony, Acting Secry. to GoB, Territorial Dpt., 20 October 1826); OSA, BoRLR 17,766 (Acting Secry. to GoB to T. Pakenham, CoCD, 3 November 1826); OSA, BoRLR 17,810 (letter to A. C. Banwell, Acting Collector of Cuttack, 23 May 1827); OSA, BoRLR 23,591 (letters on trees on Jagannath Road: Collector of Balasore to Commissioner of Cuttack, 21 April 1847, and petition of "Pudmalochun Mondul", resident of Balasore); Toynbee, *A Sketch of the History of Orissa*, 84.

[84] Maddox, *Final Report on Settlement of Orissa*, I: 33.

[85] OSA, BoRLR 18,528 (R. Hunter, Collector of Cuttack, to G. Stockwell, CoCD, 8 May 1832); OSA, BoRLR 18,529 (H. Ricketts, Collector of

However one may interpret this statement, it is clear that Orissa's leading colonial operatives did not feel inclined to include the coastal "elites" in the infrastructural policy-making processes at that time. Judging from the sources available, the zamindars appear to have been a less active party with regard to 'public works' policy and in conflicts over transport infrastructure in the Orissa plains. Both self-willed appropriations and resistance are more often ascribed to villagers though alliances with zamindars are frequently implied. In the closing paragraphs of this chapter we will, therefore, turn to the interests and relevant actions of "plebeian" or subordinated classes of society in the early colonial period—both in the directly British-controlled plains and the indirectly controlled Garhjat states.

We should again be careful not to overemphasise the effects of roads and other means of circulation on the everyday lives of Orissa's villagers in pre- and early colonial days. They were surely rather limited even if compared to contemporary standards of other Indian regions. At least some segments of the rural population appropriated, however, the existing rudimentary traffic infrastructure for their own ends to a higher degree than the usual stereotypes of isolated village communities would suggest. Various aspects of these appropriations have been mentioned before: regular patterns of labour migration between Bhadrak and Calcutta had already emerged in the eighteenth century; channels of circulation were also utilised for more localised practices such as the exchange of village and forest products on various levels of markets including the weekly haats that served a circle of localities and the annual *melas* (fairs) which functioned as subregional foci of cultural and economic exchange.[86] There seems to be little evidence (at least in colonial sources) for road works executed by village communities in Orissa. However, a British collector reported on the area of Paradip that his informants had told him "that the villagers have a fair-weather road of their own furnished with a ferry (free) on the Sonka Creek, bridged at two out of the remaining [three] creeks".[87]

Balasore, to G. Stockwell, 29 March 1832); OSA, BoRLR 18,553 (W. Wilkinson, Collector of Khoordah, to G. Stockwell, 9 April 1832).
[86] See chapter 4.
[87] OIOC, BPWP February 1867, P/432/43, Com., no. 24, 17 (memo by Mr Geddes, Special Collector with CoCD).

The construction of river embankments by Oriya village communities in precolonial times may also have facilitated local transport.[88] For roads created opportunities for dominant peasants of adjacent villages for marketing surpluses profitably—opportunities that were eagerly seized, for instance, by the raiyats of Khurda as soon as the new Cuttack–Ganjam road became passable in the early 1830s.[89] While the European "Assistant to the Superintendent of the Jugt. [Jagannath] New Road" got permission to establish "on his own private account" six bazaars along the Cuttack–Jaleshwar section of the main pilgrimage route in 1822,[90] there were also complaints about encroachments by shopkeepers who had set up illicit "chuttees" (*chatti*, here: small bazaar) on the slopes and berms of this road's embankments.[91] Moreover, cleared spaces along colonial roads (which legally belonged to the road site) were taken under cultivation, the ditches were used for fishing and villagers collected, cut and sold fruit and wood from roadside trees.[92]

There is also evidence for a very different type of appropriation: villagers frequently imposed some sort of "informal tax" on travellers in route segments where local rulers or the successive Maratha and British overlords failed to establish exclusive control. These "extortions" were condemned by British observers and took different forms in different places. On the Mahanadi route, the Khond

---

[88] Cf.: Hunter, *The Annals of Rural Bengal*, 3: 183.

[89] OSA, BoRLR 18,899 (C. A. Bushby, Secry. to Sudder BoR, to Secry. to GoB, Revenue Dpt., 10 June 1834). Also see OSA, BoRLR 18,500 (W. Wilkinson, Collector of Puri, to G. Stockwell, CoCD, 5 May 1832); OSA, BoRLR 19,253 (W. Wilkinson, Collector of Puri, to J. Master, Offg. CoCD, 6 February 1835).

[90] OSA, BoRLR 17,560 (G. Becher, Assistant Superintendent of Jagannath Road, to A. Stirling, Acting Collector of Cuttack, 2 March 1822); OSA, BoRLR 17,561 (W. Blunt, CoCD, to Holt Mackenzie, Secry. to GoB, Revenue Dpt., 12 April 1822); OSA, BoRLR 17,557 (Secry. to GoB, Territorial Dpt., to W. Blunt, CoCD, 20 June 1822); OSA, BoRLR 17,629 (Thomas Pakenham, Collector of Cuttack, to W. Blunt, CoCD, 10 June 1823); OSA, BoRLR 17,635 (W. Blunt, CoCD, to Holt Mackenzie, Secry. to GoB, Revenue Dpt., 17 June 1823).

[91] OIOC, BPWP February 1862, P/16/61, nos. 44–5, 21–24 (various relevant letters, see especially no. 44, 23: T. Armstrong, SE Cuttack Division, to CoCD, 26 January 1863).

[92] OIOC, BPWP December 1870, P/432/60, Com., nos. 21–23, 26–28. Evidence on controversies over fishing in roadside drains has already been discussed in chapter 2, hypothesis 2 of the present study.

inhabitants of the hills near the Barmul gorge, for instance, in the eighteenth century blocked the road with felled trees in order to enforce payments from merchants and other travellers.[93] Moreover, the hills of the Borasambar zamindari, which were traversed by the Sonepur–Nagpur route, were reported to be "full of robbers".[94] The Bhadrak section of Jagannath Road was, at this time, famous for its *dacoits* (brigands), highwaymen and thieves of whom hair-raising tales were told.[95] "Robberies" and "attacks and depredations committed by the Inhabitants on the Travellers" are also documented for other parts of this road.[96] Such "criminal" practices were, as Binod Sankar Das suggests, conducted under the connivance of the local authorities.[97] What is conceptualised as "dacoity" in colonial sources may thus, from another perspective, be considered in many cases a more coercive form of imposing local tolls. Such appropriations of circulatory infrastructure are in accordance with practices elsewhere in South Asia and linked to processes of late pre-colonial state formation. They conflicted with increasing efforts on the part of the colonial state since the 1830s of abolishing local tolls and of securing an exclusive control over circulation and infrastructure by means of a centralised police force.[98] In Orissa, however, these earlier and local forms of absorbing circulating surplus retained some of their viability and acceptance up to the

---

[93] Motte, "A Narrative of a Journey", 25–26.
[94] Leckie, "Journal of a Route to Nagpore", 34–35.
[95] Motte, "A Narrative of a Journey", 10; Leckie, "Journal of a Route to Nagpore", 6. Similar reports of highwaymen can be found even for the early 1860s: Senapati, *My Times and I*, 18–19.
[96] OIOC, Board's Collection F/4/315, no. 7220, 26–27 (J. Melvill to George Dowdeswell, Secry. to GoB, Revenue Dpt., extract from Bengal Revenue Consultations, 28 May 1807); and 39 (G. Webb, Collector, to T. Graham, Acting President, extract from Bengal Revenue Consultations, 4 August 1809).
[97] Das, *Studies in Economic History of Orissa*, 246.
[98] Cf. Gordon, *Marathas, Marauders and State Formation*, 3, 21–22; Sandria B. Freitag, "Crime in the Social Order of Colonial North India", *Modern Asian Studies* 25, no. 2, 1991, 232–35 and passim; Kim A. Wagner, "The Deconstructed Stranglers: A Reassessment of Thuggee", *Modern Asian Studies* 38, no. 4, 2004, 957–63. Also see Andrew J. Major, "State and Criminal Tribes in Colonial Punjab: Surveillance, Control and Reclamation of the 'Dangerous Classes'", *Modern Asian Studies* 33, no. 3, 1999, 661–66 and passim. For the abolition of local tolls, see footnote 43, in this chapter.

century's final decades. An 1883 report on the prevalence of road "crime" in Balasore district thus asserted that the "thieves" were concentrated in a few villages where they had their houses, implying some sort of community backing.[99]

While the dominated classes should thus not be viewed as passive victims of 'public works' policy, the construction or utilisation of a road certainly implied in many cases that demands on rural resources were increased and pushed through more efficiently by colonial and other authorities. More generally speaking, improved channels of circulation often meant that the level of intervention into local affairs on the part of supra-local powers rose. There were protracted proceedings concerning the appropriation of agricultural land for purposes of road construction which would merit a closer analysis but can only be briefly referred to here.[100] Yet Captain Kittoe's experience that the staves he left behind as survey marks for the future route of the Raipur Mail Road disappeared regularly was perhaps indicative for the peasants' lack of enthusiasm for roads running across their fields.[101]

Furthermore, roadworks were often associated with the large-scale utilisation of "unfree" labour. Bethi services (which will be discussed at length in chapter 8) were forced upon the subordinated, mainly "tribal" social groups of all Garhjat states—a practice so hateful to them that Kittoe felt compelled to employ one armed guard for every twenty-five corvée labourers to prevent them from absconding.[102] Moreover, convict labour was regularly employed on roadworks in colonial India, especially during the regime of the East India Company, and there is also evidence for this practice with regard to Orissa.[103] In 1834, the Government of Bengal sanctioned a proposal of the Superintendent of Public Works in Orissa that all prisoners "in the Cuttack and Pooree Jails together with 250 from

---

[99] *Balasore Sambad Bahika*, 15 February 1883, quoted in, *RNNB* for the Week Ending 3 March 1883, 93.

[100] Even Toynbee (*A Sketch of the History of Orissa*, 82) in his apologetic account mentions controversies with landholders regarding the reclamation of land for the construction on New Jagannath Road after 1818.

[101] NAI, MBP 15 January 1841, 9121–22 (Kittoe's progress report on Raipur Mail Road for November 1840).

[102] NAI, MBP 18 May 1841, 492 (Kittoe's Journal for March 1841).

[103] For convict labour on roads in other regions, see Joshi, "Working the Roads".

Midnapore and 100 from Balasore" were to work during the rains on the construction of the southern road from Cuttack to Ganjam via Khurda, while "[a]s soon as the rains are fairly closed (or from the 15th of October) all disposable Prisoners should be sent out of the Jails to level ruts and make partial repairs" to the Jagannath Road towards the north and to other unmetalled roads.[104] The 1834 Military Board report on 'public works' stated that the road from Calcutta to Cuttack had been kept in repair mainly by convict labour expressing the hope "that hired labour may be nearly dispensed with". This view was decried by the promoters of utilitarian prison reform who diagnosed, in the report for the following year, a "deteriorating influence" of such schemes on "this unhappy description of persons" and observed that "moral reform" was no objective of the "executive officers" on such works who "look on the convicts only as so many machines given to execute a certain work".[105] In this debate, a member of the Military Board admitted reluctantly that hired labour was perhaps a cheaper solution in densely populated regions but insisted that

> the case is very different, when you have to carry a Road thro a thinly inhabited Country where is a difficulty in procuring labourers and where you must frequently bring men from a distance. [O]ne great advantage of employing Convicts on the Roads, is that it often enables you to carry on work rapidly, where, but for such assistance, it must from the difficulty in procuring labourers proceed very slowly, if at all.[106]

[104] OSA, BoRLR 18,773 (W. Bell, Offg. SI of Public Works, Cuttack, to E. P. Gowan, Offg. Secry. to Military Board, 14 April 1834; W. Wilkinson, Magistrate, to W. Bell, Offg. SI of Public Works, Cuttack, 15 May 1834; Secry. to Government of Bengal to J. Master, Offg. CoCD, 2 June 1834). Later in that year the same official opined that "150 Prisoners would be ample to repair [the "station", that is, district roads of Cuttack] throughout the season, and the remainder from that Jail and of Pooree may be sent to form one Gang on the Juggernauth road, in order to reduce as much as possible the very heavy expence on its repair hitherto annually laid out." OSA, BoRLR 18,905 (W. Bell, Offg. SI of Public Works, Cuttack, to J. Master, Offg. CoCD, 5 November 1834). Other papers in this file are also relevant and clarify that prisoners were to be "managed" on road works by the "executive officers" and not by the magistrates, that is, by engineers and not by the judiciary.

[105] Both reports are summarised and excerpted in "Public Works in India", *The Times*, 12 September 1838. Also see NAI, MBP 8 December 1840, 7585–661.

[106] NAI, MBP 8 December 1840, 7605.

Such conditions certainly applied to the sections of the mail road passing though Orissa's Garhjats where up to 300 inmates of Midnapur jail were thus made to work under close supervision in the early 1840s.[107] However, even on the routes of the plains fettered prisoners remained a familiar sight: In 1859, 146 of 293 "labouring prisoners" of Cuttack Jail were reported to be employed on roads.[108] The presence of chained labour gangs consisting of men, who were deemed ritually polluted because of their inability to abide to caste codes of conduct in prison, was unlikely to make either employment on roads or the projects themselves more popular among the villagers. There is, for instance, evidence that the use of village wells by convict labourers was stiffly resisted along Raipur Mail Road.[109]

Yet even when labour was recruited on the basis of "free contract" from outside the region—like the resolutely assertive and yet sought-after *dhangur* (from *daang*, that is, hill) coolies from Chota Nagpur and Sambalpur—road works still implied for the neighbouring villages that their stores would be depleted by incessant demands for victuals.[110] Moreover, mortality rates of both "free" and "unfree" labourers on such roadworks were sometimes appalling. In 1841, it was thus reported that death rates among convict labourers on the works of the Raipur Mail Road had reached 9 per cent annually during the preceding two years, while Kittoe complained the labourers supplied by the Mayurbhanj Raja were of "such inferior kind" that "7/8th of the workmen are deceased from sickness (dysentery and fever)".[111] Artisans and workers, whether

---

[107] NAI, MBP 18 December 1840, 8084 (Secry to GoI, General Department, to Military Board, 14 November 1840); and 5 February 1841, 9855 (G. J. Shakespear, Magistrate of Midnapur, to J. A. Crommelin, Offg. SE, South Eastern Province, 28 January 1841); and 9 February 1842, 10575 (Court of Nizamut Adawlat to G. J. Shakespear, Magistrate of Midnapur, 7 January 1841).

[108] S. C. De, "Cuttack Jail in 1859", in *Cuttack One Thousand Years*, ed., Karuna S. Behera et al. (Cuttack: Cuttack City Millennium Celebrations Committee, The Universe, 1990), 195.

[109] NAI, MBP 23 April 1841, 13283–84 (J. Pagan, Civil Assistant Surgeon, to G. J. Shakespear, Magistrate of Midnapore, 29 March 1841).

[110] These "navvies" of Eastern India are mentioned in many records but see especially: *Report Showing Progress Made ... in Public Works under Bengal Government, 1861–62*, 107–8 (T. Armstrong, SE, Report on Cuttack Circle, 15 May 1862).

[111] NAI, MBP 23 April 1841, 13282 (J. Pagan, Civil Assistant Surgeon, to G. J.

pressed or employed by contract, in many cases collectively "deserted" the sites as soon as there was any sign of cholera or any other epidemic outbreak[112] and seemed with some reason, one suspects, to fear their employers' "hospital" (or rather camp dispensary) more than the disease itself.[113]

After the roadworks had been completed new problems arose. The collection of *rasad*, for instance, which could be described—according to one account—as "something between begging and compulsion", was not merely unpopular with Garhjat rulers but probably even more so with their subjects.[114] This was admitted by one colonial official on occasion of an incident in 1866 when villagers burnt down a bungalow that had been built for the convenience of British travellers in Ramgarh in the "little kingdom" of Baudh on the Mahanadi route. The background of this episode was a smouldering controversy between the *chaukidar* (customs collector) in charge of that bungalow and the villagers in which the former's assistance in providing victuals loomed large. Accordingly, the Executive Engineer observed that

> the inhabitants of [Ramgarh] all look upon as a sort of hero the man who refuses to supply russud to any European traveller who may happen to stay at the Bungalow, and that the three men in charge of the village

---

Shakespear, Magistrate of Midnapore, 12 March 1841); NAI, MBP 24 February 1841, 12973–74 (M. Kittoe to J. A. Crommelin, Offg. SE, S.E. Division). Also see OIOC, BPWP March 1863, P/16/61, Com., no. 44, 28 (T. Armstrong, SE, Cuttack Circle, to GoB, PWD).

[112] NAI, MBP 5 March 1842, 11238 (C. L. Babington, EE Raipur Mail Road, to G. J. Greene, Offg. Garrison Engineer, Fort William); *Report by the Chief Engineer of Bengal, on the Progress of Public Works, 1859–60* (Calcutta: Savielle & Cranenburgh, 1860), app. 33, diagram opp. 110 (J. Harris, SE Cuttack Circle, to C. B. Young, CE and Secry. to GoB, PWD, 22 May 1860); *Report Showing Progress Made . . . in Imperial Public Works under Bengal Government for 1862–63*, 95, 97 (T. Armstrong, SE, Report on Cuttack Circle, 26 May 1863).

[113] NAI, MBP 14 May 1841, 357 (M. Kittoe to N. McLeod, Offg. Secry. to Military Board, 6 May 1841). The widespread apprehension of colonial hospitals is reflected, for instance, in a tribal song: "In Oriya they call it *daktarakhana*//In Hindi *haspatal*//Whatever its name, it really means death." Quoted in Pati, *Resisting Domination*, 32.

[114] NAI, MBP 16 April 1841, 12988–89 (M. Kittoe's report on Raipur Mail Road, 24 February 1841).

on the part of the Rajah ... were in the habit of reviling him for having pointed out where milk and other provisions were obtainable upon various occasions.[115]

Not only little "kings"—villagers, too, had experienced that roads implied danger. Felled trees could signify a warning to travellers not to use a certain track.[116] Leckie reported that once when his party left the main track in the Sambalpur area and entered a small tribal village they found themselves surrounded by armed and furious inhabitants who, the officer chose to believe, mistook them for "burgahs" *(bargis)*, that is, Maratha horsemen.[117] Moreover, flight was a frequent reaction when foreigners approached a village. Kittoe thus observed four decades later that it was

> a common practice throughout these provinces; the instant strangers are perceived, off the people run (as if their lives were at stake) and are hid in the depths of the jungle in a moment,—it is to facilitate their escape that the jungle is never entirely cleared near the villages; a narrow belt connected with the forest is usually to be found.[118]

The unwillingness of tribals to settle near roads survived well into the twentieth century in some parts of interior Orissa.[119] In the plains, old forts were pulled down along the Jagannath Road to obtain construction material for culverts and road metal. This was, at least in some cases, not appreciated by the villagers who found themselves deprived of convenient retreats.[120] An even more serious threat was, however, created by raising an embankment for the New Jagannath Road that ran across the drainage of the country. Too little waterway was allowed since culverts were expensive. Hence flood water could not run off the fields during the monsoon, when

---

[115] OIOC, BPWP June 1868, P/432/50, Com., no. 63, 63–64 (J. T. Macnamara, Offg. EE Mahanadi Division, to SE Cuttack Circle, 29 May 1866). Also see no. 62, 63 and no. 64.
[116] Kittoe, "Account of a Journey", 379–80, 382.
[117] Leckie, "Journal of a Route to Nagpore", 33–34.
[118] Kittoe, "Account of a Journey", 607; Leckie, "Journal of a Route to Nagpore", 30. For similar strategies of villagers in the Gudem area south of the Orissa region, see Arnold, "Rebellious Hillmen", 103.
[119] Biswamoy Pati, "Survival as Resistance: Tribals in Colonial Orissa". *Indian Historical Review* 33, no. 1, 2006, 181, 184.
[120] Das, *Studies in Economic History of Orissa*, 198–99.

inundations were frequent. In such circumstances, agriculturists reacted swiftly as well as directly and there were long-drawn controversies early in the 1820s concerning the cutting-up of road embankments by villagers, especially in the Bhadrak area.[121] "Complaints regarding obstructions of drainage were common and were put forward by the zamindars" even as late as in the final decade of the century.[122]

This chapter has tried to recover the general pattern of the complex fabric of social interests and conflicts that encompassed the channels of circulation in early colonial Orissa. However sketchy and provisional this survey may be, it appears safe to conclude that no powerful socio-economic or political force in this region was interested without qualification in large-scale investment in transport infrastructure during the first four or five decades of British rule. As far as the colonial government was concerned, this was primarily due to the mode of surplus extraction by the state during this period and its evaluation of Orissa's revenue potential. Moreover, the precolonial level of commercialisation was comparatively low in this region and inherent tendencies of its societies towards "abstract space" correspondingly weak: a decline of commodity production, trade and of the classes concerned with commercial practices appears to have commenced in the eighteenth century, a process that was exacerbated by the policies prevailing during the first half-century of British rule. By the mid-century forces of change made themselves felt, while a crisis of Orissa's circulatory regime became violently evident. The following chapter develops these themes.

---

[121] Toynbee, *A Sketch of the History of Orissa*, 83; Das, *Studies in Economic History of Orissa*, 199; OSA, BoRLR 17,494 (Letter to T. Pakenham, Collector of Cuttack, 31 May 1820).
[122] Maddox, *Final Report on Settlement of Orissa*, I: 27; see also 33.

6

Early Colonialism, 'Public Works' and the Orissa Famine

In the early decades of colonial rule in Orissa, as we have argued, the tendency towards "abstract space", towards a transformation of the circulatory regime by way of investment in infrastructure was weak. This argument needs to be tested against the actual changes in the region's built environment. The year 1866 offers itself as a convenient date as the crisis of Orissa's circulatory regime became a major issue for the colonial public at that time. This year of crisis, therefore, will be used as a starting point for our discussion. From there we will proceed to a chronological account of the major 'public works' undertaken in the six decades after the British annexation of coastal Orissa. This will show, however, that the constellation of interests with regard to transport infrastructure was already in the process of being transformed in the 1850s, when key decisions for the reorganisation of the region's social space were taken.

The Orissa Famine and the Problem of Circulation

In the half-century beginning with the year 1860, devastating famines occured in India, often followed by equally fatal epidemics with an increased frequency and ferocity, killing even according to official estimates about 15 million people and probably many more.[1] The first major mortality crisis of this period was the 1866

---

[1] For an overview, see B. M. Bhatia, *Famines in India: A Study in Some Aspects of the Economic History of India with Special Reference to Food Problem, 1860–1990*, 3rd rev. ed. (Delhi: Konark Publishers, 1991 [1st ed. 1963]). As for the frequency of famines, Bhatia states that between "1860 and 1908, famine or scarcity prevailed in one part of the country or the other in twenty out of the total of forty-nine years." *Famines in India*, 8. For the death toll of late nineteenth-century famines in India, see Leela Visaria and Pravin Visaria,

famine in eastern India, which was particularly severe in coastal Orissa. According to official figures, more than 800,000 human beings died of starvation in this region alone, while more recent historical studies reckon that the death toll exceeded one million, amounting, in other words, to about 30 per cent of the population. The horrors of hunger left enduring traces in Orissa's collective memory, language and food habits. Moreover, a famine of such dimensions put an enormous strain upon social relations, broke them up temporarily or induced long-term changes. Food riots and famine crimes, transgressions of community norms and loss of caste status, religious conversions and large-scale migration, the disproportionately high mortality of landless labourers and a partial redistribution of property in land were among the consequences.[2]

If this was a moment of deep social crisis, it was also one of political delegitimation or, as the British Secretary of State for India put it—"a monument of our failure".[3] This caused considerable uneasiness in British governmental circles in both London and Calcutta as the memories of the massive insurrection of 1857 were still fresh. Hence, Orissa for once caught the attention of a British public, which discovered now that the "revenue of the province is pretty nearly all it is known by from Clive's days to our own."[4]

The famine was triggered off when the rains in September and October 1865 failed, resulting in the loss of the larger part of the

---

"Population (1757–1947)", in *The Cambridge Economic History of India*, ed. Dharma Kumar, 2: 529–31; Mike Davis, *Late Victorian Holocausts: El Niño Famines and the Making of the Third World* (London/New York: Verso, 2001), 7.

[2] Fakirmohan Senapati, who experienced the famine at the age of twenty-seven provides a glimpse of the depth of social crisis and its impact on collective memory in his autobiography (*My Times and I*, 27–31) written half a century later. The best historiographical accounts of this famine, on which much of the following discussion is based, are still Gorachand Patnaik, *The Famine and Some Aspects of the British Economic Policy in Orissa, 1866–1905* (Cuttack: Vidyapuri, 1980), 16–53; Bidyut Mohanty, "Orissa Famine of 1866: Demographic and Economic Consequences", *Economic and Political Weekly*, 28, nos. 1–2, 2–9 January 1993, 55–66. The unpublished thesis of the latter author, submitted to Delhi University in 1988, was not available. Also see Prabhat Mukherjee, *History of Orissa in Nineteenth Century*, 358–96 (for a detailed political narrative).

[3] "Parliamentary Intelligence, House of Lords" (2 August 1867), *The Times*, 3 August 1867 (speech by Sir Stafford Northcote).

[4] Editorial, *The Times*, 9 February 1867.

rice crop. The causes, however, of why a single crop failure could not be coped with and resulted in a major subsistence and mortality crisis are less obvious: this was, after all, no unforeseeable or unique event in a rice-cultivating region dependent on the quantitative as well as temporal regularity of seasonal rains. While available historical studies of this famine leave considerable scope for further research, there appears to be little doubt that an exceptionally harsh and inflexible land-revenue assessment, intensified by the overly extractive practices of "absentee landlords" (that is, zamindars residing away from their holdings, for example, in Calcutta), had resulted in a long-term decline of agricultural productivity, of investment in local irrigation, cattle and manure and even in a depletion of the traditional grain stores that would have helped to weather crop failures in earlier periods.[5] The importance of an unusually large export of about 34,000 tons of rice in 1864–65 for the reduction in these stores was a contentious issue as early as in 1867.[6] However, there seems to be a consensus that the upcoming end of a thirty-years revenue settlement and the impending revaluation of lands induced a further reduction of the area under cultivation and of investment.[7] Atrophy in agriculture was no doubt aggravated by the withering away of non-agricultural sources of income such as weaving or,

---

[5] Mohanty, "Orissa Famine of 1866", 55; Patnaik, *Famine and Some Aspects of British Economic Policy in Orissa*, 18, 30–31. For the severity of the revenue assessment, see Chaudhuri, "Agrarian Relations: Eastern India", 2: 133–34; Jit, *The Agrarian Life*, 192–224.

[6] See Robert Knight, letter to the editor, *The Times*, 23 August 1867; G. N. Barlow, letter to the editor, *The Times*, 26 August 1867; Robert Knight, letter to the editor, *The Times*, 31 August 1867. Knight argued that the volume of exported grain was strikingly small in absolute terms and that the inability to export more indicated that the people were "always treading upon the verge of famine". From another perspective, the increase of grain exports may have reflected the mounting pressure of revenue demands. Hence the volume and increase of grain exports may well have been rather a symptom of a general crisis tending towards famine than a famine cause of their own. Patnaik presents evidence for the former conclusion, fails to discuss it and endorses on the whole, like Mohanty and Arnold, the latter: Patnaik, *Famine and Some Aspects of British Economic Policy in Orissa*, 17, 26; Mohanty, "Orissa Famine of 1866", 55; David Arnold, *Famine: Social Crisis and Historical Change* (Oxford/New York: Basil Blackwell, 1988), 45.

[7] Mohanty, "Orissa Famine of 1866", 55; Patnaik, *Famine and Some Aspects of British Economic Policy in Orissa*, 17, 68.

more importantly, of salt production. The latter had come to a virtual standstill in 1863, when Liverpool salt effectively ousted Orissa's "white gold" from the Bengal market, the government's salt monopoly was lifted and the government-owned manufactures in the districts of Puri, Cuttack and Balasore were closed down. About 40,000 *malangis* had previously worked in these salt *aurangs* and were now left without subsistence.[8] The scarcity of salt for local consumption and its corresponding dearness may also have diminished a potentially considerable source of food supply by rendering the curing of fish economically unviable for Orissa.[9]

That colonial land revenue and salt policies had steered Orissa's economy into a decade-long decline was stated in the British Parliament and also in the evidence given to the commission appointed by the Government of India in 1867 to inquire into the causes of the Orissa famine.[10] However, the debate was mainly focused on the question whether the horrendous death toll was primarily caused by an inadequate management of the famine by the colonial administration or by "inexorable", mainly geographical conditions. Defenders of the Bengal Government naturalised the "calamity" and ruminated gravely about the "awful dispensation of providence" that had "appointed" a quarter of a people to die. They also asserted that a "drought in India, extending over a considerable tract of country, can no more be coped with by human agency than a hurricane or an earthquake" though it might be alleviated, to some extent, by infrastructures of irrigation and circulation.[11] Many contributors to

---

[8] Choudhury, *Economic History of Colonialism*, 54–58; Patnaik, *Famine and Some Aspects of British Economic Policy in Orissa*, 157–62; Mohanty, "Orissa Famine of 1866", 55.

[9] Colonial sources, however, contain, contradictory opinions on whether the practice of curing was referred to by fisher people because of customary food restrictions or due to the dearness of salt. See Hunter, *The Annals of Rural Bengal*, 3: 159–61; Francis Day, *Report on the Sea Fish and Fisheries of India and Burma* (Calcutta: Office of the Superintendent of Government Printing, 1873), cxv–cxxii.

[10] "Parliamentary Intelligence, House of Commons" (2 August 1867), *The Times*, 3 August 1876 (speech by H. D. Seymour); *Report of Commissioners . . . Famine in Bengal and Orissa in 1866*, 1: cli (statement by Captain A. Bond, Master Attendant and Assistant Salt Agent, Balasore, 8 February 1867). Also see Patnaik, *Famine and Some Aspects of British Economic Policy in Orissa*, 64–68.

[11] The quotes are taken from an exemplary exposition of that opinion: "An Ex-Indian Civilian", letter to the editor, *The Times*, 20 August 1867.

the British public debate including former colonial officials, held, however, that the Bengal Government's adherence to the commandment of classical political economy "thou shall not interfere with the grain market" and, more particularly, their imperturbable belief in the existence of local grain hoards, which rising prices would finally push onto the market, were responsible for a delay of government grain imports from Bengal and Burma until it was too late.[12] Others felt that the crux of the matter lay in long-term policies and particularly in the neglect of infrastructures of irrigation and transportation by the colonial government.[13] "In the Orissa famine one million human beings perished, as is but too well known—nine hundred thousand by the hands of the Government, one hundred thousand by those of inexorable fate," wrote John C. Harris.[14] Having conducted the most comprehensive survey of Orissa's river system as a senior colonial engineer, Harris clearly did not believe the famine to have been a natural phenomenon. A former Deputy Collector of Balasore complained in 1872 that "[n]o censure ... was passed upon any of the authorities responsible for this enormous butcher's bill."[15]

This verdict evidently referred to the Famine Commissioners' report of 1867, which had formulated a rather unspecific and muted critique of delayed government action[16] while emphasising the lack

---

[12] See especially H. Danby Seymour's speech in the House of Commons, which gave a detailed account of official and non-official correspondence in the Bengal Presidency with regard to famine policy in 1865 and 1866, referring to several documents that were not included in the printed evidence presented by the Famine Commissioners: "Parliamentary Intelligence, House of Commons" (2 August 1867), *The Times*, 3 August 1876. Also see Editorial, *The Times*, 2 July 1867; Editorial, 2 August 1867. This opinion was also repeatedly stated to the Famine Commissioners. See, for example, *Report of Commissioners ... Famine in Bengal and Orissa in 1866*, 1: xlv (statement by H. Levinge, Executive Engineer, Katjoree Division, East Indian Irrigation Company, 2 January 1867). For a brief summary of the Bengal Government's *laissez faire* approach towards the Orissa famine, also see Patnaik, *Famine and Some Aspects of British Economic Policy in Orissa*, 19–25.
[13] Editorial, *The Times*, 9 February 1867; letters to the editor by "An Old Indian" and "W. M. J.", and 23 August 1867.
[14] John C. Harris, letter to the editor, *The Times*, 18 December 1873.
[15] F. A. Elphinstone-Dalrymple, letter to the editor, *The Times*, 3 September 1873.
[16] This appears to have been the opinion of the majority of speakers when the report was debated in the House of Commons. See "Parliamentary

of transport facilities as a crucial factor for the extraordinary level of famine mortality.[17] "[S]hut up in a narrow province between pathless jungles and an impracticable sea," the people of Orissa were, according to them, "in the condition of passengers in a ship without provisions."[18] And in one of the most frequently quoted sentences of their report they formulated that

> [t]he whole province is geographically isolated to an excessive degree. To the north-west and west the hilly tracts merge into countries still more hilly, wild, and inaccessible, by which they are separated effectually from Central and Northern India. There is only a precarious traffic to Sumbulpore by boats of a peculiar construction which navigate the difficult river Mahanuddee in the rainy season and for a month or two after; for the rest of the year this communication is closed. On the other side, the nature of the coast and the sea is such as effectually to stop all Native traffic for the major part of the year, while during the remaining four or five months the traffic, such as it is, is conducted in rude and barbarous vessels which have deteriorated from the model of an ancient age of European adventure, but which are capable of crossing the shallow bars and entering the narrow rivers. In fact but few of these rivers are capable of so much use, and they are all inaccessible to the ordinary class of modern European vessels.[19]

While this statement has been accepted and repeated by historians as a matter-of-fact depiction of Orissa's circulatory regime before the late nineteenth century, it was rather controversial at the time of its formulation.[20] Contemporary British critics insisted that the failure of government imports for the relief of the famished was not due to any general inaccessibility of the region. It was seen rather as the effect of the Bengal Government's refusal to ship rice to Orissa before the commencement of the monsoon rains in June (at which time the roads became almost impassable and sea transport

---

Intelligence, House of Lords" (2 August 1867), *The Times*, 3 August 1867. Also see Editorial, *The Times*, 2 July 1867.

[17] For an account of the context, proceedings and recommendations of this commission, see Patnaik, *Famine and Some Aspects of British Economic Policy in Orissa*, 54–71.

[18] Quoted in Editorial, *The Times*, 2 July 1867.

[19] *Report of Commissioners ... Famine in Bengal and Orissa in 1866*, 1: 8.

[20] See for example, Samal, *Economic History of Orissa*, 126; Bhola, *British Economic Policy in Orissa*, 123.

extremely difficult) despite the fact that as early as in March, when the 'season of circulation' was still on, "the most casual observer could see that there was a severe famine in the country".[21] Some of these critics pointed out that several of the traditional minor ports along the coast of Orissa were not only adequate for Indian sailing vessels but also for steam tugboats. Andrew Henderson, an entrepreneur with a twenty-years experience of steam shipping in India, reported that at an early stage of the famine he had offered to provide a flotilla of smaller steam and sailing vessels. These could have crossed any of the bars impeding the mouths of the Orissa rivers, but his proposal had been turned down by the Bengal Government.[22] This is corroborated by testimonies to the Orissa Famine Commission, which were appended to its report.[23] As for the feasibility of overland exports G. N. Barlow, the former Collector of Balasore, asserted a year after the famine that inland trade "has been often very great".[24] With regard to intra-regional circulation there is evidence for the famine months that considerable amounts of grain were transported across the Chilka Lake, on the flooded Mahanadi and also from the interior district of Angul to Cuttack along a recently built road.[25] Hence, even colonial sources do not,

[21] *Report of the Commissioners . . . Famine in Bengal and Orissa in 1866*, 1: xlv (statement by H. Levinge, Executive Engineer, Katjoree Division, East Indian Irrigation Company, 2 January 1867). Also see the other statements referred to in footnote 12.

[22] Andrew Henderson, letter to the editor, *The Times*, 5 September 1867.

[23] *Report of Commissioners . . . Famine in Bengal and Orissa in 1866*, 1: cl-clii (statements by R. S. Evans, Bengal Pilot Service, 8 February 1867, H. S. Thomas, Chief Officer of the S. S. Nemesis, 7 February 1867, and Captain A. Bond, Master Attendant and Assistant Salt Agent, Balasore, 8 February 1867). Also see Patnaik, *Famine and Some Aspects of British Economic Policy in Orissa*, 37. The possibility of landing smaller vessels in various ports of Orissa is particularised in: *Report of Commissioners . . . Famine in Bengal and Orissa in 1866*, 2: 295–96 (T. E. Ravenshaw, Offg. Commissioner, Cuttack Division, to Secry. to Board of Revenue, Lower Provinces, 22 June 1866). Also see "Another Ex-Indian Civilian", letter to the editor, *The Times*, 29 August 1867.

[24] G. N. Barlow, letter to the editor, *The Times*, 26 August 1867. Barlow obviously referred to the dry seasons of years with good harvests.

[25] OIOC, BPWP June 1868, P/432/50, Com., no. 60, 60 (statement by Executive Engineer Bond); *Report of Commissioners . . . Famine in Bengal and Orissa in 1866*, 2: 295 (T. E. Ravenshaw, Offg. Commissioner, Cuttack Division, to

on close reading, sustain the Commissioner's claim of an *absolute* spatial disarticulation and "inaccessibility" of Orissa, though the scope of circulation was certainly restricted by its seasonal rhythm.

However, there are indications for a *declining intensity of circulation* and also for a decay of the means of transport before the famine— an aspect that has barely caught the attention of historians so far. This was pointed out graphically by the British Master Attendant (port captain) in Baleshwar who reported to the Famine Commissioners:

> I was there when the great inundations of the sea occurred in 1831 and 1832.... Rice was imported by sea and likewise from the interior for sufferers by the inundation. The suffering was very great, but timely measures were then taken. We had a large number of sea-going vessels available in the Balasore port; 246 were then fitted for sea; now only 22 are available. This is on account of the abandonment of the Government manufacture of salt. The loss of life was in those days caused by the inundation of the sea. I took people out of trees, dead and alive. I think the loss of life on that occasion was much greater than by the last famine, but there was not so much loss by starvation, for we had rice down from Calcutta immediately.[26]

W. W. Hunter observed a few years later in his encyclopaedic account of Orissa that the town of Baleshwar

> has declined since the Government abandoned the monopoly on salt trade; and rows of dismal black salt-sloops lie rotting in little channels leading out of the river, which were once docks. There are probably about 200 of these melancholy memorials of departed prosperity.[27]

Similarly, Fakirmohan Senapati, who had lived through this period, remembered sadly that in the early years of the nineteenth century "the quaysides of Balasore had bustled with people by the thousand. Yet look at them now, silent, desolate, overgrown with wild bushes and hushed as a cemetery." During the famine, he recalled, traditional sailing vessels had been unavailable since "Balasore's

---

Secry. to Board of Revenue, Lower Provinces, 22 June 1866); Mohanty, "Orissa Famine of 1866," 56.

[26] *Report of Commissioners ... Famine in Bengal and Orissa in 1866*, 1: cli (statement by Captain A. Bond, Master Attendant and Assistant Salt Agent, Balasore, 8 February 1867).

[27] Hunter, *The Annals of Rural Bengal*, appendix, 3: 41–42.

seafaring families had faded away" after the closure of the Salt Offices.[28]

Baleshwar's decline was indicative of a broader process. If commodity production requires the integration of production with circulation (see chapter 3: the commodity "is really finished only when it is on the market"), shifts in a region's regime of production can be expected to have repercussions on the circulatory regime. Seasons of agricultural production and seasons of circulation followed and determined each other (as has been shown in chapter 4) even in an agrarian society with a comparatively low level of commercialisation like that of Orissa. Hence, the disintegration of non-agricultural commodity production that rendered rice into Orissa's only exportable bulk commodity had, coupled with the simultaneous decline of agricultural productivity, disruptive effects on the patterns and means of circulation. In the seventeenth century, coastal Orissa had been a focus of mainly indigenous maritime trade in the Bay of Bengal, while its commercial textile production attracted the Dutch and English merchant companies. This implied the availability of networks and infrastructures for monetary transactions, for the supply of raw materials and for the distribution of finished goods. A considerable deterioration of these infrastructures of circulation appears to have occurred in the course of the century preceding the region's annexation by the English East India Company.[29] They appear to have further regressed beyond recognition by the 1870s when it was observed that a

> marked peculiarity in the province is the almost total absence among the Ooryahs of the bunniah or trading class which exists both in northern and southern India. At the present day throughout the length and breadth of Orissa there are only 498 markets, many of them of exceedingly minute dimensions, and these take the place of village shops or stores which may be said to have absolutely no existence.[30]

---

[28] Senapati, *My Times and I*, 15, 30. For the decline of Baleshwar, also see Patnaik, *Famine and Some Aspects of British Economic Policy in Orissa*, 158.

[29] For merchants, ports and maritime trade in seventeenth-century Orissa and their decline since the eighteenth century, see Das, *Studies in Economic History of Orissa*, 228–50. For a detailed account of Baleshwar's late seventeenth-century trade with South East Asia, Sri Lanka and the Maldives, see Prakash, *Bullion for Goods*, 209–18, 242–51, 256–57.

[30] *Papers Relating to the Orissa Coast Canal, 1869 to 1877 and 1881 to 1883*, in *Selections from the Records of the Government of India in the Public Works*

In the late 1860s and 1870s, the scarcity of boats was not only experienced in Baleshwar but in several decaying port villages along the Orissa coast also.[31] The decline of social and spatial infrastructures of exchange was particularly striking with regard to maritime trade, but could also be observed (as has been shown in the previous chapter) with regard to the region's circuits of exchange with Central and North India. If salt from Orissa's shores had been bartered for grain from Chhattisgarh in earlier periods, this circuit, which could acquire vital importance and provide some measure of relief to the people of the coastal region in periods of drought, had all but disintegrated by 1866.

The extent to which such developments affected the course of the famine cannot be established with any certainty on the basis of the present state of research. Yet some methodological observations may be in place: hence Orissa's social space and circulatory regime on the eve of the famine—a situation where the Oriyas seemed to be "shut up in a narrow province"—cannot be assumed to have been shaped by the forces of nature alone. This assumption underlay W. W. Hunter's reasoning that the 1866 famine hit Orissa particularly with force because of the absence of those "breakwaters" or "intervening influences" like secure property in land, state works of irrigation, transport infrastructure and other measures promoting "the extension of commerce and the growth of capital". By generating such safety measures modern civilisation elsewhere had rendered "the relation of actual pressure" (that is, the unavailability of

---

Department (Calcutta: Bengal Secretariat Press, 1884), 78 (note by Lieutenant J. W. Ottley, Royal Engineers, 10 December 1874). The number of bazaars in the three districts of the Cuttack Division is particularised as follows: Cuttack 278, Puri 55, Balasore 165; and 70 (Note by T. E. Ravenshaw, Esq., Commissioner of Orissa, on Colonel Gulliver's Memorandum ... dated 19 September 1874, to Joint-Secretary, Irrigation Branch). Also see OSA, R III-1/707B, General Administration Report, Orissa Division (hereafter GAROD followed by year) 1873–74, 10; Patnaik, *Famine and Some Aspects of British Economic Policy in Orissa*, 18.

[31] Cf.: *Report of Commissioners ... Famine in Bengal and Orissa in 1866*, 2: 295–96 (T. E. Ravenshaw, Offg. Commissioner, Cuttack Division, to Secry. to Board of Revenue, Lower Provinces, 22 June 1866); *Papers Relating to Orissa Canals, 1869 to 1877 and 1881 to 1883*, 69 (Note by T. E. Ravenshaw, 19 September 1874); OSA, R III-1/707B, GAROD 1874–75, 7.

food) "to natural scarcity less certain and less direct."[32] Hunter thus argued that precolonial societies were unable to counterbalance the effects of drought and were subject to the unmitigated forces of nature. This assumption, albeit accepted in later writings on the subject, needs to be questioned and qualified, however. Orissa's *relative* disarticulation from other regions of the subcontinent resulted from a physical geography upon which in the course of history many layers of socio-spatial practice (including circulation as much as production) had been superimposed. An in-depth analysis of long-term causes of the Orissa famine (which is beyond the scope of this study) thus ought to take into account the totality of interdependent productive and circulatory practices. For, even minute shifts and changes in the structure of this complex may have affected the ability of regional society to cope with famine as older strategies of countering the effects of crop failure were subverted. While a fair amount of research has been conducted with regard to the changes in Orissa's regime of production, the present study has so far identified patterns of circulation originating from early modern precolonial social formations (see chapter 4). It is now necessary to draw a balance of the changes effected by the early colonial state in the region's circulatory regime up to the famine of 1866. This is the objective of the remaining part of this chapter.

"Free Communication": Infrastructure Policy before the 1850s

That the infrastructural efforts of the early colonial state were rather limited is clearly discernible even if we turn to the most important achievement of that period—the so-called New Jagannath or Orissa Trunk Road. This unmetalled fair-weather road was raised throughout (from six to occasionally twenty-five feet), included a number of bridges across smaller watercourses and was constructed in two stages. In the first phase, the section from Midnapur via

---

[32] William W. Hunter, *The Annals of Rural Bengal,* 3rd ed. (London: Smith, Elder & Co., 1868), ("The Ethnical Frontier of Lower Bengal with the Ancient Principalities of Beerbhoom and Bishenpore"), 1: 43–56 (the quotes can be found on pp. 50, 51 and 55). Hunter dedicated this work, interestingly, to Sir Cecil Beadon who had been Lieutenant-Governor of Bengal in 1866 and was criticised at the time for insisting on "non-interference" with the grain market even in the face of a full-blown famine.

Baleshwar and Bhadrak to Cuttack and thence to Puri via Pipili was constructed between 1813 and 1825. In the Cuttack Division of the Bengal Presidency, it was 287 km long and diverged from the alignment of the former pilgrimage route from Bengal only in some segments where it kept closer to the hilly western margin of the Orissa plains.

The southward continuation of this route from Puri to Ganjam and onwards to South India had previously followed the narrow strip of land between Chilka Lake and the sea. Since the track ran over a soil of sand, water transport across the lake had been more convenient and perhaps more considerable. In the second phase, therefore, an alternative road was sanctioned and constructed from Cuttack via Khurda and the western shores of Chilka Lake to Ganjam in the decade after 1827. This section extended over 116 km within Cuttack Division, bringing up the total length of the Orissa Trunk Road to about 400 km.[33] Colonial officials entertained high expectations concerning this channel of circulation. A report written in 1815, when the construction was still in an early stage proclaimed:

> The new substantial Road now constructing thro' Orissa will facilitate a free communication between the Supreme Government and the other Presidencies which has been greatly obstructed hitherto for several Months during the year.... This Road will tend to form in a military point of view a link of connection, politically necessary between our several Establishments. It will also prove of great advantage in a Civil point of view as it increases the intercourse and may therefore be supposed to add to the prosperity of the Inhabitants of the District.... It moreover secures to the Juggunauth Pilgrims a safe and certain passage thro' the Province at every period of the year and renders more attainable the object of their devotions by affording them greater facility in their progress and return & holds forth inducements to additional

---

[33] OIOC, Board's Collection, F/4/505, no. 12139, 91–97 (John Richardson on province of Cuttack, extract from Bengal Revenue Consultations, 18 May 1815); NAI, MBP 9 March 1841, 11425 (Military Board to Governor-General, 1 December 1841, report on proceedings in Civil Dpt. for 1839/40); OSA, BoRLR 17,772 (W. Wilkinson, Collector of Puri, to T. Pakenham, Offg. CoCD, 14 September 1826); OSA, BoRLR 17,805 (Acting Secry. to GoB, Territorial Dpt., to T. Pakenham, Offg. CoCD, 22 March 1827, and other letters concerning Ganjam Road); OIOC, BPWP January 1864, P/16/66, Com., no. 39, app. I (statement of Imperial and Local Roads in Bengal); Toynbee, *A Sketch of the History of Orissa*, 82–83.

numbers to perform this Pilgrimage and thereby may probably increase the Revenue of Government.[34]

Three vital functions were thus ascribed to this road: (a) as a means of military communication, (b) as a means of commercialisation (adding sooner or later to the colonial government's revenue by raising agricultural productivity in a non-permanently settled region like the Cuttack Division), and (c) as an improved pilgrimage route (economically of limited but immediate earning power since the pilgrim tax still contributed to British revenues from Orissa). Yet, for all these attractions, Commissioner Buller in 1809 had felt that the necessary expenditure was "unreasonable" if covered by government funds alone and had, therefore, explored the willingness of Bengali notables to contribute to a subscription.[35]

A year later, Raja Sukhamoy Roy, an absentee zamindar or "tax farmer of Orissa" residing in Uttarpara (Calcutta),[36] offered to donate a substantial sum of Rs 150,000 for the construction of this road under specific conditions. The more important of these conditions were first, that no further private contributions would be accepted so that he would be the only Indian benefactor, second, that his donation would be recorded by inscriptions on all bridges in Sanskrit, Farsi and Bangla, and third, that special honours would be granted to him and his descendents. The ailing Raja's declared intention was to undertake a major pious work before his death. Like other magnates of this period he acted thus in the tradition of precolonial notables for whom (as has been pointed out in chapter 3) the endowment of sarais and other facilities of road transport served as a means of enhancing one's social standing and of displaying power and piety. Sensing that no other money of this dimension could be expected, the colonial government hastily accepted Sukhamoy Roy's conditions, insofar as they "may be consistent with the institutions of the temple".[37]

---

[34] OIOC, Board's Collection, F/4/505, no. 12139, 91–92 (John Richardson on province of Cuttack, extract from Bengal Revenue Consultations, 18 May 1815).
[35] OSA, BoRLR 17,204 (C. Buller, CoCD, to Lord Minto, Governor-General, 15 July 1809).
[36] Das, *Studies in Economic History of Orissa*, 175.
[37] OIOC, Board's Collection F/4/367, no. 9206. A leading representative of the East India Company commented this benefaction in the 1830s as

Toynbee, whose assertions have been uncritically repeated by many later historians in this respect, too, created the impression that Sukhamoy Roy merely contributed supplementary amenities (rest houses and bridges) to a larger infrastructural project that was already being implemented.[38] The available sources show, however, that this most important infrastructural project of early colonial Orissa (and virtually the *only* road development scheme in the plains before the 1850s) was sanctioned only *after* a major initial investment from a private, non-government source amounting to 10 per cent of the total outlay on the road over a period of almost two decades. Hence, a report on public works in Cuttack Division (which may well have been available to Toynbee) freely admitted that the construction of Jagannath Road "originated in a donation by Rajah Soakmoy Roy".[39] Moreover, the road paid "for itself", to some extent: the clear profit from the pilgrim tax on Jagannath Road (that is, the net margin after defraying the costs of temple maintenance) amounted to almost Rs 130,000 between 1810 and 1830 (or about Rs 6,500 per annum).[40] Henry St. George Tucker sought to fend off evangelical accusations that the East India Company was profiteering from

---

follows: "The opulent natives are well disposed to aid in the construction of roads, tanks, wells, serais, and other works of public utility; and we ought to encourage this disposition, even where it originates in personal vanity. Rajah Sookhmoy, of Calcutta, contributed 1,50,000 rupees towards the construction of the road to Jugenath: and Rajah Mittergeet Singh, of Tikàri, one of the most intelligent of our Zemindars, undertook to make a substantial road through his flourishing domain soon after he began to reap the fruits of the Permanent Settlement." Tucker, *Memorials on Indian Government*, 427. K. N. Mahapatra remarks interestingly that the donation was made by Sukhamoy together with his wife Sankari Devi. He does not give a source for a mention of the latter person, which cannot be found, to my knowledge, in the relevant British records. Did the archaeologist Mahapatra refer to the engraved stone slabs preserving the memory of the donation? Cf.: Mahapatra, *Ancient Pilgrims' Routes*, 46.

[38] Toynbee, *A Sketch of the History of Orissa*, 83.

[39] The total costs until 1830 of 262 miles of road from "Bissunpore" (Bishnupur) in Bengal to Puri are reported in the same account to have amounted to Rs. 1,521,696. NAI, MBP 9 March 1841, 11425 (Military Board to Governor-General, 1 December 1841, report on proceedings in Civil Dpt. for 1839/40).

[40] Cassels, *Religion and Pilgrim Tax*, 164.

"heathen superstition" (and backing it up in return) by asserting that the

> duty levied on the pilgrims resorting to Jugurnath, is not strictly a source of revenue: it is rather a tax of *regulation*; and the whole amount collected has been expended in constructing and keeping in repair the public road, and in other objects connected with the support of the temple.[41]

Scraping off the patina of colonial historiography discloses that less than 9 per cent of the very considerable revenue remittances from Orissa to Calcutta were reinvested in the region in the form of built environments for purposes of transport in the first three decades of British rule. The sharp increase of land revenue since the times of the proverbially rapacious Maratha regime was apparently not driven by any impulse for "improvement".[42] This approach changed little up to the middle of the century. When surfacing the road was considered in the 1820s, the costs were deemed prohibitive: they were then (for gravel metalling) estimated at about Rs 200,000, or slightly more than a quarter of the annual revenue remittances to Calcutta in the early years of colonial rule.[43] Consequently, as late as

---

[41] Tucker, *Memorials on Indian Government*, 375. Tucker was an influential director of the East India Company for many years. For a similar statement, see OSA, BoRLR 18,692, f. 13 (J. Thomason, Deputy Secry. to GoI, Revenue Dpt., to R. D. Mangles, Acting Secry. to Sudder Board of Revenue, 4 September 1832).

[42] According to Chaudhuri ("Agrarian Relations: Eastern India", 90, 94–95), net revenue collections in 1804 exceeded those of the last decade of Maratha rule by about 12 per cent and increased considerably in the following decades. While remittances from Orissa to Nagpur had rarely exceeded Rs 400,000 per annum during Maratha rule, they shot up to about Rs 750,000 on average between 1804 and 1818. Also see Jit, *The Agrarian Life*, 43–46, 199. The total construction costs of the Jagannath Road amounted, as we have seen (footnote 39), to about Rs 1,520,000 from which Sukhamoy Roy's donation of Rs 150,000 has to be subtracted. The remaining Rs 1,370,000 are equal to an annual expenditure of Rs 65,000 or 8.7 per cent of the remittances to Calcutta of annually Rs 750,000. Other 'public works' of transport were few and of a minor order (see below).

[43] OSA, BoRLR 17,719 (J. Craigie, Secry. to Military Board, to Secry. to GoB, Territorial Dpt., 22 November 1925, and other letters on the same subject); OSA, BoRLR 17,824 (G. Becher, SI of Jagannath Road, Cuttack Division, to J. Cheape, SI of Public Works, Cuttack, 10 March 1827). For remittances, see footnote 42, above. In the 1860s, the expenditure required for metalling

in 1864 there was not a single mile of *pakka* or metalled road in Orissa.[44] Moreover, even the maintenance of this Trunk Road was not regularly provided for, though repairs had to be undertaken on an annual basis as soon as the monsoon clouds dispersed and the floods drained off, if the road was to be cartable during the dry season at least. The funds required for this purpose were often not made available despite the fact that labour costs were considerably reduced, as we have seen, by the utilisation of unpaid convict labour for repairs on Jagannath Road.[45] Henry Ricketts, in the 1850s, gave vivid descriptions of the distressing conditions and tedious slowness of travel on this road (during the rains, it had once taken him nine hours to cover ten miles). He pointed out that no improvement of its state had been achieved within the twenty-five years of his experience while works were, for want of "scientific" supervision, executed "in a style of which a Mahratee mistree would have been ashamed".[46] The reference to a *mistri* (chief builder) from Maharashtra signified, of course, the uneasy feeling that, in this respect, the colonial administration was unlikely to be perceived by its Oriya subjects to be more benign or improving than the preceding Maratha rulers. In 1861, the engineer in charge of 'public works' in the Bengal Presidency put on record that "the Imperial Trunk Road between Rajghat and Cuttack ... has been left in an extraordinary state of dilapidation increasing year by year." Even major breaches of the road embankments that had occurred during the floods seven years earlier had not been repaired as yet.[47]

Toynbee mentioned that the only "other public work of any great importance ... between 1803 and 1828" was the "Churaman Canal, which was designed for the transport of salt from the

---

Orissa Trunk Road (then including 116 additional km of the Cuttack section of the Cuttack–Ganjam road) was estimated at Rs 600,000. *Report of Commissioners ... Famine in Bengal and Orissa in 1866*, 1: xli (statement by A. Crommelin, SE Cuttack Circle, 1 January 1867).

[44] OIOC, BPWP January 1864, P/16/66, Com., no. 39, app. i–ii, 114–20 (statement of Imperial and Local Roads in Bengal).

[45] See chapter 5.

[46] Ricketts, *Reports on the Districts of Midnapore ... and Cuttack*, 83–84; Ricketts, "Reports on the Districts of Pooree and Balasore", 23, 69.

[47] OIOC, BPWP August 1861, P/16/53, Com., no. 8, 5–7 (memo from J. P. Beadle, Offg. Chief Engineer, Bengal, 26 July 1861).

Dhamrah and other arangs", (that is, places of salt manufacture) to Churaman, one of the more important petty ports of Orissa, from where this commodity was shipped to Calcutta. The construction seems to have commenced in 1825 only to be abandoned again a year later—ostensibly because of difficulties in labour recruitment (which may yet also indicate that the priority of this project was not very high).[48]

It was only in the late 1830s and early 1840s that more substantial colonial efforts were made again with regard to transport infrastructure. This second major scheme before the 1850s, the Raipur Mail Road, has already been referred to in the preceding chapter: the East India Company's regime had been intent to establish direct postal communication between the two presidency towns of Calcutta and Bombay as early as in the eighteenth century, when the northern and western parts of Orissa (through which this line had to pass) were formally under the overlordship of the Berar Bhonsles.[49] After the British annexation of coastal Orissa, one so-called "Captain Johnson's road" was reported to connect Midnapur with Sambalpur, and the construction of another, more convenient mail route was considered.[50] Yet none of these roads was regularly maintained so that a new line was surveyed and constructed between 1837 and 1846 over a distance of nearly 1,000 km between Midnapur and Nagpur at a cost of Rs 493,284. Almost half of this route ran through the Garhjat states of Mayurbhanj, Kendujhar, Pal Lahera,

---

[48] Toynbee, *A Sketch of the History of Orissa*, 84. As for Churaman, Hunter quotes the Customs Collector of Baleshwar in 1809 with the statement that this port was "considered the most safe and convenient port on the coast of Orissa, and carries on a sea-going trade exceeding that of Balasore." Within a few decades, however, the port lost its significance–this demise was, according to Hunter, occasioned by the silting up of the river channel it was located at. Hunter, *A Statistical Account of Bengal*, 18: 259. Unfortunately, the original sources presently available contain no further information on this interesting project. Colonial administration was, however, confronted with labour recruitment problems in other cases and in later periods as well. Further research is required to clarify why the available means to "solve" such problems were not applied in the Churaman project.

[49] They were at that time, however, informed by the Berar Raja that no safe road through Mayurbhanj was available. Ray, *Orissa under Marathas*, 151–52.

[50] OIOC, Board's Collection, F/4/1196, no. 30905/29, 37–39 (W. R. Gilbert, Agent to Governor-General, South West Frontier, to Secry. Swinton, 29 May 1827, extract from Bengal Political Consultations, 17 August 1827).

Bonai, Bamra and Sambalpur.[51] One thousand ("free" as well as "unfree") coolies were at times employed on this section alone.

The orders of the colonial government clarified that the sole purpose of this project was to secure safe and regular *dak* communication between Calcutta and Bombay. Clearly, no priority was attached to facilitating the transport of bulk commodities or "opening up the country" to the "civilising" forces of commerce. This is evident from the mode of construction, alignment as well as further development of this road. For one, the engineer was instructed in 1841 to confine the construction works in the Orissa section to "the formation of a continuous pathway 10 feet wide through a cleared belt of jungle 100 yards wide on each side with good ferries established at the Rivers and temporary Bridges constructed across the smaller water-courses".[52] This was no cartable road implying that its capacity of promoting overland trade was rather limited. Moreover, both the Commissioner of Cuttack and the Superintending Engineer responsible pointed out that the Raipur Mail Road's contribution to the social integration of the Orissa region was necessarily limited because of its alignment. The latter argued that the economic utility of this route (and especially its capacity of serving as a channel for the profitable export of inland Orissa's forest and agricultural produce) would have been much greater if it had been directed towards Baleshwar and not towards Midnapur. Finally, the expenditure on the maintenance of this road was reduced to a minimum as soon as a new line of postal communication between Calcutta and Bombay was established via Mirzapur and

---

[51] This paragraph is based on the following sources (specific references are only given for quotations): NAI, MBP 25 May 1841, 733 (Kittoe's report for March 1841); NAI, MBP 9 March 1841, 11425 (Military Board to Governor-General, 1 December 1841, report on proceedings in Civil Dpt. for 1839–40); OIOC, BPWP 19 January 1860, P/16/37, Com., no. 14, 197–98 (J. Beadle, SI of Embankments and SE, 3rd Circle, Lower Provinces, to the Offg. CE, Lower Provinces, 19 October 1859); and 199 (G. F. Cockburn, CoCD, to SE, 3rd Circle, 27 September 1859); and no. 15, 200 (Rivers Thompson, Junior Secry. to GoB, to Offg. CE, Lower Provinces, 13 January 1860); OIOC, BPWP November 1869, P/432/56, Com., no. 5–12, 3–9 (J. Johnstone, Special Assistant in Keonjhur, to CoCD, 10 August 1869, and other relevant documents).

[52] OIOC, BPWP 19 January 1860, P/16/37, Com., no. 14, 197 (J. Beadle, SI of Embankments and SE, 3rd Circle, Lower Provinces, to the Offg. CE, Lower Provinces, 19 October 1859).

Jabalpur in 1853. Hence, in 1859, the Commissioner of Cuttack believed

> that little or nothing had been done to the road for several years past since it ceased to be the road taken by the Mails between Bombay and Calcutta, and that if not speedily attended to, its re-construction hereafter will only involve a far greater expense than necessary now if repaired at once.[53]

The Government of Bengal, however, decided that 'nothing can be done for the furtherance of this project'.[54] Ten years later in 1869 it was stated that this channel of communication, then called the old Bombay Road, had "fallen into very general decay."[55] There was, on the whole, no sustained colonial interest at that time in "opening up" the mountainous tracts of inland Orissa, in revitalising its earlier circuits of exchange with Central India, Bengal and coastal Orissa or in transforming its social space by integrating it with supraregional or transterritorial markets.

Imperial and Cotton Roads of the 1850s and 1860s

The 1850s and 1860s were (when the Raipur Mail Road was abandoned), however, simultaneously decades of major changes in colonial attitudes towards 'public works' in Orissa. The changes were connected to the overall reformulation of colonial infrastructure policies, which had commenced on a subcontinental scale at least a decade earlier. This redefinition of the colonial regime's stance towards infrastructures of circulation showed results first in other regions of "British India" as early as in the 1840s and has already been discussed at some length in chapter 3. After a delay of a decade, the drive towards a transformation of built environments also became perceivable in Orissa. Issues of transport and communication (as well as of irrigation) suddenly moved to the forefront of administrative proceedings in the 1850s. It was then that relevant

---

[53] Ibid., 199 (G. F. Cockburn, CoCD, to SE, 3rd Circle, 27 September 1859); and no. 15, 200 (Rivers Thompson, Junior Secry. to GoB, to Offg. CE, Lower Provinces, 13 January 1860).

[54] Ibid., no. 15, 200 (Rivers Thompson, Junior Secry. to GoB, to Offg. CE, Lower Provinces, 13 January 1860).

[55] OIOC, BPWP November 1869, P/432/56, Com., no. 10, 6 (extract from Proceedings of Lieutenant-Governor of Bengal in the PWD, 25 September 1869).

information was gathered more systematically and recorded in considerable detail. The material results of this transformation were here, however, far less substantial than in other regions of the subcontinent and also in the Eastern Indian macro-region itself. According to an India Office report, Orissa accounted for less than 5 per cent of the road mileage constructed in the Bengal Presidency between 1848 and 1858 and for only about 2 per cent of the expenditure on these roads, though the inhabitants of the three coastal districts of Balasore, Cuttack and Puri alone were believed to make up for almost 8 per cent of the presidency's population (see table 4).[56]

The 1850s and 1860s were not least the decades when elsewhere in India railway construction accelerated rather than slowed down by the insurrection of 1857, took off, when British capital entered the continent in considerable proportions for the first time (much

TABLE 4: Road construction in the Bengal Presidency, 1848–1858

		Roads constructed (km)	Expenditure (1,000 Rs)
First Class Roads	Bengal	104	1,099
	Orissa	0	0
Second and Third Class Roads	Bengal	6,201	1,234
	Orissa	304	51
Total	Bengal	**6,305**	**2,333**
	Orissa	**304**	**51**

Source: Calculated from data given in: British Parliamentary Papers 1859 (92. Sess. 1) xix.285, "Roads and navigable canals opened since 1848". Submitted by W. T. Thornton, India Office, Public Works Department, 25 February 1859. The exact accounting period is not given, but is here assumed to include the year 1858.

[56] No reliable population data are, of course, available for this period but it was held in colonial circles that the inhabitants of the Bengal Presidency amounted to 40 million while those of the three districts of the Cuttack Division were reckoned at 3 million. Both figures were, according to more recent calculations, too low. Since Orissa's share of the presidency's population cannot be established with any pretence of statistical accuracy, the quoted percentage gives no more and no less than a rough idea of the proportions. Visaria and Visaria, "Population (1757–1947)", 489, 529; Mohanty, "Orissa Famine of 1866", 57; Hunter, *The Annals of Rural Bengal*, appendix, 3: 5–6, 37, 76, 122–23.

of it attracted by the prospect of guaranteed dividends from railway investment).[57] It was also when Marx was induced to predict (somewhat too optimistically, as we know today) that the British rulers, for all the barbarism inherent in capitalism, could no longer deny India the progress of its productive forces.[58] As for Orissa, Stephenson's 1845 draft of an Indian railway system had included a Calcutta–Madras railroad along the subcontinent's east coast and thus across the coastal districts of Orissa (see map 2). However, Lord Dalhousie considered this line superfluous in his famous minute of 1853 and its construction was, as we shall see later in detail, repeatedly postponed until the 1890s.[59]

Yet, even if no railway lines were to be laid in Orissa for the time being, mid-nineteenth century 'public works' policy did not consist merely in filling record rooms with longwinded proceedings on various schemes of transforming the region's built environment. The major changes of direction that were to determine the development of Orissa's circulatory regime and transport infrastructure for several decades were decided upon well before the famine and were thus not causally connected with this catastrophe. The context of this transformation of dominant socio-spatial practice was, in the main, constituted rather by general tendencies in the economy and polity of colonialism in India as a whole than by specific regional conditions. Three aspects of the colonial regime's efforts to conceive and dominate Indian social space acquired particular importance for the development of Orissa's circulatory regime:

(a) an increasingly aggressive policy of imperial expansion in the years preceding the insurrection of 1857, which favoured the annexation of princely states;[60]
(b) an invigorated general drive towards cash crop production and the spatial integration of agricultural markets after the end of the agrarian depression of the 1830s and 1840s, which entailed a growing colonial interest in agricultural "improvement" including both irrigation and transport infrastructure;[61]

---

[57] Kerr, *Building the Railways of the Raj*, 17–18, 37–43, 211. Also see chapter 3 of the present study.
[58] Karl Marx, "Die künftigen Ergebnisse der britischen Herrschaft in Indien" (first publ. 1853), in *MEW* (Berlin: Dietz, 1960), 9: 222–26.
[59] Dalhousie, Minute to the Court of Director, 20 April 1853, item 174, 2: 42–43.
[60] Bayly, *Indian Society and Making of British Empire*, 133–34.
[61] Ibid., 128–32.

(c) the particular assistance offered by the colonial administration to Lancashire's textile industry in developing alternative sources of cotton supply in the run-up to and during the US Civil War.[62]

Turning to the first of these aspects, we find that the prevailing mode of studying railway development without considering the wider context of circulatory regimes and transport infrastructure (see chapter 3) has led many historians to neglect or overlook a crucial element of colonial 'public works' policy in the mid-nineteenth century. For, the "take-off" phase of Indian railway construction went along with systematic efforts to create an "imperial" road system.[63] Though reliable statistical information is hard to come by, MacGeorge estimated that 30,000 miles of road were constructed in the decade after 1848 of which 5,000 miles were metalled and bridged and that this more energetic phase went on, at least in some regions, for another fifteen years.[64] In 1857, Governor-General Lord Canning sent out a circular clarifying a new road policy, which was clearly complementary to the railway policy outlined in his predecessor Lord Dalhousie's famous minute to the East India Company's Court of Directors (cf. chapter 3). If railway trunk lines were to connect the main hubs of strategic interest on the subcontinent, a "network of Imperial roads" was to link up all districts under British rule. These roads were, in distinction to "local roads", to be managed and funded by the central government. "Imperial roads" were to be "well kept", to pass through the collectorate's "station" and the main centres of a district and connect it with all neighbouring districts. The potential commercial benefits were highlighted in particular, but the political and military advantages of improving communications between the headquarters of the key units of colonial administration had surely been considered, too. The circular was also sent to the commissioner and the collectors of Cuttack

---

[62] Indian cotton exports rose from about 60,000 tons in 1858 to almost 280,000 tons in 1866. Kirti N. Chaudhuri, "Foreign Trade and Balance of Payments (1757–1947)", in *The Cambridge Economic History of India*, 2: 849.

[63] Though these changes were noted by the geographers Varady and Munsi back in the 1970s, they appear to have attracted little attention among historians. See, for example, Varady "North Indian Banjaras", 5–6; Munsi, *Geography of Transportation in Eastern India*, 27.

[64] MacGeorge, *Ways and Works*, 104. Also see Varady, "Rail and Road Transport in Nineteenth-Century Awadh", 40.

Division who were ordered to provide detailed information on the road situation in their jurisdictions—information which was required for drawing up an "Imperial road scheme" for Bengal.[65] The state of 'public works' and especially of roads in this presidency was certainly a hotly debated problem of colonial administration and engineering in these days as is witnessed by the 1857–58 proceedings of the Institution of Civil Engineers in London.[66] The governor-general's declaration of a new road policy was, however, rather a contribution to a process already underway than its initiation. In Orissa, colonial officials had by then been reviewing the situation of transport infrastructure and the demand for means of circulation for years, and several new projects were in preparation or under construction.[67]

Turning to the roadworks that were planned and executed from the 1850s up to the Great Famine of 1866, *three categories of schemes can be distinguished*:[68]

(i) the metalling of the Jagannath or Orissa Trunk Road,
(ii) the construction of inland routes towards the Garhjats and Central India, and
(iii) the construction of local roads in the Orissa plains.

As to the *first category*, the commissioner had stressed the urgency of reconstructing the road in 1853.[69] The Government of India had supported his view and a proposal for metalling the Orissa Trunk Road had been submitted for sanction to the Court of Directors

[65] OSA, BoRLR 27,539 (W. E. Baker, Secry. to GoI, PWD, to A. R. Young, Secry. to GoB, 17 April 1857); and (Secry. to GoB, PWD, to G. F. Cockburn, CoCD, 9 May 1857). Also see Munsi, *Geography of Transportation in Eastern India*, 27.
[66] Tremenhere, *On Public Works in Bengal Presidency*.
[67] OSA, BoRLR 26,568 (H. Dixon, Offg. EE Cuttack Division, to H. Goodwyn, CE Lower Provinces, 14 June 1855); OSA, BoRLR 26,607 (letter to H. Goodwyn, CE Lower Provinces, 3 August 1855); OSA, BoRLR 26,977 (R. N. Shore, Collector of Cuttack, to E. A. Samuels, CoCD, 23 May 1856); OSA, BoRLR 27,091 (A. S. Annaud, Collector of Cuttack, to E. A. Samuels, CoCD, 17 May 1855); OSA, BoRLR 26,979 (letter to Secry. to GoB, Judicial Dpt., 25 October 1856).
[68] For a list and classification of roads in Orissa at the onset of the Great Famine, see OIOC, BPWP January 1864, P/16/66, Com., no. 39, app. i–ii, 114–20 ("Statement of Imperial and Local Roads in Bengal").
[69] OSA, BoRLR 26,568 (H. Dixon, Offg. EE Cuttack Division, to H. Goodwyn, CE Lower Provinces, 14 June 1855).

by 1856.[70] This project, which implied considerable expenditure, was deferred and reconsidered time and again, was actually commenced in 1861–62[71] and completed only after another decade.[72] This most important road of the region connected the densely populated, agriculturally most productive and directly governed districts of coastal Orissa and passed through all of its major centres of population and administration. Nonetheless, it was only brought up to the hailed "scientific standards" of British engineering after many years of excruciatingly slow progress, giving a clear indication of the low priority this region had in imperial road policy. During the insurrection of 1857–58, the Orissa plains proved to be a smooth and safe backwater. From the colonial regime's perspective, they required comparatively less investment in strategic communications, while other regions were apparently more attractive under economic considerations.

The construction of the *second category of roads*, those from Cuttack to Garhjat states and further on to Central India, was originally connected to the more aggressive policy pursued by the colonial regime against Indian princely states—a policy that was also felt in Orissa. Angul was annexed by the British in 1847 after protracted conflicts with the raja while the extensive territory of Sambalpur was taken over two years later in pursuance of Dalhousie's "doctrine of lapse".[73] The construction of the so-called "Ungool Road" north of the Mahanadi (see map 7) was clearly related to newly emerging administrative tasks and revenue prospects in these two

---

[70] OSA, BoRLR 26,979 (letter to Secry. to GoB, Judicial Dpt., 25 October 1856).
[71] *Report Showing Progress Made ... in Public Works under Bengal Government, 1861–62*, 104 (report by T. Armstrong, SE Cuttack Circle, 15 May 1862).
[72] *Progress Report of the Public Works Department, Bengal (Building and Road Branch)* for 1871–72, n.p., 1872, 21. (Also see paragraph 12 of the appended "Memorandum to accompany the Annual Report of Appropriation and Outlay on Provincial Public Works in Bengal for the year 1871–72"); OSA, R III-1/707B, GAROD 1872–73, 34; Nayak, *Development of Transport and Communication*, 31.
[73] L. S. S. O'Malley, *Bengal District Gazetteers: Angul* (Calcutta: Bengal Secretariat Book Depot, 1908), 20–21; L. S. S. O'Malley, *Bengal District Gazetteers: Sambalpur* (Calcutta: Bengal Secretariat Book Depôt, 1909), 27–28. The "doctrine of lapse" provided for the annexation of every princely state whose ruler died without a male heir.

large Garhjat states. This channel of circulation was formed between 1853 and 1855 and linked up Cuttack with the headquarters of the two newly acquired districts.[74] This road was virtually Orissa's only considerable 'public work' of transport in the decade after 1848: it made up for over 90 per cent of the total road length constructed in that period and for almost two thirds of the expenditure on road construction.[75] In 1857–58, when the limits of the Company's power were exposed in wide areas of North and Central India, the low intensity of circulation in the "Tributary Mehals" even proved to be a boon for the British: they proved to be an efficient "breakwater", a *cordon sanitaire* against the spread of insurgency towards the East despite some local insurrections, namely in Sambalpur.[76]

The next impulse for road development in this region was provided by the formidable industrial interests of Lancashire and their apprehensions of a "cotton scarcity", which would bring their textile mills to a grinding halt by cutting off their supplies with raw cotton wool—a scenario that became even more fearful after the outbreak of the American Civil War. As early as in February 1861, a resolution of the Governor-General in Council ordered the institutions of "local government" to report on practicable schemes for creating such infrastructures of transport as would render possible a massive increase of raw cotton exports to England from the next season onwards. Canning clarified that the

> attention of Government is already directed to promote these works to the utmost extent compatible with its financial means, and even so serious a calamity as an apprehension of a short supply of Cotton in

---

[74] OIOC, BPWP January 1863, P/16/61, Com., no. 90, 50–52 (T. Armstrong, SE Cuttack Circle, to Offg. CE Bengal). That expenditure on this road was mainly motivated by its providing access to "government estates" is explicitly stated in OIOC, BPWP November 1867, P/432/47, Com., no. 5, 4–6 (A. G. Crommelin, Offg. SE Cuttack Circle, to CE Bengal, 14 September 1867); and no. 7, 7 (F. H. Rundall, Joint-Secretary to GoB, PWD, to Offg. SE, Cuttack Circle, 23 November 1867); OIOC, BPWP February 1873, P/200, Com., nos. 22–26, 12 (report by T. E. Ravenshaw, CoCD, on Garhjat Roads). Also see OIOC, BPWP June 1868, P/432/50, Com., nos. 59–61, 55–62; OIOC, BPWP September 1872, P/194, Com., nos. 10–3, 6–8.

[75] British Parliamentary Papers 1859 (92. Sess. 1) xix.285, "Roads and navigable canals opened since 1848".

[76] Cf.: Praharaj, *Tribal Movements and Political History in India*, 53; Sahu *Princely States of Orissa under British Crown*, 5–6.

England, could hardly add to the desire of the Government of India to advance them as rapidly as possible.

The character of the required works was specified as follows:

> No measure will meet the object immediately in view unless it shall tell on the production of Cotton during the next season, and on our means of getting that season's crop to port. This limitation will exclude from present consideration such projects as Railways or Canals, which although the surest permanent means of increasing our power of export, could be made to tell to only a very limited degree on the exports of the next few seasons. ... It is by facilitating existing means of communication, even though it be in a rough way, that Government can best aid the merchant promptly without exceeding its legitimate functions. Projects for bridged and metalled roads are not practicable within the next year or eighteen months; but there is a great extent of country capable of producing cotton, which is now not easily accessible to ordinary country carts, even during the fair season; and probably it is by improving the present country cart and pack bullock tracks and thus extending the mileage over which an ordinary load of Cotton may be conveyed at a rate of 2 ½ or three miles per hour, that the export of the next season's crop may be most effectually aided.[77]

Three of India's most productive cotton districts were located in Central India. Considerable proportions of their crops had been transported to Western India's Konkani Coast even earlier. Canning's *ad hoc* road scheme, the completion of railway links and the construction of an extensive system of metalled feeder roads boosted the export of raw cotton from these districts via Bombay in the course of the 1860s.[78] Early in this decade, however, one of these cotton districts, Raipur, seemed to be more easily accessible from coastal Orissa, and it was for this reason that the old route along the southern bank of the Mahanadi was now improved from Cuttack to Binika, a little beyond Sonepur. From there a new link road was constructed to Sohela, a village located on the Sambalpur–Raipur Road. The expenditure on this so-called "Cotton Road" amounted to Rs 126,000. One major task consisted in opening out

---

[77] OIOC, BPWP July 1861, P/16/52, Com., no. 18, 14–16 (Governor-General's Resolution, 28 February 1861).

[78] Cf.: Amalendu Guha, "Raw Cotton of Western India, 1750–1850", *Indian Economic and Social History Review* 9, no. 1, 1972, 1–42; Laxman D. Satya, *Cotton and Famine in Berar, 1850–1900* (Delhi: Manohar, 1997), 141–51.

the Barmul ("Baramu") defile which had so far been an insurmountable barrier for the through traffic of carts on the Mahanadi route. Up to 1,500 coolies were now employed on this site alone.[79] The combined length of the new "Cotton Road" (up to Sonepur) and the Cuttack–Angul–Sambalpur route amounted to roughly 500 km. Consequently, almost 28 per cent of the so-called "imperial branch roads" in the Bengal Presidency ran through Cuttack Division in 1864—a rather disproportionate share.[80]

The Angul Road, however, which had been constructed, as we have seen, at considerable cost less than a decade earlier, fell into neglect as soon as the "Cotton Road" project was embanked upon:

---

[79] OIOC, BPWP July 1861, P/16/52, Com., no. 31, 38–39 (report by F. Bond, EE Cuttack, 15 April 1861); OIOC, BPWP July 1861, P/16/52, Com., no. 36, 41 (C. B. Young, Secry. to GoB, PWD, to SE Cuttack Circle, 3 July 1861); OIOC, BPWP January 1862, P/16/56, Com., no. 164, 126–33 (memo from T. Armstrong, SE Cuttack Circle, to Offg. CE Bengal, 22 November 1861); OIOC, BPWP January 1862, P/16/56, Com., no. 167, 135 (sanction of construction of "Cotton Road" by GoB); OIOC, BPWP April 1862, P/16/57, Com., no. 116, 75 (T. Armstrong, SE Cuttack Circle, to Offg. CE Bengal, 9 April 1862); OIOC, BPWP April 1862, P/16/57, Com., No. 281, 190–95 (T. Armstrong, SE Cuttack Circle, to Offg. CE Bengal, 7 April 1862); *Report Showing Progress Made ... in Public Works under Bengal Government* for 1861–62, 106–11 (report by T. Armstrong, SE Cuttack Circle, 15 May 1862); OIOC, BPWP December 1862, P/16/59, Com., no. 95, 83–88 (T. Armstrong, SE Cuttack Circle, to Offg. CE Bengal, 15 November 1862); OIOC, BPWP December 1862, P/16/59, Com., no. 98, 95 (J. P. Beadle, Offg. Secry. to GoB, PWD, to SE Cuttack Circle, 10 December 1782); OIOC, BPWP March 1863, P/16/61, Com., no. 44, 26–28 (T. Armstrong, SE Cuttack Circle, to GoB); *Report Showing the Progress Made ... in Imperial Public Works under the Bengal Government for 1862–63*, (Calcutta: Calcutta Gazette Office, 1863), 97–101 (T. Armstrong, SE, report on Cuttack Circle, 26 May 1863); OIOC, BPWP February 1873, P/200, Com., nos. 22–26, 11 (report by T. E. Ravenshaw, CoCD, on Garhjat Roads). Various relevant letters are to be found in OIOC, BPWP January 1875, P/200, Com., nos. 1–6, 1–4; OIOC, BPWP September 1875, P/200, Com., nos. 3–5, 3–6. The improvement of this road had already been considered before the rise in demand for Indian cotton but had received no sanction: OSA, BoRLR 28,601 (W. P. Forster, Offg. Commissioner of Sambalpur, to G. F. Cockburn, CoCD, 9 April 1859).

[80] OIOC, BPWP January 1864, P/16/66, Com., no. 39, app. v, 118 ("Statement of Imperial and Local Roads in Bengal"). In this statement, however, only 111 of the 260 km of the Cuttack–Angul–Sambalpur road were taken account of.

Early Colonialism, 'Public Works' and the Orissa Famine

its conversion into a local road and even its abandonment were under consideration from the late 1860s.[81] Moreover, plans for the "improvement" of further "Garhjat" roads, which were also to be aligned roughly along the W-ESE axis and had been under discussion from the late 1850s, were not implemented. These works were considered to be of considerable local and regional interest but were, the records leave no doubt, no major concern of the prevailing policy. The construction of a route along the valley of the Brahmani River was, for instance, discouraged since

> it is to facilitate the transit of Cotton to the seaboard that is being considered, not the improvement of routes which carry this commodity to marts or places it is consumed at, before it can reach a port of exportation.[82]

Another road of potentially great importance for regional integration (which would have connected Cuttack via Kendujhar to Chaibassa in Chota Nagpur and thereby also to North India) had been considered in the late 1850s but was not realised either.[83] Short-term extraction of raw materials to supply British industry was the goal, not the encouragement of local manufacture. These conceptions and practices of producing social space integrated mainly on a transterritorial scale ("the world market") and also within the cotton producing regions, but tended to disarticulate circulation between regions thereby enhancing the unevenness of their development. This is also borne out by the history of the Ganjam–Shankarakol road which had been completed by the

---

[81] OIOC, BPWP January 1863, P/16/61, Com., no. 90, 50–52 (T. Armstrong, SE Cuttack Circle, to Offg. CE Bengal); OIOC, BPWP November 1867, P/432/47, Com., no. 6, 6–7 (F. Bond, EE Cuttack, to SE Cuttack Circle, 15 August 1867); and no. 5, 4–6 (A. G. Crommelin, Offg. SE, Cuttack Circle, to CE Bengal, PWD, 14 September 1867); OIOC, BPWP February 1873, P/200, Com., nos. 22–26, 11–12 (report by T. E. Ravenshaw, CoCD, on Garhjat Roads).
[82] OIOC, BPWP January 1862, P/16/56, Com., no. 164, 129 (T. Armstrong, SE Cuttack Circle, to Offg. CE Bengal, 22 November 1861).
[83] OIOC, BPWP 24 September 1860, P/16/45, Com., no. 359, 306 (R. C. Birch, Senior Assistant Commissioner, Singbhoom Division, to Commissioners of Chota Nagpur, 28 July 1860); and no. 360, 307 (C. B. Young, Secry. to GoB, PWD, to Commissioner of Chota Nagpur, 24 September 1860). Also see OSA, BoRLR 28,679 (memo of "Suddanund Jachuck", Deputy Magistrate of Cuttack, 12 December 1859).

Madras Government along an old and highly frequented bullock track by the mid-1860s. In order to acquire full efficiency as a channel of the salt, grain and cotton trade between the coast of southern Orissa and Central India this route had to be extended to Sonepur, that is, through territory under the Commissioner of Cuttack. The Government of Bengal were, however, not too much interested in improved communications with Ganjam as the prevailing desolate state of traffic infrastructure worked as an effective import barrier protecting their revenues from salt manufacture. "It is supposed," wrote the Superintendent of the Tributary Mehals,

> that the people of Madras are too poor to be able to pay the same prices for their Salt as those in Bengal are compelled to do, but if true, I see no reason why the interior and central parts of India, not in Madras, should be supplied with cheap Salt to the detriment of the Government Revenue.

The construction of the short section of this road traversing the territory of the Bengal Presidency (about 80 km) was, therefore, repeatedly deferred for at least a decade, while the doctrine of non-interference with the market appeared to be of little consideration in this case.[84]

---

[84] For the quoted passage, see OIOC, BPWP August 1860, P/16/44, Com., no. 5, 5–7 (G. F. Cockburn, CoCD, to Secry. to GoB, PWD, 19 June 1860). Further evidence on this road project can be found in: OIOC, BPWP 25 May 1860, P/16/41, Com., no. 102, 442–44 (E. H. Harington, Acting District Engineer, Ganjam, to CE PWD, 17 June 1859); OIOC, BPWP December 1863, P/16/64, Com., no. 1, 1 (extract from R. N. Shore, CoCD, to Secry. to GoB, 12 June 1863); OIOC, BPWP May 1864, P/16/67, Com., no. 38, 35 (C. T. Phillips, EE Ganjam, to R. N. Shore, CoCD, 9 April 1864); OIOC, BPWP February 1865, P/16/71, Com., no. 49, 29–30 (F. B. Simson, Offg. CoCD, to Secry. to GoB, PWD, 10 February 1865); OIOC, BPWP March 1865, P/16/71, Com., no. 28–32, 16–18 (various relevant letters); OIOC, BPWP June 1865, P/16/72, Com., no. 7, 4–5 (R. N. Shore, CoCD, to Secry. to GoB, PWD, 9 May 1865); OIOC, BPWP June 1865, P/16/72, Com., no. 8, 5–6 (T. Armstrong, SE Cuttack Circle, to CoCD, 13 April 1865); OIOC, BPWP June 1865, P/16/72, Com., no. 9, 7–8 (J. E. T. Nicolls, Offg. Secry. to GoB, PWD, to Secry. to GoI, PWD, 7 June 1865). Also see the exchanges of letters between the Governments of Bengal, Madras and India in: OIOC, BPWP January 1869, P/432/54, Com., no. 16, 11; OIOC, BPWP August 1875, P/200, Com., nos. 1–2, 1–2; OIOC, BPWP November 1875, P/200, Com., no. 22, 13.

Local roads (the *third category*) were certainly even more crucial for the socio-economic, political and cultural integration of the region than metalling the Orissa Trunk Road and constructing roads towards Central India. This was clearly perceivable for contemporaries like the senior British irrigation engineer who stated before the Famine Commissioners that apart from navigable canals, "cross roads are the lines of communication most needed in this province. By cross roads I mean roads from mart to mart."[85] However, it was here that the activities of the colonial state were least energetic though several "fair-weather tracks"—i.e., raised and levelled roads for seasonal use—were improved or constructed in the years preceding the famine. This was a new departure since "[u]p to 1856 there was practically not one mile of made bye-road in either Pooree, Cuttack, or Balasore [districts]."[86] Eight years later 425 km of "local road" were recorded for Cuttack Division. This lagged, however, far behind the infrastructural developments occurring simultaneously in other parts of the Bengal Presidency in the context of the slow recovery of agricultural prices and the concomitant tendency towards commercialisation. Of the 21,527 kms of local roads existing in 1864 in the ten administrative divisions of Bengal only 2 per cent were located in Cuttack Division—all of which were unmetalled and unbridged—while the neighbouring divisions of Burdwan and Chota Nagpur accounted for 9.1 and 8.6 per cent respectively (see chart 1). One of the first local roads constructed by the colonial state in Orissa, completed in 1858, was the one from Cuttack to Aul—a place connected to Dhamra port by the Kharsua River.[87] Another simple road, about 70 kms long, was swiftly built in 1860 between Cuttack and Taldanda on the Mahanadi, not far from False Point Harbour.[88] Local road development was somewhat

---

[85] *Report of Commissioners ... Famine in Bengal and Orissa in 1866*, 1: lix (statement by Col. F. H. Rundall, Chief Engineer, East India Irrigation Company, 4 January 1867).

[86] *Report by the Chief Engineer of Bengal, on the Progress of Public Works for the Year 1860–61* (Calcutta: Savielle & Cranenburgh, 1861), app. xxi, 118 (T. Armstrong, Offg. SE Cuttack Circle, to C. B. Young, CE of Bengal, 29 May 1861).

[87] OSA, BoRLR 26,979 (letter to Secry. to GoB, Judicial Dpt., 25 October 1856); OSA, BoRLR 27,789 (J. P. Beadle, SI of Embankments, to G. F. Cockburn, CoCD, 10 July 1858).

[88] *Report by Chief Engineer of Bengal, ... 1860–61*, 17; and app. xxi, 117

more pronounced in Balasore District than in Cuttack or Puri, possibly because of its proximity to Bengal. There is evidence that the newly formed channels of communication were readily used by villagers for marketing agricultural produce and salt, which was partly exported by coastal shipping.[89]

Reconceiving a Circulatory Regime: 'Public Works' before the Famine

Up to the Orissa famine, the material results of colonial 'public works' policy were, as we have seen, mainly confined to road construction. Several phases can be distinguished: the New Jagannath or Orissa Trunk Road was reconstructed since 1813 and its southern extension completed in the 1830s; the Raipur Mail Road was the major project of the 1840s; the next decade saw the construction of a cartable road from Cuttack to the newly annexed districts of Angul and Sambalpur; "Cotton Roads" were, finally, the clear priority of the early 1860s. The focus of infrastructure policy thus kept shifting throughout this half-century, while repeated (though by no means continuous) efforts to keep constructed channels of circulation in repair are only recorded for the politically indispensable Orissa Trunk Road. Moreover, these road works were more pronounced in other regions of India since the colonial regime appears to have considered both the political risks and the economic prospects in Orissa comparatively insignificant. If the Famine Commissioners' assessment that the "whole province is geographically isolated to an excessive degree" was misleading to the extent that it

---

(T. Armstrong, Offg. SE Cuttack Circle, to C. B. Young, CE of Bengal, 29 May 1861); *Report Showing Progress Made ... in Public Works under Bengal Government for 1861–62,* 105–6 (report by T. Armstrong, SE Cuttack Circle, 15 May 1862).

[89] OIOC, BPWP 9 January 1858, P/16/19, Com., nos. 503–8 (G. F. Cockburn, CoCD, to Secry. to GoB, Judicial Dpt., 18 November 1857, and other relevant letters); OIOC, BPWP February 1858, P/16/19, Com., no. 267 (V. H. Schalch, Offg. Collector of Balasore, to G. F. Cockburn, CoCD, 31 December 1857); *Report Showing Progress Made ... in Public Works under Bengal Government for 1861–62,* 105–6, 118 (report by T. Armstrong, SE Cuttack Circle, 15 May 1862); *Report Showing Progress Made ... in Imperial Public Works under Bengal Government for 1862–63,* 180–82 (report by R. N. Shore, Offg. CoCD, on Local Works).

Early Colonialism, 'Public Works' and the Orissa Famine

suggested primordial and absolute disarticulation, it did adequately reflect the differential speed in the transformation of the circulatory regimes in the various regions of British controlled South Asia.[90] The following table, which permits a comparison of Orissa's road infrastructure in 1864 with that of other divisions of the Bengal Presidency, corroborates the notion of an uneven production of social space in colonial India, of a tendency towards a long-term "development of underdevelopment":

TABLE 5: Roads in 1864, Cuttack Division and Bengal Presidency (km and per cent)

	Imperial Roads			Local Roads	Roads (total)
	Trunk Roads	Branch Roads	Total		
Bengal Presidency (kms)	3,215	2,094	5,309	21,527	26,836
Cuttack Division (kms)	*319	*578	897	425	1,322
Cuttack Division (per cent)	9.9	27.6	16.9	2.0	4.9

* The Cuttack–Puri section of the Orissa Trunk Road was, in this statement, subsumed under the heading "Branch Roads". "Statement of Imperial and Local Roads in Bengal", OIOC: BPWP January 1864 (P/16/66), com., no. 39, app., i–ii, v, 114–20.

Table 5 also shows that road construction in Orissa was mainly confined to the two categories of "imperial roads" (that is, "trunk roads" and "branch roads"). Even a brief look on a map of the Bengal Presidency discloses that the Cuttack Division's share of 28 per cent of the "imperial branch roads" was drastically out of scale. Moreover, the proportion between these newly constructed (or reconstructed) means of interregional circulation on the one hand and the infrastructure for purposes of local and intra-regional circulation on the other diverged significantly: while local roads made up for 80 per cent of the total route mileage in the Bengal Presidency, they accounted for less than a third of that of its Cuttack Division. Chart 1 indicates correspondingly that colonial efforts in promoting circulation on the local and intra-regional scales were more marked in almost all other administrative divisions and not merely in the highly productive "rice bowls" of Bengal and Bihar or in

---

[90] *Report of Commissioners ... Famine in Bengal and Orissa in 1866*, 1: 8.

CHART 1: Local roads in the Bengal Presidency, 1864

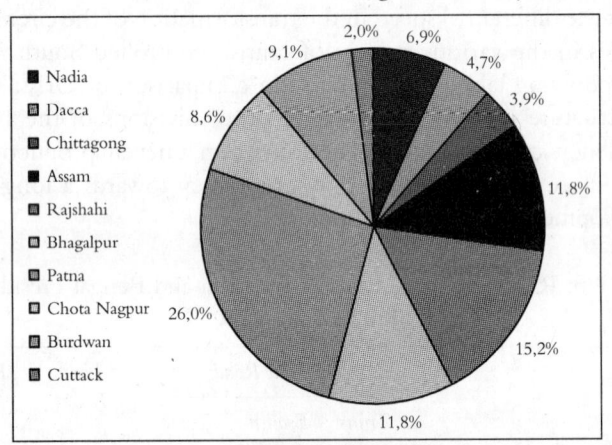

- Nadia
- Dacca
- Chittagong
- Assam
- Rajshahi
- Bhagalpur
- Patna
- Chota Nagpur
- Burdwan
- Cuttack

2,0% 6,9% 9,1% 4,7% 3,9% 8,6% 11,8% 26,0% 15,2% 11,8%

Calculated from data given in "Statement of Imperial and Local Roads in Bengal", OIOC: BPWP, January 1864(P/16/66), Com., no. 39, appendix, 118–20.

Assam, where a colonial tea plantation economy was then being established. Furthermore, Orissa's disproportionately high share of "imperial branch roads" cannot be construed into an indication for a comparatively high quality of its roads: of more than Rs 1.5 million expended on the construction of "first class" and "second class" roads in the Bengal Presidency during the decade after 1848 little more than Rs 3,000 or 0.2 per cent were allocated to this region.[91] The colonial politics of road construction in pre-famine Orissa were thus characterised by periodic, unsustained and often short-lived efforts to generate cheap channels for traversing the region for purposes of military as well as administrative communication and, by the 1860s, for draining off a strategic raw material.

Such projects became more frequent after the 1840s, when British plans and efforts for reconceiving and transforming Orissa's social space in terms of 'improvement' and 'public works' also began to expand beyond the field of road construction. Even though Dalhousie put the Calcutta–Madras railway along the shores of the Bay of Bengal on the back burner,[92] schemes for the construction of

---

[91] British Parliamentary Papers 1859 (92. Sess. 1) xix.285, "Roads and navigable canals opened since 1848".
[92] See page 206 of the present study.

railroads in Orissa continued to be framed in the 1850s.[93] A few years later, in 1865, "Messrs. Doyle & Co." applied to the Lieutenant-Governor of Bengal for the "permission to run a line of Traction Locomotive Engines, with carriages or springs, for the passenger traffic on the Midnapoor Government Road between Ooloobariah [near Calcutta] and Balasore". They planned to extend this line to Cuttack eventually.[94] There was also a "Petition of the Inhabitants of Cuttack" in 1866 for the construction of a railway line between Howrah (Calcutta) and Puri[95]—a demand repeated by Abdul Ghani, a zamindar in Bhadrak and Balasore, before the Famine Commissioners early in 1867.[96] Yet the Collector and the Commissioner of Cuttack were, in 1868, concurrently of the opinion that no railway was required in Orissa for the time being.[97]

The rejection of railway schemes in the years preceding the famine preconditioned the reorganisation of Orissa's social space in

---

[93] Hence one engineer uttered as early as in 1855 that a "Tramway with light Rails and upper works, could be constructed from Midnapore to the Madras frontier". OSA, BoRLR 26,568 (H. Dixon, Offg. EE Cuttack Division, to H. Goodwyn, CE Lower Provinces, 14 June 1855). Also see OSA, BoRLR 27,532 (V. H. Schalch, Offg. Magistrate of Balasore to G. F. Cockburn, CoCD, 8 June 1857).

[94] The proposal was discouraged by the CoCD T. E. Ravenshaw and consequently turned down. See various relevant letters in OIOC, BPWP October 1865, P/16/72, no. 24–27, 14–16.

[95] OIOC, BPWP March 1866, P/432/38, no. 16, 10 (petition of the inhabitants of Cuttack, to C. Beadon, Lieutenant-Governor of Bengal, 13 February 1866). The petition emphasised the importance of that line for the pilgrim traffic to Puri.

[96] *Report of Commissioners ... Famine in Bengal and Orissa in 1866*, 1: xcix (statement by Abdool Ghunnee, 22 January 1867). The construction of a "tramway" to Cuttack was also recommended by the President of the Calcutta Chamber of Commerce: ibid., clxxxviii (statement by F. Schiller, member of the firm Borradaile, Schiller & Co., President of Chamber of Commerce, Calcutta, 16 February 1867).

[97] OSA, BoRLR 14,454 (W. Macpherson, Collector of Cuttack, to T. E. Ravenshaw, CoCD, 30 March 1868); OSA, BoRLR 14,368 (T. E. Ravenshaw, CoCD, to Secry. to GoB, Judicial Dpt., 27 April 1868). However, the Collector of Balasore was in favour of an Orissa railway line. See OSA, BoRLR 15,522 (T. J. Bignold, Offg. Collector of Balasore, to CoCD, 28 March 1868); *Further Papers Relating to the Extension of Railway Communications in India*, reprint 14 of PWD records, (Calcutta: PWD Press, 1868), 3: 221–23 (T. E. Ravenshaw, CoCD, to Offg. Joint Secry. to GoB, PWD, Railway Branch, 27 April 1868).

subsequent decades as much as the debates on the 'improvement' of its rivers and the promotion of inland navigation. Though no major canal works were completed before the Great Famine of 1866, the fundamental decisions then taken generated the parameters of colonial infrastructure policy in this region up to the end of the century. Two large-scale schemes were considered from the late 1850s, of which only one was realised. The other project was buried in the records[98] but is still of considerable interest as it aimed at reinforcing the commercial intercourse with Central India by facilitating navigation on the Mahanadi. The Superintending Engineer of Cuttack examined about 450 km of this river in 1861 and concluded that "its rocky bed," extending over more than 200 km could never be rendered safe for navigation. Yet he remarked that a "loop river, or canal navigation" was "perfectly practicable".[99] Richard Temple, then Officiating Chief Commissioner of the Central Provinces, undertook another survey journey along the Sheonath and Mahanadi rivers early in 1863. He submitted a detailed report and an elaborate scheme which mainly consisted in excavating a canal parallel to the left bank of the Mahanadi and in creating reservoirs for surplus water during the monsoon, which could be utilised for irrigation purposes in the dry season. For this project, 418 km of river had to be "improved" and the costs were estimated at Rs 3.5 million. Temple's main objective was to create a "cheap and easy highway in the midst of rough and rugged country" in order to promote the export of raw materials from Central India such as cotton, sugar, food grains, coal, iron and timber.[100]

This first project disappeared from the colonial agenda for good when cartable roads and later railways reduced the relative distance between Central India's "cotton districts" and Bombay, turning the direction of interregional trade even further away from Orissa. The

---

[98] According to Mukherjee (*Irrigation, Inland Navigation and Flood Problems*, 19–20), Temple's project was not executed because of the financial failure of Cotton's canal scheme (see below) after which no new large projects of this type were undertaken. Further research would have to explain, however, why this project was not realised in the decade before this financial failure became manifest.

[99] *Report Showing Progress Made ... in Public Works under the Bengal Government for 1861–62*, 111 (T. Armstrong, SE, Report on Cuttack Circle, 15 May 1862).

[100] Temple, "Report on the Mahanuddy", 34–39.

second project, however, was realised in the following decades. The debate on a canal scheme in the Orissa plains, which was to combine functions of irrigation and navigation, had started in the 1850s when Arthur Cotton, the practitioner and propagator of colonial irrigation works, was invited to conduct a survey of the Mahanadi delta. In his report (submitted in 1858) he recommended

> a complete series of works similar to those constructed on the Kistna and Godavery for regulating the rivers and affording irrigation and navigation within the [Mahanadi, Brahmani and Baitarani] deltas. He further proposed a main canal which should connect the deltas with Calcutta. He estimated the cost of these works at £1,300,000, and the area capable of irrigation at 2,250,000 acres and suggested that if Government were unable or unwilling to undertake these work[s] themselves, they should be entrusted to an English company.[101]

The Commissioner of Cuttack and the irrigation officer of Bengal supported this project—the latter expected that it might provide, apart from other advantages, an alternative to the costly metalling of the Orissa Trunk Road.[102] The larger context of the Orissa Canal Scheme consisted, however, in the recovery of agricultural prices that nurtured colonial hopes of augmenting revenue by "improving" agriculture, in the search of British capital for secure investment opportunities in India and the concomitantly growing government interest in 'public works' of irrigation and transport. Accordingly, an "East India Irrigation and Canal Company" was founded in 1860 as an offshoot of the Madras Irrigation Company, which had undertaken the large irrigation schemes in South India.[103] Unlike the old one, the new company did not succeed, however, in securing a guarantee for dividends from the colonial state and consequently encountered difficulties in attracting sufficient capital. Works made, therefore, little progress before the Famine of

---

[101] *Papers Relating to Orissa Canals (1869 to 1877 and 1881 to 1883)*, 91 (note by H. W. Gulliver, Offg. CE Bengal, Irrigation Branch, on Orissa Canals, 19 February 1875).

[102] OIOC, BPWP 25 May 1860, P/16/41, no. 76, 400–2 (G. F. Cockburn, CoCD, to J. P. Beadle, SI of Embankments, Lower Provinces, 12 July 1859); and, 403–7 (memo from J. P. Beadle, SI of Embankments, Lower Provinces, 20 June 1859).

[103] For a detailed analysis of this company's dealings, see D'Souza, "Canal Irrigation and Conundrum of Flood Protection", esp. 43–48.

1866 and when they were taken over by colonial government in 1869 merely 138 km of navigable canals had been completed: 106 kms of canals providing a channel of circulation between Cuttack and the sea throughout the year and 32 km of the "High Level Canal" that was undertaken with the objective of connecting Cuttack with Calcutta.[104] Another artificial watercourse—a canal between Chilka Lake and Ganjam—had been in consideration from the mid-1850s but was taken up only in 1866 as a famine relief work.[105]

The following decades saw the materialisation of more substantial built environments for purposes of transport and there were also further important shifts in colonial infrastructure policy that will be discussed in the remaining chapters of this study. However, the colonial regime's general approach towards conceiving Orissa's circulatory regime and hence towards imposing another 'layer' upon the region's social space had already taken shape in the years preceding the catastrophe of 1866—an approach endorsed, on the whole, by the Famine Commissioners.[106] Thus three implicit yet fundamental principles appear to have underlain colonial "public works" policy in subsequent decades:[107]

First, the priority of road construction and particularly of the construction of local or village roads remained low throughout the period in comparison with the other parts of the macro-region, even though investment in this type of transport infrastructure picked up in absolute terms. This resulted in long-term regional

---

[104] *Papers Relating to Orissa Canals (1869 to 1877 and 1881 to 1883)*, 91 (note by H. W. Gulliver, Offg. CE Bengal, Irrigation Branch, on Orissa Canals, 19 February 1875). For a detailed and accurate account, see Nayak, *Development of Transport and Communication*, 180–93. Also see "The Orissa Irrigation Project", *The Statesman and Friend of India*, 22 June 1882.

[105] OIOC, BPWP August 1866, P/432/41, Com., nos. 6–8, 12–17 (various relevant letters).

[106] The Commissioners thus displayed a general preference of railways to roads, recommended the expansion of already existent railways (of which there were none in Orissa) and the construction of navigable canals in regions where major irrigation works were being implemented (which applied to Orissa). *Report of Commissioners . . . Famine in Bengal and Orissa in 1866*, 1: 161–62.

[107] Sources for the following concluding paragraphs are, unless indicated in the footnotes, presented at length in chapter 7.

disparities, in a "development of underdevelopment" with regard to road transport.

Second, in marked difference to many other regions of British India, the colonial government gave priority not to railways but to an extensive scheme of partly navigable irrigation canals. Started by a British joint stock company, this project was taken over by the state in 1869 and continued to absorb much of the resources the colonial regime was prepared to invest in Orissa's built environment. Prioritising canals thus meant postponing railway construction for decades and reducing the scope for roadworks even further. Moreover, since the Orissa canals never yielded the projected financial returns, this priority resulted in a further intensification of regional disparities.

Third, the balance of government decisions as to which schemes were to be implemented, shelved or postponed displays a distinct geographical pattern. While the Angul and Cotton roads were allowed to relapse into an indifferent state soon after their construction,[108] while Temple's scheme to "improve" the Mahanadi was consigned to oblivion, major investments in two parallel channels of circulation traversing the coastal districts of Orissa were sanctioned: (a) the High Level Canal along the western margin of the coastal plains and (b) the metalling of the similarly aligned Orissa Trunk Road. This added up to an invigoration of the axis extending from the northeast to the southwest along the shore line. It implied, at the same time, a loss of relative importance of Orissa's other axis of *ancien régime* circulation, the axis running from Central and North India in the west across the Garhjats to the coastal districts of the Cuttack Division in the east-southeast (cf. chapter 4). This invigoration of the NE-SW axis was further exacerbated by later infrastructural schemes, which resulted in three competing lines along this axis all of which were at length marginalised after the opening of the (identically aligned) East Coast Railway in the final years of the century. This spatial reorganisation amounted to Orissa's reorientation towards Calcutta, the centre of imperial administration and hub of colonial extraction. The dynamics and contradictions of this socio-spatial process will be discussed in the following chapter.

---

[108] OIOC, BPWP September 1875, P/200, Com., nos. 3–5, 3–6; and July 1877, P/915, Com., nos. 3–9, 2–13; OSA, R III-1/707B, GAROD 1875–76, 26. Also see footnote 81, in this chapter.

7

Circulation and Infrastructure in the Times of Colonial Capitalism

The production of social space is a multi-authored, accumulative process and thus irreducible to a single and unambiguously datable act of volition. It is, therefore, less than surprising that the general notion of the year 1866 as the turning point in the development of Orissa's transport infrastructure and, by extension, as the "delivery date" of the region's "modern" circulatory regime does not withstand empirical scrutiny. This conventional notion should rather be understood as one of the "heroic illusions" (or lies of life) from which the colonial oligarchy drew legitimacy and motivation. It is unsustainable because the main direction of the transformation of Orissa's circulatory regime was determined, as we have seen, in a process going back to the 1850s. The available evidence is also rather contradictory as to the intensity of infrastructural change in the immediate aftermath of the catastrophic famine of 1866. The Bengal Government thus had congratulated itself in 1877 on having achieved in that region a "striking development in the means of communication" in merely one decade.[1] This view, however, was not shared by the officials overseeing the administration of infrastructure. "Since the famine of 1865–66 in Orissa, actually nothing has been done to improve the means of communication with the province", wrote the chief executive of the Bengal Public Works Department in 1879 to his superior in the Government of India.[2]

---

[1] OSA, R III-1/707B, GoB, General Dpt., Resolution, 18 September 1877, 2.
[2] *Papers Relating to the Orissa Coast Canal* [1877 to 1881], in *Selections from the Records of the Government of India in the Public Works Department* (Calcutta: Bengal Secretariat Press, 1885), 98 (H. C. Levinge, Joint Secry. to GoB, PWD, Irrigation Branch, to Secry. to GoI, PWD, 28 April 1879). Also see *Papers Relating to Orissa Coast Canal* [1869 to 1877 and 1881 to 1883], 74 (Note by Lieutenant J. W. Ottley, Royal Engineers, 10 December 1874).

Yet the first-quoted view does not merely exemplify the colonial regime's inclination to complacency and need for self-legitimation. It is also a reflection of the considerable transformation of the region's circulatory regime—a transformation taking place *before* the major schemes of infrastructure development acquired reality. This chapter thus commences with a brief survey of the overall changes in the circulatory regime of the Orissa plains in the latter third of the nineteenth century.[3] The dominant spatial practices of generating large-scale 'public works' of transport in this area will be explored subsequently.

Commercialisation and the Circulatory Regime

When celebrating the "striking development in the means of communication" in 1877, the Government of Bengal referred mainly to the growth of Orissa's *maritime* traffic and trade, which was indeed impressive in this decade (see charts 2–4). Two infrastructural schemes of the post-famine years had no doubt facilitated this growth. First, the construction of the Kendrapara Canal (completed in 1869) provided a cheap waterway throughout the year between the regional capital of Cuttack at the apex of the Mahanadi Delta, the core areas of rice production further downstream and the delta's tidal estuaries. The canal thus constituted a permanent traffic link between Cuttack and the roadstead of False Point, which was rendered more direct and convenient when its extension to Jambu on the coast was opened in 1881. Its Patamundai and Gobri branch lines—constructed in the early 1870s and headed towards the north of the delta—facilitated the transportation and reduced shipment costs of agriculture produce to the traditional anchorage of Dhamra on the river of the same name and, most crucially, to Chandbali on the Baitarani, which emerged as Orissa's premier commercial port of the period.[4] Second, the metalling of the Orissa Trunk Road,

---

[3] Developments in the hilly areas of interior Orissa will be discussed in chapter 8.
[4] Nayak and other authors mention the Taldanda Canal from Cuttack to Paradip as an alternative waterway was constructed in the same period. The final sections, which would have connected this canal with the tidal waters, remained, however, unfinished well beyond the mid-1870s. OIOC, BPWP January 1869 (IOR P/432/54), Com., nos. 41–43, 24–26; OSA, R III-1/707B, GAROD 1872–73, 10, 32; and GAROD 1873–74, 14; and

commenced before the famine and completed by 1872, permitted wheeled traffic along the coastal plains thereby reducing intra-regional transport costs to a considerable extent.[5] Hence, three registering stations on the Orissa Trunk Road counted 99,068 loaded bullocks and 20,955 loaded carts between August 1883 and January 1884. Assuming a normal load of 250 lbs for a bullock and of 1,500 lb for a cart, the implication of this count was that the latter had surpassed the former as the predominant means of bulk transport on this road (14,000 as opposed to 11,000 lt).[6] Another count, conducted in Khurda from January to December 1879, showed that carts had virtually displaced bullocks on the trade route between Cuttack and Ganjam (16,000 as opposed to 500 lt).[7]

These infrastructural measures were necessary but not sufficient conditions for the massive growth of maritime trade and traffic. Its chief cause can rather be found in the changing conditions of agriculture—another case in point for the inextricable interdependence of circulation and production. After the famine of 1866, the land revenue settlement of 1837, which applied to the major part of the Cuttack Division, was extended on the same terms for a further thirty years. As agricultural prices were rising (they doubled in Cuttack District between the decades 1837–46 and 1887–96), the unchanged revenue assessment created incentives for an expansion of commercial, market-oriented agricultural production promising gains to certain sections of rural society.[8] Recurrent food crises in

---

GAROD 1874–75, 6; and GAROD 1875–76, 16; OSA R III-1/709, GAROD 1881–82, 18, 20–21, 54. Mukherjee, *Irrigation, Inland Navigation and Flood Problems*, 31; Nayak, *Development of Transport and Communication*, 186–95.

[5] *Progress Report of Public Works Department, Bengal (Building and Road Branch)*, for 1871–72, 21 (see also paragraph 12 of the appended "Memorandum to accompany the Annual Report of Appropriation and Outlay on Provincial Public Works in Bengal for the year 1871–72"); OSA, R III-1/707B, GAROD 1872–73, 34; Nayak, *Development of Transport and Communication*, 31.

[6] OSA, R III-1/710, GAROD 1883–84, 13. The three stations were located in Rani Talao, Nuniajori and Rajghat (on the Subarnarekha). The calculation of the volume of transported goods is based on Amalendu Guha's figures for average loads of bullocks and carts in Central India. Guha, "Raw Cotton of Western India", 21.

[7] OIOC, BPWP February 1884, P/2231, Railway, no. 1, 4 (report on a possible route of a railway line from Vishakapatnam to Cuttack).

[8] Sakti Padhi, "Property in Land, Land Market and Tenancy Relations in the Colonial Period: A Review of Theoretical Categories and Study of a

CHART 2: Orissa's maritime imports, exports and rice trade, 1868–69 to 1909–10

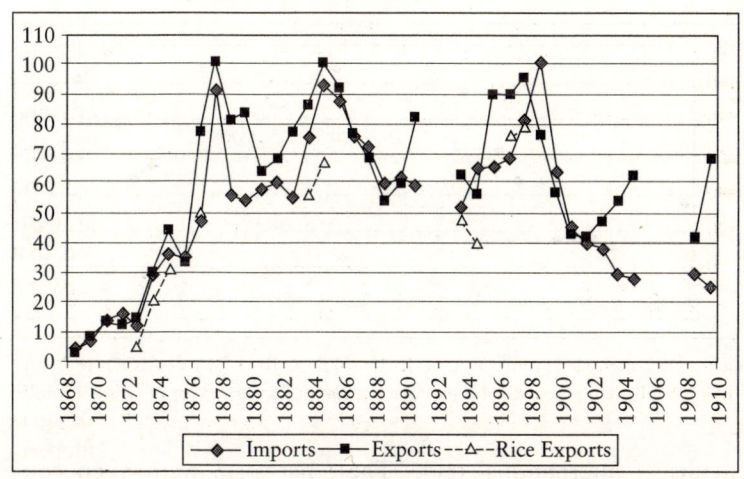

— Imports — Exports --△-- Rice Exports

(in Rs 100,000)

Source: Data compiled from OSA, R III-1/707B-R III-1/718 GAROD 1873/74–1899/1990 and various resolutions of the Goverment of Bengal on these reports; Nayak, *Development of Transport and Communication*, 156, 158, 163, 165.[9]

other Indian regions (especially the severe famine of 1876–78 in south and western India, a scarcity in 1884 in parts of Bengal and another devastating famine in several regions of the subcontinent in 1896–97) further increased sea exports of rice from Orissa (see charts 2 and 3).

Moreover, these periods of excessive demand for food grains appear to have provided the occasion for the establishment of durable commercial infrastructures, which linked up the region to

---

Zamindari District", in *Essays on the Commercialization of Agriculture*, ed. K. N. Raj et al. (Delhi: Oxford University Press [for the] Centre for Development Studies [Trivandrum], 1985), 39; Patnaik, *Famine and Some Aspects of British Economic Policy in Orissa*, 78–83. Also see Jit, *The Agrarian Life*, 214–15.

[9] Nayak's figures are drawn from records of the Bengal Government and are, when referring to the same years, identical or only marginally different from those in the Orissa Administration Reports used by the present writer. No continuous time series can be presented for the volume of rice exports but even the available data indicate (a) a strong correlation in the fluctuations of total maritime exports and of maritime rice exports and (b) that the total value of exports was made up by rice to a large extent.

CHART 3: Orissa's maritime rice exports, 1865–66 to 1897–98
(in lt 1,000)[10]

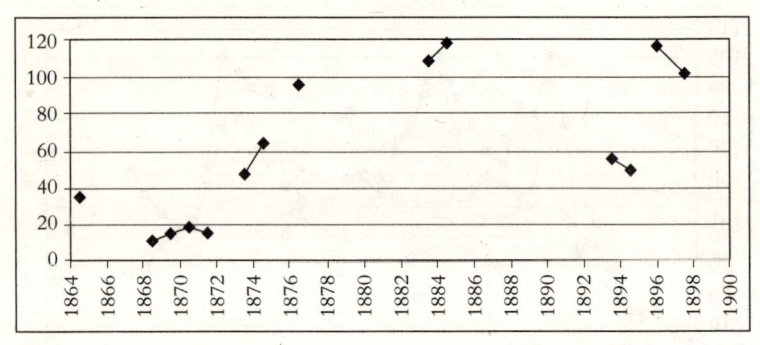

Source: Data compiled from OSA, R III–1/707B–R III–1/718 GAROD 1873/74–1896/1897; Patnaik, *Famine and Some Aspects of British Economic Policy in Orissa*, 17, 189.

circuits of interregional trade. These networks were often controlled by Marwaris and other merchants from western India, Andhra or Bengal, while Oriya traders generally acted as middlemen.[11] By and by the circuits of exchange extended into the Tributary Mehals where the growth of transregional rice trade was said to induce "a large increase of cultivation and commerce."[12] Rice accounted for the largest part of Orissa's sea export trade by far and the rest was comprised of various other raw materials such as oil seeds, hides and timber.[13] Imports, which increased in a similar proportion, consisted mainly of manufactured commodities some of which, namely salt and textiles, had been major export items of pre-

---

[10] Even though the bulk of maritime rice exports was recorded only occasionally in the reports used in this study, the available data indicate that the export of 34,000 lt of rice in 1864–65, which had been considered excessive at the time and one of the causes of the following famine, was surpassed after the mid-1870s even in years when crops and demand were moderate, while maritime rice exports could shoot up to almost 120,000 lt in years of scarcity or famine in other regions of the subcontinent.

[11] OSA, R III–1/707B, GAROD 1875–76, 10–11; and GAROD 1876–77, 8–10; OSA, R III–1/710, GAROD 1883–84, 10.

[12] OSA, R III–1/708, GAROD 1878–79, 13. Also see OSA, R III–1/710, GAROD 1883–84, 10.

[13] See, for example, OSA, R III–1/707B, GAROD 1875–76, 10; OSA, R III–1/709, GAROD 1880–81, 20.

colonial Orissa.[14] As for the spatial alignment of this circuit of exchange, 78 per cent of the region's maritime trade was with Calcutta in the four years between 1873–74 and 1876–77: all of its imports and almost two thirds of its exports.[15]

The region's closer integration with subcontinental and even transcontinental markets was thus accompanied by its being fixed to the place of a provider of natural produce in the hierarchical spatial division of labour inherent in colonial capitalism. "The trade of the district," wrote the Collector of Cuttack in 1878, "may be said to consist in the exchange of agricultural products in their raw state for foreign manufactures, metal, and articles of luxury. The staple export is rice, and all others even collectively are unimportant".[16] Risks of this reliance on one export commodity—a commodity whose availability fluctuated strongly according to even minor climatic variations—were understood and admitted by some British officials in times of crisis. "The danger of this district, as of all Orissa," wrote the Collector of Puri in 1883,

> lies in the fact that the people risk all their chances on the one single venture of rice. For all practical purposes the district has no manufactures, and has rice for its sole agricultural produce and only article of commerce. Therefore, when rice fails everything fails, and the district is left bare and destitute of all resources.... As long as the prosperity of the place hangs upon one single thread, it does not seem to me that progress can ever be more than intermittent, and must always be liable to relapses; and this single thread is peculiarly liable to disaster, for a rice crop is not a thing that can ever be counted upon in a country so unusually liable to both drought and flood as is Orissa. I am quite convinced that if progress made in Orissa is ever to be finally secured and maintained, it must be by the introduction of other agricultural products and by manufactures.[17]

Yet, such reasonings had little impact on government policy. Even what was considered Orissa's only major item of manufacture—salt—continued to be burdened with high taxes and was perceived a "dying business" by 1883 as it was displaced by cheaper

---

[14] See p. 230. For precolonial patterns of transregional trade, see chapter 4.
[15] *Papers Relating to Orissa Coast Canal* [1877 to 1881], 10 (Note by Colonel F. T. Haig, CE, Bengal PWD, Irrigation Branch, 15 February 1878).
[16] OSA, R III-1/708, GAROD 1878–79, 19.
[17] OSA, R III-1/709, GAROD 1882–83, 11–12. Also see GAROD 1881–82, 12; OSA, R III-1/708, GAROD 1878–79, 11.

Ganjam and Liverpool salt not only on the markets of neighbouring regions but also as a source of internal consumption.[18] By the 1890s, all salt aurangs in the districts of Balasore and Cuttack had been closed while the production of karkatch salt continued on the shores of the Chilka Lake in Puri District on a small scale.[19] Textiles, as we have seen, had ceased to be a major item of export even before the onset of colonial rule in Orissa, but it was cheap Lancashire and Bombay fabrics that came to be used now by "almost all classes of the people" in place of domestically produced cloth. Many artisans appear to have moved into agriculture, though some specialised muslin weavers held to their own while others adapted themselves to the use of industrially produced yarn.[20] Most importantly, a long term tendency in agrarian production towards a monoculture of rice extended well into the twentieth century. If rice fields made up for 88 per cent of the net cropped area of Cuttack District in 1897, this share rose even further to 93 per cent in 1927, implying a decline in the cultivation of other crops like, for instance, cotton.[21]

Colonial reports, especially of the 1870s and 1880s, insisted that there was "on all sides evidence of increased welfare and comfort", that the boom of rice exports had brought general prosperity to

[18] OSA, R III-1/708, GAROD 1877–78, 13–14; OSA, R III-1/709, GAROD 1880–81, 17; and GAROD 1881–82, 17; OSA, R III-1/710, GAROD 1883–84, 9; and GAROD 1884–85, 15–16; and GAROD 1885–86, 16; OSA, R III-1/714, GAROD 1887–88, 14; OSA, R III-1/714, GAROD 1888–89, 14; and GAROD 1889–90, 8. Also see Choudhury, *Economic History of Colonialism*, 111–12 and passim.
[19] OSA, R III-1/716, GAROD 1894–95, 14–16.
[20] OSA, R III-1/707B, GAROD 1872–73, 8; and GAROD 1874–75, 4–5; and GAROD 1876–77, 12; OSA, R III-1/708, GAROD 1880–81, 19–21; OSA, R III-1/709, GAROD 1881–82, 18–19; OSA, R III-1/716, GAROD 1894–95, 14. Also see Jit, *The Agrarian Life*, 90, 141–43; Patnaik, *Famine and Some Aspects of British Economic Policy in Orissa*, 187–88.
[21] Padhi, "Property in Land, Land Market and Tenancy Relations", 39. For the three coastal districts of Orissa Division about 85 per cent of the gross cropped area are said to have been used for rice cultivation in the early twentieth century. Pradipta Chaudhuri, "The Impact of Forced Commerce on the Patterns of Emigration from Orissa, 1901–1921", in *Essays on the Commercialization of Agriculture*, ed. K. N. Raj et al. (Delhi: Oxford University Press, 1985), 201, 4. For the decline of cotton cultivation in Balasore District, see Jit, *The Agrarian Life*, 90.

Orissa, which had "filtered down to the lowest classes".[22] Yet times of crisis revealed that this prosperity was rather shallow, unevenly distributed and accrued mainly to traders, zamindars and the richer strata of the peasantry. When the price of rice soared due to deficient crops or unusually high demand in neighbouring regions (both frequent events in that period of recurrent famines), a large proportion of the urban population and all others dependent on money wages suffered in particular.[23] Hence, during the first winter of the severe famine of 1876–78 in South India considerable distress was experienced even though the late-year harvest of 1876 was said to have been "abundant" in Baleshwar and "a fair average" in the districts of Cuttack and Puri. In Baleshwar, it was reported, "some people expected that rice would be purchasable for a song, as had hitherto been the case under similar circumstances, and were vastly indignant when they found this was not to be."[24] Two years later, the collector of that district admitted that the "poorer artisans and day laborers have sometimes had to forego one of their two daily meals and their children stinted [sic]. The distress has been most conspicuously observed in towns".[25] To townspeople of Puri, which was one of the region's largest urban settlements and a busy export harbour at the same time, the burgeoning export of food supplies appeared rather as iniquitous machinations than as contributions to general prosperity and many were reported to have participated in a major food riot:

> the popular discontent at the high prices there was aggravated by the sight of the grain stored for export on the beach, and by the operations of the whole-sale merchants, who established a cordon round the town and bought up all rice as it was being carted in. The result was that the

[22] OSA, R III-1/707B, GAROD 1876–77, 4. Also see GAROD 1872–73, 7; and GAROD 1875–76, 4; OSA, R III-1/708, GAROD 1878–79, 12; OSA, R III-1/709, GAROD 1882–83, 11.
[23] OSA, R III-1/707B, GAROD 1875–76, 7; OSA, R III-1/708, GAROD 1877–78, 18–19; and GAROD 1878–79, 22; and GAROD 1879–80, 11–12.
[24] OSA, R III-1/707B, GAROD 1875–76, 8.
[25] The collector was, however, reluctant to admit any scarcity of grain. Looking down from the heights of civilisational superiority, urban distress resulted, in his view, not only from particularly high prices of rice but also from the waste of money on opium, that is, the improvidence and lacking frugality of the poor. OSA, R III-1/708, GAROD 1877–78, 10.

supply, even at the enhanced prices, was somewhat scanty; and the people took advantage of the absence of the European officers at the Cuttack Durbar on the 1st January 1877 to plunder grain to the value of nearly half a lakh of rupees. The riot was suppressed after two days, and more than half of the rice recovered.[26]

The unevenness of socio-spatial integration flashes up in this account most graphically: the intensification of transregional circulation entailed the establishment of a "cordon" separating town and country; the "annihilation" of spatial distance between regional grain markets was thus accompanied by constraints on local access to food (cf. hypothesis 6 in chapter 2).

Agricultural labourers, it was often pointed out, were less immediately affected by such increase in rice prices as they were customarily paid in kind—a practice that was being undermined to a larger extent only by the end of the century. Even so, their incomes also dropped below the requirements of sheer subsistence in years of drought, when employment was hard to come by.[27] The curtailment of customary rights to use marginal ("scrub waste") lands and forest produce by a colonial legislation deprived them, moreover, of subsidiary sources of income.[28] Nor did the boom of rice exports benefit the lower strata of the landholding peasantry to an extent that would have permitted them to generate reserves that could provide a cushion against risk. This was admitted by colonial officials only reluctantly in times of acute crises of subsistence and generally ascribed to an alleged "inborn improvidence" of the Oriya cultivator.[29] At times, however, other explanations were considered, which hinted at causes for the lack of food security intrinsic to the

---

[26] OSA, R III-1/707B, GoB, General Dpt., Resolution, 18 September 1877, 3. Also see GAROD 1876–77, 6–7, 10. Complaints in Puri against the exportation of rice by "Bombay merchants" who had "offered a price which brought up all the grain in the bazaar" are again recorded for 1884–85: OSA, R III-1/710, GAROD 1884–85, 9.

[27] OSA, R III-1/707B, GAROD 1872–73, 8; OSA, R III-1/708, GAROD 1878–79, 2, 12; OSA, R III-1/714, GAROD 1887–88, 12; OSA, R III-1/719, GAROD 1899–1900, 8.

[28] OSA, R III-1/714, GAROD 1888–89, 10–11. Also see OIOC, BPWP October 1890 (P/3632), Railway, no. 25, 23–40 (tour report by Sir John Edgar to GoB, Revenue Dpt., 19 August 1889).

[29] See, for example, OSA, R III-1/718, GAROD 1897–98, 10.

structure of agrarian relations under colonial rule. Hence, it was pointed out that participation in the burgeoning rice trade permitted an accumulation of sustainable assets only to certain sections of rural society and particularly to the mahajans, while the lower strata of the peasantry were extremely vulnerable to annual variations in crop yield:

> The bulk of the population being indebted agriculturists, who are under advances to sell their crops before they are harvested at rates fixed beforehand, and labourers dependent on them, a small harvest sweeps off all their grain into their mahajans' golas [store-houses], and dearness of food-grains is generally very keenly felt.[30]

Similarly, Romesh Chunder Dutt, commissioner of Orissa in the mid-1890s and soon to become the leading protagonist of Indian economic nationalism, found that poorer peasants were often highly indebted to their zamindars. They were rarely able to stock upon rice supplies large enough to tide over a season of scarcity until the next harvest and, therefore, were at risk of being reduced to the status of landless labourers.[31] Several official enquiries—the earliest conducted in the 1890s, the latest in 1929–30—"showed that 75 to 80 per cent of the total agricultural population was indebted" to dominant peasants, zamindars or traders.[32]

Rural discontent with the scarcity of food supplies was expressed in various forms as even a cursory reading of the more general official records shows. In 1877 the Collector of Cuttack thus reported that

> the people complained about this state of things, and in their ignorance abused not only the merchants but Government, too, for not stopping exportation. ... In one instance, in order to thwart the petty dealers who are collecting rice for the merchants, the villagers of four or five neighbouring villages combined and, in broad daylight, robbed four carts

---

[30] OSA, R III-1/714, GAROD 1888–89, 10. Also see OSA, R III-1/707B, GAROD 1873–74, 5
[31] OSA, R III-1/716, GAROD 1890–91, 10–11. For R. C. Dutt's commissionership in Orissa, see Tapan Raychaudhuri, "Dutt, Romesh Chunder [Rameshchandra Datta] (1849–1909)", *Oxford Dictionary of National Biography* (Oxford: Oxford University Press, 2004).
[32] Chaudhuri, "Impact of Forced Commerce", 184. Also see Jit, *The Agrarian Life*, 224–34.

of rice while in transit to the merchant's godown. Thirteen of the perpetrators were on conviction sentenced to one year's rigorous imprisonment and to pay a fine of Rs. 5 each. No other instance of grain robbery carried out by any large number, occurred during the year, though there were numerous small thefts of that nature.[33]

During the same period of scarcity it was also reported that

> several of those superstitious rumours which spring no one knows whence have been current in Orissa. A monster was to appear who, unless appeased by an offering of rice begged from seven houses, would destroy the owners of every house it came to; whereupon for some days people went about begging rice from their neighbours.[34]

This may be interpreted as an assertion of customary rights to charity and, conversely, as an indication that the transformation of the circulatory regime was experienced as a crisis of an established "moral economy". However, the most telling if gruesome evidence for the differential impact of the increasing commercialisation of Orissa's agriculture on its largely rural population can be found in accounts of annual fluctuations in mortality. Though no major crop failure occurred in the Orissa plains between the famine of 1866 and the end of the century, poor harvests and years of soaring rice exports were followed repeatedly by years of increased mortality. While grain exports were being continued in such seasons, colonial officials, notwithstanding their claims to general prosperity, ascribed the rising incidence of terminal diseases (most prominently cholera) to widespread malnutrition among the poor and their recourse to inferior "famine foods"—that is, to plants that were avoided as long as rice was affordable.[35] That Orissa's integration in supraregional markets as a rice exporter benefited some classes more than others is also indicated by the development of real wages for "unskilled" coolie labourers. The official reports of the final three decades of the nineteenth century hence generally concurred in that the price of

---

[33] OSA, R III-1/708, GAROD 1877–78, 16. Also see OSA, R III-1/707B, GAROD 1872–73, 7.
[34] OSA, R III-1/707B, GAROD 1876–77, 12.
[35] OSA, R III-1/708, GAROD 1878–79, 10–11; OSA, R III-1/714, GAROD 1889–90, 5–6; OSA, R III-1/716, GAROD 1894–95, 8.

rice fluctuated and tended to increase, while money wages remained almost stable.[36] As for the wages of agricultural labourers, they appear to have stagnated at 2 to 2.5 seers of rice per day (if paid in kind) and at 1.5 to 2.5 annas per day (if paid in cash) from the 1810s right to the end of the century.[37]

The transformed circulatory regime and the infrastructural schemes of these decades did provide relief to some extent in seasons when the price of rice soared or the demand for agricultural labour was slack. Tens of thousands found work on road, canal and (in the 1890s) railway sites. These employment opportunities though provided only temporary safety valves for as long as construction went on and were also confined to supposedly 'unskilled' labour for earth moving, since 'skilled' workers were recruited outside the region, mainly in western India and Punjab.[38] In seasons of scarcity additional funds were made available for minor "relief works".[39] More importantly, the expansion of coastal shipping—increasingly controlled by British companies and rendered less costly as well as more independent from the monsoons by the development of steamship technology—resulted not merely in a swift growth of coastal trade but also in a massive boost of maritime passenger traffic between Calcutta and the ports of Orissa (see chart 4).[40]

While pilgrims to Puri made up for a large proportion of the passengers until the opening of the East Coast Railway at the end of the century, the other large group, it was officially held, consisted of

---

[36] OSA, R III-1/707B, GAROD 1875–76, 8; OSA, R III-1/708, GAROD 1879–80, 13–14; OSA, R III-1/709, GAROD 1880–81, 16; OSA, R III-1/714, GAROD 1890–91, 7; OSA, R III-1/719, GAROD 1899–1900, 8.

[37] Padhi, "Property in Land, Land Market and Tenancy Relations", 40.

[38] OSA, R III-1/707B, GAROD 1873–74, 2; and GAROD 1876–77, 5; OSA, R III-1/709, GAROD 1881–82, 15; OSA, R III-1/710, GAROD 1883–84, 7; and GAROD 1884–85, 11; OSA, R III-1/716, GAROD 1894–95, 11; OSA, R III-1/718, GAROD 1897–98, 10–11; OSA, R III-1/719, GAROD 1899–1900, 7.

[39] OSA, R III-1/707B, GAROD 1873–74, 31; OSA, R III-1/708, GAROD 1878–79, 1–2; OSA, R III-1/714, GAROD 1887–88, 11; OSA, R III-1/714, GAROD 1889–90, 7; OSA, R III-1/718, GAROD 1897–98, 10.

[40] OSA, R III-1/709, GAROD 1880–81, 20. With regard to the growing utilisation of steam technologies of navigation, it was reported that 295 of 380 vessels entering the Orissa ports in 1893–94 were steamers. "The Orissa Ports", The Indian Engineer 22/396, 10 November 1894.

CHART 4: Orissa's maritime passenger traffic (1873–74 to 1890–91)[41]

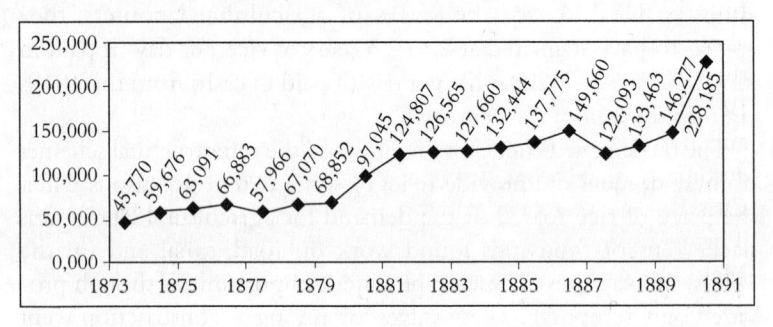

Year	Passengers
1873	45,770
1874	59,676
1875	63,091
1876	66,883
1877	57,966
1878	67,070
1879	68,852
1880	97,045
1881	124,807
1882	126,565
1883	127,660
1884	132,444
1885	137,775
1886	149,660
1887	122,093
1888	133,463
1889	146,277
1890	228,185

Source: Data compiled from OSA, R III–1/707B–R III–1/714, GAROD, 1873–74 to 1890–91.

migrant workers, mainly from Balasore District.[42] These workers took one of the several ships leaving Chandbali each week to find jobs in Calcutta or its neighbourhood as *palki* (palanquin) bearers, domestic servants, coolies, dock workers or, towards the end of the century, as factory hands in one of the mushrooming jute mills along the Hugli. Most of these workers were seasonal migrants who regularly returned to their families, often before the harvest. Though this pattern of transregional and seasonal migration to Cuttack, as mentioned before, was well established as early as in the eighteenth century, the availability of coastal steamers had facilitated, cheapened and accelerated the journey.[43] By the mid-1890s, moreover, the number of these migrant workers had swelled to 100,000

---

[41] Figures comprise both arrivals and departures. Most passengers travelled to and from Chandbali. Balasore was of minor importance while passenger traffic of other seaports was considered insignificant and, therefore, not registered. Also see Nayak, *Development of Transport and Communication*, 160, whose figures, based on provincial records, are identical or marginally different for most years but considerably lower (118, 187) for 1890–91.

[42] See the final section of this chapter.

[43] *Further Papers Relating to Extension of Railway Communications*, 219 (W. J. Herschel, Offg. Commissioner, Burdwan Division, to Offg. Joint Secry. to Government of Bengal, PWD, Railway Branch, 15 April 1868); OSA, R III–1/707B, GAROD 1872–73, 5; and GAROD 1873–74, 6; and GAROD 1874–75, 4; ibid., GAROD 1875–76, 6; and GAROD 1876–77, 4, 7; OSA, R III–1/710, GAROD 1884–85, 13; OSA, R III–1/714, GAROD 1888–89, 12; and GAROD, 1889–90, 8. For eighteenth-century labour migration to Calcutta, see chapter 4 of the present study.

according to a calculation of Orissa's chief colonial official of that time, Romesh Chunder Dutt. If correct, these numbers imply that about one in ten of the coastal districts' households relied in part on their incomes.[44] An older pattern of seasonal circulation between Bengal and Orissa had thus been intensified and adapted to a faster and more 'serialised' rhythm (cf. hypothesis 7 in chapter 2). The colonial state also encouraged permanent labour emigration from Orissa as a safety valve to alleviate subsistence crises and poverty. This exodus was sometimes (and conveniently) accounted for in Malthusian terms of "overpopulation"—a path of causation religiously followed notwithstanding that the famine of 1866–67 had already cut down a quarter of the coastal districts' inhabitants.[45] Until the end of the century, the recruitment of coolies on long-term contracts for the plantations of Assam or the Caribbean seems to have acquired, however, considerable proportions only in the southern Ganjam District and in several 'little kingdoms' of the interior, especially after the famine of 1888–89 in this area. It was only after the turn of the century that tens of thousands of Oriyas from the coastal plains, many of them migrating as families, waited in the "coolie depots" to be transported to the plantations of the Northeast.[46]

'Public Works' and the Reorganisation of Social Space: Roads and Canals

We have argued that the transformation of the circulatory regime *preceded* massive productions of built environment. Yet, investment

---

[44] OSA, R III-1/716, GAROD 1894–95, 12–13. In 1884, it was even speculated that the number of labour migrants to Calcutta had risen to no less than 150,000 after the establishment of regular steamer service to Chandbali and Balasore. OSA, R III-1/710, GAROD 1883–84, 7.
[45] See, for example, OSA, R III-1/714, GAROD 1889–90, 8.
[46] OSA, R III-1/707B, GAROD 1872–73, 5; and GAROD 1876–77, 5; OSA, R III-1/714, GAROD 1888–89, 12; and GAROD 1890–91, 7; OSA, R III-1/716, GAROD 1894–95, 12–13; OSA, R III-1/719, GAROD 1899–1900, 7; RNNB, 26 January 1889 (*Bangabasi*, 19 January 1889), 73–74; *RATMO* 1896–97, 16; OSA, R III-1/797, *Report on Administration of Mourbhanj, 1906–1907*, 97; OSA, R III-1/800, *Report on Administration of Mourbhanj 1909–1910*; Chaudhuri, "Impact of Forced Commerce", 184–209. The present author's evidence contradicts Biswamoy Pati's claim that emigration from the coastal districts began in the late nineteenth century and from the interior areas not before the 1920s. Pati, *Resisting Domination*, 37–38.

in infrastructure followed suit and soon assumed much larger dimensions than in the early part of the century. The metalling of the Orissa Trunk Road and the construction of the Kendrapara (and Taldanda) canals have been mentioned already.[47] There were also some investments in port infrastructure such as the creation of goods-handling facilities in Chandbali and the construction of lighthouses, though these measures were hardly substantial enough to counter the perennial problem of siltation and to produce shipping charges to a level that would have made a lasting impact.[48] Orissa's ports thus suffered from the competition of the Coast Canal immediately after its completion in 1887 and faced a sharp decline after the East Coast Railway was opened just before the end of the century.[49] By the mid-1920s, the number of passengers using the steamer service between Chandbali and Calcutta had dipped to 38,000 (see chart 4), while the formerly busy harbour of False Point was abandoned altogether.[50]

Road policy, for all its limitations, sustained the transformation of the circulatory regime. Metalling the Orissa Trunk Road, as has been shown earlier, entailed a considerable reduction of transport costs on that line by allowing for wheeled traffic throughout the year.[51] But even less far-reaching schemes contributed to rendering circulation more intensive. The "improvement" of the old road from Cuttack to Sambalpur and Central India along the southern bank of the Mahanadi in the early 1860s, for instance, and particularly the widening and levelling of the difficult Barmul defile facilitated traffic even though the road remained unmetalled through the period under review.[52] Hence, in the three winter months between December 1882 and February 1883 no less than 5,252 carts (carrying mainly Ganjam salt and oilseed) were counted traversing this

---

[47] See page 225f, above.
[48] Cf, Jit, *The Agrarian Life*, 100–3; Nayak, *Development of Transport and Communication* 140–42, 152–53. Also see OSA, R III-1/707B, GAROD 1874–75, 6.
[49] OSA, R III-1/714, GAROD 1887–88, 15; and GAROD 1888–89, 10; and GAROD 1889–90, 9; OSA, R III-1/716, GAROD 1894–95, 24; OSA, R III-1/719, GAROD 1899–1900, 10.
[50] Government of Bihar and Orissa, *Bihar and Orissa in 1924–25* [hereafter *Bihar and Orissa in* followed by year] (Patna: Superintendent of Government Printing, Bihar and Orissa, 1926), 73. Also see the final section of this chapter.
[51] See page 226, above.
[52] See chapter 6.

mountain pass, which had been inaccessible for wheeled traffic before. Moreover, the commercialisation of agriculture appears to have revitalised trade along this route in general. More than 600 boats were reported to have passed Barmul each month between July 1882 and February 1883, the bulk of the transported commodities being rice (7,200 lt).[53] This route (as well as others along the W-ESE axis) served, under certain conditions, even as an infrastructure for the temporary spatial redirection of circulatory movements. Hence, during the 1888–89 famine in Central India and the Garhjats a "complete reversal of the ordinary course of trade" was reported, since rice was carried up the inland routes to an extent severely affecting the region's maritime trade.[54]

Furthermore, a new financial and institutional foundation for the construction and maintenance of intraregional roads was established since the 1870s. A "road cess" was imposed upon all houseowners in 1871, its proceeds were administered by local Road Cess Committees and used for funding district roads and to some extent for the improvement of village roads also. A large proportion of the earnings from the leases of ferry concessions that had so far been used for purposes of road improvement and maintenance within the division were, however, simultaneously diverted to the treasury of the Government of India. This meant, in the view of the commissioner, that "by a refinement of cruelty what Orissa had in one pocket to pay for her roads is annexed under pretext that the other pocket may be ultimately filled from road cess and local taxation".[55] The inadequacy of the road funds available to the Road Cess Committees and, after their establishment in 1887, to District Boards seemed a longstanding grievance to local colonial officials throughout the period.[56] For over half a century no funds could be found,

[53] OSA, R III-1/709, GAROD 1882–83, 18–20. Also see OSA, R III-1/710, GAROD 1883–84, 13; OIOC, BPWP December 1884 (P/2235), Railway, no. 30, app. B, 21 ("Cuttack-Pooree Railway. Preliminary Reports and Estimates": "A. Smith, CoCD, to Secry. to GoB, PWD, 14 August 1883").
[54] OSA, R III-1/714, GAROD 1888–89, 15. Also see chart 2.
[55] OSA, R III-1/707B, GAROD 1871–72, 7.
[56] See, for instance, OSA, R III-1/708, GAROD 1877–78, 32; OSA, R III-1/709, GAROD 1880–81, 51; OSA, R III-1/710, GAROD 1884–85, 45; and GAROD 1885–86, 47; and GAROD 1886–87, 44. For the organisation and problems of district road administration in late nineteenth-century Orissa, see Kartik C. Rout, *Local Self-Government in British Orissa, 1869–*

for instance, for the metalling of the road connecting Bhadrak on the Orissa Trunk Road with the region's principal port of Chandbali, though its crucial importance as a feeder for coastal traffic and its impracticability during the rains was officially acknowledged time and again.[57] In 1898, the District Boards were advised to generally abstain from the construction of new roads as they "have already a greater length of roads than they can keep in proper repair".[58] Statistical evidence suggests that restraints on road construction operated more severely in Orissa than elsewhere. The total length of roads in the Cuttack Division more than doubled between 1864 and the turn of the century from 1,322 to 2,703 km. Even so, the division's share of the Bengal Presidency's total road length declined from 4.9 to 4.3 per cent in the same period. Not only the Orissa region as a whole but also the coastal plain, its most densely populated and intensively cultivated part, fell far behind the neighbouring regions of British India regarding the development of roads. While the three coastal districts of Balasore, Cuttack and Puri made up for 5.4 per cent of the area of the Bengal Presidency, their share of the presidency's road mileage amounted to merely 3.7 per cent in 1901. At this time, the road density of the three districts did not exceed 18 road miles per one hundred square miles, 30 per cent below the Presidency's average of 26.[59] Social space continued to be

1935 (Delhi: Daya Publishing House, 1988), 275–90; Nayak, *Development of Transport and Communication*, 34–56.

[57] OSA, R III-1/707B, GAROD 1875–76, 35; OSA, R III-1/708, GAROD 1877–78, 16; and GAROD 1878–79, 5; OSA, R III-1/710, GAROD 1883–84, 10; and GAROD 1884–85, 45; and GAROD 1885–86, 47; and GAROD 1886–87, 44–45; OSA: BoRLR, 10,469 Bd.Doc (Commissioner's Office, Revenue Dpt., to Secry. to GoB, General Dpt., 13 July 1886); Nayak, *Development of Transport and Communication*, 53; Maddox, *Final Report on Settlement of Orissa*, 1: 29; *Report of the Orissa Flood Committee* (Patna: Superintendent, Government Printing, Bihar and Orissa, 1928), 26–27; Sarma, *Report on Road Development*, 13.

[58] OSA, R III-1/718, GAROD 1897–98, 11.

[59] OIOC, BPWP January 1864 (P/16/66), Com., no. 39, app., i–ii, v, 114–20; Government of Bengal, Public Works Department (henceforth GoB, PWD) *Annual Administration Report for Roads and Buildings, Irrigation and Railways, 1900–1901* (Calcutta: Government Press, 1901), 15; *Statistical Abstracts Relating to British India from 1894–95 to 1903–4* (London: HMSO, 1905), 1; William W. Hunter et al., eds., *Imperial Gazetteer of India* (Oxford: Clarendon Press, 1908), 19: 249.

produced unevenly in this respect in the remaining half-century of British rule: in 1948, Orissa's road mileage per one hundred square miles amounted to no more than 12.3 (including the former Tributary States) while the corresponding figures for West Bengal, Bihar and (post-partition) India as a whole came to 74.5, 43.8 and 20.1 respectively.[60]

This tendency materialised despite a growing interest of sections of late nineteenth-century Oriya society in road infrastructure: apart from the continuation of traditional pious practices of zamindars and other notables of endowing bridges, sarais, roadside wells or dispensaries,[61] a Baleshwar merchant, Mothur Mohun Parhi, was reported to have made efforts for improving the "old port of Churaman and removing the silt".[62] Interestingly, there is also evidence of applications made by both zamindars and "villagers" for the amelioration of village roads and for their active participation in such schemes to the colonial authorities.[63] This change in attitude may well have been connected to the tendency towards agricultural commercialisation and it would be useful, in this context, to explore which sections of rural society partook voluntarily in the generation of local transport infrastructure and to which extent. Future studies, relying on district and local level material, may shed new light on this crucial "field of force" of infrastructural development.

For our present purposes, the emphasis of the investigation has to remain, however, with major developments on a regional scale.

---

[60] Sinha, "Transport and Communications Problems in Orissa", 41. Also see Sarma, *Report on Road Development*, 14–15.

[61] Such endowments were mainly undertaken by Oriya notables in the coastal plains and often pertained to the new Jagannath Road (that is, Orissa Trunk Road). See, for example, OSA, R III-1/707B, GAROD 1873–74, 28; and GAROD 1875–76, 30; OSA, R III-1/708, GAROD 1878–79, 11, 40. However, a major offer for the improvement of the Mahanadi route was also made even before the famine: "The Rajah of Rewah who experienced the great difficulties of the Ghat road on his pilgrimage to Pooree in 1857, suffered [sic] Rupees 6,000 for the opening out of a proper road and the construction of a Serai at Puddumtolah on the top of the Pass." OIOC, BPWP July 1861 (P/16/52), Com., no. 31, 39 (Report by F. Bond, 15 April 1861).

[62] OSA, R III-1/707B, GAROD 1873–74, 21.

[63] OSA, R III-1/707B, GAROD 1873–74, 29; and GAROD 1875–76, 26; and GAROD 1876–77, 23; OSA, R III-1/709, GAROD 1880–81, 50–51; OSA, R III-1/710, GAROD 1885–86, 47.

These were, well into the 1880s, focused on the excavation of navigable canals and from the middle of that decade up to the turn of the century on the construction of railways. The construction of the Kendrapara Canal and its extension and branch canals as well as of the smaller Taldanda Canal, all of them constructed in the decade after the Orissa famine to feed the produce of the delta region of the Mahanadi, Brahmani and Baitarani rivers into the maritime channels of a growing transregional trade, has already been mentioned. Yet there were also major schemes for canals paralleling the coastline rather than hitting it at right angles. The first of these was a short line of canal between the southern shore of the Chilka Lake and Ganjam, which reduced transport costs considerably between the district of Puri and the northernmost port of the Madras Presidency. This canal had probably the most lasting effects of all "famine relief works" executed after the first half of the catastrophic year of 1866.[64] According to the plans, upon which colonial officials pondered extensively, it was meant to be merely one link in a continuous chain of canals taking off from the Hugli River below Calcutta, passing through Bengal's Midnapur District and the whole length of the Cuttack Division, ending as far south as Vishakapatnam in the Madras Presidency.[65] Though this scheme was never completed in its entirety, two major projects were conducted on its lines. The first project was the High Level Canal, which was aligned along the western margin of the Orissa plains and designed to provide irrigation as well as a waterway for steamers and other vessels. Yet, when the section connecting Cuttack and Bhadrak was opened to traffic in 1878–79 and about 240 km of canal were still missing to link it up with the canals of Bengal proper, it was found that the supply of sufficient water to render the canal navigable throughout the year was more difficult and expensive than anticipated.[66] Hence the project was given up, a few steamers plied the completed ranges between Cuttack and Bhadrak until the end of the century, when the East Coast Railway pushed them out of competition and the

[64] OIOC, BPWP August 1866 (P/432/41), Communications, nos. 6–8, 12–17.
[65] *Papers Relating to Orissa Coast Canal* [1877 to 1881], 104–5 (note by A. Fraser, Secry. to GoI, PWD, on the East Coast Canal, 23 January 1880).
[66] Hunter, *The Annals of Rural Bengal*, 3: 193, and appendix, 110–11; Maddox, *Final Report on Settlement of Orissa*, 1: 31. Also see "The Orissa Irrigation Project", *The Statesman and Friend of India*, 22 June 1882.

utilisation of the canal became confined to purposes of local transport. Planned as a "productive public work", the High Level Canal proved to be an unprofitable investment as the receipts from both irrigation and navigations remained far below expectations.[67] The same was true for the second major scheme, the construction of a cheaper Orissa Coast Canal, which was sanctioned instead in 1880, taken in hand in the following year and completed by 1887.[68] Following the shoreline closely, often at a distance of less than 10 km, this canal was supplied with brackish tidal water and, therefore, usable only for purposes of transport. It linked up to the canals of Midnapur District, traversed the whole length of Orissa's Balasore District terminating after a length of about 150 km at the village of Charibatia on the Matai Nadi, thereby connecting to the sea and to the waterways of the conjoint deltas of the Baitarani, Brahmani and Mahanadi rivers (see map 8). On the part of the colonial administration and many of their loyalist Indian associates, expectations were particularly high with regard to this scheme.[69] After the Coast Canal was opened fully in 1887, traffic seemed, however, to build up rather slowly and colonial officials noticed two years later that "the trade along this canal has not yet developed to anything like its capacity".[70] However, the figures did not improve materially until the turn of the century when the East Coast Railway rendered it at last, like the High Level Canal, redundant except for local purposes. Fourteen years after the start of construction in 1880 Rs 4.5 million had been invested on this scheme, a balance not including the substantial interest payments. This amounted to more than Rs 320,000 per year or about four times the annual expenditure of Orissa's Road Cess Committees on district and local roads in the early 1880s. As opposed to roads, the Coast Canal was, of course, classified as a

[67] Maddox, *Final Report on Settlement of Orissa*, 1: 24, 31–32.
[68] *Papers Relating to the Orissa Coast Canal* [1877 to 1881], 106 (Secry. of State for India to GoI, 30 November 1880); *Papers Relating to the Orissa Coast Canal*, second series, in Selections from the Records of the Government of India in the Public Works Department (Calcutta: Bengal Secretariat Press, 1889), 2 (note by C. W. I. Harrison, Offg. CE, on revised estimate for Orissa Coast Canal, 5 October 1888).
[69] For a collection of documents assessing the probable effects of the Coast Canal and its supposed advantages to both coastal navigation and railway transport, see *Papers Relating to Orissa Coast Canal* [1877 to 1881].
[70] OSA, R III-1/714, GAROD 1888–89, 16.

"productive public work". By the end of the century colonial authorities admitted, however, that the canal was a "failure" as a "commercial enterprise": its revenue from tolls, far from turning the canal into a profitable investment, did not cover working expenses in most years even before the opening of the railway, when it was further reduced by half.[71] The largest single investment in Orissa's transport infrastructure since the famine thus seeped away into the alluvial soil and into the bank accounts of British creditors. When the Orissa Flood Committee took stock of the Coast Canal four decades after its opening they painted a gloomy picture:

> All the gates, and in some cases the gearing also, of the seven locks in this portion are worn out to such an extent that repair is impossible and nothing but complete renewal will avail. In many stretches, the banks are no more than a series of mounds, through the gaps between which water flows in some cases from the canal in to the fields, in others from the fields into the canal. In long reaches the canal is silted and fails to afford the depth of water required for navigation.

The committee estimated that a major investment of about Rs 400,000 was necessary to restore the canal, but recommended instead to give up altogether several of its ranges. "[T]he traffic upon it is negligible," they felt, "and enquiry among the villages [sic] educed no expression of any general desire for its retention. The popular feeling seemed to be that, viewed as a means of transport, it was already out of action for so large a portion of the year that it would make little difference were it abandoned altogether."[72]

The failure of the longitudinal canals of Orissa's coastal strip as infrastructural measures reveals the limits of "abstract space", the limits of policies seeking to impose upon a supposedly stationary and inactive *tabula rasa* an entirely novel spatial order in the image of capital (see hypothesis 4 in chapter 2). For the colonial system of flood embankments and canals for purposes of irrigation and navigation conflicted with fundamental socio-spatial practices of Orissa's agrarian society, with a historically formed social ecology based on

---

[71] Maddox, *Final Report on Settlement of Orissa*, 1: 30–31; OSA, R III-1/718, GAROD 1899–1900, 32; GoB, PWD, *Annual Administration Report for Roads and Buildings, Irrigation and Railways, 1899–1900* (Calcutta: Government Press, 1900), 9–10, 31–37.
[72] *Report of Orissa Flood Committee*, 25–26.

the flexible appropriation of the region's hydrology: like the road embankments of the new Jagannath Road in the early half of the century, the embankments of these canals impeded the drainage of the country in the event of both inundation on account of heavy rainfalls (which was a regular environmental feature) and of periodic cyclonic surges. River inundation had, of course, been one of the foundations of agriculture in the Mahanadi Delta with its vast drainage area of more than 130,000 sq km. Yet if the water was retained by embankments and could not drain off quickly enough, it destroyed the crops instead of irrigating and fertilising the fields, while raising the incidence of malaria and other waterborne diseases. An even spread of the fertile silt contained in the flood water was prevented at the same time, which entailed a decline in soil quality. In case of cyclonic surges, the embankments hardly prevented the salt water from flooding the coastal country, but again impeded the drainage thus increasing the danger of salinisation. These problems were known at the time of the construction of the High Level and Orissa Coast canals and rendered these schemes highly unpopular in the adjacent villages.[73] The misgivings of locals were shared by a few colonial administrators like the Collector of Balasore in the early 1880s though their arguments were indignantly brushed aside by the engineering experts of the Bengal PWD.[74] However, the opinion of the Collector of Balasore may still be quoted at some length since it particularised vividly why a scheme like the Coast Canal met with the hostility of a large part of the people concerned:

> It crosses the drainage of the country, and many are the fears expressed by the owners of the neighbouring lands that the drainage of the country

---

[73] Maddox, *Final Report on Settlement of Orissa*, 1: 31; *Report of Orissa Flood Committee*, 26; D'Souza, *Flood, Embankments and Canals*, 14–21, 39–50; and "Colonialism, Capitalism and Nature", 1261–72; and "Canal Irrigation and Conundrum of Flood Protection", 46–64. For complaints of villagers, also see OSA, R III-1/710, GAROD 1884–85, 4. For a critical view of the canal system in the contemporary Oriya press, see *RNNB*, 14 August 1886 (*Sebaka*, 31 July 1886).

[74] See, for instance, *Papers Relating to Orissa Coast Canal* [1877 to 1881], 95–97 (note by H. C. Levinge, CE, PWD, Irrigation Branch, Bengal, 15 February 1879); and 97 (H. C. Levinge, Joint Secry. to GoB, PWD, Irrigation Branch, to Secry. to GOI, PWD, 28 April 1879); OSA, R III-1/709, GAROD 1882–83, 57.

will be interfered with, and that loss to them and unhealthiness to the district will result. On such a matter it is of course impossible for me to express opinion. In this country great public works previous to construction are considered only from the Government point of view. A work is sanctioned according or not to its supposed necessity and the probable financial results, and complaints and remonstrances of the inhabitants are unknown or unheeded.... I confess I know nothing about engineering: but when I find that a canal crosses the drainage of the country with a high bank; that many rivers are absolutely closed, while the passage of their waters is secured by running two or three of them into one channel, which in high flood is insufficient to carry off its own waters; when all the drainage spills are apparently on the highest ground that can be selected, leaving intermediate depressions apparently for water to rest in them; and when for about 14 miles of country only in two places is outlet for water provided, I confess I am not surprised that the inhabitants consider they have reasonable grounds for their anxiety, and I fear that hereafter some further expensive works may be found necessary in order to repair unforeseen mischief.[75]

If the notion of civilisational superiority prompted colonial administrators to override local experience and knowledge of Orissa's surface water hydrology, the problem of drainage continued to haunt all canal schemes in this region.[76] While additional outlets and culverts were supposed to solve the problem their main effect appears to have been to push the actual expenditure far beyond the original estimates—in the case of the Coast Canal from Rs 3.6 million to Rs 4.5 million exclusive of interest charges. Receipts from both irrigation and navigation were at the same time much less than had been anticipated.[77] Peasants were reluctant to irrigate their fields with canal water (which lacked the fertilising silt of the rivers), found the water rates demanded from them excessive and were antagonised by administrative attempts to force canal water upon them.[78]

The expectation that canal navigation on the East Coast Canal and coastal shipping would rather supplement than compete with each other was also disappointed. It was found instead that seaborne trade was diverted to some extent to the canal in the years after its

[75] OSA, R III-1/709, GAROD 1881–82, 54–55. For a similar view, see "The Orissa Irrigation Project", *The Statesman and Friend of India*, 22 June 1882.
[76] Cf.: Hill, "Ideology and Public Works", 52 and passim.
[77] Maddox, *Final Report on Settlement of Orissa*, 1: 30.
[78] OSA, R III-1/714, GAROD 1887–88, 16.

opening.[79] A dual pattern emerged: the canals were plied mainly by small "country boats", while steamers, offering larger space and lower rates to traders, predominantly continued to use the coastal route.[80] As for passenger transport, the steamship companies running coastal services between Chandbali and Calcutta would retain the lion's share until the completion of the East Coast Railway by cutting their fares, especially since canal navigation was even less convenient for travellers.[81] The colonial administration attempted at times to make up for the smaller volume of traffic by enhancing the tollage, which resulted, however, only in a further reduction of canal navigation.[82] In sum, the financial losses of the canal schemes indicated the limits of abstract space or, the historical impossibility of creating a fully commercialised circulatory regime *de novo*, regardless of the multilayered social space generated by interacting forces in the *longue durée*.

'Public Works' and the Reorganisation of Social Space: Railways

Railway tracks reached coastal Orissa, it has been mentioned before, as late as at the turn of the century when the other major regions of eastern India had been linked to the railway system for up to four decades.[83] The Indian railway network had, however, a direct and unmediated impact on the region's circulatory regime ever since the mainline of the Bengal–Nagpur Railway (BNR) was opened in 1891. This railroad constituted a second and shorter rail link between Calcutta and Bombay, which passed the coal fields of Chota Nagpur, skirted and partly traversed the north-western margin of Orissa on its way to Raipur and Nagpur (see map 8).[84]

---

[79] OSA, R III-1/714, GAROD 1888–89, 15; and GoB, General Dpt., Resolution, 2 September 1889, 2.
[80] Maddox, *Final Report on Settlement of Orissa*, 1: 30.
[81] *Papers Relating to Orissa Coast Canal*, second series, 49 (Collector of Balasore to Executive Engineer, Balasore, 17 July 1886); Maddox, *Final Report on Settlement of Orissa*, 1: 30. For travelling conditions of canal steamers, see P. W. O'Gorman, *Puri Pilgrim Canal Traffic*, n.p., n.d. [c. 1895], 5–7.
[82] OSA, R III-1/708, GAROD 1878–79, 40–41; OSA, R III-1/709, GAROD 1881–82, 21.
[83] For a summary of the expansion of railways in Eastern India, see Munsi, *Geography of Transportation in Eastern India*, 99–100, 115.
[84] The only, thoroughly conventional but fortunately very informative history of the BNR was written by a former railway official who became the

This resulted in a shift in the structure of interregional transport costs implying that the Mahanadi route's attraction as a channel of Central India's transregional trade was further diminished.[85] In the terms developed in the first part of this study (see hypothesis 6 in chapter 2): while "time-space" was "compressed" between Central India and western Bengal (or their *relative* distance reduced), Orissa moved away as it were from the neighbouring region of Central India, which had been such an important reference area of its *ancien régime* of circulation. The structure of relative distances and spatial scales was transformed, which is also evident in the development of pilgrim traffic from Central India: the road along the southern bank of the Mahanadi had been the most important route for *yatris* to Jagannath from this region and their number apparently increased after it was opened out for carts. More than 30,000 passengers were reported to have reached Cuttack via the Mahanadi route in one year of the early 1880s.[86] However, when the Bengal–Nagpur mainline was complemented by the East Coast Railway in 1899–1900, the enormous detour over Calcutta turned into a shortcut in terms of travel time, while the much more direct Mahanadi route lost its attraction for many pilgrims (see map 8).

Effects of disarticulation also pertained to the patterns of circulation within the region of the present state of Orissa: The BNR

---

curator of India's National Rail Museum. While the print edition of this book was not available, an internet edition which has no pagination however could be consulted. For this reason, the title of the relevant chapter is referred to wherever this book is cited in the present study: "Bengal–Nagpur Railway", in *South Eastern Railway–March to the Millenium*, Bhandari, Ratan R. (Calcutta: South Eastern Railway, 2001) (the first edition of 1987 was entitled *The Blue Chip Railway*), http://www.serailway.gov.in/General/Book_RRB/index.htm.

[85] Inglis, *Canals and Flood Banks of Bengal*, 13. Also see "The Orissa Ports", *The Indian Engineer* 22/396, 10 November 1894.

[86] The traffic count was made for the period between 1 July 1882 and 30 June 1883, when 31,826 passengers and 10,123 conveyances were reported to reach Cuttack on that route. OIOC, BPWP December 1884 (P/2235), Railway, no. 30, app. B, 21 ("Cuttack–Pooree Railway. Preliminary Reports and Estimates": "A. Smith, CoCD, to Secry. to GoB, PWD, 14 August 1883"). Also see Temple, "Report on the Mahanuddy", 40; OIOC, BPWP December 1863 (P/16/64), Com., no. 1, 1; OIOC, BPWP June 1868 (P/432/50), Com., no. 59, 56; OSA, R III-1/709, GAROD 1880–81, 51, OIOC, BPWP August 1882 (P/1831), Railway, no. 3, 3 and chapter 6 of the present study.

connected the north-western Garhjats to Calcutta and contributed to their spatial reorientation towards the imperial capital. Sambalpur, always a subregional space between Central India and Orissa, was linked up to the BNR by a branch line in 1893, which induced a rapid commercialisation of agriculture, benefiting local dominant landowners and immigrant traders, by further accentuating its ties with the Central Provinces as well as with Calcutta: "the Jharsuguda–Sambalpur Branch Railway changed the run of trade and doubled the price of rice."[87] This diversion was not lost on contemporaries and officially acknowledged in the 1909 district gazetteer: "The river Mahanadi was formerly the main outlet for the trade of the district, and boat transport is still carried on as far as Sonepur; but since the opening of the railway, river-borne trade with Cuttack has greatly diminished."[88]

As for the extension of railways to the Orissa plains, we have seen that the idea of a railroad connecting the two presidency towns of Calcutta and Madras along the coast of the Bay of Bengal dated back to Stephenson's 1845 plan for an Indian railway network (see map 2 and chapter 6). We have also seen that, in marked difference to colonial 'public works' policies regarding other regions of the subcontinent, the protagonists of navigable canals prevailed over those of railways during the crucial transitional period of the 1850s and 1860s (see chapter 6). However, there were always voices not only in the colonial oligarchy, but also from the dominant Indian classes calling for the construction of a railway link to coastal Orissa. Appeals to this effect by Oriya notables thus continued to be written and turned down in the 1870s.[89] It was only in the following decade though that the debate intensified: a "Balasore Railway Committee" was founded in 1881, which comprised much of northern Orissa's high society including Maharaja Krushna Chandra of Mayurbhanj (r. 1867–1882) with Baikuntha Nath De, an influential zamindar, as its honorary secretary. The committee sent a carefully prepared memorial to the Government of Bengal calling for the

---

[87] Bal G. Baboo, *Economic History of Sambalpur District, 1849–1947* (MS., 21 pages.), n.p., n.d., 3. These links were further reinforced by Sambalpur's being administered as a part of the "Central Provinces" between 1862 and 1905. Also see *RATMO* 1897–98, 11.

[88] O'Malley, *Bengal District Gazetteers: Sambalpur*, 161–62; also see 155–57.

[89] Nayak, *Development of Transport and Communication*, 74–75.

construction of a direct rail link between Calcutta and Madras through the Orissa coastal plains and of a branch line to Puri. This railway, they argued, would not only provide a faster and safer means of transport to Jagannath pilgrims, but would also reduce the incidence of cholera epidemics by improving the pilgrims' lot and could, furthermore, serve as a famine protection line. The large number of pilgrims travelling to Puri, which they believed to be between 500,000 and 600,000 annually, would guarantee handsome profits to investors.[90]

From the early 1880s these arguments were repeated time and again in Oriya (and sometimes also in Bangla) newspapers. The colonial government was urged to introduce a railway line to Cuttack and Puri either from Varanasi (Benares) via Chota Nagpur and the Garhjat States of Orissa or from Calcutta across the coastal plains. An analysis of official summaries of relevant articles reveals a growing sense of exasperation among the largely loyalist correspondents: interventions from a newly emerging Indian public sphere were clearly not appreciated and usually ignored by the British administration.[91]

---

[90] OIOC, BPWP August 1882 (P/1831), Railway, no. 4, 3–7: "An Appeal for a Light Passenger Railroad from Ranigunge to Pooree through Bankoora, Midnapore, Balasore, Cuttack, and Khorda". These figures appear to be exaggerated by far. OIOC, BPWP August 1882 (P/1831), Railway, no. 3, 3 (CoCD to Secry. to GoB, PWD, 15 October 1881). Also see footnote 124, in this chapter.

[91] See *RNNB* for: 17 September 1881 (*Balasore Sambad Bahika*, 4 August 1881), 11; 1 October 1881 (*Balasore Sambad Bahika*, 1 September 1881), 6–7; 3 December 1881 (*Utkal Dipika*, 12 November 1881), 7; 18 February 1882 (*Balasore Sambad Bahika*, 2 February 1882), 58; 22 July 1882 (*Utkal Dipika*, 9 July 1882), 254; 29 July 1882 (*Utkal Dipika*, 22 July 1882), 270–71; 12/8/1882 (*Utkal Dipika*, 5 August 1882), 293; 19 August 1882 (*Medini*, 14 August 1882); 9 September 1882 (*Utkal Dipika*, 26 August 1882); 23 December 1882 (*Utkal Dipika*, 16 December 1882), 471; 17 February 1883 (*Utkal Dipika*, 3 February 1883), 74; 4 August 1883 (*Utkal Darpan*, 15 July 1883), 474; 5 January 1884 (*Utkal Dipika*, 15 December 1883), 23; 12 January 1884 (*Utkal Dipika*, 22 December 1883), 52; 19 January 1884 (*Purusottam Patrika*, 31 December 1883), 76; 2 February 1884 (*Utkal Dipika*, 12 January 1884), 133; 1 March 1884 (*Samvad Bahika*, 7 February 1884), 252; 15 March 1884 (*Samvad Bahika*, 21 February 1884), 312; 20 September 1884 (*Utkal Darpan*, 2 September 1884), 1209; 1 November 1884 (*Samvad Bahika*, 16 October 1884), 1343; 16 January 1886 (*Utkal Dipika*, 2 January 1886), 92; 14 August 1886 (*Sebaka*, 31 July 1886), 922–23; 23 October 1886 (*Utkal Dipika*, 25 September 1886), 1157; 23 April 1887 (*Sanskaraka*, 7/4/1887), 441.

The point was not that Orissa's colonial administrators were totally averse to the construction of a railway line at that time. In fact, they argued on similar lines as the Indian notables did. Yet the Commissioner of Cuttack plainly refused to cooperate with the "Balasore Railway Committee".[92]

In 1887, the campaign for an Orissa railway reached a new pitch when the *Sir John Lawrence*, a seagoing steamer that had left Calcutta for Puri with over eight hundred passengers, sank on 25 May due to the shipmaster's irresponsible navigation. Hundreds of predominantly female pilgrims were drowned, many of whom were from well-to do Calcutta *bhadralok* families.[93] It was now that more widely distributed Bangla newspapers took the lead in the campaign and that the tone became more insistent: "Railway lines have been constructed in all directions for the benefit of Europeans and of their trade. The interests of natives of India have been sacrificed to the interests of Europeans", wrote the *Bangabasi*. And it went on to present the Orissa railway as an issue of the whole "Hindu community": "A railway line to Puri will be hailed with delight by 16 crores[94] of Hindus, for it will lessen the dangers and difficulties, and put an end to their sorrows and fears."[95] The *Dainik* argued on similar lines:

> It is the fault of Government that a railway to Puri has not yet been opened. The Darjeeling Railway has been constructed for the convenience of hill-going Europeans; railways have been constructed in Assam for the benefit of tea-planters; and arrangements are in progress for constructing railways to the different sanatoriums of the different Governments. But no railway has yet been constructed for the safety of the hundreds of thousands of Hindu pilgrims to Puri. In vain have the people of Orissa and the whole Hindu Community of 16 crores of people repeatedly prayed for a railway to Puri.[96]

---

[92] OIOC, BPWP August 1882 (P/1831), Railway, no. 3, 2–3 (CoCD to Secry. to GoB, PWD, 15 October 1881).
[93] "A Great Disaster in Bengal—Loss of the Sir John Lawrence", in *The Indian Mirror*, 5 June 1887.
[94] Crore: corrupted transliteration of *karor* (that is, ten million).
[95] *RNNB*, 18 June 1887 (*Bangabasi*, 11 June 1887), 621–22.
[96] *RNNB*, 11 June 1887 (*Dainik*, 9 June 1887), 595. For further relevant summaries of articles, see 18 June 1887 (*Sahachar*, 8 June 1887), 621; 18 June 1887 (*Som Prakash*, 13 June 1887), 622; 18 June 1887 (*Dacca Gazette*, 13 June 1887), 622; 25 June 1887 (*Charu Varta*, 13 June 1887), 651; 25 June 1887 (*Burdwan Sanjiwani*, 11 June 1887), 651; 25 June 1887 (*Navasamvad*, 11 June

The British railway policy was, in other words, identified as the pursuit of a particular interest and not, as the colonial oligarchy claimed, as an activity for the benefit of "the community at large" (cf. chapter 3). The self-representation of the colonial government as the impartial promoter of universal 'civilisation' was, thereby, put into question. The short-term political fallout of these debates consisted, however, merely in the upper echelons of regional society trying to convince the British that they should be included in processes of decision-making with regard to infrastructure. The point thus was not to democratise the production of social space, but to co-opt Indian notables to the colonial circles that "conceived", planned and engineered social space. Yet even this moderate demand went against the grain of a colonial policy that sought to keep 'public works' beyond public control (cf. chapter 3).

The proposals of Indian notables were thus disregarded out of larger political considerations and not because the extension of railways to the Orissa coastal districts was unthinkable or because the colonial administration was generally disinclined to sanction railway schemes that would have facilitated Hindu pilgrimage. In fact, very similarly argued proposals from British administrators and businessmen gave occasion to lengthy official deliberations.[97] In the

---

1887), 651; 16 July 1887 (*Sahachar*, 6 July 1887), 723; 16 July 1887 (*Samvad Bahika*, 6 June 1887), 737; 22 October 1887 (*Sanskaraka*, 8 September 1887), 1037; 22 October 1887 (*Navasamvad*, 15 September 1887), 1038; 3 December 1887 (*Sanskaraka*, 10 November 1887), 1206; 21 April 1888 (*Utkal Dipika* and *Samvadbahika*, 31 March 1888), 430; 30 June 1888 (*Utkal Dipika*, 26 May 1888), 647; 4 August 1888 (*Utkal Dipika*, 30 June 1888), 779; 25 August 1888 (*Utkal Dipika*, 4 August 1888), 857; 17 November 1888 (*Sahachar*, 7 November 1888), 1129; 8 December 1888 (*Sahachar*, 28 November 1888), 1189; 29 June 1889 (*Dipaka* and *Utkal Dipika*, 15 June 1889), 576; 17 January 1891 (*Bengal Exchange Gazette*, 12 January 1891), 82–83; 28 March 1891 (*Sahachar*, 18 March 1891), 373.

[97] OSA, R III-1/709, GoB, General Dpt., Resolution, 13 August 1881, 5; OSA, R III-1/708, GAROD 1881–82, 56–57; NAI, GoI, Railway Dpt., November 1881, nos. 139–162A, Office Note no. 1, 14 October 1881; OIOC, PWRC November 1881 (P/1705), no. 157, 1289 (correspondence between Hoare, Miller & Co. and GoI); "Report from Select Committee on East India Railway Communication", British Parliamentary Papers 1884 (284) xi.1, 34, 463 (statements by J. Caird and W. W. Hunter); OIOC, BPWP January 1884 (P/2231), Railway, nos. 66–68, 62–64 and February 1884 (P/2231), Railway, no. 1, 1–11 (correspondence on proposals from "certain

late 1880s (when the BNR mainline was planned and constructed) the colonial Government of India thus also considered a "Benares–Cuttack–Pooree pilgrim line" and had two alternative routes surveyed and estimated. The first, more direct line via the coal fields of Chota Nagpur and Chaibassa was soon rejected as it would have crossed the Kendujhar plateau, which was then deemed an "extremely poor, unproductive and unimprovable country".[98] In hindsight this is ironical as at the time of writing large tracts of this area are being torn up for their rich iron ore deposits at the behest of transnational steel corporations.[99] The second route was considered more seriously. Branching off from the BNR mainline at Panchpara towards Sambalpur, following thence the Mahanadi all the way down to Cuttack, the line would have terminated at Puri.[100] Again, there were high expectations: apart from its administrative benefits the railway "would open out the province of Orissa, enhance the prosperity of Bengal, and add to the revenue of the Bengal–Nagpore

---

English promoters for a metre-gauge railway from Vizagapatnam through Ganjam to Cuttack in Orissa, with a branch to Pooree"). For earlier railway schemes, see chapter 6.

[98] OIOC, BPWP March 1888 (P/3170), Railway, no. 45, Appendix A: GoB, PWD, Railway Branch: Benares–Cuttack–Puri Railway Reports, Estimates, and Correspondence from the Commencement up to the End of 1883–84 (Calcutta: Bengal Secretariat Press, 1886), 103–12 (F. J. E. Spring, Under-Secry. to Government of Bengal, PWD, on the Report and Estimates of the Benares–Cuttack–Puri Railway with a Branch to Gya, 30 August 1884); OIOC, BPWP October 1890 (P/3632), Railway, no. 38, 51–53 (note by Mr. Bestic, Under-Secry. to GoB, PWD, 21 February 1889). Also see the other papers compiled in the two volumes on the "Benares–Cuttack–Puri Railway" (cf.: footnote 100, in this chapter).

[99] Manshi Asher, "Steel not Enough?" *Economic and Political Weekly* 41, no. 7, 18–24 February 2006, 555–56.

[100] This scheme was documented extensively. See especially OIOC, BPWP August 1882 (P/1831), Railway, no. 3, 3 (CoCD to Secry. to GoB, PWD, 15 October 1881); OIOC, BPWP March 1888 (P/3170), Railway, no. 45, Appendix A, 1–125 (GoB, PWD, Railway Branch: Benares–Cuttack–Puri Railway, vol. 1); OIOC, BPWP March 1888 (P/3170), Railway, no. 46, Appendix B, 1–250 (GoB, PWD, Railway Branch: Benares–Cuttack–Puri Railway, Reports of the Engineers upon the Work of 1883–84, 1884–85 and 1885–86, and Estimates and Correspondence up to the Closure of the Work in November 1886, vol. 2 (Calcutta: Bengal Secretariat Press, 1887); OIOC, BPWP October 1890 (P/3632), Railway, no. 38, 51–53 (note by Mr. Bestic, Under-Secry. to GoB, PWD, 21 February 1889).

Railway", especially by attracting large numbers of pilgrims; it would also protect Orissa against famine and even dispel its bad reputation as the "home of Cholera".[101] In 1884, the chief official in Cuttack even believed that a Benares–Cuttack line would "benefit Orissa more than all possible schemes for canals and irrigation."[102] Such speculations on an unbuilt railway are, of course, unverifiable, but they do indicate a feasible historical alternative, which may well have entailed a course of interregional integration and the emergence of a circulatory regime substantially different from the one that actually shaped social practice and experience in Orissa for many decades. Originally planned as a state work it was, nonetheless, given low priority and re-scheduled in 1884 as a project to be undertaken by a private company, which was to receive government support in the form of free land, but no guarantee for annual interest payments to the shareholders.[103] The Bengal–Nagpur Railway Company, which received a government guarantee of 4 per cent in 1887 and would have been the agency constructing and operating this railway, had other priorities, too, and "postponed" this scheme in 1893–94 "for want of funds."[104] Postponement turned permanent when the company obtained the permission to establish its own terminus in Calcutta as well as to construct an important part of the East Coast Railway since these schemes required considerable capital and promised higher returns.[105] The direct railway link between

---

[101] Lord Ripon, Governor-General, to Secry. of State for India, 29 September 1884, quoted in *Railway Construction in India*, ed.Setter and Misra, item 321, 3: 218; OIOC, BPWP December 1884 (P/2235), Railway, no. 30, app. B, 13 ("Cuttack–Pooree Railway, Preliminary Reports and Estimates": "A. Smith, CoCD, to Secry. to GoB, PWD, 14 August 1883"); OIOC, BPWP October 1890 (P/3632), Railway, no. 38, 51–53 (note by Mr Bestic, Under-Secry. to GoB, PWD, 21 February 1889); "Railway Communications in Orissa", *The Indian Engineer* 21/382, 4 August 1894, 421–22.

[102] OSA, R III-1/710, GAROD 1883–84, 41. One of the predecessors of the quoted commissioner had asserted as early as in 1873 that the "most favourable line for a railway tapping the heart of Orissa, would be from the Central Provinces down the Mahanuddy valley to Cuttack and Pooree". OSA, R III-1/707B, GAROD 1872–73, 32. Also see GAROD 1873–74, 20; OSA, R III-1/709, GAROD 1881–82, 57.

[103] Settar and Misra, *Railway Construction in India*, item 321, 3: 218 (Lord Ripon, Governor-General, to Secry. of State for India, 29 September 1884).

[104] "Sambalpur Khurda Connection", in *South Eastern Railway*.

[105] *The Indian & Eastern Engineer: An Illustrated Weekly Journal for Engineers in*

Central India and the Orissa plains, the Mahanadi railroad between Sambalpur (connected to the BNR system in 1893) and Cuttack, was, therefore, shelved for a century and opened as late as in 1999.[106]

The construction of the Midnapur–Cuttack section of the East Coast Railway, sanctioned by the Government of India in 1895 and opened to traffic in successive stages between 1898 and 1900,[107] was thus the largest single investment in Orissa's transport infrastructure in the period under review. It followed the northeast-southwest axis of the region's circulatory regime, which connected Calcutta with Orissa's coastal districts. This axis had already been supplied with built environments for three modes of transport: the metalled Orissa Trunk Road, the High Level and Coast canals and the feeders and facilities of the ports of Chandbali and False Point. While the East Coast Railway marginalised the latter two of these competing lines within a few years,[108] the Orissa Trunk Road persisted as an important channel of transport. The latter became even more heavily frequented when motorised road traffic acquired considerable proportions in the interwar period. By then, "road and railway competition" had emerged as a major issue of 'public works' policy. The findings of a committee appointed in the early 1930s by the colonial government to investigate this problem on an all-India scale were particularly pertinent to the state of transport infrastructure in Orissa: the major channels of circulation were, on the whole, not complementary but in competition with each other. The only main line of railway doubled the only metalled transregional road.[109]

India and the East, 24/440, 14 September 1895, 555 (report on extraordinary meeting of the BNR Company in London).

[106] Keshab Das, "Underdevelopment by Design? Undermining Vital Infrastructure in Orissa", *Economic and Political Weekly* 41, no. 7, 18–24 February 2006, 647.

[107] "East Coast Railway" and "Extensions to Calcutta and Cuttack", in *South Eastern Railway*. Also see *The Indian & Eastern Engineer*, 24/433, 27 July 1895, 449; *The Indian & Eastern Engineer*, new series 4/3, March 1899, 77. The southern section of the East Coast Railway, which connected Cuttack and the Ganjam District with "Bezwada" (Vijayawada) on the Krishna River (and thereby with Madras) was constructed as a state railway since 1892.

[108] Maddox, *Final Report on Settlement of Orissa*, 1: 30–32; *Report of Orissa Flood Committee*, 25; Mukherjee, *Irrigation, Inland Navigation and Flood Problems*, 31.

[109] Mitchell and Kirkness, *Report on Present State of Road and Railway Competition*, 1–2, 7; Sarma, *Report on Road Development*, 16–17.

This line, the East Coast Railway, was constructed despite extremely costly engineering works, which were required for taking it across the numerous and sometimes vast riverbeds of the coastal plains. The spans of the bridges across the Mahanadi and her distributaries alone added up to a combined length of almost 4.5 km. The senior engineer in charge of their construction noted that this project "entailed no great engineering difficulties" but "was perhaps the largest of its kind ever undertaken in India, and certainly comprised the greatest amount of waterway in so short a length of railway".[110] Hence, bridges and other provisions for waterway made up for 42 per cent of the estimated outlay on the line between Cuttack and Balasore. The mileage rate for constructing the East Coast Railway increased far beyond the average as a result, while filling the order books of the British engineering companies who supplied the steel structures.[111]

A comprehensive view of the railway debates of the late 1890s discloses that the colonial administration pondered over two alternatives of connecting Orissa to the Indian railway network. Both alternatives—the coastal line from Midnapur to Cuttack and the Mahanadi line from Sambalpur to Khurda/Cuttack—were almost equal with regard to length (193 and 190 miles respectively) and estimated costs (Rs 22 and 23 million respectively).[112] Both alternatives

---

[110] William T. C. Beckett, "The Bridges over the Orissa Rivers on the East Coast Extension of the Bengal–Nagpur Railway", in *Minutes of Proceedings of the Institution of Civil Engineers* CXLV, 1901, 269, also see 268–91. The combined girder length of all bridges in the Orissa sections of the East Coast Railway added up to 6.7 km. *Summary of the Administration of Indian Railways during the Viceroyalty of Lord Curzon of Kedleston* (Calcutta: Office of the Superintendent of Government Printing, 1906), part II, 30.

[111] The mileage rate for the Orissa sections of the East Coast Railway was estimated at Rs 134,352 and thus more than 50 per cent in excess of that for the BNR mainline (Rs 87,220). The estimated mileage rate for the Sambalpur–Cuttack railway would also have been less (about Rs 119,000). "The Cuttack–Midnapur–Calcutta Railway" (part III), *The Indian Engineer* 20/367, 21 April 1894; OIOC, BPWP January 1885 (P/2231), Railways, app. (GoB, PWD, Railway Branch, Progress and Administration Report of the State Railways in Bengal for 1883–84); "Sambalpur Khurda Connection", in *South Eastern Railway*. Supplier of steel structures for the Orissa railway were following companies: P. & W. MacLellan Ltd., Braithwaite & Kirk and Horsehay Co. Ltd.: "East Coast Railway", in ibid.

[112] *The Indian Engineer* 20/367, 21 April 1894; "Sambalpur Khurda Connection", in Bhandari, *South Eastern Railway*.

were to be constructed by the BNR Company which had secured a 4 per cent guarantee for their shareholders in 1887. This implied an equal financial commitment on the part of the Government of India in each case, especially since both lines had been estimated to be "productive" (defined at that time as earning an annual profit of at least 4 per cent). Even if a greater "productivity" may have been expected from the East Coast Railway in terms of traffic receipts (which could have generated a larger revenue not only for the shareholders but also for the colonial state) purely financial considerations might still have recommended the Sambalpur–Cuttack line.[113] For the construction of the East Coast Railway dispelled any hope of recovering an appreciable portion of the large state investments in navigable canals along the NE–SW axis (amounting only for the Coast Canal, as we have seen, to Rs 4.5 million exclusive of interest charges).[114] Why one railway scheme was implemented and the other shelved cannot, therefore, be explained as the immediate and inescapable upshot of financial compulsions. Moreover, the availability of these canals and of other means of circulation along this axis also suggests that the decision for the coastal railway was no unmitigated response to a supposedly "objective" regional demand for transport infrastructure. It reflected rather a pattern in the 'public works' policy of the powerful—a pattern resonating with the interests dominating a colonial economy and with the socio-spatial dynamics of an age of imperialism. This pattern was pervasive despite all complexities and contradictions of 'public works policy'. In 1880, when the construction of the Coast Canal was the "project of the day", the Collector of Cuttack specified that one of its main objectives was to "convert Orissa (especially Balasore) from a remote and inaccessible region into a rural appanage of the metropolis."[115] Fifteen years on, a contribution to the *Indian Engineer*, a

---

[113] For the legal definition of "productive public works" in 1884, see "Report from the Select Committee on East India Railway Communication", British Parliamentary Papers 1884 (284) xi.1, iv. For the BNR's terms of contract with the GoI, see "Origins", "Bengal Nagpur Railway" and "Main Contract of BNR" in Bhandari, *South Eastern Railway*.

[114] See page 243, above.

[115] The other main objective was, in the collector's view, to provide a "means of transit for grain on the occasion of the next Orissa famine." OSA, BoRLR 4889 (draft for the General Administrative Report for Orissa Division, 1879–80, extract from a letter).

mouthpiece of imperial engineering, displayed less fondness for neofeudal jargon but still put Orissa in its supposedly preordained place: "*The mart* for the produce of the districts traversed by the East Coast line is Calcutta, and no time should be lost in bringing these districts into touch with *their mart* through the railway."[116] Summing up somewhat uneasily the material results of this policy, the provincial government of Bihar and Orissa stated in 1928 that "[a]ll the railways of the province are primarily designed to feed the great port of Calcutta."[117]

Pilgrims and Railways: An "Unreasonable" Appropriation

Social space, including the built environment, is not merely *produced* in a field of force by conflicting social agencies. As soon as transport infrastructure is opened to traffic, its polyvalence is realised by numerous appropriations for potentially conflicting purposes. The Indian railway system was thus immediately appropriated by large numbers of pilgrims to Hindu shrines and even by those who ventured to Puri. In the early 1880s it was believed that pilgrimage to Gaya had more than doubled after the construction of the railway.[118] From the same decade onwards, there was also a marked increase of pilgrimage to Jagannath which was at least partly due to improved railway communications: pilgrims from North or Central India could travel by rail to locations in Bengal or (after the opening of the BNR in 1891) in Chhattisgarh from where they continued their journey by road or waterway.[119] As for the large number of pilgrims from Bengal it was obvious by then that the expansion of steamer traffic (along the coast and on the canal) had brought little relief as far as travelling conditions were concerned: steamers were

---

[116] "The East Coast Railway Extension", *Indian Engineer* 23/409, 9 February 1895, emphasis added.

[117] Govt. of Bihar and Orissa, *Bihar and Orissa in 1927–28*, 108.

[118] OIOC, BPWP August 1882 (P/1831), Railway, no. 4, 4.

[119] See, for example, *RNNB*, 29 July 1882 (*Utkal Dipika*, 22 July 1882), 270: "From Bombay, the Punjab, from east and west, and from Bengal, pilgrims come by rail to Calcutta, and thence by steamer to Cuttack." The conclusion that Jagannath pilgrimage increased from the 1880s can be drawn from the available figures though they are far from reliable. Yet even contemporaries sensed this increase. See, for instance, ibid., 12 July 1884 (*Samvad Bahika*, 19 June 1884), 844.

extensively used by pilgrims[120] but still reported to be "exceedingly inconvenient and distasteful to natives".[121] A "Jagannath Pilgrim Fund Committee" of Balasore calculated in 1887 that approximately 6,000 pilgrims died annually on their journey to Puri on both overland routes and waterways (many of them due to insanitary travel facilities and the resulting epidemic outbreaks of waterborne diseases like cholera).[122] There was hence little doubt that an Orissa railway would readily be embraced as an alternative by a large number of pilgrims. And so it was. Although statistical evidence for nineteenth-century pilgrimage is far from reliable and considerable fluctuations in the number of *yatris* could occur from one year to the next (since certain festivals were only performed in certain years),[123] the following statement may provide an idea of the general trend: about 340,000 pilgrims were reported to have

[120] See footnote 136, in this chapter.
[121] *Papers Relating to Orissa Coast Canal* [1877 to 1881], 14 (Note by Colonel F. T. Haig, CE, Bengal PWD, Irrigation Branch, 15 February 1878). This quote related to the coastal steamers but reports on conditions on board the canal steamers do not suggest that they were any more acceptable: "That much suffering, discomfort, exposure, starvation, sickness and actual loss of life, direct and indirect, to passengers themselves, and afterwards to inhabitants of their native villages and districts, result are [sic] only far too evident. ... Speaking of the canal routes particularly, it is well-known that the steamers, and towed barges and flats especially, were overcrowded with human beings. And, as was discovered, it would appear to have been at once fatal for any passenger to have got sick of such a disease as cholera on board some of these vessels as he was apt to be abandoned on the most convenient canal bank, and if he happened to have expired before this happy consummation his body was as promptly thrown overboard. Bodies have thus been picked up in the canals by the Police; those in the rivers of course never return to tell tales." O'Gorman, *Puri Pilgrim Canal Traffic*, 5–7.
[122] *RNNB*, 7 January 1888 (*Uriya*, 7 December 1887), 28–29. Hunter's estimate in the early 1870s had even amounted to an annual mortality of 10,000 pilgrims. See Hunter, *The Annals of Rural Bengal*, 2: 157.
[123] Extraordinary numbers of pilgrims assemble, for instance, when the rath yatra, the most important annual festival, coincides with the *naba kalebar* festival, which usually takes place every twelve years. Particularly large rath yatras were recorded for 1893 (200,000) and 1912 (250,000). W. H. Gregg, *26th Annual Report of the Sanitary Commissioner for Bengal 1893* (Calcutta: Government Press, 1894), 21; O'Gorman, *Puri Pilgrim Canal Traffic*, 3; E. C. Hare, *Annual Sanitary Report of the Province of Bihar and Orissa (1912)* (Patna: Bihar and Orissa Government Press, 1913), 6.

reached Puri in an unusually active year of pilgrimage in the 1870s, whereas the most reliable source for the early 1910s, the report of a "Pilgrim Committee", appointed by the Government of Bihar and Orissa in 1913, indicates an average figure of more than half a million.[124]

Yet the appropriation of the railways by yatris not only entailed a considerable quantitative growth but also qualitative changes in the spatial, temporal and social patterns of Puri pilgrimage.[125] For the time when the yatris set out for a slow journey of several months to approach Jagannath along an extensive chain of numerous minor pilgrimage sites drew to a close. As late as in 1881 the road journey from the railhead of Raniganj in western Bengal to Puri had taken twenty-six days;[126] by the turn of the century the journey from Calcutta to Puri could be done in twelve hours.[127] This instance of "time–space compression" implied a considerable transformation of the religious landscape: pilgrimage to Puri had earlier required a densely knit network of dharamsalas, bazaars, temples and ferries, that afforded shelter, food and various other services after every day's journey, a network that had involved and sustained an intermediate level of less prominent pilgrimage centres like Kantilo or Jajpur, where several minor routes converged. Many of these nodal

---

[124] Late nineteenth-century estimates of the annual number of pilgrims reaching Puri varied widely but were usually between 50,000 and 350,000. Hunter, *The Annals of Rural Bengal*, 2: 150; OSA, 14,922 BoRLR (R. L. Mangles, Offg. Secry. to GoB, Judicial Dpt., to CoCD, 29 March 1877); *Papers Relating to Orissa Coast Canal* [1877 to 1881], 14 (Note by Colonel F. T. Haig, CE, Bengal PWD, Irrigation Branch, 15 February 1878); W. H. Gregg, *27th Annual Report of the Sanitary Commissioner for Bengal, 1894* (Calcutta: Government Press, 1895), 29. Police counts in Puri indicated that "the average number of pilgrims visiting the shrine at Puri for nine years from 1874 to 1882 was 210,605, the largest number in any one year being 337,235". OIOC, BPWP March 1888 (P/3170), Railway, no. 46, Appendix B, 160 (GoB, PWD, Railway Branch: Benares–Cuttack–Puri Railway, vol. II). For the 1913 estimate quoted above, see *Report of the Pilgrim Committee, Bihar and Orissa* (Simla: Government Central Branch Press, 1913), 52.

[125] For a suggestive discussion of qualitative changes in pilgrimage patterns on an all-India level, see Kerr, "Reworking a Popular Religious Practice", 313–17.

[126] OIOC, BPWP August 1882 (P/1831), Railway, no. 4, 4.

[127] W. Wesley Clemesha, *37th Annual Report of the Sanitary Commissioner for Bengal, 1904* (Calcutta: Bengal Secretariat Press, 1905), 12.

points of an older sacred landscape were now bypassed by the increasingly rail-borne pilgrim traffic between India's regions, which did not necessarily imply dilapidation but surely a redefinition of their position in social space.[128]

Moreover, the "Pilgrim Committee" of 1913 noted that the temporal patterns or the annual rhythm of pilgrimage had changed: participation in great festivals like the rath yatra (car festival) increased markedly, but not as steeply as the annual figures. Pilgrim traffic thus came to be distributed more evenly over the year though in certain seasons, when work was less in agriculture, unexpected rushes occurred as villagers used the opportunity for a short pilgrimage to Puri.[129] This temporal transformation had several social implications. For one, the social base of pilgrimage seems to have widened as a yatra to Jagannath became feasible for larger sections of the peasantry and also for the female population in terms of both expenditure and the time required. Moreover, as Calcutta's middle classes acquired a taste for trips to Puri that combined traditional pilgrimage with modern tourism, clever entrepreneurs began to develop the facilities of a holiday resort.[130]

---

[128] This appears to be a major field of India's cultural history that has hardly been explored so far. The present study can only hint at this phenomenon of a dynamic religious landscape and emphasise the complexities of the processes involved. Hence it is not suggested here that the imposition of new transport networks upon South Asia's social space resulted in a whole scale decline of minor sacred centres. The tendency towards concentration appears to have been rather coupled with a countervailing tendency, which generated new minor foci of ritual practice. Hermann Kulke has, for instance, drawn my attention to the phenomenon that the expansion of the network of motorable roads in Orissa has been accompanied by a sometimes spectacular rise of roadside temples.

[129] *Report of Pilgrim Committee*, 4–5. Also see Kerr, "Reworking a Popular Religious Practice", 315.

[130] Jakob Rösel, "The Evolution and Organization of Pilgrimage to Jagannatha at Puri", in *Pilgrimage Studies: Text and Context,* eds. D. P. Dubey and L. Gopal, Sri Phalahari Baba Commemoration Volume (Allahabad: The Society of Pilgrimage Studies, 1990), 112. Consider also the following interesting report of the British "civil medical officer" in Puri from the year of the opening of the East Coast Railway: "Nearly all the people I questioned said they had been told by the pandas that they would be able to come all the way by rail, and that, for this reason, they would require only to bring very little food or money with them, and that they would thus be able to do the whole pilgrimage and return to their houses within a few days. In this way

This entanglement of pilgrimage with new commercial pursuits was merely one facet of a larger process, in which the economy and spatial practice of pilgrimage was transformed after the extension of railway tracks to Puri. This is particularly evident with regard to the changed role of the *pandas* (temple priests) of Jagannath in the organisation of pilgrimage. Previously, a panda would have visited a few villages annually where his family had been recruiting pilgrims for generations, had been donated land and had, thereby, knit close networks with local society. These spatial linkages had been viewed by the British with suspicion and the pandas had been perceived as "pilgrim-hunters".[131] Far from rendering these old networks obsolete, the opening of the East Coast Railway now permitted pandas to operate on a larger social and spatial scale: Powerful pilgrimage entrepreneurs emerged who bought, rented or simply invaded the rights and privileges of other pandas. Pilgrim registers, in which such claims were carefully entered, became valuable and transferable assets. More powerful pandas ceased to go to the villages themselves and preferred to send agents while they diversified their economic activities in Puri town. Older layers of social space and the social relations constituting them were recast rather than conserved or dissolved by the establishment of the new transport infrastructure. Those pandas, who were able to grasp the opportunities emerging from rising levels of geographical and social integration, transformed the organisation of pilgrimage into commercial enterprises.[132]

Not all Hindu notables appreciated the changes accompanying "railway pilgrimage". Insisting famously in 1909 that "[g]ood travels at a snail's pace" and charging the railways with having rendered

---

many poor women were induced to leave their houses, their husbands and their families surreptitiously." H. J. Dyson, *32nd Annual Report of the Sanitary Commissioner for Bengal, 1899* (Calcutta: Bengal Secretariat Press, 1900), 26.

[131] See, for example, John Beames, *Memoirs of a Bengal Civilian* (London: Chatto & Windus, 1961), 196.

[132] Such changes in the practices of pilgrimage seem to have rarely attracted the interest of social historians. An exception, on which the present discussion is mainly based, is Jakob Rösel's excellent essay "Evolution and Organization of Pilgrimage to Jagannatha"; see especially, 110–13. Rösel, however, assumes a steady growth of the Jagannath pilgrimage during the whole of the nineteenth century, while the present writer could not find evidence for any substantial increase prior to the 1880s.

the "holy places of India . . . unholy",[133] Gandhi echoed ideas that had been aired for years. One Bangla newspaper correspondent had warned, for instance, in 1895 that "all means of rapid locomotion are . . . impediments in the way of acquiring religious merit".[134] R. C. Dutt, who had turned into a formidable critic of colonial railway policy after his spell as a Commissioner of Orissa, also underscored the superior value of traditional modes of pilgrimage to Jagannath by having the protagonists of his novel *The Lake of Palms* (1902) prefer the slow pilgrimage by palanquin and horse to the railway journey. These traditional modes consumed, of course, both funds and time to an extent more easily affordable by the moneyed and leisured classes, particularly if they were to be tolerably comfortable ("Two bullock carts carried few servants and the cooking vessels, always going ahead by night to have things ready in time at each successive stage of the journey", described Dutt the travel arrangements of rich pilgrims).[135] Be that as it may, the steamer and later the railway largely displaced older modes of overland pilgrimage to Puri in an amazingly short time, notwithstanding the perceived antagonism between material acceleration and spiritual progress.[136]

The appropriation of the railways by pilgrims also met with an ambivalent response from the colonial oligarchy. Of all pilgrim destinations of India, Puri had drawn upon itself the maximum of evangelical venom and "Juggernaut" had become a byword for heathen monstrosity and India's lack of 'civilisation'. This had not

---

[133] Mohandas K. Gandhi, *Collected Works of Mahatma Gandhi*, vol. 10 (New Delhi: Publications Division, Ministry of Information and Broadcasting, Govt. of India, 1966), 267 (the quote is from the 1939 edition of "Hind Swaraj", which was first published in 1909).

[134] *RNNB*, 9 November 1895 (*Dainik-o-Samachar Chandrika*, 31 October 1895), 983.

[135] Romesh Chunder Dutt, *The Lake of Palms* (London: T. F. Unwin, 1902), especially 154–55, 189–90.

[136] Hence it was reported in 1894 that "during the year under report about 25,000 pilgrims passed by Jagarnath Trunk road on their way to and from Puri, and about 206,271 pilgrims are reported to have taken the Orissa Coast Canal and sea routes." Gregg, *27th Annual Report of Sanitary Commissioner, 1894*, 29. In 1912 it was known that of the 250,000 pilgrims who had visited Puri during the latter half of July and the beginning of August over 150,000 had been carried by the railway. Hare, *Annual Sanitary Report of Bihar and Orissa, 1912*, 6.

prevented colonial officials from including pilgrim traffic in their calculations regarding the "productivity" of investments in Orissa's transport infrastructure, nor did it stop the BNR Company from advertising the East Coast Railway as a facility permitting Hindus "to reach the place of their heart's desire" without incurring the risks of pre-railway travel[137]. There had also been an expectation of future changes that was most evocatively articulated by Kipling in 1893 in his story "The Bridge-Builders".[138] According to Kipling though railways might temporarily reinforce pilgrimage and the brahmanical order in general, the cunning of a technicistic and authoritarian reason would work its way in the long run: the sheer and quasi-magical power of European science and technology would confine the gods of the Hindus to the jungles; the ideological hegemony of the brahmans would be replaced by the hegemony of British technocrats; the homogenising force of the overcrowded third-class railway carriage would undermine irrational caste hierarchies (while the compartmentalisation of spaces in trains and stations according to race and class guaranteed a social order that was considered more reasonable). Yet, as the above account of the panda's adaptation to the new circulatory regime exemplifies, these hopes were to be disappointed on many counts: the pursuit of the 'civilising mission' frequently yielded results very different from the intentions of the colonial rulers.[139]

Therefore, despite the fact that pilgrim traffic was a profitable business for the colonial state, for British-owned railway companies and other entrepreneurs, British officials were never quite at ease with the prompt appropriation of the railway network by Indian pilgrims. If they had argued, before the construction of the Orissa railway, that steam locomotion would relieve the region from the scourge of cholera as pilgrims would be removed from the unhealthy conditions of Puri much faster,[140] they soon came to perceive the

---

[137] St. Nihal Singh, *The Changing Scene in India* (Calcutta: Bengal Nagpur Railway, n.d.), 48 (published in the 1920s).
[138] Rudyard Kipling, *The Writings in Prose and Verse of Rudyard Kipling* (London/New York: Macmillan, 1899), 13: 3–56.
[139] This paragraph summarises a more elaborate discussion in my essay "'The Bridge-Builders'", but also draws on interpretations from Goswami, *Producing India*, 103–9 and 116–27.
[140] See, for example, OIOC, BPWP December 1884 (P/2235), Railway, no. 30, Appendix B, Cuttack, A. Smith, CoCD, to Secry. to GoB, PWD, 14

threat that, as Kipling put it, the sickness might be attached "to the wheels of the fire-carriages",[141] that cholera epidemics might be spread from Puri to distant parts of the subcontinent.[142] These perceptions appear to have been exaggerated but were not totally unfounded. In 1912, for instance, when the rath yatra was attended by almost a quarter of a million of pilgrims, the minimum number of Puri pilgrims who had died of cholera on the train during their return journey was 251.[143] Yet British railway and government officials, like those in the Bihar and Orissa "Pilgrim Committee" of 1913, were not prepared to admit that appalling sanitary conditions in trains and stations were important contributing factors to such outbreaks of diseases. Rather, according to their view, pilgrimage and epidemics were inevitably connected.

Interestingly, this inevitability theory seems to have sounded far less plausible to many pilgrims. A round trip experience to various pilgrimage sites in Bihar and Orissa left the members of the committee completely bewildered that Indian pilgrims, the gentlemen discovered, were far from being awe struck and grateful in the face of the new "fire-carriages" that had been bestowed on them by their colonial masters. Instead, they found that "[w]herever we went we were inundated with complaints regarding the manner in which pilgrims are carried and treated in their journeys by rail."[144] What annoyed the committee is particularly interesting for our purposes

---

August 1883, 13; Gregg, *27th Annual Report of Sanitary Commissioner, 1894*, 29; H. J. Dyson, *31st Annual Report of the Sanitary Commissioner for Bengal, 1898* (Calcutta: Bengal Secretariat Press, 1899), 24.

[141] Kipling, *Writings in Prose and Verse*, 13: 40.

[142] *Report of Pilgrim Committee*, 4.

[143] Ibid., 3. On the role of railways (and not only of pilgrim rail traffic) in spreading cholera, see Ira Klein, "Imperialism, Ecology and Disease: Cholera in India, 1850–1950", *Indian Economic and Social History Review* 31, no. 4, 1994, 505–10, and Ira Klein, "Death in India, 1871–1921", *Journal of Asian Studies* 32, no. 4, 1973, 649.

[144] *Report of Pilgrim Committee*, 31. Complaints against practices of railway administration were also frequent in other regions. See, for example, Manjiri N. Kamat, "'The Palkhi as Plague Carrier': The Pandharpur Fair and the Sanitary Fixation of the Colonial State; British India, 1908–1916", in *Health, Medicine and Empire: Perspectives on Colonial India*, ed. Biswamoy Pati and Mark Harrison (London: Sangam, 2001), 306–7.

and may, therefore, be worth quoting the report's relevant passages at some length:

> Quick to appreciate the comforts and advantages of railway travelling in these days, the educated and well-to-do people of this country have interested themselves greatly in all matters of railway administration. This branch of public affairs occupies their attention very largely and they are continually asking for the extension and improvement of the railway system throughout the country. The numerous questions in the Legislative Council show how keenly the shortcomings of the railway are scrutinised all over India. It is not strange then that the railway arrangements during the festivals at places of pilgrimage should come in for a good deal of adverse comment. The trains are crowded to their utmost; often there is no seat to be found; it is very difficult to get a ticket; trains are frequently delayed; food and water are not readily procurable: the discomforts are too well known to every one to need detailed enumeration. The educated passenger finds that travelling at the time of a great religious festival is a very different thing from an ordinary railway journey. His acquaintance with the railway, however, is too short for him to understand that much of this discomfort is unavoidable and that, go where you will in the world, wherever there is a rush of travellers there will, and must, be similar discomforts. Railways are new and it is not fully realised in this country as elsewhere that at times the rush and the overcrowding are inevitable. The Indian has a trusting belief that he has but to make a complaint and someone will find the remedy.

What was even worse, however, was that these complaints were not confined to babus or "educated classes" whose demands were generally considered to be unrepresentative of the "true mind" of the people:

> The patient villager is slow to voice his grievances but will, if questioned, likewise add his protest against the railway arrangements. The same villager who will cheerfully submit to any overcrowding in his panda's house, to any sort of shelter at the fair, to any crushing or weary waiting at the temple door, to any exactions from his priest, reserves his grumble for the railway. This seems strange but is largely due to the newness of the railways: it has always been his experience that fairs are crowded and priests greedy but that railways are generally comfortable; his acquaintance with the latter is too short for him to understand that there are times when lapses from the normal must be expected.[145]

---

[145] *Report of Pilgrim Committee*, 31.

The committee did not deny that many complaints were based on real grievances. They conceded, for instance, that yatris were herded into goods wagons covered with the grime of previous transports of coal, chillies or hides and bones. Nor did they deny that "trucks used for carrying cattle are much better provided with ventilation than those generally used in the pilgrim traffic".[146] The gentlemen's irritation arose rather from the fact that the complaints with regard to pilgrim traffic (and railway transport in general) were uttered openly and publicly by large sections of various social groups in Bihar and Orissa. This appropriation of the transformed social space did not content itself with merely using the pathways conceived by the colonial oligarchy. It went beyond a submissive utilisation of an imposed infrastructure—the only appropriation becoming to colonial subjects. For the complainants implicitly claimed, with regard to the presumably 'public' works, an accountability of the authorities to a 'public', of which the claimants were part and which they constituted by voicing their complaints. This was at odds with the colonial assumption that most Indian subjects were incapable and would remain incapable for an undefined period to be members of a 'public' exerting effective control over the authorities (see chapter 3). In response, the committee's report deplored that colonial authorities could not instil the same kind of unquestioning obedience in their subjects' minds as the representatives of 'traditional' hierarchy (the pandas and priests) presumably could. In other words, there was a sense of inadequate "basic legitimacy" and lacking hegemony. Moreover, the committee saw the main reason for the persistent and general criticism of railway arrangements for pilgrims in the brief "acquaintance" of both "educated passengers" and "patient villagers" with railways: Indians were lacking in experience—therefore, they just could not understand. The refusal of Indians to accept social minority was used as a proof for their continuing incapability of political participation and need of paternal regulation. Hence, the members of the committee did not feel obliged to explain why railway companies were adverse to the use of volunteers in the organisation of pilgrim traffic, though "Indian gentlemen" had offered assistance at various places.[147]

---

[146] Ibid., 36–37.
[147] *Report of Pilgrim Committee*, 51. For the frequency of such complaints, also see Kerr, "Reworking a Popular Religious Practice", 316–19.

This seems to have been typical of the prevailing attitude of railway authorities towards Indian pilgrims—an attitude that relied more heavily on the enforcement of obedience and less effort made to muster cooperation. This attitude expressed itself in numerous quotidian practices of authority which were experienced and sometimes resisted by thousands. One of these practices, tried out in Puri for instance before being applied to all major pilgrimage sites of India, consisted of subjecting incoming pilgrims to compulsory cholera inoculations before permitting them to leave the railway station.[148] A study of such experiences may well permit new insights into the everyday structures of colonial power but is beyond the scope of this study. However, the following quotes from the memoirs of John W. Mitchell, a railway official who had once been in charge of the Puri section of the BNR, provide a telling glimpse of such structures. "The Bengal–Nagpur Railway," wrote Mitchell proudly, "has built up a most efficient system of handling the masses of ignorant, illiterate, grown-up children who crowd its trains to Puri bound."[149] And he also gave an example for the workings of this system at Puri's railway terminal:

> Four huge roofed steel pens, permanent and solid, each capable of accommodating 1,500 pilgrims, have been erected. To prevent overcrowding and possible chaos, never more than approximately 1,000 passengers are allowed to enter at one time. No one is admitted to the platforms without first passing through these pens which segregate the pilgrims according to their ticket colours. One can hardly imagine an English Railway administration attempting to pen off its football crowds and shoe traffic passengers this way. Steel bars would never suffice for them. They would have to be reinforced by asbestos to withstand the sulphurous language from the enraged inmates. This is India, however, and other countries, other peoples, other ways.[150]

---

[148] Central Advisory Board of Health, *Report of the Sub-Committee Appointed by the Central Advisory Board of Health to Examine the Possibility of Introducing a System of Compulsory Inoculation of Pilgrims against Cholera* (Simla: Government of India Press, 1940), 7. For conflicts over compulsory measures of plague prevention in Maharashtra's most important pilgrimage centre in the early years of the twentieth century, see Kamat, "Palkhi as Plague Carrier", 299–316.

[149] John W. Mitchell, *Wheels of India: Autobiographical Reminiscences of a Railway Official in India* (London: Thornton Butterworth, 1934), 268–69.

[150] Mitchell, *Wheels of India*, 306.

"Handling the masses", Mitchell reassured his British readers, was still an easier task in India than in England. However, the conditions of railborne pilgrim traffic and the authoritarian measures imposed by the colonial administration had long since given rise to numerous complaints and demands for accountability. Infrastructural development, the construction of the railways with their monumental iron girder bridges and stations had been intended to enhance the "basic legitimacy" of British rule (see chapter 3). Yet, the new circulatory regime generated conflicts over the control of social space: the colonial ruling block failed to hegemonise "public opinion" on the railways, on one of their main achievements in transforming India's social space. Instead, the shared quotidian experience of racial discrimination and authoritarian "systems of handling the masses" raised questions of political legitimacy and participation.

8

Kings, Commerce and Corvée
in the Tributary States

The transformation of Orissa's circulatory patterns and transport infrastructure started in the coastal plains and along the region's western margin. These processes have been outlined in the preceding chapter. The emerging new circulatory regime of the region as a whole cannot be understood, however, if directly connected developments in the hills and valleys of interior Orissa are ignored. For since the 1870s, the colonial oligarchy, Indian entrepreneurs and also the rajas and chiefs of the Tributary States increasingly looked for means of commercially exploiting the agricultural potential of the interior valleys and the rich forest and mineral resources of the surrounding hills[1]. By the end of the century, the infrastructure policy of the little kingdoms and the circulatory regime were undergoing major changes—a process whose contradictory implications for the various social groups of western and northern Orissa stood out with particular clarity. These are the themes that run through this chapter.

Commercial Kingdoms and Improving Rajas

When agriculture in the plains was commercialised after the Orissa famine and ports were turned into major transshipment centres for rice trade in the Bay of Bengal, repercussions were almost immediately felt in the interior Garhjat region of Orissa. The *ancien régime* of circulation, briefly outlined in chapter 4, had, of course, integrated the plains with the hills in various ways. This was done not

---

[1] The princely states of Orissa were also designated as Garhjat States, Tributary Mahals and, since the end of the nineteenth century, as Feudatory States. They will here be referred to as Tributary States consistently for the convenience of readers.

only by way of an integrated religious and political landscape consisting of numerous interdependent ritual sites and centres of pilgrimage, but also through an economic complementarity based, roughly speaking, on the exchange of salt for various types of forest produce. Socio-spatial integration of the two subregions as such was thus no achievement of the later nineteenth century. Some areas of western Orissa such as Sambalpur were even to some extent disarticulated from the coastal plains when their traffic was rerouted to the BNR mainline.[2] In other Garhjat areas, the intensity, content and modality of circulatory exchange with the districts of Balasore, Cuttack and Puri was transformed in a different way. The growing export demand for food grains entailed not only an expansion of cultivation on the alluvial soil of the river deltas. Valleys of Orissa's interior tracts were also integrated more closely into the circuits of transregional grain trade since the 1870s.[3] The resulting intensification of commercial agriculture in this area was further reinforced by the uneven distribution of the gains of commercialisation in the coastal districts. As marginal peasants found it increasingly difficult to make ends meet and to hold on to their ancestral lands, many were drawn towards the Garhjat kingdoms where land was more easily accessible.[4] One reason for the comparatively low intensity of permanent transregional emigration from the Orissa plains in the late nineteenth century (for instance to Assam, see chapter 7) may well be found in the drive towards intraregional resettlement in combination with a large-scale and permanent conversion of forest into (permanent) agricultural crop land. Moreover, this expansion of settled agriculture was not the only effect of commercialisation: as the networks and infrastructures of export trade became established more firmly, the possibilities of commercially exploiting the natural resources of Orissa's hill area expanded, too. Up to the end of the century the focus of commercial interest rested not on the rich mineral deposits of the interior in the first place. The coal beds of the Tributary State of Talcher were, for instance, first explored by

---

[2] OSA, R III-1/716, GAROD 1894–95, 19.
[3] OSA, R III-1/708, GAROD 1878–79, 13; OSA, R III-1/709, GAROD 1883–84, 10; OSA, R III-1/714, GAROD 1888–89, 15–16.
[4] P. C. Tallents, *Census of India, 1921: Bihar and Orissa*, Vol. VII (Patna: n.p., 1923), part I: "Report", 63–64. Also see table 6.

a British engineer in 1838,[5] surveyed by a prominent colonial geologist in the 1870s,[6] but mining commenced only in the mid-1920s.[7] Kendujhar was similarly renowned as a source for high-quality iron ore without attracting mining companies for decades.[8] "[T]hroughout these Gurjat States, the great natural resource is timber,"[9] believed a senior colonial official in 1863 and slow-growing hardwood came to be, indeed, the prime object of commercial desires in the following half-century. The extensive sal forests of Orissa were thus, like teak and *deodar* populations elsewhere in India, converted to railway sleepers (railroad ties) in large proportions. The demand for hardwood was enormous in these decades of a swiftly expanding Indian railway network, especially since the sleepers had to be replaced every few years.[10] As early as in 1879 colonial officials had warned

---

[5] Kittoe, "Mr. Kittoe's Journal", 1061–62.

[6] Valentine Ball, *Jungle Life in India or the Journeys and Journals of an Indian Geologist* (London: De La Rue, 1880), 512–13.

[7] *Review of the Annual Report on the Administration of the Feudatory States of Orissa and Chota Nagpur* [hereafter *RARAFS* followed by year] *1923–24*, 24, 33; Government of Bihar and Orissa, *Bihar and Orissa in 1925–26* (Patna: Superintendent of Government Printing, Bihar and Orissa, 1927), 18; *General Review of the Administration of the Feudatory States of Orissa* [hereafter: *GRAFSO* followed by year] *1926–27*, 22, 26.

[8] OIOC, BPWP March 1888 (P/3170), Railway, no. 46, Appendix B, 42 (Report by J. M. Luff, Temporary Engineer [sic], on the Keunjhar Division of 1884–85, in: GoB, PWD, Railway Branch: Benares–Cuttack–Puri Railway, vol. II: Reports of the Engineers upon the Work of 1883–84, 1884–85 and 1885–86, and Estimates and Correspondence up to the Closure of the Work in November 1886 (Calcutta: Bengal Secretariat Press, 1887).

[9] Temple, "Report on the Mahanuddy", 19.

[10] For Orissa, see *RATMO 1897–98*, 11; *Report on the Administration of the Feudatory States of Orissa and Chota Nagpur* [hereafter *RAFSOC* followed by year] *1916–17* (Patna: Superintendent of Government Printing, 1917), 10–11; *RARAFS 1923–24*, 8; *GRAFSO 1925–26*, 10; *GRAFSO 1926–27*, 8; *GRAFSO 1928–29*, 17. For the exploitation of hardwood populations in other Indian regions for the production of railway sleepers, see Madhav Gadgil and Ramachandra Guha, *This Fissured Land: An Ecological History of India* (New Delhi/Oxford: Oxford University Press, 1992), 120–22, 137–38; E. P. Flint, "Deforestation and Land Use in Northern India with a Focus on Sal (Shorea robusta) Forests, 1880–1980", in *Nature and the Orient: The Environmental History of South and South East Asia*, ed. Richard H. Grove, Vinita Damodaran and Satpal Sangwan (Delhi: Oxford University Press, 1998), 437–39.

that a coherent forest policy was required in the Tributary States to avoid "the reckless destruction of the forest".[11] In some states forests were damaged to an extent that prompted rajas and their British overlords to impose forest regulations. However, these forest regulations were often primarily not directed against the commercial overexploitation by large Calcutta-based timber companies but rather against traditional practices of forest utilisation such as shifting cultivation.[12] By the end of the century, deforestation in the hill tracts had severe ecological consequences: the discharge volume of the rivers increased considerably and the ensuing inundations in the plains became more destructive.[13] Even so, the colonial government acknowledged well into the 1920s that these extremely wasteful and damaging practices of converting sal forests into sleepers were being continued, since long-term contracts of timber companies with certain Garhjat kingdoms could not be interfered with.[14]

The dominant strata of Garhjat society and particularly the various types of chiefs nevertheless experienced commercialisation as a new chance for self-assertion and aggrandisement in a period when older sources of power were drying up (see below). As a consequence, the rajas moved away gradually but radically from the policies of social space, circulation and infrastructure their *ancien régime* ancestors had pursued (see chapter 5). This departure was gradual because changes in the patterns of circulation were initially achievable without major investments in roads or railways. Timber was rafted down the rivers as before, only in larger proportions, while an increasing number of pack bullocks carried rice to plains on well-beaten tracks.[15] It was only when new circulatory needs and networks had

[11] *Papers Relating to Orissa Coast Canal* [1877 to 1881], 61 (report by J. C. Vertannes, EE, Balasore, 10 January 1879).
[12] OSA, R III-1/709, GAROD 1881–82, 4; *RATMO 1896–97*, 32–33; *RATMO 1898–99*, 2; Cobden-Ramsay, *Feudatory States*, 95–97; *GRAFSO 1925–26*, 28. Also see Praharaj, *Tribal Movements and Political History*, 131; Kanchanmoy Mojumdar, *Changing Tribal Life in British Orissa* (New Delhi: Kaveri Books, 1998), 39.
[13] Hill, "Ideology and Public Works", 59–60.
[14] *GRAFSO 1928–29*, 17.
[15] OSA, R III-1/709, GAROD 1883–84, 10; OSA, R III-1/714, GAROD 1889–90, 10. Only general observations of colonial officials can be found as evidence for the growth of grain and timber transports from the Tributary States. "What is usually regarded as the trade of Orissa is such portion of that

established themselves to some extent that investment in infrastructure and a corresponding reconstruction of the Garhjat polities as a whole became the *sine qua non* of further commercialisation.

In anticipation of the current standard indictment against historians who take notice of material processes: it is, of course, not suggested here that the "economic logic" of colonial capitalism enforced itself "path-dependently", mechanically and irrespective of social agency upon all spheres of political and social life. Economic, political and ideological aspirations and practices rather generated a historically distinctive and potentially conflictual field of force in which a new "layer" of social space was produced. The point is that the variously motivated aspirations and practices of Orissa's princes came to *reinforce each other* by the turn of the century with respect to transport infrastructure. This had not been the case as long as the *ancien régime* of circulation (outlined in chapter 4) had held sway: even though the control of channels of circulation provided political leverage and sources of revenue, inaccessibility was the best protection of local rulers against overbearing overlords, while the social demand for means of circulation did not call for heavy expenditure on built environment. In other words, even if local rulers had been able to extract sufficient revenue from their subjects to afford a costly transport infrastructure this would not have been the most promising strategy to preserve or expand their social and political power.

This historical constellation was gradually transformed in the last third of the nineteenth century. By then British power had been consolidated to an extent that it could no longer be eschewed by retreating to remote hill forts. John Beames, a senior colonial official in Orissa between 1869 and 1877, summarised the political relationship between the Garhjat rajas and the colonial administration of Orissa as follows:

> The system in force in 1877 when I took charge [as commissioner] was as follows. The Rajas were allowed the general administration of their territories, but any of the subjects who felt himself aggrieved by any act

---

trade as enters and leaves the Orissa ports", remarked Commissioner R. C. Dutt in 1895 criticising that no statistics were available for the overland trade between British-ruled Orissa, the Tributary States and the neighbouring districts. Relying on the available quantitative data, historians have, therefore, often missed out on this very significant segment of Orissa's circuits of exchange. See OSA, R III-1/716, GAROD 1894–95, 17–18.

of his Raja might appeal to the Commissioner, who asked for an explanation from the Raja, and finally decided what ought to be done and communicated his decision to the Raja. If the Raja refused to obey, no one exactly knew what would have happened. But it was tacitly understood that he would not refuse and, as a matter of fact, he knew better than to do so. This is what is called "moral influence". When backed by bayonets it is a great power. Moreover each Raja had a minister. This is a very ancient native institution. ... Ravenshaw[16] and his predecessors had in a great number of cases induced the Rajas to appoint as Mantri[17] persons of their own choosing, and by selecting men who were natives of British territory and had in many instances served in our courts and offices, he secured a partisan at every Raja's court, and one, moreover, who could be relied on to keep his Raja straight.[18]

Fakirmohan Senapati, who is regarded as the founder of modern Oriya literature and served as one of these ministers in various states between 1871 and 1896, left no doubt in his memoirs that the decision of who was to be a raja's next *diwan* (or *mantri*) was more often than not taken by the collector or commissioner.[19] He also recalled that the colonial government was particularly careful to make sure that the new generation of rajas received a British education and imbibed the spirit of "improvement" at an early age.[20] They would be sent to the "Princes' School for Minors" in Calcutta while being *takoit* (heir apparent) or, if they were raised to the *gaddi* (seat of royalty) in the course of their minority. Placing minors on thrones had the additional advantage that the interim administrators—most of them British—were answerable to a colonial "Court of Wards". They would take care that strategic roads were constructed to facilitate communication with the centres of colonial power in the plains: more than 300 km of road were reported in 1897 to have been built within two years in the "Wards' States".[21] More and

---

[16] Thomas Edward Ravenshaw became Orissa's chief administrator just before the famine of 1866 and held the office of Commissioner of Cuttack and Superintendent of the Tributary Mehals for more than a decade.
[17] "Mantri" is the Sanskrit term for minister. The more commonly used designation for this office in nineteenth-century Orissa (used in colonial records but also, for instance, by Fakirmohan Senapati in his memoirs) was the Persian term *diwan*.
[18] Beames, *Memoirs of a Bengal Civilian*, 261.
[19] Senapati, *My Times and I*, 45, 52, 66–67, 75, 87.
[20] Ibid., 53.
[21] *RATMO 1896–97*, 6, 26–27; also see *RATMO 1897–98*, 18.

more rajas streamlined their administrations to the British model, conducted revenue settlements, decreed forest laws and also embarked on "public works" programmes.[22] The Garhjat raja of the late nineteenth century had to present himself as an 'improving' and, therefore, fully "civilised" ruler to convince his colonial overlords of his aptitude, to avert interference or even deposition and to enhance his status in the finely tuned imperial hierarchy. The Raja of Athmallik, for instance, received good marks in 1876, when Commissioner Ravenshaw reported:

> The new road ... has proved a source of profit to the Raja, who is now working the fine forests opened out. He has obtained some well constructed timber trucks made at the Cuttack workshops. The Raja takes personal interest in the management of his estate, and continues to deserve the confidence of his people.[23]

Conversely the British administration after the "great rebellion" of 1857 was unlikely to annex princely territories or dethrone their rulers as long as they operated within the parameters set for them.[24] An 'improving' conformism thus lent itself to the rajas of the Tributary States as the most effective political survival strategy. This implied, among other things, that the construction of roads and other 'public works' of transportation had turned from being an impolitic security risk into an indispensable ingredient of opportunistic state policy.

Moreover, it seems likely that such policies were not pursued for tactical reasons alone, though further research is required to ascertain in how far the image of the 'enlightened and improving ruler' came to be integrated with conceptions of kingship in the hills of Orissa. Visible indications for such changes can, however, be found in the increasing presence of permanent and more expensive built

---

[22] The official gazetteer for the Feudatory States, published in 1910, particularises this process for each State: Cobden-Ramsay, *Feudatory States, passim*. Also see *RAFSOC 1910–11*, 4–5.

[23] NAI, Foreign Dpt., Pol. A, September 1876, nos. 91–95 (T. E. Ravenshaw, SI Tributary Mehals, Cuttack, to R. L. Mangles, Offg. Secry. to Government of Bengal, Pol. Department, 9 June 1876).

[24] For a good summary of British policies towards Indian princely States after 1857, see Jacques Pouchepadass, "Princely India, 1858–1950," in *A History of Modern India, 1480–1950*, ed. Claude Markovits (London: Anthem Press, 2002), 386–98.

environments, in their growing importance for the functioning and the self-representation of these princely states. The times when rajas resided in remote, often hardly accessible and changing parts of their domains in what was known as *garhs* (but called disparagingly "mud forts" by the British) came to an end (see chapter 4)—some rajas actually resided for long periods in Cuttack or even Calcutta.[25] In the kingdoms themselves, more stately palaces and buildings "of public utility" were erected in the final decades of the nineteenth century, occasionally under the supervision of British engineers.[26] The "capitals" or principal towns of the Tributary States, where this newly built environment was concentrated, also became the pivot from which a modest but growing number of levelled and widened, sometimes raised and bridged roads radiated into subordinate areas and extended to the seats of the colonial administration in the plains.[27] "The steady increase in expenditure on public works during the last few years has been remarkable," wrote the British "Political Agent" who supervised the Tributary States in 1910 ascribing this change to

> the enlightened policy and zeal of the Chiefs who are all of them striving to developc [*sic*] their States by the erection of good public buildings, construction and improvement of lines of communication and schemes of irrigation.[28]

Such 'improvements' and changes in royal habitus required an augmentation of state revenues, for which the overall processes of commercialisation had generated economic preconditions. Several rajas, therefore, involved themselves, as we shall see in some detail for the kingdom of Mayurbhanj, more actively with trade and the commercial exploitation of the natural resources of their domains. The nexus between the local landowning aristocracy on the one hand and often external traders and contractors on the other thus became a defining property of the Garhjat polities: the 'improving' raja was a commercial raja.

---

[25] Senapati, *My Times and I*, 54, 118.
[26] Cobden-Ramsay, *Feudatory States*, 103–04. Also see the case study on the State of Mayurbhanj, in this chapter.
[27] See, for example, OSA, R III-1/707B, GAROD 1875–76, 26.
[28] *RAFSOC 1909–10*, 9.

By the first decade of the twentieth century, the combined impact of these ideological, political and economic drives for 'improvement' and, by implication, for 'public works' of transport was observable in most Tributary States of Orissa, as the reports of their self-satisfied colonial overseers indicate.[29] This process had set in earlier than in most other principalities and with the most substantial effects in the kingdom of Mayurbhanj, which bordered on Balasore District in the east, on Bengal in the north and on the coal belt of Chota Nagpur in the west (see map 9). Mayurbhanj's rulers were not merely the odd ones out with regard to late nineteenth-century 'public works' of transport but set an important and comparatively successful example to the rajas of other Tributary States. This example was particularly influential since Mayurbhanj was by the turn of the century the largest of the Orissa principalities in the Bengal Presidency in terms of area (4,243 square miles or 15 per cent of their area), population (610,000 or 19 per cent) and even more markedly in terms of revenue (almost Rs 1.3 million or 29 per cent). Moreover, it was surpassed by no other Tributary State of Orissa in the imperial status hierarchy.[30] The developments in Mayurbhanj will, therefore, be looked at more closely in the following paragraphs rather as a paradigmatic case for qualitative developments in this subregion than as a representative sample in terms of quantity.

Infrastructural and institutional transformation commenced in Mayurbhanj as early as in the 1870s. Its ruler, Raja Krushna Chandra Bhanj (r. 1867–1882), had a metalled and thoroughly bridged road constructed under the supervision of a British engineer between his capital Baripada and the colonial district headquarter in Baleshwar. Apart from this technically difficult and, therefore, rather expensive project a few other surfaced roads to administrative divisions of the kingdom were constructed under his reign and also numerous "public buildings" including a new palace. A Public Works Department, headed by an Englishman, was created in the process of a

[29] See footnote 28. Also see *RAFSOC 1910–11*, 4–5; *Annual Reports on the Administration of the Feudatory States of Orissa and Chota Nagpur* [hereafter: *ARAFS* followed by year] *1911–12* (Ranchi: Bihar and Orissa Govt. Press, 1912), 14–16; *Report on Administration of Bihar and Orissa, 1912–13*, 5; *ARAFS 1914–15*, 16.
[30] *RAFSOC 1909–10*, 7.

comprehensive administrative adaptation to the governmental and judicial structures of the colonial state.[31] The raja in the early 1880s even offered to provide sleepers from his forests without royalty for 125 kms of permanent way, if a railway line was constructed between Bengal and Puri.[32] When Krushna Chandra died at a young age in 1882, the kingdom came under the administration of the Court of Wards, while his successor Sri Ram Chandra Bhanj Deo (r. 1890–1912) received schooling at Baleshwar under the close tutelage of a British educationist and continued to study science in Calcutta up to the B.A. level.[33] In the meantime, the English manager appointed by the Court of Wards pushed forward with road construction in Mayurbhanj, completing 179 km of surfaced and 114 km of unsurfaced road until Sri Ram Chandra became an adult legally and ascended the gaddi in 1890.[34] In the twenty-two years of his reign, he became the epitome of the 'improving' raja ("the most enlightened of the Garhjat Chiefs"),[35] for which the British raised him to the imperial rank of a Maharaja in 1903, a title made hereditary in 1911. Numerous agricultural, administrative, judicial, educational and health reforms were implemented during his reign.[36] The state's total income had more than tripled between 1890–91 and 1910–11, to which the much faster, almost ninefold increase of the forest revenue—mainly derived from the exploitation of the rich sal populations of the Simlipal range—contributed in no small way.[37] The momentum was kept up with regard

---

[31] OSA, R III-1/707B, GAROD 1872–73, 34; and GAROD 1873–74, 32; and GAROD 1875–76, 26; Praharaj, *Tribal Movements and Political History*, 77–79.
[32] OIOC, BPWP August 1882 (P/1831), Railway, no. 4, 5 ("An Appeal for a Light Passenger Railroad from Ranigunge to Pooree through Bankoora, Midnapore, Balasore, Cuttack, and Khorda").
[33] *RATMO 1895–96*, 9; Praharaj, *Tribal Movements and Political History*, 80.
[34] OSA, Mayurbhanja Records, M 111 (British administration of Mayurbanj, 1882–1890, no. 195, "Engineer of Mourbhanj Raj to the Manager of Mourbhanj Raj", 5 November 1890, 6).
[35] Cobden-Ramsay, *Feudatory States*, 241.
[36] Praharaj, *Tribal Movements and Political History*, 80–84.
[37] Mayurbhanj's gross revenue amounted to Rs. 364,754 in 1890–91 and to Rs 1,267,892 in 1910–11, the annual forest revenue was reported to have never exceeded Rs 30,000 in the decade after 1884 and to have risen to almost Rs 250,000 by the end of the first decade of the new century. OSA, Mayurbhanja Records, M 111 (British administration of Mayurbanj, 1882–

to the transformation of built environment and transport infrastructure: R. C. Dutt, who was "Superintendent of the Tributary Mehals" in the mid-1890s, showed himself

> greatly pleased with the scheme which has been prepared under the Raja's directions to open out the country with roads, not only for the convenience of the people, but also with a view to the working of the forests in the interior.[38]

More than 800 km of road were reported to have been built during his reign, of which 240 km were metalled.[39] Most strikingly, a "Mayurbhanj State Light Railway" with a length of about 50 km was constructed at the expense of the kingdom. It was opened for traffic in 1905 between the state's capital Baripada and Rupsa, a junction town on the East Coast Railway near Balasore, and managed by the Bengal–Nagpur Railway Company.[40] This railway proved instrumental in the commercialisation of Mayurbhanj's agriculture: as early as in the first year of its operation a massive increase of rice exports was officially recorded, which entailed an increase of more than 50 per cent in the price of rice. Furthermore there was "a large influx of traders from various parts of India who penetrated even into remote villages to export rice" and the immigration of cultivators who intended to reclaim forest for permanent agriculture.[41] Mayurbhanj's population growth between 1891 and 1921 was, according to census figures, even more impressive than that of the Tributary States of Orissa as a whole in comparison with both

---

1890, no. 401P, 1: G. Toynbee, SI Tributary Mahals of Orissa, to Chief Secry. to Government of Bengal, 18 February 1892); *RAFSOC 1910–11*, 7; Cobden-Ramsay, *Feudatory States*, 254.

[38] R. C. Dutt, Offg. SI Tributary Mahals, to Chief Secry., GoB, 31 August 1896. *RATMO 1895–96*, 27.

[39] Sailendra N. Sarkar, *Biography of Maharaja Sri Ram Chandra Bhanj Deo, Feudatory Chief of Mayurbhanj* (Calcutta: n.p., 1918), 127.

[40] OSA, Mayurbhanja Records, 266M ("Mourbhanj State Light Railway", 1905); OSA, R III-1/796, Report on the Administration of Mourbhanj 1905–6, 25; "Mayurbhanj State Railway", in *South Eastern Railway*; Sarkar, *Biography of Maharaja Sri Ram Chandra*, 128.

[41] OSA, R III-1/796, Report on the Administration of Mourbhanj 1905–6, 3–5, 23, 25–28. Also see OSA, R III-1/797, Report on the Administration of Mourbhanj 1906–7, 3–5; Cobden-Ramsay, *Feudatory States*, 241, 250.

the Orissa Division and the greater region of eastern India. The differential between the variations of the population in Mayurbhanj and the neighbouring Balasore District were particularly large. This remarkable growth (slowed down only in the second half of the 1910s because of a series of bad crops and the influenza pandemic of 1918) was ascribed to the expansion of cultivation and a correspondingly high rate of immigration (see table 6).[42]

TABLE 6: Variations in the population of selected areas of eastern India, 1891–1921 (in per cent)[43]

1	2	3	4	5	6
	Mayurbhanj	Balasore District	Orissa Feudatory States	Orissa Division (Brit. Territory)	Eastern India
1891–1901	+ 14.7	+ 7.7	+ 9.5	+ 6.8	+ 7.3
1901–1911	+ 19.5	– 1.7	+ 19.6	+ 3.0	+ 7.2
1911–1921	+ 3.4	– 7.1	+ 0.3	– 3.2	+ 1.9

Source: Tallents, Census of India, 1921: Bihar and Orissa, Vol. 7, part II: "Tables" (Patna: n.p., 1923). The Figures in columns 2–5 are calculated from data on pp. 6 and 8. Figures for the regions of eastern Indian (comprising the Bengal Province and States, Bihar and Orissa Province and States and Assam Province and States) are calculated from data given in Visaria and Visaria, "Population (1757–1947)", 2: 490.

Sri Ram Chandra did not, however, stop at having his capital connected with the British district headquarter. As his official biographer noted, "it was with the object of providing an efficient means of export that the Maharaja in conjunction with Mr. Barooah formulated a project for extension of the State light railway into the Simlipal Hills, where the best and largest quantity of sal and other timber is to be found."[44] B. Barooah & Co., it should be added, were

[42] Tallents, Census of India, 1921: Bihar and Orissa, Vol. VII, part I: "Report", 63–64.
[43] Earlier census data from 1872 and 1881 have not been used as they were later believed to be far too low. Yet the census commissioners believed that real growth rates had been very considerable in Mayurbhanj and the Feudatory States in these earlier decades. See Tallents, Census of India, 1921, part I: "Report", 63–64.
[44] Sarkar, Biography of Maharaja Sri Ram Chandra, 119. The Maharaja had been deeply involved with the timber business since the late 1890s when he established a saw mill in Bangriposi with machines imported from England. It was then that he first considered the idea of a railway for supplying the

among the largest timber contractors from Calcutta.[45] Sri Ram Chandra died in 1912 but the "forest extension" to Talband was sanctioned during the ensuing period of administration under the Court of Wards and opened to traffic in 1920.[46]

The Mayurbhanj Railway did not extend to the western tracts of this large state, which were, however, skirted by the BNR mainline. These tracts moved into the focus of commercial interest because of their iron deposits when the Tatas, one of Bombay's premier entrepreneurial families, established India's first steel works in 1908 in a village called Sakchi that was to become the steel city of Jamshedpur. The maharaja granted exclusive mining rights in Mayurbhanj to the Tatas and the BNR opened a broad-gauge branch to Gurumahisani from its mainline in 1911, thereby connecting the iron deposits of Orissa's most commercial king with the steelworks of one of India's kings of industry.[47] Mayurbhanj's mines in and about Gurumahisani furnished iron ore at "less than one-half the cost of production of any other major ore-producing district in the world", since opencast mining was possible, which required little capital and predominantly "unskilled" labour.[48] Mayurbhanj accounted for almost two thirds of India's total output of iron ore (1.5 million lt) in 1925.[49]

By the first decade of the twentieth century, investment in transport infrastructure appears to have been accepted as a policy issue by most rajas and the combined expenditure on "communications" more than doubled in the Tributary States of Orissa from Rs 440,000 in 1905–6 to Rs. 950,000 in 1910–11.[50] Even Maharaja Sri Ram Chandra's efforts of linking up his territory to the Indian railway network in alliance with Indian or British capital were not totally

---

saw mill with sal timber. See *RATMO 1897–98* (Calcutta: Bengal Secretariat Press, 1898), 11.

[45] See *GRAFSO 1926–27*, 8; *GRAFSO 1928–29*, 17.

[46] *Report on Administration of Bihar and Orissa, 1914–15*, ii; "Mayurbhanj State Railway", in *South Eastern Railway*.

[47] OSA, R III-1/796, Report on the Administration of Mourbhanj 1905–6, 17–18; Sarkar, *Biography of Maharaja Sri Ram Chandra*, 120–21; Maya Dutta, *Jamshedpur: The Growth of the City and Its Regions* (Calcutta: The Asiatic Society, 1977), 3–4.

[48] Morris D. Morris, "The Growth of Large-scale Industry to 1947", in *The Cambridge Economic History of India*, 2: 589.

[49] Govt. of Bihar and Orissa, *Bihar and Orissa in 1925–26*, 122.

[50] *RAFSOC 1910–11*, 7. Also see *Report on Administration of Bihar and Orissa, 1912–13*, 5.

unparalleled. The Raja of Parlakimedi, a major estate in southern Orissa, had also promoted the construction of a light railway in his territory, which was opened five years earlier than its Mayurbhanj counterpart.[51] The Raja of Gangpur claimed in 1926 that the beneficial effects of the BNR mainline, which traversed the whole length of his state, had been anticipated already by his grandfather who had willingly supplied the required land in the 1890s without demanding any payment. This had increased Gangpur's revenues since the 1910s by turning its limestone and dolomite quarries into profitable businesses: these minerals were required for the production of steel as so-called "flux stones" and haulage costs to the next steel works were low since Jamshedpur was a mere 130 km to the northeast and directly connected by the BNR mainline.[52] There was also a short narrow-gauge railway from Baleshwar to the granite quarries of the princely state of Nilgiri, which was constructed before 1910 by K. M. Dey & Co., the Calcutta-based owners of these quarries.[53] The seachange in princely policies of circulation and infrastructure amounted to a reversal of roles in the 1920s. The colonial Governor of Bihar and Orissa put off the urgent requests of chiefs and rajas of Tributary States for a speedy extension of the railways to their territories due to insufficient funds.[54]

Unsanctioned Mobilities and the Violence of 'Public Works'

If Garhjat rajas turned into fervent 'improvers', beneficiaries of commercialisation and key producers of abstract space, the implications for their subjects were more differentiated and contradictory. As in the coastal districts, the gains of commercialisation and the benefits of the transformed circulatory regime were unevenly distributed. Certain plebeian groups could no doubt successfully appropriate these processes to their own purposes. Cultivators who could not hold on to their land or were excluded from acquiring land in the intensively farmed plains migrated, for instance, in

---

[51] "Parlakimedi Light Railway", in Bhandari, *South Eastern Railway*.
[52] *GRAFSO 1925–26*, 28 (address by Raja Bhawani Shankar Deo of Gangpur to Henry Wheeler, Governor of Bihar and Orissa); Dutta, *Jamshedpur: The Growth of the City*, 4.
[53] "Mayurbhanj State Railway", in Bhandari, *South Eastern Railway*.
[54] *RARAFS 1922–23*, 32–34 (addresses by the Chief of Kalahandi and the Maharaja of Patna and the replies of Governor Wheeler).

appreciable numbers to the Tributary States.[55] The spaces these immigrants appropriated were far from empty in terms of social practice. Long-established practices of forest utilisation and of shifting cultivation, integral to the way of living of the largely "tribal" population of the interior tracts, were not only cut into (quite literally) by the newcomers from the plains but also increasingly suppressed by the local powerholders, who were intent on benefiting from the higher surpluses of market-oriented agri- and silviculture.[56] As Bhuiyans, Oraons, Panas, Kols, Khonds, Santals and members of many other "tribal" communities felt invaded and deprived, tensions between native *deshlog* (people of the land) and *dikkus* (the foreign peasants) moneylenders and contractors, were inevitable and could materialise in violent clashes.[57]

However, it is evident that at least a considerable section of the plebeian classes participated to some extent in the gains of commercialisation—gains that could be made not only in market-oriented agriculture, but also by way of employment in the expanding building and transport sectors.[58] As for the local, often "tribal" communities, the expansion of transport infrastructure also opened channels of labour migration that had not existed previously. It was the tribal population of the Garhjats who turned first (as we have seen) to transregional emigration in large numbers—a process actively encouraged by the colonial administration (see chapter 7). Like the migrants of neighbouring Chota Nagpur,[59] tribal people of Orissa's

---

[55] Cobden-Ramsay, *Feudatory States*, 35–36 and passim and table 6. Also see Pati, "Survival as Resistance", 177–78; Sanjukta Das Gupta, "The Changing World of the Singhbhum Hos, 1820–1932", *Indian Historical Review* 33, no. 1, 2006, 92.

[56] OIOC, BPWP October 1890 (P/3632), Railway, no. 25, 23–40 (report by John Edgar to GoB, Revenue Dpt., 19 August 1889); *RATMO 1896–97*, 32; *RATMO 1898–99*, 17.

[57] For cases in point from Mayurbhanj, Kalahandi and Chinnakimedi, see Chandi Prasad Nanda, *Textualising Mayurbhanja: Social Mobility Movement of the Kudmi-Mohantas of Orissa*, unpublished manuscript; Mojumdar, *Changing Tribal Life*, 77, 80–83, 98 and passim.

[58] See, for example, *RATMO 1895–96*, 13.

[59] Several excellent studies of coolie migration from Chota Nagpur are available. See especially: Prabhu P. Mohapatra, "Coolies and Colliers: A Study of the Agrarian Context of Labour Migration from Chotanagpur, 1880–1920", *Studies in History*, new series, vol. 1, no. 2, 1985, 247–303; Kaushik

Tributary States may well have agreed to indentured labour in the tea plantations of the Northeast rather under severe economic pressure than out of their liking. Be that as it may, these new forms of circulation implied a mobility that could not be controlled comprehensively by state authorities, landlords and contractors. The circulation of labour was a polyvalent socio-spatial practice and this polyvalence could be appropriated by subordinated social groups to their own purposes. Observations of a colonial official in the early 1920s hint, for instance, at interesting patterns of intraregional labour migration, which had evolved in the preceding decades:

> Besides the usual emigration to the tea gardens of Assam and the seasonal emigration to the dockyards of Calcutta and Rangoon, there is an increasing proportion of the labouring classes who move off after the harvests and are gathered to work on the mines and railways. A curious feature of this movement is that this labour often prefers to work elsewhere than in its own State. Gangpur coolies, for instance, will rather go to Singhbhum for work than quarry limestone and manganese near their own homes. Dhenkanal coolies like better to go to Calcutta and elsewhere than work on the Talcher railway which runs through the State. Labourers from Baud are reported to have gone to the Talcher railway though there was plenty of work for them in the State. Mayurbhanj Santals and Kohls [Kols] work very largely on the local iron mines, but large numbers leave the State for work on the railways outside and it is difficult to get local labour for earthwork on the roads. It is not a question entirely of higher wages for these are much the same everywhere, but there is a greater spirit of adventure abroad; the outside world is no longer unknown and feared but is a place where perhaps greater results can be achieved than at home.[60]

The subtext of the official's statement raises interesting questions: what may these achievable "greater results" have been if no higher wages were to be expected? And more generally, what rendered the "outside world" more attractive than the "inside world"? Though these questions require further research one obvious unstated reason for moving to a neighbouring kingdom was that customary, yet

---

Ghosh, "A Market for Aboriginality: Primitivism and Race Qualification in the Indentured Labour Market of Colonial India", in *Subaltern Studies X. Writings on South Asian History and Society*, ed. G. Bhadra, G. Prakash and Susie Tharu (New Delhi: Oxford University Press, 1999), 8–48.
[60] *RARAFS 1923–24*, 26.

historically contingent obligations to local communities and authorities became less easily enforceable. The "protection" offered by such bonds of community and clientship did not prevent segments of labour force from withdrawing from the pressures inherent in these relationships, for instance, the chiefs' claim to often very considerable amounts of unpaid work for various purposes—an issue we shall return to before long. At this stage of our argument the point is simply that the tendency towards spatial integration and "abstract space" bred contradictory effects: the very process that reinforced the scope and the means of domination generated simultaneously new techniques of negotiating, evading and resisting this power structure. The emergence of new modalities of "criminal activity" (or deviant social behaviour) is another case in point. Consider, for instance, the following report on police proceedings in the State of Gangpur during the early decades of the twentieth century:

> the State is peculiarly situated, being traversed for 80 miles by the main line of the Bengal–Nagpur Railway; it is also surrounded on three sides by British districts and is also bordered by three Native States, one of which is in the jurisdiction of the Central Provinces: these facts naturally throw special difficulties on the police of this State . . .; a few years ago the police of the Gangpur State rendered very special assistance in bringing to book a very dangerous and numerous gang of Eranga Kol dacoits who had been operating in the Ranchi and Sambalpur districts, and also in Gangpur, Bamra and Bonai States. During the year under review some of the members of this gang were released on expiry of sentence and were joined by other members who migrated to Assam and returned from the gardens to join their old associates and commenced operations in the Gangpur State; the State police however again did excellent work and rendered further assistance by bringing to book members of the new gang.[61]

If 'improved communications' and mobility were usually portrayed in colonial accounts as a 'civilising' influence, the availability of railway transport is here (together with a politically segmented landscape) perceived as a "special difficulty" for the police: the railways were appropriated as 'vehicles of crime', which enabled 'dacoits' to operate in an even more extensive geographic area, while long-distance networks of labour circulation (unthinkable without

[61] *ARAFS 1915–16*, 6.

the transformation of transport infrastructure) provided new avenues of retreat in periods of mounting pressure. This was no isolated case[62] and a police official from Madras even published a long treatise in 1915 on the "history of the railway thieves", which assumed a special propensity of certain "criminal tribes" for this type of offence. As for Orissa, he specifically mentioned the Koravar, a nomadic community notified under the Criminal Tribe Act of 1911, who he accused of having been involved with "railway theft" since the opening of the East Coast Railway in 1899.[63]

For all possibilities of plebeian appropriation of the new circulatory regime, the limits of such 'self-willed takeovers' can only be ignored at the cost of relativising (and thereby belittling) the facticity of domination, that is, of asymmetric structures of social power. Transport infrastructure was not forged in an open, inclusive 'public space' but rather in a highly exclusive, asymmetric field of force—this appears to have been the shared experience of the labouring poor in Orissa's hill region, too. The available evidence suggests that 'public works' and the accompanying technologies of transport were frequently associated, even equated with acts of intrusion, seizure and violence. This menacing impact of the new means of circulation flashes up in an Oraon magic spell, used for extracting *bhut*s (evil spirits): "Pull father, pull, pull,//Pull the railway train" runs one of its verses.[64]

---

[62] See, for instance, another report which asserted that emigration "in some cases ... rids the States of the habitual criminals who have found that by changing their names and, if possible, their castes, they can by emigration to various labour districts free themselves of the attentions of the police so long as they abstain from committing offences in their adopted home. The Superintendent of Patna State, for one instance, ascribes the great decrease in crime in the last few years to be in the main due to the emigration of the bad characters of the Ganda caste to the tea gardens of Assam." *GRAFSO 1925–26*, 24.

[63] M. Pauparao Naidu, *The History of the Railway Thieves with Illustrations & Hints of Detection* The Criminal Tribes of India Series No. 1 (Madras: Higginbothams, 1915), 1, 61–62. For wider implications of the Criminal Tribes Act of 1911 for the Koravar and other nomadic communities of South India, see Radhakrishna, *Dishonoured by History*. For another Indian region (Punjab), the policing of itinerant communities has been discussed in: Major, "State and Criminal Tribes" and Sauli, "Circulation and Authority".

[64] The full content of this spell is presented by Biswamoy Pati as follows: "Pull, father, pull, pull,//Pull the *bhut*s to whom,//Vows were by our fathers

There is no way of knowing at the present state of research in how far the dangers of roads and railways outweighed their attractions in the perceptions of labourers, peasants and forest dwellers. Yet the sense of an imminent threat recurs in various ways. Let us return for a moment to that curious article, which a small Oriya newspaper published in 1896 (and which has already been quoted and discussed in a more general context in chapter 2). Its author recounted with a sense of outrage and embarrassment that a "rumour has found such a wide circulation in all the districts of Orissa, that ... the very name of a railway creates a shudder in the mind of the commonest peasant". The rumour was, in the version transcribed and thereby fixed by the writer, to the effect that

> Government wants a certain number of men and women to be offered up as human sacrifices to the deities that preside over the rivers that are to be bridged over and the mountains that are to be crossed, as those deities can never be propitiated without human blood.[65]

While this rumour may have had a richness and variety of meanings and allusions that cannot be recovered because of the scantiness, nature and bias of our evidence, it seems clear that it resonated with widespread anxieties among the subordinate classes in both the coastal plains and the hills of the interior. How serious these fears were and how far they circulated is indicated by a corroborative report from a remote Tributary State in western Orissa:

> The Manager of Pal Lahera ... reports that about 300 families of Pans of the State left in a body in the month of October last and fled to the neighbouring States, when Mr. Daly, the District Superintendent of the Angul Police, visited the State. The reason was that a rumour was spread that Mr. Daly's visit was made for the purpose of transporting some men for sacrificial purposes on the Railway works going on in Cuttack. They, however, soon returned to their homes when they saw their own mistakes.[66]

---

made.//Pull father, pull, pull,//Pull the *bhuts* to whom,//Vows were by our grandfathers,//and great-grandfathers made.//Pull, father, pull, pull,//Pull the steam boat.//Pull father, pull, pull.//Pull the railway train.//Pull, father, pull, pull,//Pull the bicycle.//Pull father, pull." Pati, *Resisting Domination*, 42 (see also p. 58).

[65] *Samvadvahika* (Baleshwar), 28 May 1896, quoted in *RNNB*, 18 July 1896, 702.
[66] *RATMO 1896–97*, 18.

Local culture and oral traditions, a wide range of everyday experiences with the realities of colonial rule may have fed this rumour in a variety of ways. The frequency of epidemic outbreaks of waterborne diseases like cholera and malaria on colonial construction sites, which regularly resulted in the collective flight of the coolies, may, for instance, have contributed to the plausibility of the rumour.[67] Yet more important for our present purpose is that 'public works' (railways, in this case) were associated with compulsion and violence in more than one way: the report on the incident in Pal Lahera reveals not merely that families of the Pana community believed that the British would not shrink from offering human sacrifices for the sake of their railways (and that the suppression of the practice of *meriah,* that is, human sacrifices in the Khond hills, which the British saw as an incontrovertible proof for the benignity of their rule in Orissa, had hardly earned them the trust of their subjects).[68] The report also shows that the visit of a British official raised fears of forcible impressment for 'public works'.

Such fears became extremely virulent during World War I, when the British tried to recruit members of several tribal communities from the Tributary States for so-called "Labour Corps" who were to be employed on particularly unpopular infrastructure schemes: they were meant to excavate trenches on the battlefields of France and Mesopotamia. Colonial officials, sometimes assisted in their efforts by missionaries, experienced "extreme timidity" at first. Further research is required with regard to the actual practices of recruitment, but many potential recruits evidently found it hard to believe that service in the labour corps was voluntary. By the summer of 1918, 1,453 coolies had been sent to the trenches[69] but only after the recruitment operations had sparked off a major *meli*

---

[67] OIOC, BPWP May 1861 (P/432/39), nos. 15–16, 8–10; *Report by Chief Engineer of Bengal on Progress of Public Works, 1859–60,* appendix, chart after page 110; *Report Showing Progress Made . . . in Imperial Public Works under Bengal Government for 1862–63,* 95–96. For a more general discussion of epidemic outbreaks on railway construction sites also see Kerr, *Building the Railways,* 159–66.

[68] For a critical study of the British campaigns against meriah sacrifices in the 1840s and 1850s, see Felix Padel, *The Sacrifice of Human Being: British Rule and the Konds of Orissa* (Delhi: Oxford University Press, 2000 [1st ed. 1995]), 64–163.

[69] *RARAFS 1917–18* [no page numbers].

(rebellion) among the Santals in Mayurbhanj in May and June 1917. The rebellion could only be suppressed after the Military Police and an infantry detachment had been sent in twice. In the year after the meli, 264 "volunteers" were enlisted for the Labour Corps in Mayurbhanj, but 977 persons were convicted for offences committed in the course of the rebellion, of which four faced the death penalty, 34 were transported or jailed for life, while most others were sentenced to long terms of imprisonment between one and fourteen years. The harshness of judicial repression reflects the bitterness of this conflict. It cannot be explained exclusively with the apprehension of forcible impressment, as the issues of the insurgents appear to have broadened in the course of the movement. Yet 'public works' continued to be a core issue since they were also clearly perceived as infrastructures of counter-insurgency. Hence, forms of protests included not only mass meetings, physical attacks on recruitment officials and police stations or the looting of bazaars, but also the cutting of the State Railway line and the demolition of road bridges.[70] These latter forms were also utilised in the 1942 popular movement in the State of Talcher, when railway, telephone and telegraph lines were destroyed to impede the intervention of colonial armed forces.[71]

The Reinvention of Bethi

If 'public works' of transport were perceived by the subordinate classes of the Tributary States as inseparable from practices of domination involving compulsion and violence, this was not least due to the widespread utilisation of forced and unpaid (or only partially paid) labour for the construction and maintenance of roads and other infrastructures. Rendering labour services without remuneration

---

[70] *Report on Administration of Bihar and Orissa, 1917–18*, 5; Praharaj, *Tribal Movements and Political History*, 119–20, 126–28; Nanda, *Textualising Mayurbhanja*. Praharaj gives a much higher figure for enrolment for war services from Mayurbhanj (2,452). He relies on a curious publication, which this author has been unable to trace: Somerset Playnee, *Indian States* (London, 1917 [sic]). The figure of 264 seems more reliable and is based on *RARAFS 1917–18*.

[71] Pati, *Resisting Domination*, 177. Similarly roads had been blocked in Ranpur in 1939 to prevent the intervention of the British Political Agent for the Orissa States. Ibid., 127.

or for a *khoraki* (mere food allowance) was clearly an established claim on Orissa's plebeian classes, to which the British had to relate. Colonial sources implicitly distinguished between two basic forms of such services, namely unpaid labour for the village community and unpaid labour as a form of tribute demanded by rajas and other local powerholders from their subjects. The last-mentioned category of unremunerated labour was akin to the practice of corvée in Europe and locally covered by the terms bethi and begar. Since a critical historical study of unpaid labour services in pre-colonial Orissa is so far wanting, it cannot be ascertained at present whether the 'communitarian' and the 'feudal' varieties of unpaid labour services were clearly separable basic forms (even the latter variety was, after all, utilised for the repair of village bunds and irrigation tanks). The question of how far claims to bethi/begar services were perceived legitimate by the subjects of *precolonial* polities (and not merely by their rulers) also requires further research.[72] The evidence available for the colonial period suggests, however, a comparatively low intensity of community-based unpaid labour services paired with a remarkable reinforcement of bethi, which was now demanded by Garhjat rulers from their subjects not only for customary purposes, but also and in ever growing proportions for the pursuit of 'public works'.[73] When the first systematic investigations into unpaid compulsory labour in the Tributary States were made in the last decade of British rule in India, bethi was found to be demanded for a wide range of tasks. The laborious tasks included the transport of the raja's luggage, his officials and British masters,

---

[72] By way of example, Jagannath Patnaik's contentions that "mutual understanding between the feudal chief and the tenants about free [i.e., unpaid] labour gave rise to the system of Bethi" or that "Bethi was not formerly considered force[d] labour" are, judging from his references, solely based on interpretations contained in nationalist and provincial government reports of the final years of British rule. Unless corroborated by strong evidence from the relevant period this notion of a kind of "contract social" on *bethi* remains unhistorically abstract and raises the suspicion to reflect merely the ideological commitments of the authors of these reports. Jagannath Patnaik, *Feudatory States of Orissa, 1803–1857* (Allahabad: Vohra, 1988), 2: 551–53.

[73] The argument that bethi was extended both in quantitative terms and in respect of the purposes for which these services were to be rendered has been forwarded convincingly in an excellent study of the colonial impact on the Khond hills of southern Orissa: Mojumdar, *Changing Tribal Life*, 41, 60–64.

the conduct of *shikar* beats (that is, driving game towards the guns of aristocratic or colonial hunters), carrying timber for Jagannath's ceremonial car, the erection of temples and palaces, the extinction of forest fires, the repair of local irrigation tanks and, very prominently, the construction and maintenance of roads and connected facilities.[74] These demands had by then become a major issue of conflict between Orissa's rajas and their subjects, many of whom joined massive and partly militant *prajamandal*[75] movements in this period.[76] Bethi was perceived not only as degrading in terms of status but also as a major economic burden: according to the report of the Orissa States Enquiry Committee, which had been appointed by the largely Gandhian Orissa States People's Conference in 1937,

> [a] *peasant spends over one hundred days of the year in doing forced labour for the states or its officials.* He is liable to be called up at any time of the day or night. He must leave his own work, however urgent it may be, on pain of being beaten, fined, or even imprisoned. If it is harvest season, the crops must wait.[77]

The quoted nationalist document and an equally revealing confidential report for the colonial government were prepared more than two decades after the end of the period covered by the present study. They are relevant nevertheless as they are the only available systematic surveys of the characteristics and extent of unpaid compulsory labour in the Orissa States during the colonial period. That they were the first reports of their kind is, furthermore, an important piece of information in itself. While colonial records contain very similar descriptions of bethi and related practices since the early nineteenth century,[78] no such systematic investigation of the

---

[74] *Report of the Enquiry Committee, Orissa States, 1939* (Cuttack: Orissa Mission Press, n.d.), 108–9, 118–19, 124, 131–32, 140, 158–59, 166, 172, 177, 179, 183, 190, 192–93, 197, 204, 210, 216, 219–20; NAI, Orissa States Agency Files, CS Branch, file no. XXVI-35–CS/1941–42, vols. I and II, items 2, 5, 7, 9, 11, 14, 15, 16, 20, 22, 23, 25, 37, 66, 78, 89, 104. Also see Patnaik, *Feudatory States of Orissa*, 2: 551–52.

[75] "People's associations" in Indian princely states.

[76] For a succinct account of these conflicts, see Pati, *Resisting Domination*, 108–29.

[77] *Report of Enquiry Committee, Orissa States*, 15, emphasis in the original.

[78] OSA, BoRLR 18,167 (CoCD, to H. Shakespear, Secry. to GoB, Judicial Dpt., 19 July 1830). This document has already been quoted at length in chapter 5 of the present study.

issue was apparently considered necessary or politic before the upsurge of popular movements in the interwar period. In fact (as we have seen in chapter 5) the Commissioner of Orissa in 1840 specifically recommended "not to look into matters such as these" and settle the accounts with the Raja of Mayurbhanj for the labour provided for the construction of the Raipur Mail Road, even though it was apparent that the workers would not be paid or be underpaid.[79] There is more detailed evidence from the Khond hills in the "Ganjam Agency" of the Madras Presidency. *Patros* and *bissoyis* (local chiefs who were usually Oriyas) for many decades since the 1860s were road contractors for the British, who were very much aware that the cheapness of road construction in these districts was due to an extended enforcement of bethi.[80] That several Garhjat kings insisted at that time to have only their own subjects employed in their dominions on colonial road works may indicate the spread of such practices.[81] Jadunath Bhanja (r. 1828–1863) of Mayurbhanj was thus not the only ruler to discover that the recruitment of coolies for colonial road works in his dominion could be turned into a source of revenue by means of a contradictory social arrangement: his engagement with the colonial administration with regard to road construction was ultimately that of a commercial labour contractor, who sought to fulfil his commitments, however, by drawing upon the politically defined obligations *prajas* (subjects) owed, in his view, to their raja and patron. This arrangement tended to strain relationships on which the polity rested by changing their social content. Moreover, the extension of bethi obligations to the new and extremely labour-intensive task of constructing raised, levelled and bridged roads also implied that the demand for unpaid labour services increased and that these services had to be rendered at a greater distance from home and became more burdensome. Both

---

[79] NAI, MBP 5 January 1841, 8562–63 (A. J. Moffat Mills, CoCD, to GoI, General Dpt., 23 October 1840).

[80] See especially: Mojumdar, *Changing Tribal Life*, 60–69. Also see Dandapani Behara, *Freedom Movement in the State of Ghumsar in Orissa, 1836–1866* (Calcutta: Punthi Pustak, 1984), 115–16. The Ganjam Agency was the colonial department in charge of controlling the Khond chiefdoms of southern Orissa.

[81] OIOC, BPWP December 1862 (P/16/59), Com., no. 95, 84 (T. W. Armstrong, SE, Cuttack, to Offg. CE Bengal, 15 November 1862). Also see chapter 5 of the present study.

the qualitative and quantitative aspects of the transformation of bethi/begar may have underlain rural resistance against such claims in the nineteenth century. When local chiefs demanded from their Kuttia Khond subjects in 1865 to render bethi over long periods on distant colonial roads in the middle of the agricultural season, they provoked a major uprising, which targeted not merely their Oriya patros but sought to drive out all Oriyas from the Chinnakimedi hills of the "Ganjam Agency".[82] Fakirmohan Senapati recalled in his memoirs the Bhuiyan rebellion of 1891 in Kendujhar, which he had experienced as the diwan of that state. He had little sympathy for this insurrection and even prided himself (whether justly or not) of having been instrumental in suppressing it. Given this background, Senapati represented the rebellion's immediate cause as having been connected to a 'public work' initiated by him personally, namely the excavation of a channel for purposes of 'river improvement':

> The Bhuiyan peasants were conscripted to dig the channel. Vicitrananda [the engineer who was also the raja's assistant manager in this area] wanted them to be as hardworking as himself. They were set to swinging thirty-pound shovels to smash the rock. It was no easy job. The least slacking earned a beating. They had to keep at it from dawn to dusk with only a two-hour midday break for dinner. Those who had brought rice with them cooked and ate it. The poor chaps who had none at home went without and slept. That they should actually be given any was unthinkable. Goaded by this excessive hardship the Bhuiyans rebelled to a man, aiming to kill the Assistant Manager, Vicitrananda Dasa, and depose the Maharaja. Had they laid hands on him, Vicitrananda would certainly have been killed, but flight saved him.[83]

Senapati defended the channel scheme and chose to ascribe the cause of the rebellion to the exaggerated zeal of a well-meaning younger official (Vichitrananda). The official's mistake was merely in wanting the conscripted raiyats "to be as hardworking as himself"—a line of reasoning that resonated with colonial notions of a

---

[82] Mojumdar, *Changing Tribal Life*, 75–83; Padel, *Sacrifice of Human Being*, 165–66.

[83] Senapati, *My Times and I*, 99 (for the whole account of the rebellion: 93–114. For a critical appraisal of this account and its interpretation by historians, see Barbara Lotz, *Rebels, Rajas and the British Raj: Situating Fakirmohan Senapati in the Bhuyan Revolt of 1891–92* (unpublished manuscript.).

deficient work ethic among the tribal population of Orissa, and thus returned the fault for the rebellion implicitly to the rebels. The refusal to provide food, the imposition of long working hours and the regular use of corporal punishments as an instrument for the intensification of the labour process are mentioned as specific grievances, suggesting that the attempt to adjust the modalities of bethi to the parameters of a new industrial work regime may have added to the violence of this conflict. Moreover, Senapati evaded the obvious question of why the insurgents turned not only against the engineer, but even sought to overturn the raja. He, however, writes somewhat unspecifically that the Bhuiyans were under the "delusion" that "the kingdom of Keonjhar was theirs and that they had the right to depose kings and crown new ones"—a delusion that "had already caused numerous revolts and was not entirely ungrounded."[84] This suggests a more general sense of status loss on the part of the Bhuiyan tribals, which was further heightened by the imposition of particularly coercive forms of bethi for purposes other than those that may have been legitimised by customary practice.

Full-scale tribal rebellions like those of the Kuttia Khonds of the "Ganjam Agency" in 1865 or of the Bhuiyans of Kendujhar in 1891 were, however, extremely dangerous forms of resistance. For the rajas could count on the assistance of the armed forces and the judiciary of their colonial overlords in the event of insurgency: the risings were ruthlessly suppressed, retribution meted out to the involved communities and participants sentenced to long spells of imprisonment and transportation.[85] Moreover, a standard British response to rebellion was to press ahead with infrastructural schemes and thereby increase the very burden the insurgents had sought to shake off. The British Superintendent of the Tributary States insisted, for instance, after the Bhuiyan rebellion that it

> is not too much to ask from a Chief who has twice been involved in protracted civil disturbances, necessitating for intervention on a large scale, to keep open good communications from the British districts from whence assistance will be derived.[86]

---

[84] Senapati, *My Times and I*, 97.
[85] Mojumdar, *Changing Tribal Life*, 77–78; Senapati, *My Times and I*, 110–12.
[86] *RATMO 1896–97*, 27.

Armed rebellions were certainly an important form of expressing rural resentment of unpaid forced labour, but considering the risks it is hardly surprising that they were rather uncommon. Among the less spectacular but more quotidian responses was the unwillingness of most Garhjat inhabitants to accept even voluntary and paid employment on roads and other 'public works'.[87] "They had an idea that their labour was to be forced, and were at first most unwilling to work," reported a British engineer in 1862. He went on to complain that "I never came across so impracticable a set of people, or Districts so difficult to work in" and added that they had had to rely on specialised navvies (earth-workers) from outside the states they were working in.[88] "It is this bethi," wrote a colonial official when commenting on his tour of the Tributary States in 1898, "which has ruined free labour and taught people to regard it as degrading."[89] Three decades later members of the Pana community of southern Orissa refused to render bethi on the grounds that their "changed social status after conversion to Christianity should free them from their traditional obligation."[90]

If employment on 'public works' was usually associated with bethi to some extent (both in perception and practice), plebeians resorted more commonly to tactics of evasion than of open confrontation: hiding from press gangs, dragging one's feet or escaping from the camps were more feasible methods of resistance than open defiance. Orissa's Superintending Engineer of the early 1860s, already quoted above, was enraged by the "ignorant and lazy jungle coolies" provided by the rajas who "do not even understand the common obedience work people ought to yield". They were "the worst and laziest workmen I ever came across", but he hoped that they would "become useful and willing laborers" after being exposed to examples of free "imported" labour.[91] More than thirty

---

[87] *RATMO 1897–98*, 10.
[88] *Report Showing Progress Made … in Public Works under Bengal Government for 1861–62*, 107 (T. Armstrong, SE, Report on Cuttack Circle, 15 May 1862).
[89] *RATMO 1897–98*, 3.
[90] Mojumdar, *Changing Tribal Life*, 65.
[91] OIOC, BPWP December 1862 (P/16/59), Com., no. 95, 84–85 (T. W. Armstrong, SE, to Offg. CE Bengal, 15 November 1862); OIOC, BPWP December 1862 (P/16/72), Com., no. 8, 7 (T. W. Armstrong, SE, to CoCD, 13 April 1865).

years later, however, it was reported that "the Garjatis are averse to work on roads or tanks, except in the case of the lowest classes".[92] It was also pointed out that "contractors have not succeeded in getting many coolies from the Garhjats" for the construction of the East Coast Railway "in spite of proclamations and the offer of very fair wages".[93]

In 1898, the British Superintendent of the Tributary States still repeated the old complaint of the "obstructiveness on the part of the people to all road work" and added that these were "very preposterous pretensions on the part of the low-caste population, and should be resisted".[94] He did not specify, however, the means to be used by the colonial administration for resisting these "low-caste" "pretensions". This vagueness as to how people were made to work for the infrastructural development of the Tributary States was typical for the official accounts of that period: the network of social relations, which permitted the production of abstract space in Orissa's "little kingdoms" remained strictly and literally off the record in its contentious particulars. The official picture was on the whole that of a direct march towards general progress: the Garhjat hills were opened up to the civilising forces of commerce and exchange,[95] the 'wild' (or absolute) spaces of their forests were rendered 'productive' (or relative) as they were converted into countable assets,[96] the rulers of the Tributary States were slowly but surely remoulded into enlightened managers of their people's welfare,[97] and even the "aborigines" let go of irrational practices like shifting cultivation, shed their habitual improvidence and were turned into useful labourers.[98] The idea of 'civilisation', in its nineteenth- and twentieth-century historical context, implied the reformulation of all social relations in the terms of bourgeois contract law. 'Free labour', a contractual relation between legally (and only legally)

[92] *RATMO 1896–97*, 13, see also p. 17.
[93] *RATMO 1895–96*, 16.
[94] *RATMO 1897–98*, 3.
[95] See, for example, *Report on the Administration of the Feudatory States of Orissa 1908–9* (Calcutta: Bengal Secretariat Book Depot, 1909), 53–54.
[96] See, for example, *RAFSOC 1910–11*, 11; *RARAFS 1922–23*, 33.
[97] See, for example, ibid., 4–5.
[98] See, for example, *RARAFS 1922–23*, 23; *GRAFSO 1926–27*, 24. Also see OSA, R III-1/796, *Report on the Administration of Mourbhanj* 1905–6, 5.

equal parties, and a similarly formal 'freedom of movement' was at the heart of this notion of 'civilisation'. Yet bethi was based on the normatively as well as factually unequal relationship between ruler and subject, which included the right (though not always the ability) of the former to determine the whereabouts of the latter. The existence of bethi in a British-controlled area was, therefore, a political embarrassment and the abolition of forced labour a topos of the rhetoric of civilisation triumphant. In 1895, Sri Ram Chandra Bhanj Deo took the lead and banned begar and bethi in his State of Mayurbhanj.[99] Other rulers followed this example in subsequent decades, usually rather converting bethi into monetary tributes like "road cesses" than abolishing this mode of surplus extraction altogether.[100] As for colonial public works, the official reports created the impression that they were largely conducted on the basis of voluntary and fully paid work and that both rajas and prajas appreciated by and by the advantages of (formally) free wage labour.[101]

It was only in the political context of the interwar period, when the late colonial regime faced massive popular movements and lost much of the limited hegemony it had been able to establish to the various strands of Indian nationalism that the issue of bethi could no longer be kept off the record. That the news of bethi in the British-controlled Tributary States of Orissa spread as far as to the International Labor Organization in Geneva in a period when forced labour in colonies became an international anathema may have further increased the pressure.[102] The proverbial 'elephant in the room' thus had to be acknowledged even officially since the 1930s, when it was found that bethi/begar was being continued in most of the

---

[99] Praharaj, *Tribal Movements and Political History*, 130.
[100] *Report of Enquiry Committee, Orissa States*, 16–17, 108–9, 118–19, 166, 197; NAI, Orissa States Agency Files, CS Branch, file no. XXVI-35–CS/1941–42, vols. 1 and 2, item 2.
[101] See, for example, *GRAFSO 1924–25*, 26–27; *GRAFSO 1926–27*, 24.
[102] ILO, N206/1/33/0 ("Forced Labour in India"); various documents including a letter from Sarangadhar Das, Secry. of the Orissa States People's Conference to the editor of the International Labour Review, 9 August 1939, forwarding the 1st vol. of the report of the Orissa States Enquiry Committee and drawing his "attention specially to the wide prevalence of unpaid forced labour, which the British Government, although a signatory to the Geneva Convention on forced labour, supports in these States". Also see Mojumdar, *Changing Tribal Life*, 66.

Tributary States. The ostensible "commutation" of bethi into monetary obligations had generally entailed no more than the imposition of a new tax, while unpaid labour services continued to be claimed.[103] According to villagers, who had walked three days to submit their complaints to the Orissa States Enquiry Committee in 1939, this was even the case in the model State of Mayurbhanj.[104] The volume of labour power forcibly extracted by rajas and their officials was reported to have been expanded enormously in several states, the most extreme case being Ranpur: "the poor peasants ... are forced to work nearly five months of the year without wages and there are 27 varieties of *bethi*."[105] Moreover, it now became public that British administrators had not tried to suppress practices of unpaid compulsory labour altogether but rather used their power in the Tributary States to codify bethi, that is to define by way of regulation legitimate claims of rajas to their subjects' unpaid services. This policy was defended with the argument that, "it is far better to regulate 'Begar' as has in fact been done by the Political Agents or the Local Governments than to attempt in the present circumstances to eradicate it, when this attempt is foredoomed for failure."[106] The debates of the interwar-period revealed that a tacit acceptance and utilisation of unpaid compulsory labour had been a stable feature of colonial policy in the Tributary States for a century.[107] Yet no-one stated the crux of the issue more clearly than the

---

[103] See the evidence compiled in *Report of Enquiry Committee, Orissa States* and NAI, Orissa States Agency Files, CS Branch, file no. XXVI-35–CS/1941–42, vols. I and II.

[104] *Report of Enquiry Committee, Orissa States*, 219–20. also see Praharaj, *Tribal Movements and Political History*, 130–33.

[105] *Report of Enquiry Committee, Orissa States*, 158–59; see also 108–9, 172, 177, 210.

[106] Mr. Lothian, Special Political Officer, quoted in *Report of Enquiry Committee, Orissa States*, 16; see also 131–32, 140, 179; NAI, Orissa States Agency Files, CS Branch, file no. XXVI-35–CS/1941–42, vols. I and II, items 7, 9, 22, 37, 66, 79, 85 (item 66 is of particular interest as it consists of a letter from A. N. Mitchell, the Political Agent of the Orissa States Agency, dated 18 August 1942, which defines "further principles on the subject of Begar").

[107] For a subtle belittlement of bethi see, for instance, Cobden-Ramsay, *Feudatory States of Orissa*, 80. Also see the cautious statement of C. L. Philip, Political Agent of the Orissa Feudatory States in 1925, who emphasised the

British official in charge in 1933 of the "Ganjam Agency", which comprised the Khond hills of southern Orissa:

> without *vetti* [bethi] labour, the administration of the agency would either break down or the Government would have to foot a surprisingly large bill. The abolition of compulsory labour is no doubt a necessary concomitant of the march of civilisation, but its abolition in the agency will . . . leave civilisation with no roads to march on.[108]

Thus the advent of 'civilisation' had to be postponed even after almost a century of British rule and road construction. "Opening up the country" had not entailed the complete eradication of *ancien régime* modes of social domination. Rather, the conversion of the valleys, forests and hills of interior Orissa into alienable items of an abstract space and the generation of a corresponding circulatory regime had at once preserved, transformed and exacerbated customary forms of compulsory unpaid labour. Bethi was preserved as a prerogative of local rulers, transformed into a means of entrepreneurial activity and exacerbated in quantity and modality. Stripped of all content that was not measurable in terms of exchange value, bethi also lost all use value it may ever have possessed as a device of generating bonds of clientship and its legitimacy as a royal prerogative. Turned into an economic device in the pursuit of profit, it became, as the *prajamandal* movements revealed, a political liability to Orissa's increasingly beleaguered rajas.

---

benefits of the (largely nominal) abolition of bethi by several states but added that "the system of bethi has undoubted advantages in the more remote States where markets are distant and the means of communication difficult." *GRAFSO 1924–25*, 26–27.

[108] *Ganjam Agency Administration Report, 1932–33* (Tamil Nadu State Archives, Chennai), quoted in Mojumdar, *Changing Tribal Life*, 68.

Conclusion

This book has been an attempt to write a history of how an *ancien régime* of circulation and its infrastructure were radically transformed in the course of the long nineteenth century, of how an increasingly abstract, relational space was produced in Orissa and of how this region was turned into a periphery of the colonial metropolis of Calcutta. This attempt was confined, however, by the present state of research to a preliminary exploration of such concepts and problems that may be critical for opening new perspectives on India's social history of circulation and infrastructure. More questions have, therefore, been raised than could be answered. The study has looked at a period beginning in the late eighteenth century. But the importance of *longue durée* processes for problems of circulation and transport infrastructure (emphasised at its outset) renders a better understanding of the dynamics of the precolonial circulatory regime(s) desirable, of which little is known at present with regard to the whole subcontinent. The period under review extends over almost one-and-a-half-century to World War I, but the postulate of the long term also begs the question, whether lines of continuity extended to subsequent infrastructural developments. More recent conflicts in Orissa over river damming and road construction in connection with issues of development or "law and order" point, for instance, to a problematic inheritance of colonial 'public works' policies. Moreover, the study has looked closely at a region that was clearly not the focus of attention of the colonial regime's infrastructural efforts. Comparable researches are required for other regions of the subcontinent before we can state with any certainty in how far the transformation of Orissa's circulatory regime was a singular phenomenon or indicative of more general, supra-regional tendencies. Furthermore, the two-pronged approach of the present study—the examination of critical conceptual fields and the empirical reconstruction of predominantly social and economic processes on a regional scale—covers merely two of many possible perspectives.

The present writer's hope is, therefore, that micro-historical studies of local circulatory regimes, explorations of the cultural history of transport and other contributions to a new social history of circulation will provide necessary correctives to his interpretations.

In the categories developed in the first part of this study, the findings of its second part may be briefly summarised as follows. In Orissa, as in many other parts of the subcontinent, the circulation of commodities, and also of people and information, had acquired distinct social, spatial and temporal patterns well before the onset of colonial rule: seasonal trade in salt, manufactured goods and various types of agricultural and forest produce was conducted between the coastal plains and the hilly interior as well as with areas beyond the lands of the Oriyas by interlinked commercial circuits of large-scale merchants, nomadic traders and local dealers. Commercial circulation was doubled by and interwoven with the yatras of numerous pilgrims from various parts of India, who circulated through Orissa's rich sacred landscape with the intent of reaching the Jagannath temple in Puri—a form of mobility that appears to have increased, too, in the early modern period with a widening of the social base of pilgrimage. Orissa's *ancien régime* of circulation had been organised in geographical space by two intersecting axes and, with regard to time, by a complex rhythm reflecting climatic seasons, cycles of production and calendars of rural culture. The first half-century of British rule effected little change in these overall patterns and appears to have even intensified the attrition of Orissa's circulatory channels that had set in during the latter half of the eighteenth century, when the region was controlled by the Maratha rulers of Nagpur. The consolidation of the colonial state, an aggressively annexationist policy of its operatives and a growing importance of India for the British economy as a provider of raw materials and as a market for industrial products entailed that a colonial policy change with regard to transport infrastructure extended to Orissa from the 1850s onwards. A specific colonial variety of capitalism thus constituted the crucial context of the reorganisation of social space even though this region moved into the centre neither of imperial strategy nor of colonial commercial interest. In the last quarter of the century, the patterns of circulation were fundamentally transformed by a tendency towards monoculture, which turned rice into the bulk of Orissa's growing exports, and by major infrastructural schemes that favoured canals and, from the late 1880s onwards, railways but had little regard for roads. In effect, the intensity of circulation was increased considerably and the northeast-southwest axis of the previous circulatory regime, that is, the region's link to Bengal and the colonial metropolis of Calcutta, was given clear priority over the axis that connected Orissa's coastal districts with Central India. The "time–space" between Calcutta and Puri was compressed from a journey of almost four weeks to twelve hours when the East Coast Railway was at last opened to traffic fully in 1900. This implied not merely savings in cost and time, but also the imposition of a fast, industrial, repetitive rhythm of circulation, since travel and transport on this route were rendered independent from the seasonal shifts of climate, which had so far been attended with considerable risks and pains. This "time–space compression" applied, however, only to a limited area and, as the density of the new transport infrastructure was particularly low in Orissa, disparities with other regions of the subcontinent were further accentuated. The mainline of the Bengal–Nagpur Railway diverted, at the same time, traffic from Central India and western Orissa towards Bengal and disarticulated older intraregional as well as transregional circuits. This transformation and re-scaling of social space did not merely affect the circulation of commodities, but also the patterns of passenger traffic and the modalities of pilgrimage in particular.

The imposition of a new circulatory regime and of capital-intensive infrastructures upon Orissa's social space was conceived, planned, engineered and dominated by the colonial oligarchy, that is by British administrators and connected commercial interests. And this dominance was only too real—it was experienced as unrelenting by wide sections of society such as salt manufacturers and nomadic traders (who lost their means of subsistence), townspeople (who could not afford to buy rice when exports soared), peasants (whose lands were confiscated for infrastructural purposes) and the labouring poor (who were made to toil on works that served a "public" they were clearly no part of). Yet the actual transformation and reorganisation of social space was never fully congruent with colonial blueprints—and could never be—for two reasons.

For one, dominant efforts of generating a relational and abstract space of commercialising 'improvement' superimposed themselves upon a complex social space. They could harness the absolute and concrete qualities of the older 'layers' but could not replace them in their entirety. This was observable for both the natural and the socially produced aspects of Orissa's concrete space. Aligning almost all major traffic channels towards Calcutta against the drainage of a vast river delta, building a canal system according to allegedly universal rules of engineering and converting hitherto 'unimproved' sal forests into commercial assets made sense from the vantage point of an abstract spatial economy of colonial capitalism, but these impositions upon an assumedly empty space or *tabula rasa* were often no more than transient, sometimes Pyrrhic victories over nature: they were expensive, destructive and frequently unsustainable in the long run. Nor were the concrete social qualities of the *ancien régime* of circulation, the accretions of earlier circulatory practices, wiped out in their entirety by colonial attempts at newly inventing Orissa's regime of circulation. Old intraregional circuits between the coastal plains and the Garhjat area, for instance, ceased to be viable after the ruin of Orissa's salt manufacture, but the old pathways and networks were now employed for exporting timber and rice from the Tributary States to Calcutta and other destinations outside the region. Several nodal points of the *ancien régime* of circulation were disarticulated and marginalised, while others acquired new circulatory functions like some of the headquarters of the western Tributary States on the Bengal–Nagpur Railway mainline. The region's differentiated sacred landscape was further focused on Puri by steam navigation and the East Coast Railway, but minor centres of pilgrimage and commerce (such as Kantilo) were not necessarily lost to oblivion if they were not directly linked to the railway system. Most crucially, steam locomotion depended on older modes and patterns of circulation; the availability or non-availability of bullock tracks and "unproductive works" like cartable roads delimited the scope for the profitability of the prioritised "productive works".

The second reason why the British capacity of engineering social space in the image of empire and capital met with limitations consists in that the new circulatory regime was both the result of contradictory processes and polyvalent in its uses. It was produced in a conflictual field of force, that is through simultaneous and overlapping spatial practices of a wide range of (unequally powerful) regional and extraregional social agencies—through practices not always in accord with the plans of the colonial administration. Garhjat rajas thwarted colonial road projects well into the second half of the nineteenth century, British investors struggled with colonial bureaucrats over guaranteed interest payments from Indian revenues, Bengali newspapers politicised the issue of railway construction in Orissa by turning it into a touchstone of the benignity of colonial rule, peasants were openly hostile against canal projects and the labouring poor more than reluctant of being employed on 'public works'. These and other attitudes and activities contributed to the production of social space in nineteenth-century Orissa, even though the colonial regime ruled out any formal participation of their subjects in the determination of 'public works' policy. This field of force was itself subject to transformation: whereas few social and political agencies were in favour of and had an unmitigated interest in the formation of built environment for purposes of transport in the former half of the period under review, there was a marked change in attitudes, policies and practices as well as a realignment of social forces with regard to 'public works' in the last decades of the nineteenth century.

The scope for an effective deviance from the dominant colonial conceptualisations and politics of social space was, however, far greater in the utilisation than in the formation of transport infrastructure. Once opened for traffic, the polyvalence of metalled roads, navigable canals and railways revealed itself in numerous practices of purposeful appropriation, which amounted not necessarily or predominantly to acts of resistance but were still at variance with the dominant ideology and practice of space. The appropriation of the railways by *pandas* or temple priests of Puri for the generation of more powerful means of organising pilgrimage implied, paradigmatically, neither a critique nor a confrontation of British rule, but rather an attempt to partake of the potentials of establishing social control that had been extended by the new circulatory regime. Nor was the immediate and massive appropriation of the railways by the yatris themselves perceived as a direct threat to British authority but in rather more ambivalent terms: it was a practice that contributed to the "productivity" of railways by increasing the ratio of utilisation and, at the same time, a landmark defining the limits of the 'civilising mission' or, in other words, of the regime's ability to establish its hegemony over society. "Railway pilgrimage" was, from the perspective of the colonial regime, no assault on the state but an affront to the values of 'improvement' and a danger for 'public health'. The increased spatial mobility of the subordinated classes displayed a similar ambivalence from the points of view of both the rulers and the ruled: for labour migrants, the polarising effects of commercialisation made migration a necessity rather than a choice between several feasible alternatives. Yet, there was also a possibility, if only for a part of the concerned households, to secure and enhance their status and material position by additional incomes from labour migration. Moreover, the new avenues of mobility could also be used for withdrawing from oppressive constellations of local power. Colonial administrators (and 'improving *rajas*') perceived migration, conversely, as a means to alleviate 'population pressure' and food crises and to supply Calcutta's services and industries as well as the colonial plantation economy with labour power, but simultaneously as a potential threat to the fixity of a socio-spatial order they wished to preserve, since increased mobility could be 'abused' for 'irrational' or even 'criminal' purposes.

Building the pathways of Empire, the transformation of the circulatory regime and of transport infrastructure contributed, then, to the production of a social space that was riven with contradictions and, therefore, at once determined by structures of subordination and rife with historical possibility. It was a hierarchically ordered, dominated social space dedicated to the pursuit of 'productivity'. The policies of social space, including the policies of infrastructure, acquired, furthermore, a particularly authoritarian form in a colonial field of force. Yet the hierarchies were in motion, domination never total and there were even rare moments of emancipatory hope. Thus, when a militant popular movement against bethi and other practices of the 'improving *rajas*' spread across large areas of interior Orissa in the final decade of colonial rule, it became apparent that the 'little kingdoms' had ceased to be the compartmentalised *cordon sanitaire* against political unrest they had been in 1857.

Conclusion

It was in such moments that the notion of space as the eternal "suitcase of the world", where each and all had their fixed places, revealed itself as an illusion.

- - - Present external boundary
of India

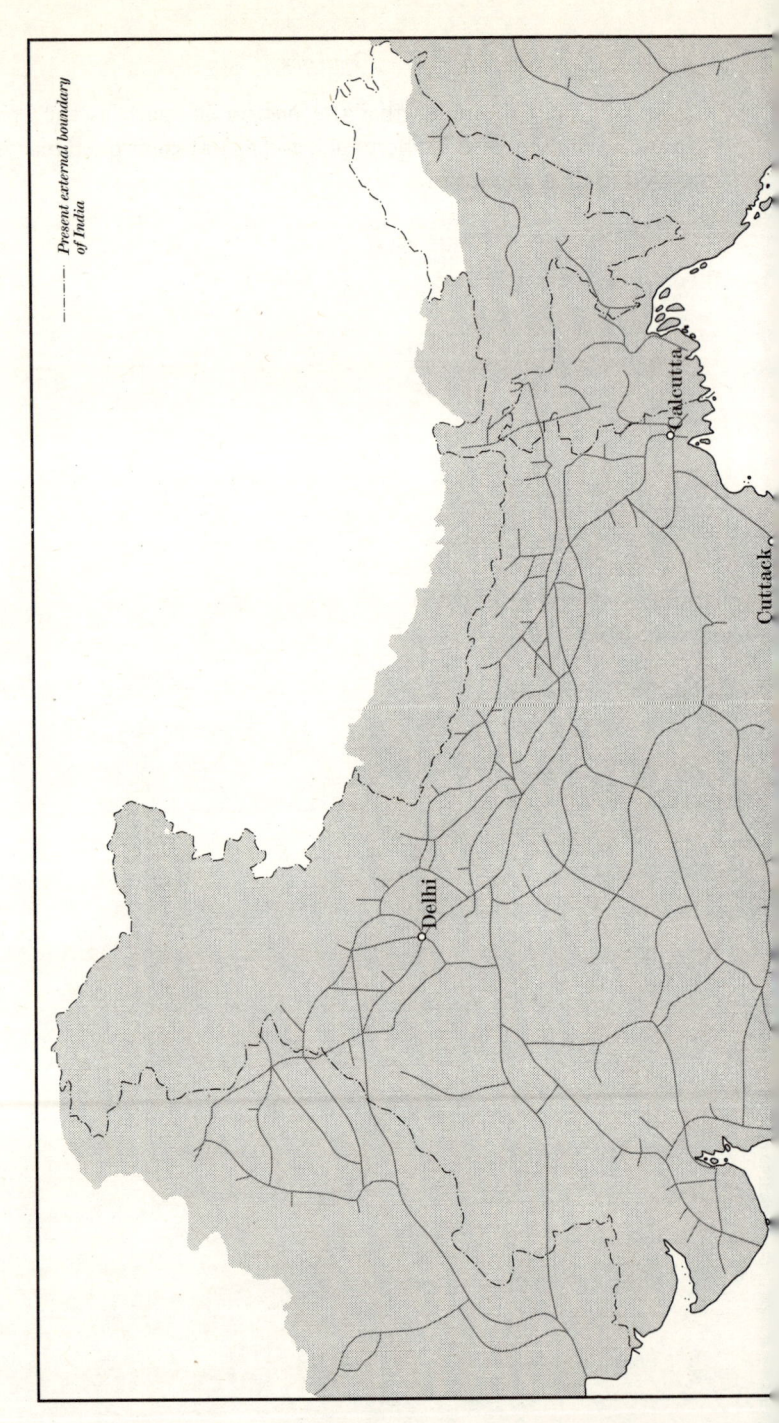

Calcutta

Cuttack

Delhi

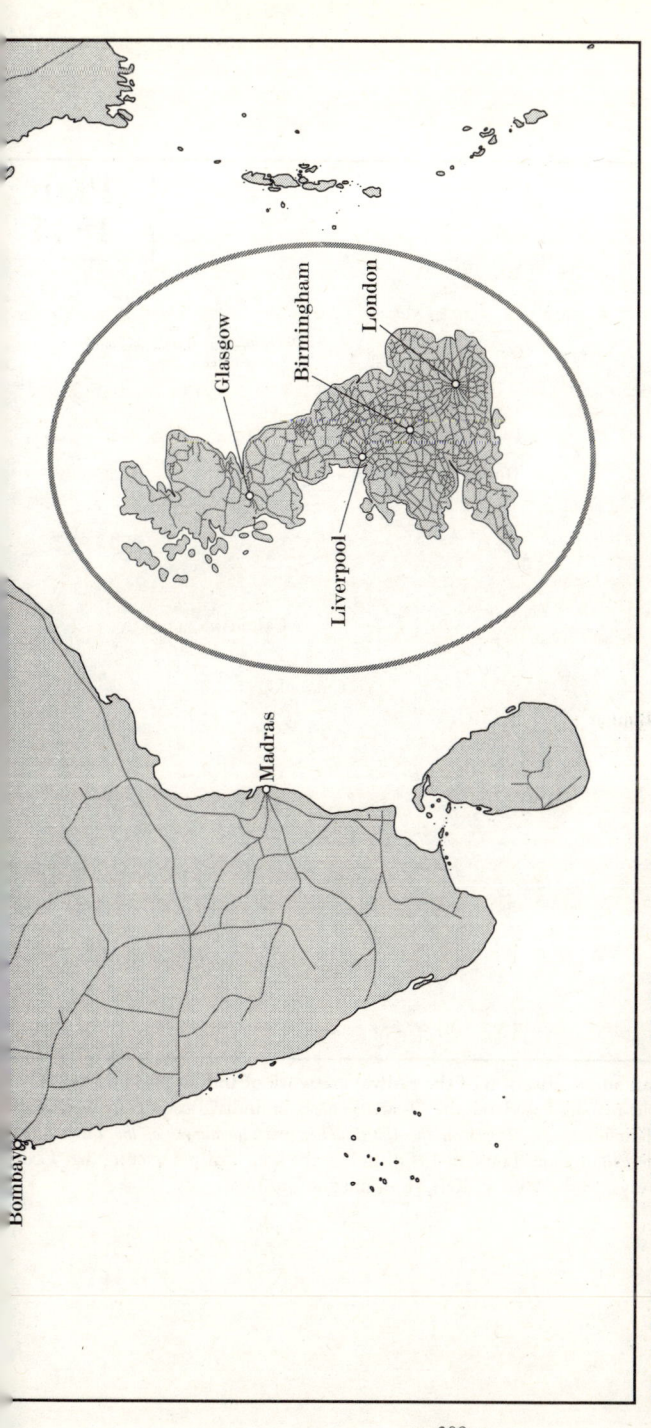

MAP 1: **Railway networks of India and Britain around 1900.**
Both maps are drawn to the same scale. *Sources*: Kerr, "Introduction", p. 2, and Thrift, "Transport and Communication", p. 462. Both railway systems were, at that time, of a comparable size of between 30,000 and 40,000 route kilometres (the Indian networks being more extensive). The marked difference between the radial Indian and the cellular British system is clearly discernible (see ch. 3).

* 309 *

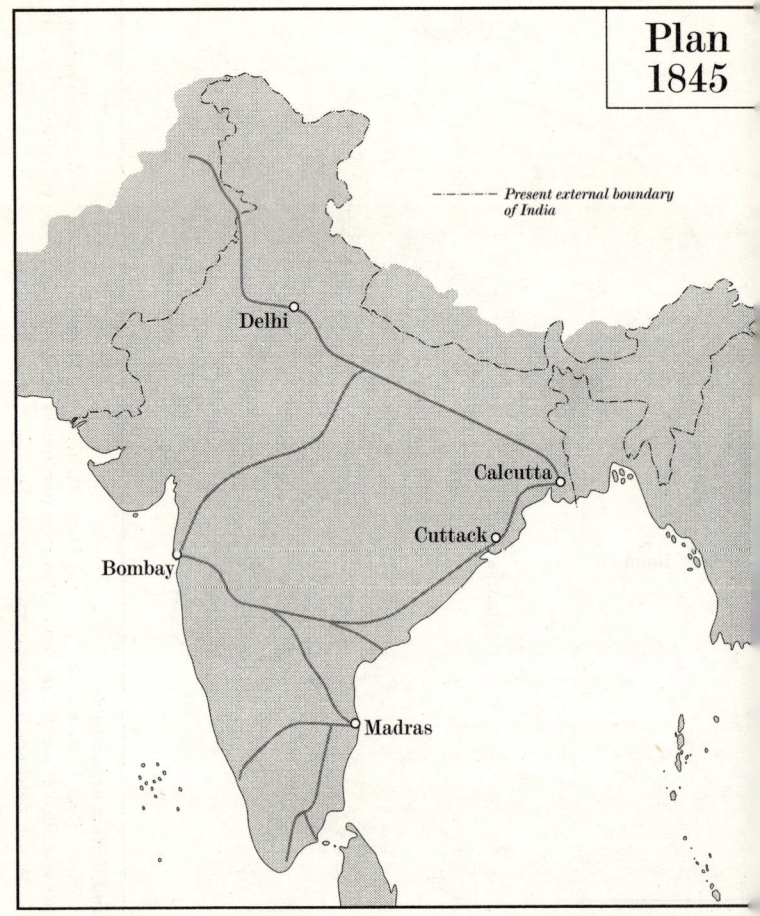

MAP 2: Plan and realisation of the railway network of India (1845 and 1881).
This double map is based on the "Railway Map of India" accompanying Rowland Macdonald Stephenson, *Report on the Practicability and Advantages of the Introduction Railways into British India* (London, 1845), and on the sketch map depicting the "Growth of the Railways, 1861–1901", in Kerr, "Introduction", p. 2.

Reality 1881

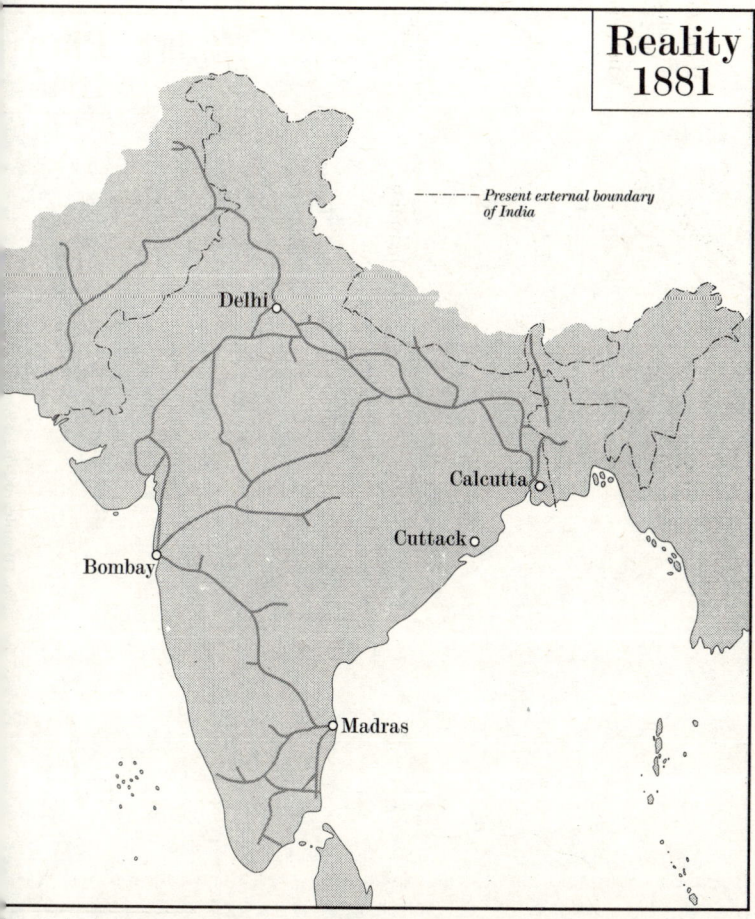

----- Present external boundary of India

By 1881, the system of "trunk lines" between the "Presidency" towns of Calcutta, Bombay and Madras, which had been projected by Stephenson in the 1840s, had been realised. The remarkably planned character of the Indian railway system and its orientation towards the colonial port metropolises is clearly distinguishable. The only major digression in the actual layout of the "trunk lines" was that the trunk line along the East Coast had not been built in 1881 and was only opened for traffic two decades later (see chs. 3, 6 and 7).

* 312 *

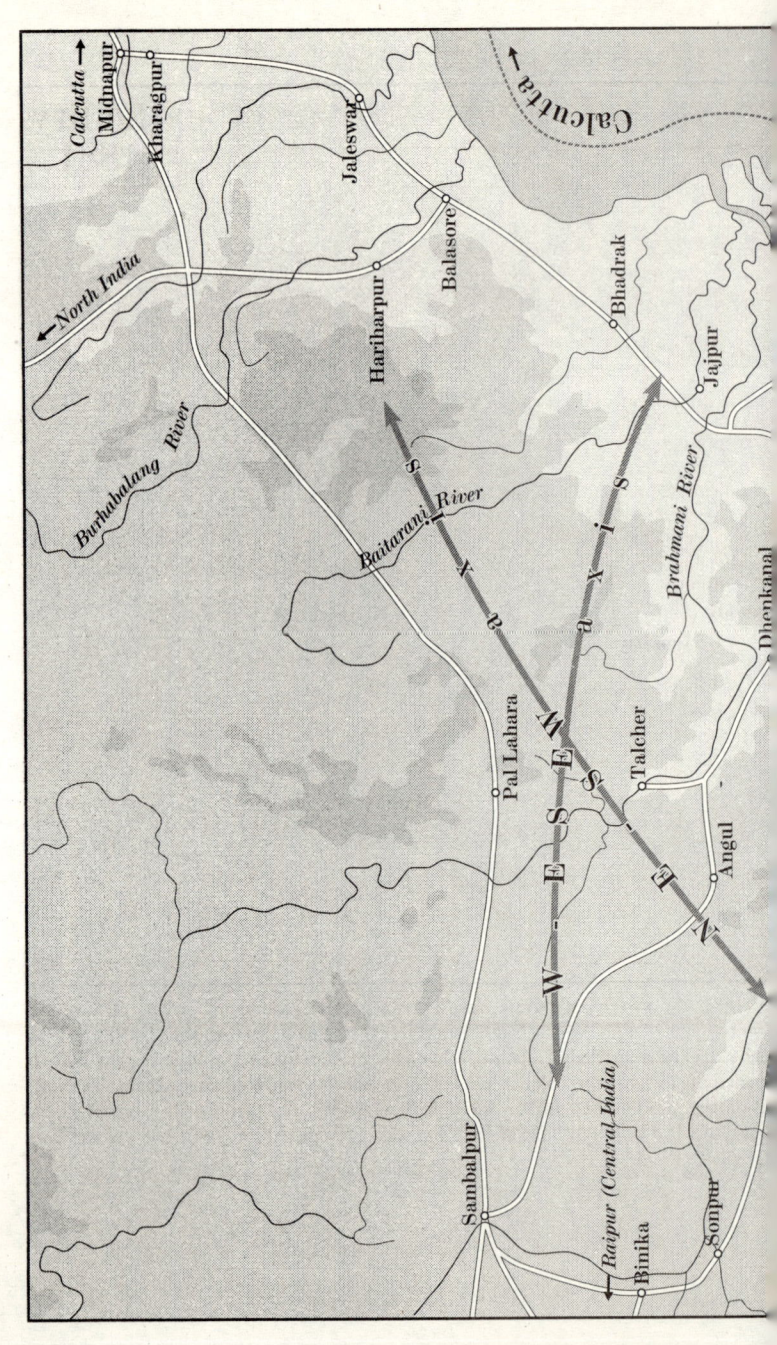

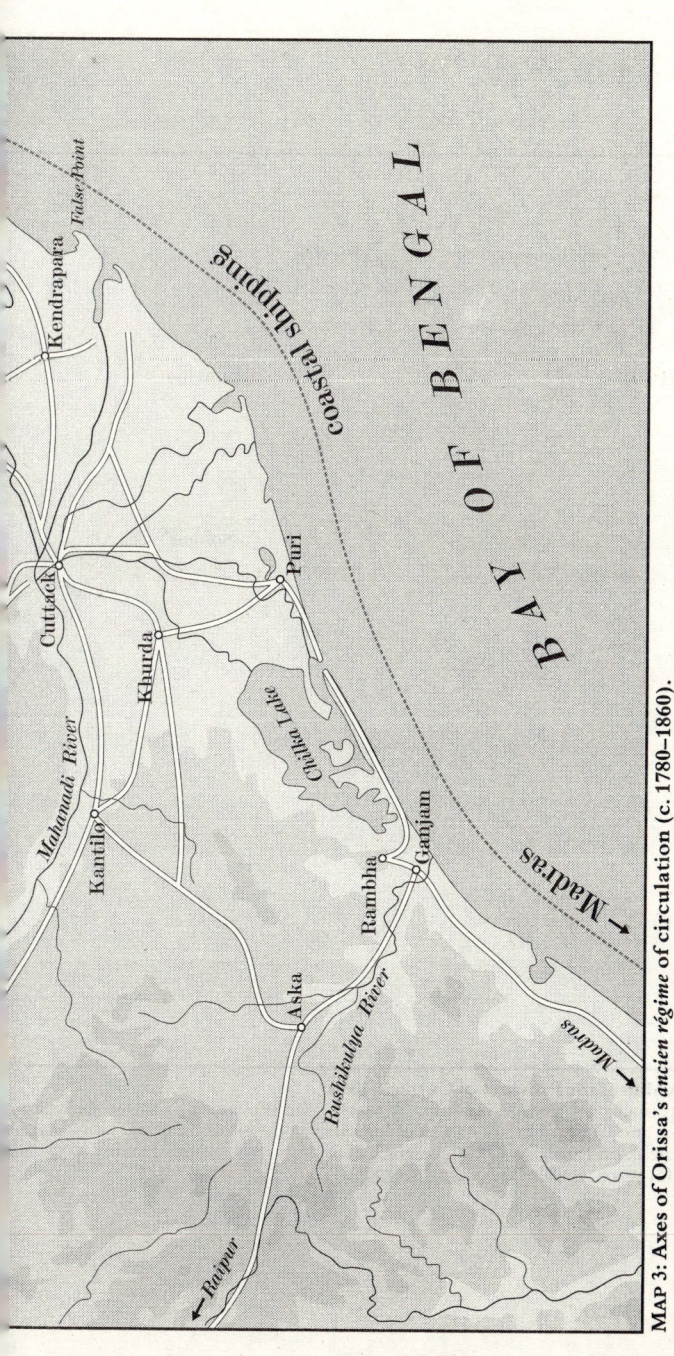

MAP 3: Axes of Orissa's *ancien régime* of circulation (c. 1780–1860).
This map combines information from various maps of the early half of the nineteenth century (see the references given in maps 4 to 7) and also from textual sources discussed in ch. 4 in order to present a schematic view of the alignment of major traffic routes and hence of Orissa's older patterns of circulation (see Part II of the present study).

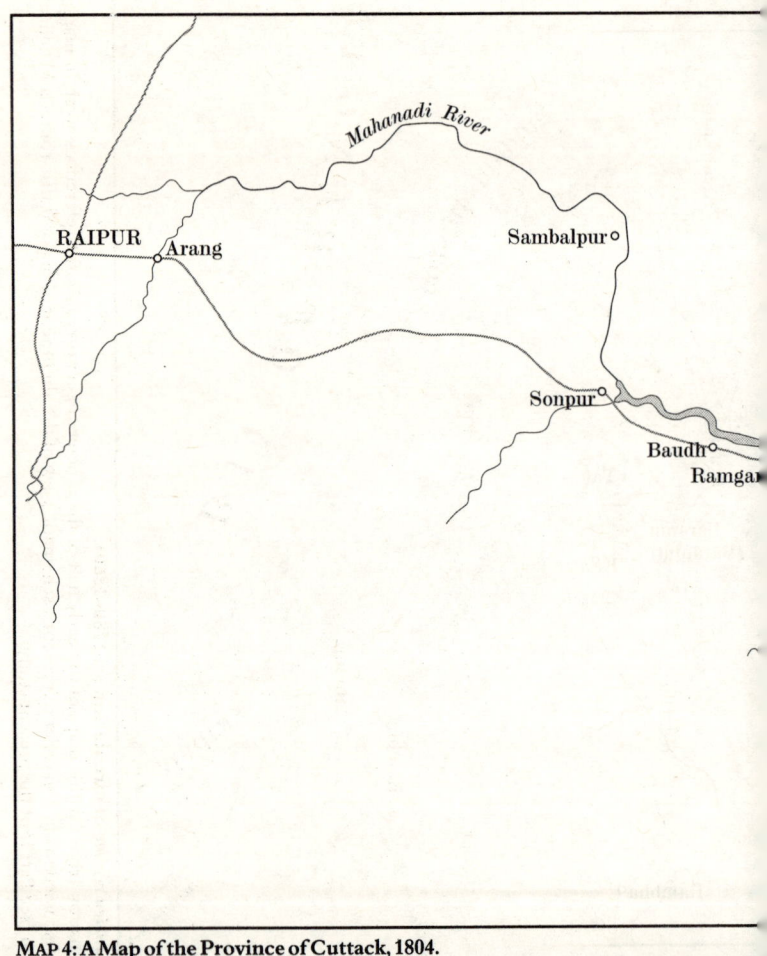

MAP 4: A Map of the Province of Cuttack, 1804.
This map is adapted from J. T. Blunt, "A Map of the Province of Cuttack with part of Goomsoor and Choteesgur, the ranges of hills exhibit the situation of the Hilly Districts Dependencies on Kuttack and Choteesgur", 26 March 1804, British Library, MSS. Add. 13,903c (for an extract from the original see map 5).

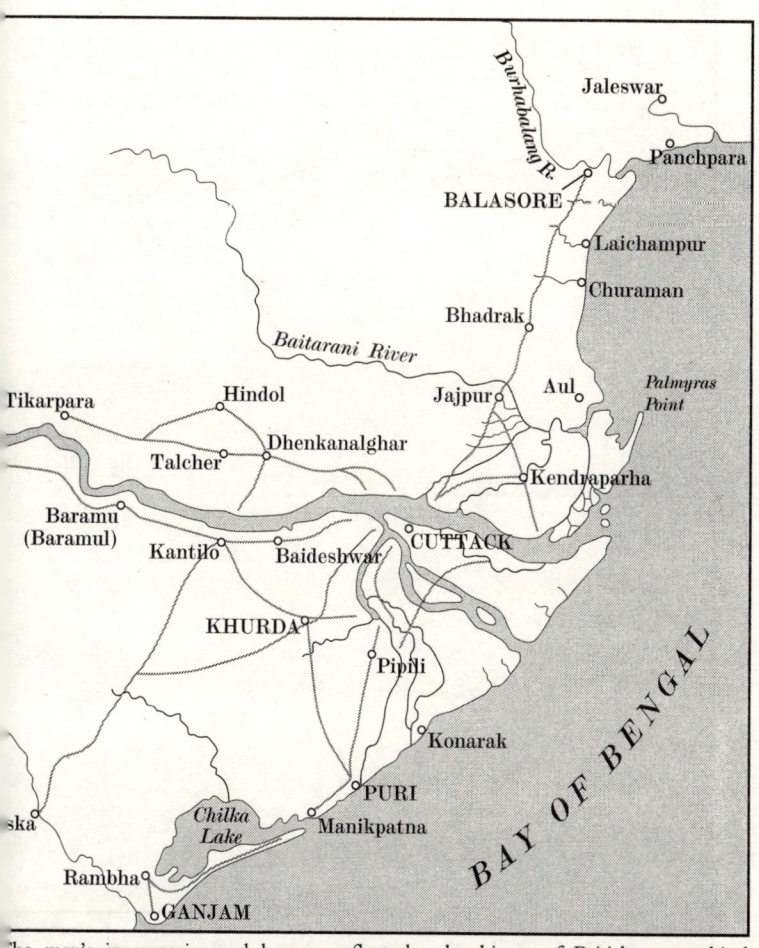

The map's inaccuracies and lacunae reflect the sketchiness of British geographical information on Orissa at the time of annexation (see Part II of the present study).

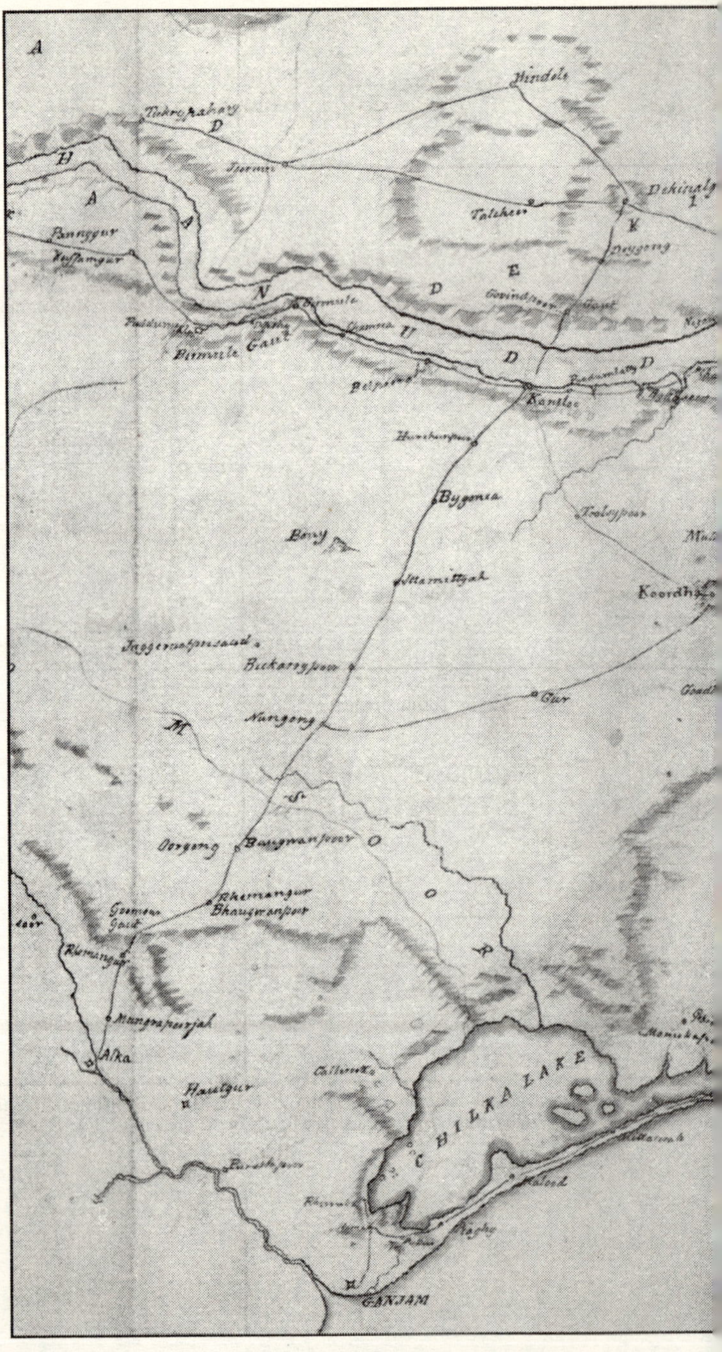
A
Hindole
Talcheer
Byganea
Boory
Koordha
Gur
Oorgong
Alka
Haulgur
CHILKA LAKE
GANJAM

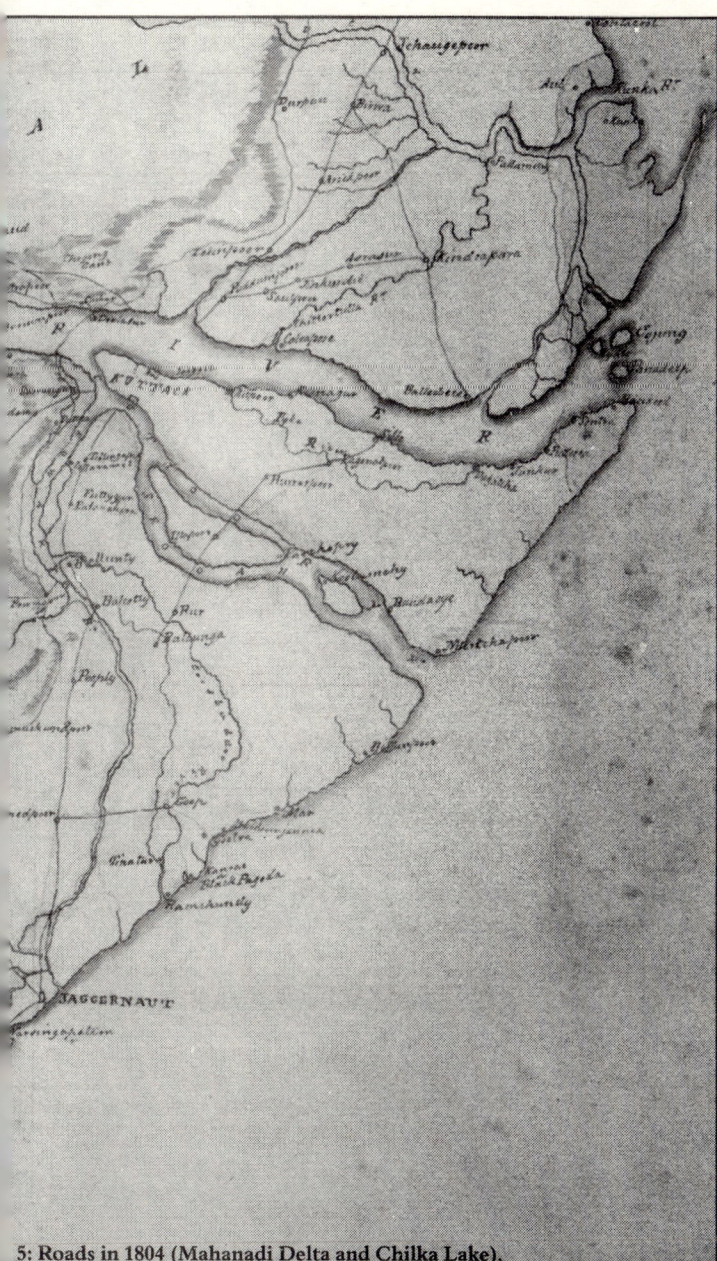

5: Roads in 1804 (Mahanadi Delta and Chilka Lake).
ct from J. T. Blunt, "A Map of the Province of Cuttack with part of Gooms hills
it the situation of the Hilly Districts Dependencies on Kuttack and Choteesgur",
arch 1804, British Library, MSS. Add. 13,903c (see ch. 4 of the present study).

MAP 6: Orissa according to Rennell (1788).

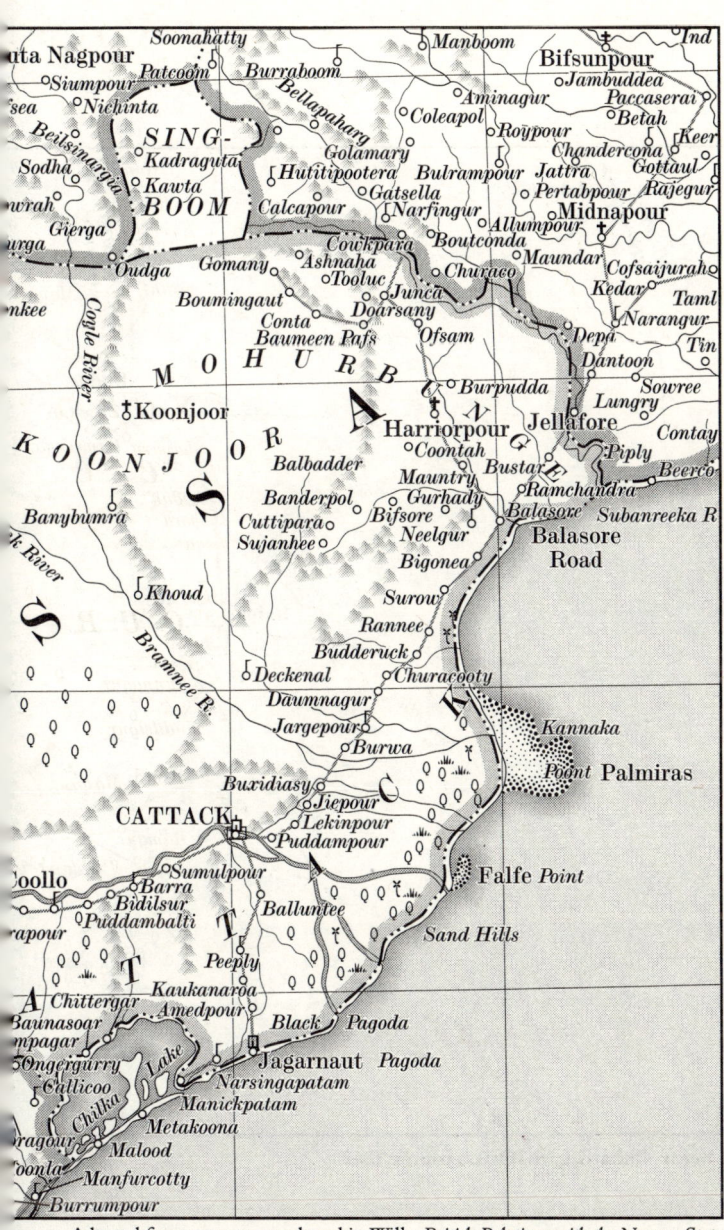

Adapted from a map reproduced in Wills, *British Relations with the Nagpur State*
(see ch. 4 of the present study)

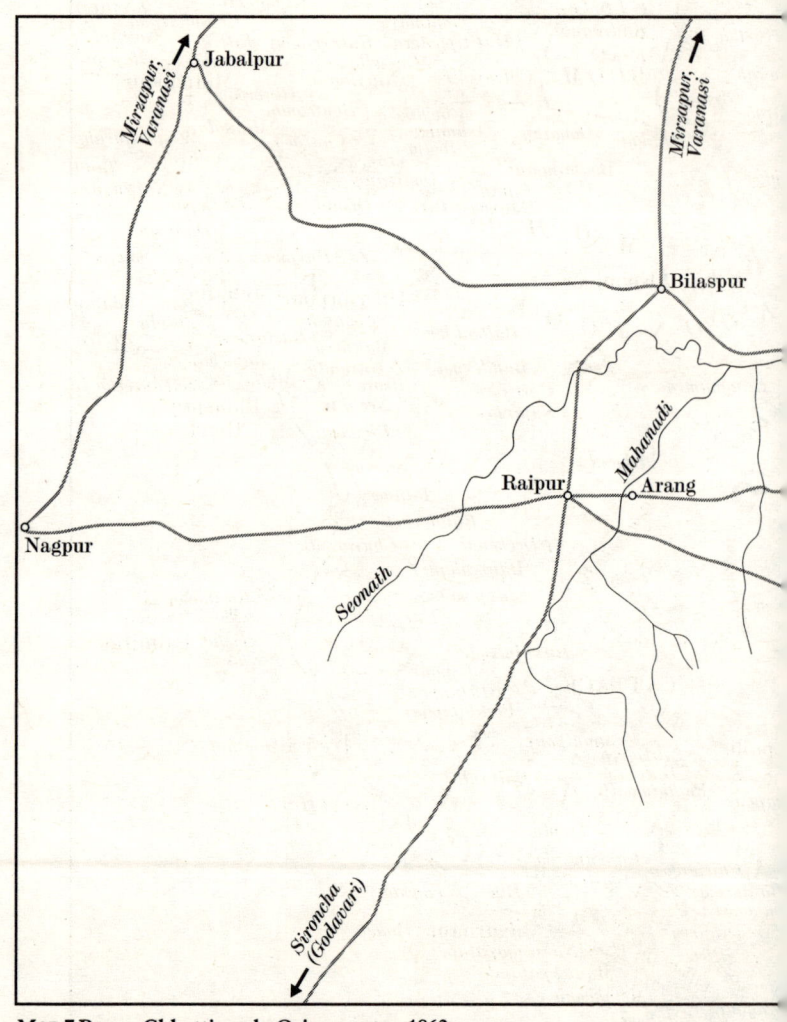

MAP 7 Berar–Chhattisgarh–Orissa routes, 1862.

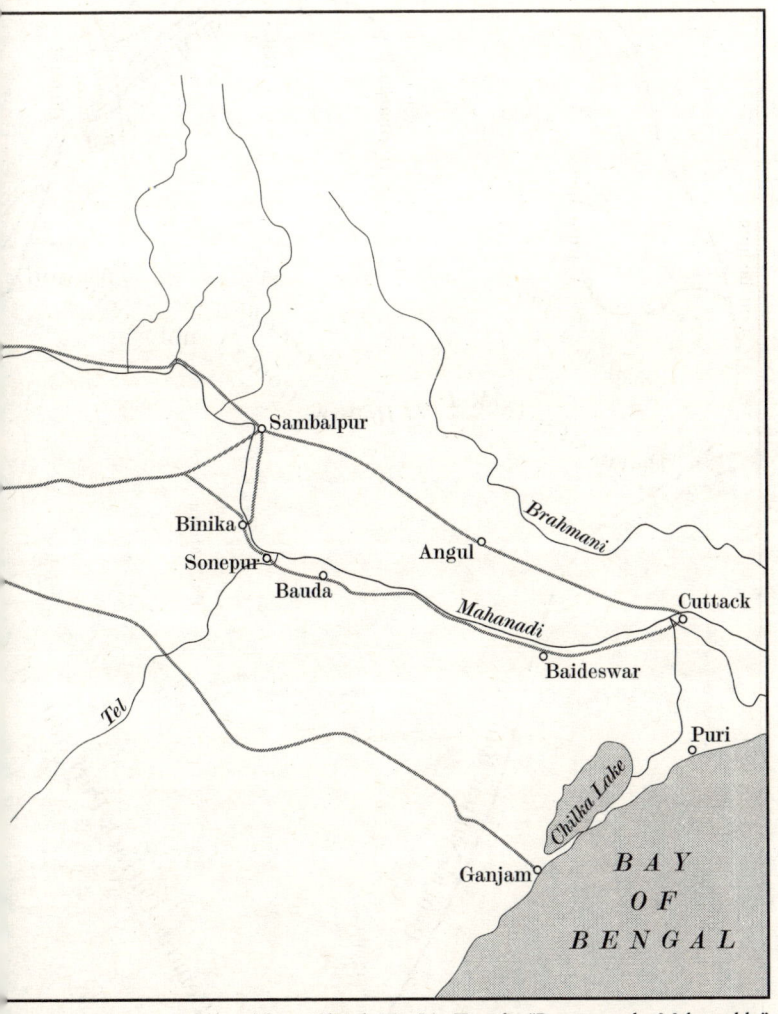

Adapted from "Sketch Map" in Temple, "Report on the Mahanuddy" (see chs. 4 and 6 of the present study).

* 322 *

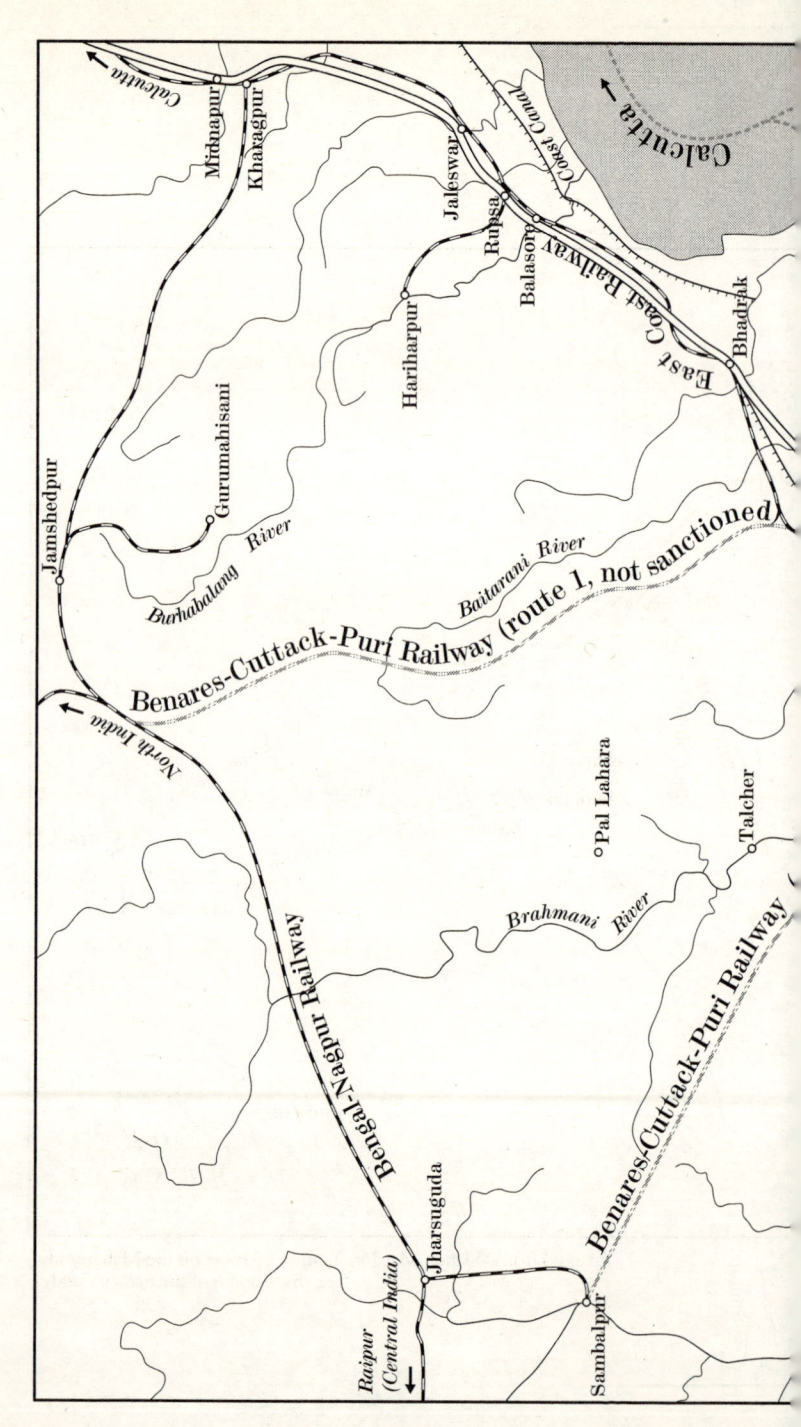

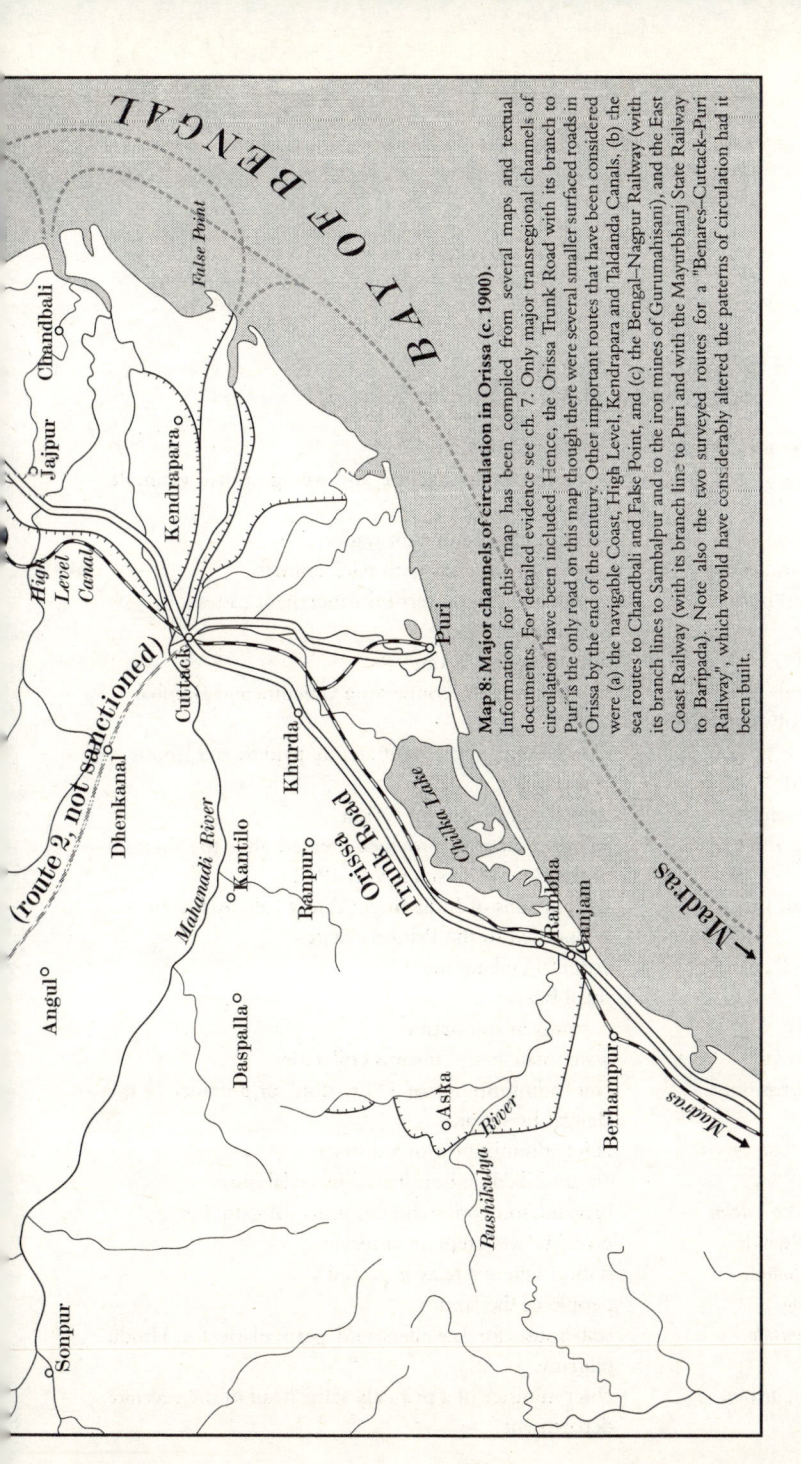

Map 8: Major channels of circulation in Orissa (c. 1900). Information for this map has been compiled from several maps and textual documents. For detailed evidence see ch. 7. Only major transregional channels of circulation have been included. Hence, the Orissa Trunk Road with its branch to Puri is the only road on this map though there were several smaller surfaced roads in Orissa by the end of the century. Other important routes that have been considered were (a) the navigable Coast, High Level, Kendrapara and Taldanda Canals, (b) the sea routes to Chandbali and False Point, and (c) the Bengal–Nagpur Railway (with its branch lines to Sambalpur and to the iron mines of Gurumahisani), and the East Coast Railway (with its branch line to Puri and with the Mayurbhanj State Railway to Baripada). Note also the two surveyed routes for a "Benares–Cuttack–Puri Railway", which would have considerably altered the patterns of circulation had it been built.

Glossary

Athara-nala Bridge	eighteen channel bridge
aurang	location of manufacture and storage (form example, salt)
Banjara	community of itinerant traders
Banjara *tanda*	convoy of Banjaras with pack animals
bania, "bunniah"	merchant, generic term for merchant castes
bargis	Maratha horseman
begar	unpaid forced labour
Bengal–Nagpur Railway (BNR)	opened in 1891, connecting Calcutta and Bombay
bethi	Corvee unpaid or insufficiently paid forced labour
bhut(s)	evil spirits
Bhuiyan	'tribal' community in Orissa
Bihar and Orissa	an administrative province created after the division of the Bengal Presidency in 1912
British India	the portions of India under direct rule by the British as opposed to the Princely States
"bund", bandh	artificial embankment
chatti	small bazaar
chauki	customs or toll station
chaukidar	watchman; here: customs collector
commissioner	chief administrator of a "division" or province of the Bengal Presidency
collector	chief administrator of a district
coolie	an 'unskilled', subordinated wage labourer
"dacoit", *daku*	brigand; someone who commits gang-robbery
dak, "dawk"	postal relay system, mail service
dak chauki	station where a relay is posted
deshlog	people of the land
dharamsala	rest-house for travellers and particularly for Hindu pilgrims
diwan, dewan	chief minister of a princely state; head of the revenue department

* 324 *

Glossary

dikku	Hindu settlers in 'tribal' area
doab	region situated between two rivers
East Coast Railway	railway line traversing the coastal districts of Orissa, opened to traffic from 1898–1900
East India Company	founded in 1600 as the first joint-stock company; transformed from a trading company into a territorial power in the second half of the eighteenth century; controlled by the British parliament and dissolved in 1858
faujdar	military commander
gaddi	seat of royalty
garh	(minor) fort, especially a hill fort
garhjat	(Persian plural of *garh*), Tributary State ruled in the Orissa hill tracts
ghat	here: mountan pass or range
Governor-General of India	chief colonial administrator of British India, see: Viceroy
haat, hat	temporary market; fair
hajj	pilgrimage to Mecca
jagirdar	(Farsi) holder of a hereditary assignation to a territory's revenue
jalkar	fishing tax
karkatch	salt manufacture by solar evaporation
"Khond Maliah"	literally Khond hills; hill areas of southern Orissa
Khond, Kond	'tribal' community
khorakhi	food allowance
Kol	'tribal' community
kos	two statute miles
kotwal	town magistrate
lakh	100,000
Lieutenant-Governor	chief administrator of the Bengal Presidency
malangil	saltwater
mahajan, "Mahajun"	merchant, moneylender
mahal, mehal	administrative subdivision
mahjis	steerman and/or owner of ferry boat
mofussil	subordinate or separate district; the country or province; also adjectively: provincial, rural
mela	a fair, often associated with a religious festival
meli	rebellion
meriah	practice of human sacrifice in southern Orissa
minar	tower
mukaddam	village headmen
mukhtar, "Mooktar"	authorised agent or attorney

Glossary

nawab	governor of a province in Mughal India; in the eighteenth century increasingly independent
Oraon	'tribal' community
pakka	literally ripe, mature, cooked, here "pakka road", that is, surfaced road
palki	palanquin
Pana	'tribal' community in Orissa
panda	hereditary and resident temple priest
panga	salt manufacture by boiling
parwana	written government order
praja	subject
Prajamandal	People's Association/in a princely state
Presidency	the three main administrative divisions of British India under the EIC: the Bengal, Madras and Bombay Presidencies; also their capital cities
raiyat	a subject; in the Anglo-Indian usage particularly a peasant
raj	kingdom, principality, also: reign
raja	king, prince
rasad	forage and victuals
rath yatra	annual "car festival" in Puri on which the images of deities are taken outside the temple
sal	north Indian hardwood tree
salami	complimentary present
Santal	'tribal' community of eastern India
saradh	winter rice crop
sarai	inn building forming an enclosed yard for the lodging of travellers with their pack animals
sayer	transit duties
Secretary of State for India	head of the India Office, the cabinet office in London controlling the Government of India
shikar	hunting
takoit	heir apparent
tanda	convoy
Viceroy	the Governor-General and Viceroy of India, official designation of the chief colonial administrator from 1858 to 1947; appointed by the Crown
yatra, jatra	pilgrimage to a venerated spot or festival; religious march
yatri, jatri	a pilgrim
zamindar	literally landholder; various types of local rulers, landlords and revenue collectors

Bibliography

PRIMARY SOURCES

Archival Material

British Library, Oriental and India Office Collections (OIOC)
    Board of Control, "Board's Collection", 1807–1825.
    Government of Bengal, Public Works Proceedings (BPWP), 1860–1890.
    Government of India, Public Works Proceedings, Railway Construction (PWRC), 1881.
    European Manuscripts (Eur.MSS)
British Library, Additional Manuscripts (Add. MSS.)
Orissa State Archives (OSA), Bhubaneswar
    Cuttack District Records, Board of Revenue Proceedings, 1805.
    Cuttack Division, Board of Revenue Loose Records (BoRLR), 1805–1925.
    General Administration Report, Orissa Division (GAROD), 1871/72–1899/1900.
    Mayurbhanja Records, 1890–1905.
National Archives of India (NAI), New Delhi
    Government of India, Military Board Proceedings (MBP), 1840–1841.
    Government of India, Railway Department, 1881.
    Government of India, Foreign Department, 1876.
    Orissa States Agency Files, 1941–42.
International Labor Organisation (ILO), Geneva
    Archives, 1939 files.

Official publications

Annual Reports on the Administration of the Feudatory States of Orissa and Chota Nagpur [ARAFS], Ranchi/Patna: Bihar and Orissa Govt. Press, 1911/12–1915/16.
British Parliamentary Papers
    1847 (68.) (151.) xli.233.257, Railway Reports from India.

Bibliography

1884 (284) xi.1, Report from the Select Committee on East India Railway Communication.

1859 (92. Sess. 1) xix.285, "Roads and navigable canals opened since 1848."

Central Advisory Board of Health. *Report of the Sub-Committee Appointed by the Central Advisory Board of Health to Examine the Possibility of Introducing a System of Compulsory Inoculation of Pilgrims against Cholera.* Simla: Government of India Press, 1940.

Clemesha, W. Wesley. *37th Annual Report of the Sanitary Commissioner for Bengal (1904).* Calcutta: Bengal Secretariat Press, 1905.

Cobden-Ramsay, L. E. B. *Feudatory States of Orissa.* Bengal Gazetteers, vol. XXI. Calcutta: Bengal Secretariat Book Depot, 1910.

Dyson, H. J. *31st Annual Report of the Sanitary Commissioner for Bengal, 1898.* Calcutta: Bengal Secretariat Press, 1899.

———. *32nd Annual Report of the Sanitary Commissioner for Bengal (1899).* Calcutta: Bengal Secretariat Press, 1900.

Further Papers Relating to the Extension of Railway Communications in India (reprint 14 of PWD records). Vol. III. Calcutta: PWD Press, 1868.

General Review of the Administration of the Feudatory States of Orissa [GRAFSO], Patna: Superintendent of Government Printing, Bihar and Orissa, 1924/25—1928/29.

Government of Bengal (GoB), Public Works Department (PWD). *Annual Administration Report for Roads and Buildings, Irrigation and Railways,* 1899–1900, 1900–1901. Calcutta: Government Press, 1900–1.

——— Railway Branch: Benares–Cuttack–Puri Railway: Reports, Estimates, and Correspondence from the Commencement up to the End of 1883–84. Calcutta: Bengal Secretariat Press, 1886.

Government of Bihar and Orissa. *Bihar and Orissa,*

——— *in 1924–25.* Patna: Superintendent of Govt. Printing, Bihar and Orissa, 1926.

——— *in 1925–26.* Patna: Superintendent of Govt. Printing, Bihar and Orissa, 1927.

——— *in 1927–28.* Patna: Superintendent of Govt. Printing, Bihar and Orissa, 1929.

Gregg, W. H. *26th Annual Report of the Sanitary Commissioner for Bengal, 1893.* Calcutta: Government Press, 1894.

———. *27th Annual Report of the Sanitary Commissioner for Bengal, 1894.* Calcutta: Government Press, 1895.

Hare, E. C., *Annual Sanitary Report of the Province of Bihar and Orissa, 1912.* Patna: Bihar and Orissa Government Press, 1913.

History of the Rise and Progress of the Operations for the Suppression of Human Sacrifice and Female Infanticide in the Hill Tracts of Orissa. Selections from the Records of the Government of India [Home Department] No. V. Calcutta: Bengal Military Orphan Press, 1854.

Bibliography

Hunter, William W. *The Annals of Rural Bengal.* Vol. I ("The Ethnical Frontier of Lower Bengal with the Ancient Principalities of Beerbhoom and Bishenpore"). 1st ed. London: Smith, Elder & Co., 1868.

———. *The Annals of Rural Bengal: Orissa.* Vols. 2 and 3: London: Smith, Elder & Co., 1872.

———. *A Statistical Account of Bengal.* vols. 18, 19. Delhi: Concept Publishing Company, 1976 (1st ed. 1875–1877).

Hunter, William W., et al., eds. *Imperial Gazetteer of India.* Vol. 19. Oxford: Clarendon Press, 1908.

Mitchell, K. G., and L. H. Kirkness. *Report on the Present State of Road and Railway Competition and the Possibilities of their Future Co-Ordination and Development, and Cognate Matters, in Governor's Provinces.* Calcutta: Government of India Central Publication Branch, 1933.

Maddox, S. L. *Final Report on the Settlement of the Province of Orissa (Temporary Settled Areas), 1890–1900.* Vol. I. N.p., n.d.

O'Malley, L. S. S. *Bengal District Gazetteers: Cuttack.* Calcutta: Bengal Secretariat Book Depot, 1906.

———. *Bengal District Gazetteers: Angul.* Calcutta: Bengal Secretariat Book Depot, 1908.

———. *Bengal District Gazetteers: Sambalpur.* Calcutta: Bengal Secretariat Book Depot, 1909.

Maltby, T. J. *The Ganjam District Manual.* Ed. by G. D. Leman. Madras: Government Press, 1918 (1st ed. 1882).

Papers on the Settlement of Cuttack and the State of the Tributary Mehals. In Selections from the Records of Government III. Calcutta: W. Palmer, Military Orphan Press, 1851.

Papers Relating to the Orissa Canals [1869 to 1877 and 1881 to 1883]. In *Selections from the Records of the Government of Bengal.* Calcutta: Bengal Secretariat Press, 1884.

Papers Relating to the Orissa Coast Canal [1869 to 1877 and 1881 to 1883]. In Selections from the Records of the Government of India in the Public Works Department. Calcutta: Bengal Secretariat Press, 1884.

Papers Relating to the Orissa Coast Canal [1877 to 1881]. In Selections from the Records of the Government of India in the Public Works Department. Calcutta: Bengal Secretariat Press, 1885.

Papers Relating to the Orissa Coast Canal [second series]. In Selections from the Records of the Government of India in the Public Works Department. Calcutta: Superindentent of Government Printing, 1889.

Progress Report of the Public Works Department, Bengal (Building and Road Branch) for 1871–72. N.p., 1872.

Rennell, James. *A Bengal Atlas Containing Maps of the Theatre of War and Commerce on that Side of Hindoostan. Compiled from the Original Surveys; and published by Order of the Honourable the Court of Directors for the Affairs of the East India Company.* [London:] n.p., 1781.

Bibliography

Report by the Chief Engineer of Bengal on the Progress of Public Works for the Year 1859–60. Calcutta: Savielle & Cranenburgh, 1860.

Report by the Chief Engineer of Bengal, on the Progress of Public Works for the Year 1860–61. Calcutta: Savielle & Cranenburgh, 1861.

Report of the Commissioners Appointed to Enquire into the Famine in Bengal and Orissa in 1866. 2 vols. Calcutta: Office Superintendent Government Printing, 1867.

Report of the Enquiry Committee, Orissa States, 1939. Cuttack: Orissa Mission Press, n.d.

Report of the Indian Road Development Committee, 1927–28. Vol. 1. Calcutta: Government of India Press, 1928.

Report of the Orissa Flood Committee. Patna: Superintendent, Government Printing, Bihar and Orissa, 1928.

Report of the Pilgrim Committee, Bihar and Orissa. Simla: Government Central Branch Press, 1913.

Report on Native Newspapers, Bengal (RNNB), 1882–1896.

Report on the Administration of Bihar and Orissa, 1912/13–1917/18. Patna: Bihar and Orissa Secretariat Book Depot, 1913–1918.

Report on the Administration of the Feudatory States of Orissa, 1908–9. Calcutta: Bengal Secretariat Book Depot, 1909.

Report on the Administration of the Feudatory States of Orissa and Chota Nagpur [RAFSOC],
—— 1909–10. Calcutta: Bengal Secretariat Book Depot, 1910.
—— 1910–11. Calcutta: Bengal Secretariat Book Depot, 1911.
—— 1916–17. Patna: Superintendent of Government Printing, 1917.

Report on the Administration of the Tributary Mahals of Orissa [RATMO], 1893/94–1898/99. Calcutta: Bengal Secretariat Press, 1894–1899.

Report Showing the Progress Made ... in Public Works under the Bengal Government, 1861–62. Calcutta: Savielle & Cranenburgh, 1862.

Report Showing the Progress Made ... in Public Works under the Bengal Government, 1862–63. Calcutta: Calcutta Gazette Office, 1863.

Report Showing the Progress Made ... in Imperial Public Works under the Bengal Government for 1862–63. Calcutta: Calcutta Gazette Office, 1863.

Review of the Annual Report on the Administration of the Feudatory States of Orissa and Chota Nagpur [RARAFS] 1917/18–1923/24. Patna: Superintendent of Govt. Printing, Bihar and Orissa, 1918–1924.

Ricketts, Henry. "Reports on the Districts of Pooree and Balasore". In *Selections from the Records of the Bengal Government*. Vol. XXX. Calcutta: John Gray, 1859.

Ricketts, Henry. *Reports on the Districts of Midnapore (Including Hijelee) and Cuttack*. Calcutta: John Gray, 1858.

Sarma, E. Satyanarayana. *Report on Road Development for the Orissa Province*. Cuttack: Government Press Orissa, 1942.

Selections from the Records of the Bengal Government. Vol. XXX. Calcutta: John Gray, 1859.

Statistical Abstracts Relating to British India from 1894–95 to 1903–4. London: HMSO, 1905.

Summary of the Administration of Indian Railways during the Viceroyalty of Lord Curzon of Kedleston. Calcutta: Office of the Superintendent of Government Printing, 1906.

Tallents, P. C., *Census of India, 1921: Bihar and Orissa* Vol. VII (2 parts). Patna: n.p., 1923.

Temple, Richard. "Report on the Mahanuddy and its Tributaries; the Resources and Trade of the Adjacent Countries and the Proposed Works for the Improvement of Navigation and Irrigation...". In *Selections from the Records of the Government of India, in the Public Works Department*, Vol. XLIII. Calcutta: John G. Hirons, PWD Press, 1864.

Newspapers and journals

The Calcutta Review (Calcutta), 1870.
The Economic Times (New Delhi), 2005.
Frontline (Chennai), 2005.
The Indian Engineer. An Illustrated Weekly Journal for Engineers in India and the East (Calcutta), 11 Nov. 1893–30 March 1895 (continued as:)
The Indian & Eastern Engineer: An Illustrated Weekly Journal for Engineers in India and the East (Calcutta), new series, April 1895–December 1921.
The Statesman and Friend of India (Calcutta), 1882.
The Times (London), 1838–1876.

SECONDARY SOURCES

Articles and books

Adas, Michael. *Machines as the Measure of Men: Science, Technology, and Ideologies of Western Dominance.* Ithaca/London: Cornell University Press, 1989.

Agarwal, Anil, and Sunita Narain. *Dying Wisdom: Rise, Fall and Potential of India's Traditional Water Harvesting Systems.* New Delhi: Centre for Science and Environment, 1997.

Ahuja, Ravi. "Labour Unsettled: Mobility and Protest in the Madras Region, 1750–1800." *Indian Economic and Social History Review* 35, no. 4, 1998, 381–404.

———. *Die Erzeugung kolonialer Staatlichkeit und das Problem der Arbeit: Eine Studie zur Sozialgeschichte der Stadt Madras und ihres Hinterlandes zwischen 1750 und 1800*, Stuttgart: Steiner, 1999.

———. "'The Bridge-Builders:' Some Notes on Railways, Pilgrimage and the British 'Civilizing Mission' in Colonial India." In *Colonialism as Civilizing Mission: The Case of British India*, ed. Fischer-Tiné and Mann, 195–216.

Bibliography

———. "'Opening up the Country'? Orissan Society and Early Colonial Communications Policies (1803–1866)." *Studies in History*, new series, vol. 20, no. 1, 2004, 73–130.

———. "Lateinsegel und Dampfturbinen: Der Schiffsverkehr des Indischen Ozeans im Zeitalter des Imperialismus." In *Der Indische Ozean: Das afroasiatische Mittelmeer als Kultur-und Wirtschaftsraum*, ed. Dietmar Rothermund and Susanne Weigelin-Schwiedrzik, 207–25. Vienna: Promedia, 2004.

———. "Erkenntnisdruck und Denkbarrieren: Anmerkungen zur indischen Arbeitshistoriographie." In *Konfigurationen der Moderne: Diskurse zu Indien* (Soziale Welt, Sonderband 15), ed. Shalini Randeria, Martin Fuchs, and Antje Linkenbach, 349–66. Baden Baden: Nomos, 2004.

———. "'Captain Kittoe's Road': Early Colonialism and the Politics of Road Construction in Nineteenth-Century Peripheral Orissa." In *Periphery and Centre in Orissa: Groups, Categories, Values*, ed. Georg Pfeffer, 291–318. New Delhi: Manohar, in press.

Alavi, Seema. *The Sepoys and the Company: Tradition and Transition in Northern India, 1770–1830.* Delhi: Oxford University Press, 1998.

———. Introduction. to *The Eighteenth Century in India*, ed. Seema Alavi, 1–56. Delhi: Oxford University Press, 2002.

Ambirajan, S. *Classical Political Economy and British Policy in India.* Cambridge: Cambridge University Press, 1978.

Andrew, William P. *Indian Railways and their Probable Results . . ., by an old Indian Postmaster.* London: T. C. Newby, 1848 (1st ed. 1846).

Anstey, Vera. *The Economic Development of India:* London et al.: Longmans, Green and Co., 1929.

Arasaratnam, Sinnappah. *Maritime Commerce and English Power: Southeast India, 1750–1800.* New Delhi: Sterling Publications, 1996.

Arbuthnot., A. J. "Cotton, Sir Arthur Thomas, 1803–1899." In *Oxford Dictionary of National Biography*, ed. H. C. G. Mathew and Brian Harrison. Oxford: Oxford University Press, 2004.

Arnold, David. "Rebellious Hillmen: The Gudem-Rampa Risings, 1839–1924." In *Subaltern Studies I*, ed. Ranajit Guha, 88–142. New Delhi: Oxford University Press, 1982.

———. "Famine in Peasant Consciousness and Peasant Action: Madras, 1876–8." In *Subaltern Studies III*, ed. Ranajit Guha, 62–115. New Delhi: Oxford University Press, 1984.

———. *Famine: Social Crisis and Historical Change.* Oxford/New York: Basil Blackwell, 1988.

———. *Science, Technology and Medicine in Colonial India.* New Cambridge History of India III.5. Cambridge: Cambridge University Press, 2000.

———. "Europe, Technology and Colonialism in the Twentieth Century". *History and Technology* 21, no.1, 2005, 85–106.

Arnold, David, and Ramachandra Guha, eds. *Nature, Culture, Imperialism: Essays on the Environmental History of South Asia.* Delhi: Oxford University Press, 1996.

Bibliography

Arnold, Edwin. *The Marquis of Dalhousie's Administration of British India*, The Annexation of Pegu, Nagpore and Oudh, and a general Revenue of Lord Dalhousie's Rule in India. Vol. II. London: Saunders, Otley and Co., 1865.

Asher, Catherine B. *Architecture of Mughal India*. New Cambridge History of India I: 4. Cambridge: Cambridge University Press, 1992.

Asher, Manshi. "Steel not Enough?" *Economic and Political Weekly* 41, no. 7, 18–24 February 2006, 555–56.

Baboo, Bal G. *Economic History of Sambalpur District, 1849–1947* (MS., 21 pages). N.p., n.d.

Bagchi, Amiya K. *The Political Economy of Underdevelopment*. Cambridge/New York: Cambridge University Press, 1982.

———. "The Other Side of Foreign Investment by Imperial Powers: Transfer of Surplus from Colonies". *Economic and Political Weekly* 37, no. 23, 8 June 2002, 2229–38.

Bagwell, Philip S. *The Transport Revolution*. London: Routledge, 1988 (1st ed. 1974).

Bailey, Damien, and John McGuire. "Railways, Exchange Banks and the World Economy: Capitalist Development in India, 1850– 1873." In *27 Down: New Departures in Indian Railway Studies*, ed. Ian J. Kerr, 101–88. Delhi: Orient Longman, 2007.

Ball, Valentine. *Jungle Life in India or the Journeys and Journals of an Indian Geologist*. London: De La Rue, 1880.

Banerji, Arun. *Finances in the Early Raj: Investments and the External Sector*. New Delhi: Sage Publications, 1995.

Basu, K. K. "Tour-Diary of J. R. Ouseley" [1840]. *Orissa Historcial Research Journal* 5, no. 3, 1956, 166–78.

Bayly, Christopher A. *Indian Society and the Making of the British Empire*. New Cambridge History of India II. 1. Cambridge: Cambridge University Press, 1988.

———. *Rulers, Townsmen and Bazaars: North Indian Society in the Age of British Expansion, 1770–1870*. Delhi: Oxford University Press, 1992.

Beames, John. *Memoirs of a Bengal Civilian*. London: Chatto & Windus, 1961.

Beckett, William T. C. "The Bridges over the Orissa Rivers on the East Coast Extension of the Bengal–Nagpur Railway". In *Minutes of Proceedings of the Institution of Civil Engineers* CXLV, 1901, 268–91.

Begley, Wayne E. "Four Mughal Caravanserais Built during the Reigns of Jahangir and Shah Jahan". In *Muqarnas: An Annual on the Visual Culture of the Islamic World* 1, 1983, 167–79.

Behara, Dandapani. *Freedom Movement in the State of Ghumsar in Orissa, 1836–1866*. Calcutta: Punthi Pustak, 1984.

Behera, Karuna S., et al., eds. *Cuttack One Thousand Years*. Cuttack: Cuttack City Millennium Celebrations Committee, The Universe, 1990.

Bell, Duncan S. A., "Dissolving Distance: Technology, Space, and Empire in British Political Thought, 1770–1900". *Journal of Modern History* 77, 2005, 523–63.

Bibliography

Bernstein, Henry T. *Steamboats on the Ganges: An Exploration in the History of India's Modernization through Science and Technology.* Bombay: Orient Longman, 1960.

Bhandari, Ratan R. *South Eastern Railway—March to the Millenium.* Calcutta: South Eastern Railway, 2001. http://www.serailway.gov.in/General/Book_RRB/index.htm.

Bhatia, B. M. *Famines in India: A Study in Some Aspects of the Economic History of India with Special Reference to Food Problem, 1860–1990.* 3rd rev. ed. Delhi: Konark Publishers, 1991 (1st ed. 1963).

Bhattacharya, Neeladri. "Predicaments of Mobility: Peddlers and Itinerants in Nineteenth-century Northwestern India." In *Society and Circulation: Mobile People and Itinerant Cultures in South Asia, 1750–1950,* ed. Markovits, et. al.163–214.

Bhattacharya, Sabyasachi. "Regional Economy (1757–1857): Eastern India." In *The Cambridge Economic History of India,* c. 1757—c. 1970, vol. 2, ed. Dharma Kumar, 270–95.

Bhola, Sudhira C. *British Economic Policy in Orissa.* New Delhi: Discovery Publishing House, 1990.

Blith, Walter. *The English Improver Improved . . .* London: John Wright, 1653.

Bloch, Ernst. *Experimentum Mundi: Frage, Kategorien des Herausbringens, Praxis.* Frankfurt a. M.: Suhrkamp, 1985.

Boer, Roland. *The Sanctuary and the Womb: Henri Lefebvre and the Production of Space.* http://www.cwru.edu/affil/GAIR/papers/2000papers/Boer.html.

Braudel, Fernand. *La Méditerranée et le monde méditerranéen à l'époque de Philippe II.* Paris: Colin, 1949.

———. *Sozialgeschichte des 15.-18. Jahrhunderts.* Vol. I. Munich: Kindler, 1990. (1st French ed.: *Civilisation matérielle, économie et capitalisme, XVe–XVIIIe siècle,* Paris: Colin, 1979.

Brenner, Neil. "Global, Fragmented, Hierarchical: Henri Lefebvre's Geographies of Globalization." *Public Culture* 10, no. 1, 1997, 135–67.

Broeze, Frank. "Underdevelopment and Dependency: Maritime India during the Raj". *Modern Asian Studies* 18, 1984, 429–57.

———. "From Imperialism to Independence: The Decline and Re-emergence of Asian Shipping". *The Great Circle* 9, no. 2, 1987, 73–95.

Burnet, Gilbert. *Three Letters Concerning the Present State of Italy* [. . .]. N.p., 1688.

Cain, P. J., and A. G. Hopkins. *British Imperialism, 1688–2000.* 2nd ed. Harlow: Longman, 2002.

Campbell, Henry. *The Law of Land Acquisition in British India: Being a Full Commentary on the Land Acquisition Act (Act No. I of 1894).* Bombay: N. M. Tripathi & Co., 1911.

Campbell, John. *A Personal Narrative of Thirteen Years Service amongst the Wild Tribes of Khondistan for the Supression of Human Sacrifice.* N.p., 1864.

Bibliography

Cassels, Nancy Gardner. *Religion and Pilgrim Tax under the Company Raj*. South Asian Studies 17. New Delhi: Manohar, 1988.

Chandra, Bipan. *The Rise and Growth of Economic Nationalism in India: Economic Policies of Indian National Leadership, 1880–1905*. New Delhi: People's Publishing House, 1966.

Chakrabarty, Dipesh. "The Colonial Context of the Bengal Renaissance: A Note on Early Railway-Thinking in Bengal." *Indian Economic and Social History Review* 11, no. 1, 1974, 92–111.

Chapman, John. *The Cotton and Commerce of India, Considered in Relation to the Interests of Great Britain: with Remarks on Railway Communication in the Bombay Presidency*. London: John Chapman, 1851.

———. *Principles of Indian Reform: Being Hints together with a Plan for the Improvement of the Constituency of the East India Company, and for the Promotion of Indian Public Works*. 2nd ed. London: John Chapman, 1853.

Chatterjee, Partha. *The Nation and Its Fragments: Colonial and Postcolonial Histories*. Princeton: Princeton University Press, 1993.

Chaudhuri, Binay. "Agrarian Relations: Eastern India." In *The Cambridge Economic History of India*, c. 1757—c. 1970, 2: 86–177.

Chaudhuri, Kirti N. *Asia before Europe: Economy and Civilisation of the Indian Ocean from the Rise of Islam to 1750*. Cambridge, et al.: Cambridge University Press, 1990.

———. "Foreign Trade and Balance of Payments (1757– 1947)." In *The Cambridge Economic History of India*, c. 1757—c. 1970, 804–77.

Chaudhuri, Pradipta. "The Impact of Forced Commerce on the Patterns of Emigration from Orissa, 1901–1921." In *Essays on the Commercialization of Agriculture*, 184– 209.

Choudhury, Sadananda. *Economic History of Colonialism: A Study of British Salt Policy in Orissa*. Delhi: Inter-India Publications, 1979.

Chowdhury-Zilly, Aditee Nag. *The Vagrant Peasant: Agrarian Distress and Desertion in Bengal, 1770–1830*. Beiträge zur Südasienforschung 71. Wiesbaden: Franz Steiner, 1982.

Clarke, Hyde. *Practical and Theoretical Considerations on the Management of Railways in India*. N.p. [1847?].

Cooper, Frederick. "What is the Concept of Globalization Good for? An African Historian's Perspective." *African Affairs* 100, 2001, 189–214.

Cotton, Arthur. *Public Works in India, their Importance; with Suggestions for their Extension and Improvement*. 2nd ed. London: Richardson Brothers, 1854.

Dalhousie, Lord. "Minute to the Court of Directors of the East India Company, 20 April 1853." In *Railway Construction in India: Select Document*, vol. 2, ed. S. Settar and Bhubanes Mishra.

Danvers, Juland. *Indian Railways: Their Past History, Present Condition, and Future Prospects*. London: Effingham Wilson, 1877.

Das, Bhaskar. *Social and Economic Life of Southern Orissa: A Glimpse into Nineteenth Century*: Orissa Studies Project 23. Calcutta: Punthi Pustak, 1985.

Bibliography

Das, Binod S. *Studies in the Economic History of Orissa from Ancient Times to 1833.* Calcutta: KLM, 1978.

Das, Keshab. "Underdevelopment by Design? Undermining Vital Infrastructure in Orissa." *Economic and Political Weekly* 41, no. 7, 18–24 February 2006, 642–48.

Das, Purna C. *The Economic History of Orissa in the Nineteenth Century.* New Delhi: Commonwealth Publishers, 1989.

Das Gupta, Sanjukta. "The Changing World of the Singhbhum Hos, 1820–1932." *Indian Historical Review* 33, no. 1, 2006, 76–98.

Davidson, Edward. *The Railways of India: With an Account of their Rise, Progress, and Construction.* London: E. & F. N. Spon, 1868.

Davis, Mike. *Late Victorian Holocausts: El Niño Famines and the Making of the Third World.* London/New York: Verso, 2001.

Day, Francis. *Report on the Sea Fish and Fisheries of India and Burma.* Calcutta: Office of the Superintendent of Government Printing, 1873.

De, S. C. "Cowry Currency in Orissa." *Orissa Historcial Research Journal* 1, no. 2, 1952, 10–21.

———. "Cuttack Jail in 1859." In *Cuttack One Thousand Years,* ed. Karuna S. Behera et al. Cuttack: Cuttack City Millennium Celebrations Committee, The Universe, 1990.

Deloche, Jean, *The Ancient Bridges of India.* 1st Engl. ed. New Delhi: Sitaram Bhartia Institute of Scientific Research, 1984.

———. "Études sur la circulation en Inde. VIII. De la trouée de Palghat et du plateau de Maisur a la pédipleine Tamoule: Liaisons routières anciennes et vestiges de chemins." *Bulletin de l'École Fran?aise d'Extrême-Orient* 78, 1991, 52–85.

———. *Transport and Communication in India Prior to Steam Locomotion: Land Transport.* vol. 1. Delhi: Oxford University Press, 1993.

———*Transport and Communication in India Prior to Steam Locomotion: Water Transport.* Vol. 2. Delhi: Oxford University Press, 1994.

Derbyshire, Ian D. "Economic Change and the Railways in North India." *Modern Asian Studies* 21, no. 3, 1987, 521–45.

Diderot, Denis, and Jean Le Rond d'Alembert. *L" Encyclopédie ou Dictionnaire raisonné des sciences, des arts et des métiers.* Marsanne: Redon, 2000. http://portail.atilf.fr/encyclopedie/. Originally published in 17 vols. Paris, 1751–1772.

Dodgshon, Robert A. "Human Geography at the End of Time? Some Thoughts on the Notion of Time-Space Compression." *Environment and Planning D: Society and Space* 17, no. 5, 1999, 607–20.

D'Souza, Rohan. *Flood, Embankments and Canals: The Colonial Experience in Orissa, 1803–1928.* Nehru Memorial Museum and Library, Research-in-Progress Papers "History and Society", third series, No. 6. New Delhi: Centre for Contemporary Studies, 1996.

———. "Colonialism, Capitalism and Nature: Debating the Origins of Mahanadi Delta's Hydraulic Crisis, 1803–1928." *Economic and Political Weekly* 37, no. 13, 2002, 1261–72.

———. "Canal Irrigation and the Conundrum of Flood Protection: The Failure of the Orissa Scheme of 1863 in Eastern India." *Studies in History* 19, no. 1, 2003, 41–68.

Dubey, D. P., and L. Gopal, eds. *Pilgrimage Studies: Text and Context.* Sri Phalahari Baba Commemoration Volume. Allahabad: The Society of Pilgrimage Studies, 1990.

Dugdale, William. *The History of Imbanking and Drayning of Divers Fenns and Marshes, both in Forein Parts and in this Kingdom, and of the Improvements thereby ....* London: Alice Warren, 1662.

Dupin, Charles. *Du commerce et de ses travaux publics en Angleterre et en France: discours prononcé le 2 juin 1823, Paris: n.p., 1823.*

——— *The Commercial Power of Great Britain Exhibiting a Complete View of the Public Works of this Country ....* London: Knight, 1825.

Dupuit, Jules. "De la mesure de l'utilité des travaux publics." In *De l'utilité et de sa mesure,* edited by Mario de Bernardi, 29–65. Torini: La Riforma sociale, 1934 (Firshed published 1844).

Dutt, Romesh Chunder. *The Lake of Palms.* London: T. F. Unwin, 1902.

———. *The Economic History of India in the Victorian Age: From the Accession of Queen Victoria in 1837 to the Commencement of the Twentieth Century.* 7th ed. London: Routledge & Kegan Paul, 1950 (1st ed. 1903).

———. *The Economic History of India: Under Early British Rule, 1757–1837.* 2nd reprint Delhi: Publications Division, Ministry of Information and Broadcasting, Govt. of India, 1970 (1st ed. 1903).

Dutta, Arup K. *Indian Railways, the Final Frontier: Genesis and Growth of the North-East Frontier Railway.* Guwahati: Northeast Frontier Railway, 2002.

Dutta, Maya. *Jamshedpur: The Growth of the City and Its Regions.* Calcutta: The Asiatic Society, 1977.

Edney, Matthew H. *Mapping an Empire: The Geographical Construction of India, 1765–1843.* Chicago: University of Chicago Press, 1997.

Encyclopaedia; or, A dictionary of arts, sciences, and miscellaneous literature .... 18 vols. 1st American ed. Philadelphia: Dobson, 1798. Thomson Gale Databases, "Eighteenth Century Collections Online."

Eusebius of Caesarea. *The History of the Church from our Lords Incarnation, to the Twelth Year of the Emperour Maricius Tiberius, or the Year of Christ 594 ... also, The Life of Constantine in Four Books ....* Cambridge: Printed by John Hayes ... for Han. Sawbridge, 1683.

Farooque, Abul Khair M. *Roads and Communications in Mughal India.* Delhi: Idarah-i Adabiyat-i Delli, 1977.

Febvre, Lucien. *A Geographical Introduction to History: An Introduction to Human Geography.* London: Kegan Paul, 2003 (1st ed. 1924).

Fergusson, James. *History of Indian and Eastern Architecture*. 2 vols. Rev. and edited with additions. London: John Murray, 1910 (1st ed. 1876).

Fischbach, Rainer. *Mythos Netz*. Zürich: Rotpunktverlag, 2005.

Fischer-Tiné, Harald, and Michael Mann, eds. *Colonialism as Civilizing Mission: The Case of British India*. London: Anthem, 2004.

Fisher, Michael H. "The East India Company's 'Suppression of the Native Dak'. *Indian Economic and Social History Review* 31, no. 3, 1994, 311–48.

Flint, E. P. "Deforestation and Land Use in Northern India with a Focus on Sal (Shorea robusta) Forests, 1880–1980." In *Nature and the Orient: The Environmental History of South and South East Asia*, ed. Richard H. Grove, Vinita Damodaran, and Satpal Sangwan, 421–58. Delhi: Oxford University Press, 1998.

Freeman, Michael J., and Derek H. Aldcroft, eds. *Transport in Victorian Britain*. Manchester: Manchester University Press, 1988.

Freeman, Michael J. Introduction to *Transport in Victorian Britain*, 1–56.

Freitag, Sandria B. "Crime in the Social Order of Colonial North India." *Modern Asian Studies* 25, no. 2, 1991, 227–61.

Frey, René L. *Infrastruktur: Grundlagen der Planung öffentlicher Investitionen*. Tübingen/Zürich: Mohr et al., 1970.

Gadgil, Dhananjay R. *The Industrial Evolution of India in Recent Times, 1860–1939*. 5th ed. Delhi: Oxford University Press, 1972 (1st ed. 1924).

Gadgil, Madhav, and Ramachandra Guha. *This Fissured Land: An Ecological History of India*. New Delhi/Oxford: Oxford University Press, 1992.

Gandhi, Mohandas K. *Collected Works of Mahatma Gandhi*. Vol. 10. New Delhi: Publications Division, Ministry Information and Broadcasting, Govt. of India, 1966.

Gat, Azar. *A History of Military Thought: From the Enlightenment to the Cold War*. Oxford: Oxford University Press, 2001.

Geppert, Alexander C. T., Uffa Jensen, and Jörn Weinhold. "Verräumlichung: Kommunikative Praktiken in historischer Perspektive, 1840–1930." In *Ortsgespräche: Raum und Kommunikation im 19. und 20. Jahrhundert*, ed. idem, 15–49. Bielefeld: Transcript, 2005.

Ghosh, Kaushik. "A Market for Aboriginality: Primitivism and Race Qualification in the Indentured Labour Market of Colonial India." In *Subaltern Studies X: Writings on South Asian History and Society*, ed. G. Bhadra, G. Prakash and Susie Tharu, 8–48. New Delhi: Oxford University Press, 1999.

Gilmartin, David. "Models of Hydraulic Environment: Colonial Irrigation, State Power and Community in the Indus Basin." In *Nature, Culture, Imperialism. Essays on the Environmental History of South Asia*, ed. David Arnold and Ramachandra Guha, 210–236. Delhi: Oxford University Press, 1996.

Gole, Susan. *Indian Maps and Plans from Earliest Times to the Advent of European Surveys*. New Delhi: Manohar, 1989.

Gommans, Jos. *Mughal Warfare: Indian Frontiers and High Roads to Empire, 1500–1700*. London/New York: Routledge, 2002.

Gopal, Sarvepalli. *British Policy in India, 1858–1905*. Cambridge: Cambridge University Press, 1965.

Gordon, Stewart. *Marathas, Marauders, and State Formation in Eighteenth-Century India*. Delhi/Oxford: Oxford University Press, 1994.

Goswami, Manu. "From Swadeshi to Swaraj: Nation, Economy, Territory in Colonial South Asia, 1870 to 1907." *Comparative Studies in Society and History* 40, no. 4, 1998, 609–36.

———. *Producing India: From Colonial Economy to National Space*. Chicago: University of Chicago Press, 2004.

Gosztonyi, Alexander. *Der Raum. Geschichte seiner Probleme in Philosophie und Wissenschaften*. 2 vols. Freiburg/Munich: Alber, 1976.

Gourvish, T. R. "Railways, 1830–1870: The Formative Years." In *Transport in Victorian Britain*, ed. Michael J. Freeman and Derek H. Aldcroft, 57–91. Manchester: Manchester University Press, 1988.

Grove, Richard H., Vinita Damodaran, and Satpal Sangwan, eds. *Nature and the Orient: The Environmental History of South and South East Asia*. Delhi et al.: Oxford University Press, 1998.

Guha, Amalendu. "Raw Cotton of Western India, 1750–1850." *Indian Economic and Social History Review* 9, no. 1, 1972, 1–42.

Guha, Ranajit. "The Prose of Counterinsurgency." In *Subaltern Studies II: Writings on South Asian History and Society*, ed. Ranajit Guha, 1–42. New Delhi: Oxford University Press, 1983.

Habib, Irfan. "The Technology and Economy of Mughal India". *Indian Economic and Social History Review* 17, no. 1, 1980, 1–34.

———. "Merchant Communities in Precolonial India." In *The Rise of Merchant Empires: Long-distance Trade in the Early Modern World, 1350–1750*, ed. James D. Tracy 371–99. Cambridge: Cambridge University Press, 1990.

———. *The Agrarian System of Mughal India, 1556–1707*. 2nd rev. ed. New Delhi: Oxford University Press, 1999.

Hallett, Holt S. *New Markets and Extension of Railways in India and Burmah*. London: P. S. King & Son, 1887.

Hamilton, Alexander. *A New Account of the East Indies*. Vol. 1. Edited, with notes by William Foster. London: Argonaut Press, 1930 (1st ed. 1727).

Hamilton, Ivie G. J. *An Outline of Postal History and Practice with a History of the Post Office of India*. Calcutta: Thacker, Spink & Co., 1910.

Harley, John B., and David Woodward. *The History of Cartography: Cartography in the Traditional Islamic and South Asian Societies*. Vol. 2, book 1. Chicago/London: University of Chicago Press, 1992.

Harrison, Mark. *Public Health in British India: Anglo-Indian Preventive Medicine 1859–1914*. Cambridge: Cambridge University Press, 1994.

Harvey, David. *The Limits to Capital*. Oxford: Basil Blackwell, 1982.

———. *The Condition of Postmodernity: An Enquiry into the Origins of Cultural Change*. Oxford/Cambridge, MA: Basil Blackwell, 1989.

Bibliography

———. "Between Space and Time: Reflections on the Geographical Imagination." *Annals of the Association of American Geographers* 80, no. 3, 1990, 418–34.

———. *Spaces of Capital: Towards a Critical Geography.* Edinburgh: Edinburgh University Press, 2001.

Haly, George T. *Appeal for the Sufferers by the Present Famine in Orissa.* London: Smith, Elder & Co., 1866.

Haynes, Douglas E. "Market Formation in Khandesh, c. 1820– 1930." *Indian Economic and Social History Review* 36, no. 3, 1999, 275–302.

Haynes, Douglas E., and Tirthankar Roy. "Conceiving Mobility: Weavers' Migrations in Precolonial and Colonial India." *Indian Economic and Social History Review* 36, no. 1, 1999, 35–67.

Headrick, Daniel R. *The Tentacles of Progress: Technology Transfer in the Age of Imperialism, 1850–1940.* New York/Oxford: Oxford University Press, 1988.

Hill, Christopher V. "Ideology and Public Works: 'Managing' the Mahanadi River in Colonial North India." *Capitalism, Nature, Socialism* 6, no. 4, 1995, 51–64.

Hobsbawm, Eric J. "Looking Forward: History and the Future." *New Left Review* 125, 1981, 3–19.

"H.O." *Railways in India, Being Four Articles Reprinted from the Railway Register for July, August, September, and November, 1845.* London: Madden & Malcolm, 1845.

Hurd, John M. "Irrigation and Railways: Railways." In *The Cambridge Economic History of India, c. 1757—c. 1970,* vol. 2, ed. Dharma Kumar, 737–61. Cambridge: Cambridge University Press, 1982.

Inglis, W. A. *The Canals and Flood Banks of Bengal.* Calcutta: Bengal Secretariat Press, 1909.

Irschick, Eugene F. *Dialogue and History, Constructing South-India, 1795–1895.* Delhi/Oxford: Oxford University Press, 1994.

Iyer, G. Subramania. *Economic Aspects of British Rule in India.* 1903. Reprint Delhi: Gian Publishing House, 1988.

Jagga, Lajpat. "Colonial Railwaymen and British Rule: A Probe into Railway Labour Agitation in India, 1919–1922." *Studies in History* 3, nos 1–2, 1981, 102–45.

Jenks, Leland H. *The Migration of British Capital to 1875.* London: Jonathan Cape, 1938 (1st ed. 1927).

Jit, Nabin K. *The Agrarian Life and Economy of Orissa—A Survey, 1833–1897.* Calcutta: Punthi Pustak, 1984.

Joshi, Chitra. "Working the Roads: Convicts, Runaways in Nineteenth-Century India." Unpublished paper for the 4th International Conference of the Association of Indian Labour Historians, 18–20 March 2004, Noida.

Kamat, Manjiri N. "'The Palkhi as Plague Carrier': The Pandharpur Fair and the Sanitary Fixation of the Colonial State; British India, 1908–1916." In *Health, Medicine and Empire: Perspectives on Colonial India,* ed. Biswamoy Pati, and Mark Harrison, 299–316. London: Sangam, 2001.

Bibliography

Kern, Stephen. *The Culture of Time and Space, 1880–1918*. Cambridge, MA: Harvard University Press, 1983.

Kerr, Ian J. *Building the Railways of the Raj, 1850–1900*. Delhi: Oxford University Press, 1997.

———. ed. *Railways in Modern India*, New York: Oxford University Press, 2001.

———. Introduction to *Railways in Modern India*, 1–61.

———. "Reworking a Popular Religious Practice: The Effects of Railways on Pilgrimage in Nineteenth and Twentieth Century South Asia." In *Railways in Modern India*, 304– 27.

———. "Representation and Representations of the Railways of Colonial and Post-colonial South Asia." *Modern Asian Studies* 37, no. 2, 2003, 287–326.

———, ed. *27 Down: New Departures in Indian Railway Studies*. Delhi: Orient Longman, 2007.

Khosla, G. S. *A History of Indian Railways*. New Delhi: Ministry of Railways (Railway Board), Govt. of India, 1988.

Kipling, Rudyard. *The Writings in Prose and Verse of Rudyard Kipling*. Vol. 13. London/New York: Macmillan, 1899.

Kittoe, Markham. "Mr. Kittoe's Journal of his Tour in the Province of Orissa." *Journal of the Asiatic Society of Bengal* VII, 1838, 669–85, 1060–63.

———. "Extracts from the Journal of Lieut. Markham Kittoe, submitted to the Asiatic Society at the Meeting of the 6th Oct. 1836." [sic 1837?]. *Journal of the Asiatic Society of Bengal* VII, 1838, 53–56, 200–6, 660–62.

———. "Account of a Journey from Calcutta via Cuttack and Pooree to Sumbulpúr, and from thence to Mednipúr through the Forests of Orissa." *Journal of the Asiatic Society of Bengal* VIII, 1839, 367–83, 474–80, 606–20, 671–81.

———. "Report on the Coal and Iron Mines of Tálcheer and Ungool. . . ." *Journal of the Asiatic Society of Bengal* VIII, 1839, 137–44.

Klein, Ira. "Imperialism, Ecology and Disease: Cholera in India, 1850–1950." *Indian Economic and Social History Review* 31, no. 4, 1994, 491–518.

———. "Death in India, 1871–1921." *Journal of Asian Studies* 32, no. 4, 1973, 639–59.

Koch, Ebba. *Mughal Architecture: An Outline of Its History and Development, 1526–1858*. Munich: Prestel, 1991.

Kolff, Dirk. *Naukar, Rajput and Sepoy: The Ethnohistory of the Military Labour Market in Hindustan, 1450–1850*. Cambridge: Cambridge University Press, 1990.

Koselleck, Reinhart. *Zeitschichten: Studien zur Historik*. Frankfurt a.M.: Suhrkamp, 2003 (1st ed. 2000).

Kubicek, Robert. "British Expansion, Empire, and Technological Change." In *The Oxford History of the British Empire:*, Nineteenth Century, vol. 3 ed. Andrew Porter, 247–69. Oxford: Oxford University Press, 1999.

Bibliography

Kulke, Hermann. "The Struggle between the Rajas of Khurda and the Muslim Subahdars of Cuttack for the Dominance of the Jagannatha Temple." In *The Cult of Jagannath and the Regional Tradition of Orissa*. South Asian Studies No. 8, ed. Anncharlott Eschmann Hermann Kulke, and Gaya C. Tripati, 321–357. Delhi: Manohar, 1986 (1st ed. 1978).

Kumar, Dharma, ed. *The Cambridge Economic History of India*, c. 1757—c. 1970. Vol. 2. Cambridge: Cambridge University Press, 1982.

———. "The Fiscal System." In *The Cambridge Economic History of India*, c. 1757—c. 1970, 2: 905– 44.

Langins, Janis. *La République avait besoin de savants: Les débuts de l'École polytechnique: l'École centrale des travaux publics et les cours révolutionnaires de l'an III*. Paris: Belin, 1987.

Leckie, Daniel R. *Journal of a Route to Nagpore by the Way of Cuttae, Burrosumber, and the Southern Bunjare Ghautin the Year 1790: With an Account of Nagpore and a Journal from that Place to Benares by the Sohagee Pass*. London: John Stockdale, 1800.

Lefebvre, Henri. *The Production of Space*. Translated by Donald Nicholson-Smith. Oxford/Cambridge, MA: Basil Blackwell, 1991 (1st French ed. 1974).

——— *Rhythmanalysis: Space, Time and Everyday Life*. Tran stated by Stuart Elden and Gerald Moore. London/New York: Continuum, 2004 (1st French ed. 1992).

Lehmann, Frederick. "Great Britain and the Supply of Railway Locomotives of India: A Case Study of 'Economic Imperialism'." *Indian Economic and Social History Review* 2, no. 4, 1965, 297–306.

Livingstone, David N. *The Geographical Tradition: Episodes in the History of a Contested Enterprise*. Oxford/Cambridge, MA: Blackwell Publishers, 1992.

Livy. *The Romane Historie Written by T. Livius of Padua. Also, the Breviaries of L. Florus: with a Chronologie to the Whole Historie: and the Topographie of Rome in Old Time*. Translated out of Latine into English, by Philemon Holland. London: A. Islip, 1600.

Lotz, Barbara. *Rebels, Rajas and the British Raj: Situating Fakirmohan Senapati in the Bhuyan Revolt of 1891/92*. Unpublished MS. Orissa Research Programme.

Löw, Martina. *Raumsoziologie*. Frankfurt a.M.: Suhrkamp, 2001.

Ludden, David. *An Agrarian History of South Asia*. New Cambridge History of India IV.4. Cambridge: Cambridge University Press, 1999.

———. "History Outside Civilization and the Mobility of South Asia". *South Asia* 17, no.1, 1994, 1–23.

Lyotard, Jean-François. *The Postmodern Condition: A Report on Knowledge*. Manchester: Manchester University Press, 1993 (1st ed. 1984).

MacGeorge, G. W. *Ways and Works in India: Being an Account of the Public Works in that Country from the Earliest Times up to the Present Day*. Westminster: Archibald Constable & Co., 1894.

Bibliography

MacPherson, Samuel C. *Report upon the Khonds of the Districts of Ganjam and Cuttack.* Calcutta: n.p., 1842.

Mahapatra, K. N. *Ancient Pilgrims' Routes of Orissa.* Bhubaneswar, 1972. Xeroxed MS., Orissa Archive, South Asia Institute, Heidelberg, 265 mss 16/146.

Major, Andrew J. "State and Criminal Tribes in Colonial Punjab: Surveillance, Control and Reclamation of the 'Dangerous Classes'". *Modern Asian Studies* 33, no. 3, 1999, 657–88.

Malapert, M. F. *Histoire de la législation des travaux publics.* Paris: Ducher et ci, 1880.

Manrique, Sebastien. *Travels of Fray Sebastien Manrique, 1629–1643*, vol. II. Hakluyt Society, 2nd series, 61. Introduced and annotated by C. Eckford Luard. Oxford: Hakluyt Society, 1927.

Markovits, Claude, ed. *A History of Modern India, 1480–1950.* Trans. Nisha George and Maggie Hendry. London: Anthem, 2002.

Markovits, Claude, Jacques Pouchepadass, and Sanjay Subrahmanyam, eds. *Society and Circulation: Mobile People and Itinerant Cultures in South Asia, 1750–1950.* Delhi: Permanent Black, 2003.

———. "Introduction: Circulation and Society under Colonial Rule." In *Society and Circulation: Mobile People and Itinerant Cultures in South Asia, 1750–1950*, 1–22.

Marx, Karl. *Grundrisse: Foundations of the Political Economy (Rough Draft).* Translated by Martin Nicolaus. London: Penguin Books, 1973.

Marx, Karl, and Friedrich Engels, *Werke* (MEW)

Vol. 9, 220–26 (Marx, Karl, "Die künftigen Ergebnisse der britischen Herrschaft in Indien", August 1853). Berlin: Dietz, 1960.

Vol. 24 (Karl Marx, Das Kapital, vol. II, ed. Friedrich Engels). Berlin: Dietz, 1963.

Vol. 42 (Karl Marx, Ökonomische Manuskripte 1857/1858). Berlin: Dietz, 1983.

McAlpin, Michelle Burge. "Railroads, Prices, and Peasant Rationality: India, 1860–1900." *Journal of Economic History* 34, no. 3, 1974, 662–84.

McPherson, Kenneth, Frank Broeze, Joan Wardrop, and Peter Reeves, "The Social Expansion of the Maritime World of the Indian Ocean, Passenger Traffic and Community Building, 1815–1939." In *Maritime Aspects of Migration*, ed. Klaus Friedland, 427–40. Cologne/Vienna: Böhlau, 1989.

Meiksins Wood, Ellen, and Neal Wood. *A Trumpet of Sedition: Political Theory and the Rise of Capitalism, 1509–1688.* London/New York: Pluto Press, 1997.

Metcalf, Thomas R. *Ideologies of the Raj.* New Cambridge History of India III.4. Cambridge: Cambridge University Press, 1994.

Mill, John Stuart. *Principles of Political Economy with Some of Their Applications to Social Philosophy*, Books III–V. Introduction by V. W. Bladen, textual ed. J. M. Robson. Toronto: University of Toronto Press, 1968.

Bibliography

Misro, R. C., and L. K. Patnaik. "Salt Monopoly in South Orissa under the British Raj." *Quarterly Review of Historical Studies* (Calcutta) 39, nos. 1–2, 1999, 36–45.

Mitchell, John W. *Wheels of India: Autobiographical Reminiscences of a Railway Official in India*. London: Thornton Butterworth, 1934.

Mohanty, Bidyut. "Orissa Famine of 1866: Demographic and Economic Consequences." *Economic and Political Weekly* 28, nos. 1–2, 2–9 January 1993, 55–66.

Mohapatra, Prabhu P. "Coolies and Colliers: A Study of the Agrarian Context of Labour Migration from Chotanagpur, 1880– 1920." *Studies in History*, new series, vol. 1, no. 2, 1985, 247–303.

Mojumdar, Kanchanmoy. *Changing Tribal Life in British Orissa*. New Delhi: Kaveri Books 1998.

Morris, Morris David. "The Growth of Large-scale Industry to 1947." In *The Cambridge Economic History of India*, c. 1757—c. 1970, 2: 553–676.

Motte, Thomas. "A Narrative of a Journey to the Diamond Mines at Sumbhulpoor." Reprint of a 1766 Diary. *Orissa Historical Research Journal* 1, no. 3, 1952, appendix, 1–49.

Mukerji, Amit, and R. C. Sharma. "Acquisition of Land for Railway Construction in the Agra District." In *Proceedings of the Indian History Congress*, 51st Session (Calcutta). Delhi: Indian History Congress, 1991.

Mukherjee, Hena. *The Early History of the East Indian Railway, 1845–1879*. Calcutta: KLM, 1994.

Mukherjee, Mukul. "Railways and Their Impact on Bengal's Economy, 1870–1920." *Indian Economic and Social History Review* 17, no. 2, 1980, 191–209.

Mukherjee, Prabhat. *History of Orissa in the Nineteenth Century*. Cuttack: Utkal University, 1964.

———. *Irrigation, Inland Navigation and Flood Problems in North Orissa durig the British Rule*. N.p., n.d.

———. *History of te Jaganath Temple in the Nineteenth Century*. Calcutta: KLM, 1977.

Munsi, Sunil K. "Railway Network and Nodes in Eastern India: The First Fifty Years of Interaction." In *International Geography* 6, 1976, 234–38. 23rd International Geographical Congress, Moscow, section 6: General Economic Geography.

———. *Geography of Transportation in Eastern India under the British Raj*. CSSSC Monograph 1. Calcutta: K. P. Bagchi, 1980.

Naidu, M. Pauparao. *The History of the Railway Thieves with Illustrations & Hints of Detection*. The Criminal Tribes of India Series 1. Madras: Higginbothams, 1915.

Nair, Janaki. *The Promise of the Metropolis: Bangalore's Twentieth Century*. New Delhi/Oxford: Oxford University Press, 2005.

Nair, P. Thankappan, ed. *Bruton's Visit to Lord Jagannatha 350 Years Ago: British Beginnings in Orissa*. Calcutta: Minerva Associates, 1985.

Bibliography

Nanda, Chandi Prasad. *Textualising Mayurbhanja: Social Mobility Movement of the Kudmi-Mohantas of Orissa*. Unpublished manuscript.

Naoroji, Dadabhai. *Poverty and Un-British Rule in India*. New Delhi: Publications Division, Ministry of Information and Broadcasting, Govt. of India, 1996. 1st ed. 1901.

Nayak, Ganeswar. *Development of Transport and Communication: A Case Study*. New Delhi: Anmol Publishing, 2000.

Notes on the History of Mayurbhanj. N.p., n.d.

O'Gorman, P.W. *Puri Pilgrim Canal Traffic*. N.p., n.d. [c. 1895].

O'Malley, L. S. S. "Mechanism and Transport." In *Modern India and the West: A Study of the Interaction of their Civilizations,* ed. L. S. S. O'Malley, XXXI–XX. London: Oxford University Press, 1941.

"The Organization of the Public Works Department". *The Calcutta Review* L, 1870, 48–72.

Osterhammel, Jürgen. "Die Wiederkehr des Raumes: Geopolitik, Geohistorie und historische Geographie." *Neue Politische Literatur* 43, no. 3, 1998, 374–98.

Padel, Felix. *The Sacrifice of Human Being: British Rule and the Konds of Orissa*. Delhi: Oxford University Press, 2000. 1st ed. 1995.

Padhi, Sakti. "Property in Land, Land Market and Tenancy Relations in the Colonial Period: A Review of Theoretical Categories and Study of a Zamindari District." In *Essays on the Commercialization of Agriculture*, ed. K. N. Raj et al. 1–50.

Pati, Biswamoy. *Resisting Domination: Peasants, Tribals and the National Movement in Orissa, 1920–50*. Delhi: Manohar, 1993.

———. "Survival as Resistance: Tribals in Colonial Orissa". *Indian Historical Review* 33, no. 1, 2006, 175–201.

Patnaik, Gorachand. *The Famine and Some Aspects of the British Economic Policy in Orissa, 1866–1905*. Cuttack: Vidyapuri, 1980.

Patnaik, Jagannath. *Feudatory States of Orissa (1803–1857)*. 2 vols. Allahabad: Vohra, 1988.

Popper, Karl. *Das Elend des Historizismus*. 6th rev. ed. Tübingen: Mohr, 1987.

Pouchepadass, Jacques. "Itinerant Kings and Touring Officials: Circulation as a Modality of Power in India, 1700– 1947." In *Society and Circulation: Mobile People and Itinerant Cultures in South Asia, 1750–1950*, 240–74.

Praharaj, Debendra M. *Tribal Movements and Political History in India—A Case Study from Orissa, 1803–1949*. New Delhi: Inter-India Publications, 1988.

Prakash, Gyan. *Another Reason: Science and the Imagination of Modern India*. Delhi: Oxford University Press, 2000.

Prakash, Om. *Bullion for Goods: European and Indian Merchants in the Indian Ocean Trade, 1500–1800*. Delhi: Manohar, 2004.

"Princely India", 1858–1950. In *A History of Modern India, 1480–1950*, ed. Claude Markovits, 386–409. London: Anthem Press, 2002.

Radhakrishna, Meena. *Dishonoured by History: Criminal Tribes and British Colonial Policy*. New Delhi: Orient Longman, 2001.

Bibliography

Raj, Kapil. "Circulation and the Emergence of Modern Mapping: Great Britain and Early Colonial India, 1764–1820." In *Society and Circulation: Mobile People and Itinerant Cultures in South Asia, 1750–1950*, 23–54.

Raj, K. N. Neeladri Bhattacharya, Sumit Guha and Sakti Padhi, eds. *Essays on the Commercialization of Agriculture*. Delhi: Oxford University Press [for the] Centre for Development Studies, Trivandrum, 1985.

Ray, Bhabani C. *Orissa under Marathas, 1751–1803*. Allahabad: Kitab Mahal, 1960.

Raychaudhuri, Tapan. "Inland Trade." In *The Cambridge Economic History of India*, c. 1200—c. 1750, vol. 1, ed. idem and Irfan Habib, 325–59. Cambridge: Cambridge University Press, 1982.

———. "Dutt, Romesh Chunder [Rameshchandra Datta] (1849–1909)", In *Oxford Dictionary of National Biography*. Oxford: Oxford University Press, 2004.

Raynal, Guillaume T. F. *A Philosophical and Political History of the Settlements and Trade of the Europeans in the East and West Indies*. Vol. 8. London: W. Strahan and T. Cadell, 1783 (1st French ed. 1770).

Reinwald, Brigitte. *Routen, Koordinaten und Konturen einer seascape: Überlegungen zur Historiographie des modernen Indischen Ozeans*. Unpublished mnuscript, Berlin.

Rennell, James. *Memoir of a Map of Hindostan or the Mogul Empire*. 3rd ed. London: G. Nicol, 1793.

Reynolds, Edward. *The Rich Mans Charge Delivered in a Sermon at the Spittle . . . .* London: G. Thomason, 1658.

[Lieutenant] Righy. "Memorandum on the Usual Building Materials of the District of Cuttack. . . ." *Journal of the Asiatic Society of Bengal* XI, no. 129, 1842, 836–38.

Robinson, Ronald E. "Introduction: Railway Imperialism." In *Railway Imperialism*, ed. Clarence B. Davis and Kenneth E. Wilburn, 1–6. New York, Westport, Conn., London: Greenwood Press, 1991.

Rogers, James E. T., ed. *Speeches on Questions of Public Policy by John Bright, M.P.* 2nd ed. Vol. I. London: Macmillan, 1869.

Rösel, Jakob. "The Evolution and Organization of Pilgrimage to Jagannatha at Puri." In *Pilgrimage Studies: Text and Context* (Sri Phalahari Baba Commemoration Volume), ed. D. P. Dubey, and Lallanji Gopal, 94–117. Allahabad: The Society of Pilgrimage Studies, 1990.

Rothermund, Dietmar. *An Economic History of India: From Precolonial Times to 1991*. 2nd ed. London/New York: Routledge, 2000.

Rout, Kartik C. *Local Self-Government in British Orissa, 1869–1935*. Delhi: Daya Publishing House, 1988.

Roy, Tirthankar. *The Economic History of India, 1857–194*. New Delhi/Oxford: Oxford University Press, 2000.

Sahu, Bhagabana. *Princely States of Orissa under the British Crown (1858–1905)*. Cuttack: Vidyapuri, 1993.

Bibliography

Samal, J. K. *Economic History of Orissa , 1866–1912.* New Delhi: Mittal, 1990.

Sarkar, Bejoy Kumar. *Inland Transport and Communication in Mediaeval India.* Calcutta: Calcutta University Press, 1925.

Sarkar, Sailendra N. *Biography of Maharaja Sri Ram Chandra Bhanj Deo, Feudatory Chief of Mayurbhanj.* Calcutta: n.p., 1918.

Sarkar, Sumit. "Postmodernism and the Writing of History." In *Beyond Nationalist Frames: Relocating Postmodernism, Hindutva, History,* by Sumit Sarkar, 154–94. Delhi: Permanent Black, 2002.

Satya, Laxman D. "Colonial Sedentarisation and Subjugation: The Case of the Banjaras of Berar, 1850–1900." *Journal of Peasant Studies* 24, no. 4, 1997, 314–36.

———. *Cotton and Famine in Berar, 1850–1900.* New Delhi: Manohar, 1997.

Satyanarayana, Adapa, "'Birds of Passage': Migration of South Indian Laborers to Southeast Asia." *Critical Asian Studies* 34, no. 1, 2002, 89–115.

Sauli, Arnaud. "Circulation and Authority: Police, Public Space and Territorial Control in Punjab, 1861–1920." In *Society and Circulation: Mobile People and Itinerant Cultures in South Asia, 1750–1950,* 215–39.

Savage, Richard. "Of Public Spirit in Regard to Public Works: An Epistle." In *The Works of Richard Savage . . . .* With an Account of the Life and Writings of the Author, by Samuel Johnson vol. 2, 131–43. London: T. Evans, 1775.

Schivelbusch, Wolfgang. *Geschichte der Eisenbahnreise: Zur Industrialisierung von Raum und Zeit im 19. Jahrhundert.* Frankfurt a.M.: Fischer-Taschenbuch-Verlag, 2004 1st ed. 1977.

Schröder, Iris, and Sabine Höhler. "Welt-Räume: Annäherungen an eine Geschichte der Globalität im 20. Jahrhundert." In *Welt-Räume: Geschichte, Geographie und Globalisierung seit 1900,* ed. idem, 9–47. Frankfurt a.M.: Campus-Verlag, 2005.

Schwartzberg, Joseph E., ed. *A Historical Atlas of South Asia.* The Association of Asian Studies reference series 2. 2nd ed. New York/Oxford: Oxford University Press, 1992.

———. "South Asian Cartography." In *The History of Cartography: Cartography in the Traditional Islamic and South Asian Societies,* Vol. 2, book 1, ed. J. B. Harley and David Woodward, 295–509 Chicago/London: University of Chicago Press, 1992.

Seeley, J. R. *The Expansion of England: Two Courses of Lectures.* London: Macmillan, 1885. 1st ed. 1883.

Senapati, Phakirmohana. *My Times and I (Atma-Jivana-Carita).* Trans. by John Boulton. Bhubaneswar: Orissa Sahitya Academy, 1985.

Settar, S., and Bhubanes Misra, eds. *Railway Construction in India: Select Documents.* 3 vols. New Delhi: Northern Book Centre/Indian Council of Historical Research, 1999.

Sharma, Sanjay. *Famine, Philanthropy and the Colonial State: North India in the Early Nineteenth Century.* Delhi/Oxford: Oxford University Press, 2001.

Sidebottom, John K. *The Overland Mail to India: A Postal Historical Study of the Mail Route to India.* London: Allen and Unwin Ltd., 1948.

Bibliography

Singh, St. Nihal. *The Changing Scene in India*. Calcutta: Bengal Nagpur Railway, n.d.

Sinha, B. N. "Transport and Communications Problems in Orissa." *The National Geographical Journal of India* 3, no. 1, 1957, 27–45.

———. "Railway Transport and Its Problems in Orissa." *The National Geographical Journal of India* 3, no. 2, 1957, 93–103.

———. *Geography of Orissa*. 3rd rev. ed. New Delhi: National Book Trust, 1999.

Smith, David. *Report on Pilgrimage to Juggernauth, in 1868*. Calcutta: E. M. Lewis, Calcutta Central Press, 1868.

Smith, Adam. *The Wealth of Nations, Books IV–V.* Ed. and with an introduction by Andrew Skinner. London: Penguin Books Ltd, 1999.

Smith, Neil. *Uneven Development: Nature, Capital and the Production of Space*. Oxford/New York: Blackwell Publishing, 1984.

Soja, Edward W. "The Postmodernization of Geography: A Review." *Annals of the Association of American Geographers* 77, no. 2, 1987, 289–94.

———. *Postmodern Geographies: The Reassertion of Space in Critical Social Theory*, London: Verso, 1989.

Sopher, David. "The Geographic Patterning of Culture in India." In *An Exploration of India: Geographical Perspectives on Society and Culture*, ed. David Sopher 289–326. New York: Cornell University Press, 1980.

Stein, Burton. "Circulation and the Historical Geography of Tamil Country." *Journal of Asian Studies* 37, no. 1, 1977, 7–26.

Stephenson, Rowland M. *Railways: An Introductory Sketch with Suggestions in Reference to their Extension to British Colonies*. London: John Wale, 1850.

———. *Report upon the Practicability and Advantages of the Introduction of Railways into British India . . . .* London: Kelly & Co., 1845.

Stirling, Andrew. "An Account, Geographical, Statistical and Historical of Orissa Proper, or Cuttack." *Asiatic Researches* XV, 1825, 163–338.

Stöckler, Manfred. "Raum und Zeit." In *Enzyklopädie Philosophie*, ed. Hans J. Sandkühler, 1343–46. Hamburg: Meiner, 1999.

Stokes, Eric. *The English Utilitarians and India*. Delhi: Oxford University Press, 1989 (1st ed. 1955).

Strachey, John. *India: Its Administration and Progress*. 4th ed., rev. by T. W. Holderness. London, 1911 (1st ed. 1888).

Strachey, John, and Richard Strachey. *The Finances and Public Works of India from 1869 to 1881*. London: Kegan Paul & Co., 1882.

Srivastava, S. K. *Transport Development in India*. New Delhi: Chand, 1964.

Tchitcherov, Alexander I. *India: Changing Economic Structure in the Sixteenth to Eighteenth Centuries. Outline History of Crafts and Trade*. 2nd ed. New Delhi: Manohar, 1998.

Thompson, Edward P. *The Making of the English Working Class*. 1st edition 1963. London: Penguin, 1991.

Bibliography

Thorner, Daniel. *Investment in Empire: British Railway and Steam Shipping Enterprise in India, 1825–1849*. Philadelphia: University of Pennsylvania Press, 1950.

———. "The Pattern of Railway Development in India." Reprinted in *Railways in Modern India*, 80–96. New Delhi: Oxford University Press, 2001. First published in 1955.

Thornton, William T. *The Economic Writings of William Thornton*. Vol. 5. Edited by Philip Mirowski and Steven Tradewell. London: Pickering & Chatto, 1999.

Thrift, Nigel. "Transport and Communication, 1730–1914." In *An Historical Geography of England and Wales*, ed. Robert A. Dodgshon and R. A. Butlin, 453–86. 2nd ed. London: Academic, 1990.

Tomlinson, B. R. *The Economy of Modern India, 1860–1970*. New Cambridge History of India III.3. Cambridge: Cambridge University Press, 1993.

Toynbee, George. *A Sketch of the History of Orissa from 1803 to 1828*. Calcutta: Bengal Secretariat Press, 1873.

Tracy, James D., ed. *The Rise of Merchant Empires: Long-distance Trade in the Early Modern World, 1350–1750*. Cambridge: Cambridge University Press, 1990.

Tremenhere, George B. *On Public Works in the Bengal Presidency (with an Abstract of the Discussion upon the Paper)*. Excerpt Minutes of Proceedings of the Institution of Civil Engineers, vol. XVII, session 1857–58. London: William Clowes & Sons, 1858.

Tucker, Henry St. G. *Memorials on Indian Government*. Edited by John William Kaye. London: Bentley, 1853.

Tyrell, Frederick. *Public Works Reform in India*. London, Edward Bumpus, 1873.

Van Laak, Dirk "Infra-Strukturgeschichte." *Geschichte und Gesellschaft* 27, no. 3, 2001, 367–94.

———. "Der Begriff 'Infrastruktur' und was er vor seiner Erfindung besagte." *Archiv für Begriffsgeschichte* 41, 1999, 280–99.

———. *Imperiale Infrastruktur: Deutsche Planungen für eine Erschließung Afrikas 1880 bis 1960*. Paderborn et al.: Schöningh, 2004.

Von Trotha, Trutz "Über den Erfolg und die Brüchigkeit der Utopie staatlicher Herrschaft. Herrschaftssoziologische Beobachtungen über den kolonialen und nachkolonialen Staat in Westafrika." In *Verstaatlichung der Welt? Europäische Staatsmodelle und außereuropäische Machtprozesse*, ed. Wolfgang Reinhard, 223–51. Munich: Oldenbourg Verlag, 1999.

Varady, Robert G. "North Indian Banjaras: Their Evolution as Transporters." *South Asia* 2, nos. 1–2, 1979, 1–18.

———. Rail and Road Transport in Nineteenth-Century Awadh: Competition in a North Indian Province. Ph.D. diss. University of Arizona, 1981.

Verghese, K. E. *The Development and Significance of Transport in India, 1834–1882*. New Delhi: N. V., 1976.

Ville, Simon P. *Transport and the Development of the European Economy, 1750–1918*. Houndmills/London: Macmillan, 1990.

Bibliography

———. "British Transport History: Shifting Perspectives and New Agendas." In *Studies in Economic and Social History: Essays in Honour of Derek J. Aldcroft*, ed. Michael J. Oliver 1–29. Aldershot: Ashgate, 2002.

Visaria, Leela, and Pravin Visaria. "Population (1757– 1947)." In Kumar, *The Cambridge Economic History of India*, c. 1757—c. 1970, 2: 529–31.

Wagner, Kim A. "The Deconstructed Stranglers: A Reassessment of Thuggee." *Modern Asian Studies* 38, no. 4, 2004, 931–63.

Washbrook, David. "Progress and Problems: South Asian Economic and Social History, c. 1720–1860." *Modern Asian Studies* 22, no. 1, 1988, 57–96.

Whitcombe, Elizabeth. "Irrigation and Railways: Irrigation." In Kumar, *The Cambridge Economic History of India*, c. 1757—c. 1970, 2: 677–737.

Wills, C. U. *British Relations with the Nagpur State in the Eighteenth Century: An Account, Mainly Based on Contemporary English Records*. Nagpur: Central Provinces Government Press, 1926.

Wilson, Horace H. *A Glossary of Judicial and Revenue Terms*. Repr. of 1855 ed. New Delhi: Munshiram Manoharlal, 1997.

Wilson, Jon E. "'A Thousand Countries to Go to': Peasants and Rulers in Late Eighteenth-Century Bengal." *Past and Present* 189, 2005, 81–109.

World Bank, *Project Information Document: India Orissa State Roads Project*. 24 October 2005. http://www-wds.worldbank.org.

Yang, Anand A. *Bazaar India: Markets, Society, and the Colonial State in Gangetic Bihar*. Berkeley: University of California Press, 1998.

Yule, Henry, and A. C. Burnell. *Hobson-Jobson: A Glossary of Colloquial Anglo-Indian Words*. New Delhi: Munshiram Manoharlal, 1984.

Index

accountability, 111, 267, 269
Agra, 148
Ahom dynasty, 86
Allahabad, 43n63
Anandpur, 131, 132n42
Ancient Rome, 28, 80, 81n40, 82n42, 83
Andhra, 63, 228
Angul Road, 209–10, 212–13, 216, 223
Annales "school", 24, 67n2
Annexation
  Angul, 209
  Mughalbandi districts, 164
  Orissa, 129, 156n7, 168, 186, 202
  princely states, 206, 209n73
Arang, 127–28, 130
Arnold, David, 64, 188n6
Arthashastra, 4
artisans, 70, 73, 88, 182, 230–31. *See also* weavers
Aska, 131
Asoka, 151
Assam, 32n71, 86, 218, 237, 251, 271, 285, 286, 287n62
Athara-nala bridge, 121, 163
aurang, 189, 204, 230
Awadh, 5n10, 96n90, 145n89

Bahmangatti, 169, 175
Bailey, Damien, 76n28, 103
Bailparra (Belparapatnà), 166
Balasore (Baleshwar), 125n19, 126, 129, 132–34, 138n62, 140n68, 149, 151n107, 159, 162–63, 176, 180–81, 189, 190, 192–95, 197, 202n48, 203, 205, 215–16, 219, 230–31, 236, 240–41, 243, 256–57, 259, 271, 278–81, 283
"Balasore bearers", 140, 236
Balasore Railway Committee, 249, 251
Balianta, 131
bamboo, 139, 168
bamboo fortifications (palisades), 134, 166–68
Banerji, Arun, 97
Bangabasi, 251
Bangriposi, 281n44
Baripada, 278, 280
Barmul (Baramu) Pass, 128n29, 166, 179, 212, 238–39
barter, 139, 143, 195
Basta, 164
Bay of Bengal, 63, 126, 131–33, 138, 144, 194, 218, 249, 270
bazaars, 75, 126, 159n76, 174, 178, 195n30, 232n26, 260, 290
Beadon, Sir Cecil, 196n32
Beames, John, 274
begar. *See* forced labour
betel, 143
bethi. *See* forced labour
Benares (Varanasi), 43n63, 128n29, 132n44, 138n62, 145, 148, 250, 253–54
"Benares–Cuttack–Pooree pilgrim line", 253–54

Index

Bengal, 40, 43–45, 54, 57n106, 70, 88n64, 119, 128n29, 131–32, 137n60, 140, 145, 148–49, 152, 156–57, 159, 162, 164–65, 167, 189–90, 197, 199n39, 204–5, 208, 214–18, 227–28, 237, 240–42, 248, 253, 258, 260, 278–79, 303
Bengal–Assam Railway, 47n71
Bengal–Nagpur Railway (BNR), 127, 247–49, 253–58, 264, 268, 271, 280, 282–83, 286, 303–4
Bengali newspapers, 33n36, 250–51, 263, 305
Bengal troops, 157
Berar, 127, 135n57, 138, 141, 148, 156, 158, 164, 166, 202
Bhadrak, 126, 134, 140, 177, 179, 185, 197, 219, 240, 242
Bhattacharya, Neeladri, 37
Bhonsle dynasty (of Berar), 156–57, 202.
Bhopal, 134
Bhubaneswar, 11
Bihar, 5n10, 98n104, 132, 149n100, 150, 217, 241, 258, 265, 267
Binika, 128, 130, 146, 148, 211
Bisoi, 142n77
Bloch, Ernst, 19n2, 20–21, 30
boatmen, 148, 179n45
boats. *See* inland navigation or maritime transport
Bombay, 46, 51, 59–60, 62, 202–4, 211, 220, 230, 232n26, 247, 258n119, 282
Borasambar (zamindari), 179
Braudel, Fernand, 26–27, 39
brass utensils, 139n65, 141
Brenner, Neil, 26n19
bridges, 33, 47n71, 61, 69, 79, 81n39, 85, 86n58, 87n59, 88n64, 90, 99, 105n132, 120–21, 126, 161, 163, 177, 196, 198–99, 203, 207, 211, 241, 256, 269, 277–78, 288, 290, 293

Bright, John, 92
Britain, 28, 49, 51–52, 55, 57–58, 62, 73, 75, 76n28, 82n43, 91, 99, 103n126, 105, 112
British capital, 6, 43, 55–56, 75, 76n28, 93, 95, 102–4, 108–9, 205, 221, 282
British Engineers, 121, 141, 169, 173, 209, 256, 272, 277–78, 296
Bruton, William, 137n60
Buckingham Canal, 77
Bülow, Adam von, 78n34
Burdwan (Bardhaman), 145n89, 215
Burma, 63, 152, 190

Cain, P. J., 75n27, 91–92
Calcutta, 40, 43n63, 46, 51, 57, 59–60, 62n123, 63n126, 68, 78, 140, 145, 148, 152, 177, 181, 187–88, 193, 198–200, 202–4, 218–19, 221–23, 229, 235–38, 242, 247–51, 254–55, 258, 260–61, 273, 275, 277, 279, 282–83, 285, 301, 303–4, 306
Calcutta Review, 84
canals, 2, 6, 29, 31, 44n66, 45, 48, 51, 57–58, 60, 76–77, 90, 98–100, 104n127, 106, 110, 201, 211, 215, 220–25, 235, 238, 242–47, 249, 254–55, 257–59, 263n136, 303–5
Caribbean, 237
cartography, 41
carts, 52, 59, 68, 98n104, 120, 132n43, 137–39, 143n81, 153, 161, 201, 203, 211–12, 216, 220, 226, 233, 238, 248, 263, 304
Central India, 51, 127, 129, 131, 141–48, 150, 152, 156, 159, 161, 165, 204, 208–11, 214–15, 220, 226n6, 238–39, 248–49, 255, 258, 303
Chaibassa, 132n42, 213, 253
Chandbali, 225, 236–38, 240, 247, 255

* 352 *

Index

chaos, spatial, 38, 55
Chapman, John, 84
Charibatia, 243
chatti (small market), 178
chaukidar, 183
chauki. *See* toll station
Chhattisgarh, 127, 134, 135n57, 138, 141, 145–50, 195, 258
Chilka Lake, 125–26, 143n81, 144–45, 192, 197, 222, 230, 242
Chinnakimedi, 139n65, 284n57, 294
cholera, 183, 234, 250, 254, 259, 264–65, 268, 289
Chota Nagpur, 127, 134, 138, 173, 182, 213, 215, 247, 250, 253, 278, 284
Churaman, 125n19, 202, 241
Churaman Canal, 201
circulatory regime,
  conceptualisation, 71–76, 301–6
  Orissa, 1, 12, 122, 185–86, 191, 194–96, 206–7, 222, 224–25, 234, 238, 247, 254–55, 270, 283, 287, 300, 301–6
civilisation, 2, 29, 31, 63, 91–93, 100n113, 101, 106–7, 155, 170–71, 195, 203, 231n25, 246, 252, 263–64, 276, 286, 297–98, 300, 304
Clarke, Hyde, 77
Clive, Robert, 156n7, 201
coal, 220, 247, 253, 267, 271–72, 278
Cockburn, G. F., 143
coconuts, 141, 143
Colombo, 133
colonial capitalism, 8, 58, 117, 134, 224, 229, 274, 302, 304
commercialisation, 3n4, 12–13, 54, 57, 117, 151, 185, 194, 198, 215, 225, 234, 239, 241, 247, 249, 270–271, 273–74, 277, 280, 283–84, 304, 306
Commissioner of Cuttack (i.e., of Orissa), 120, 130n39, 143, 155, 159–60, 168, 170, 172–73, 198, 203–4, 207–8, 214, 219, 221, 233, 239, 251, 254n102, 263, 274–76, 293
commodity
  circulation, 12, 41, 52, 65, 74, 129, 134, 137, 152, 302–3
  exchange, 42, 87, 90, 143, 145
  form, 73, 76
  market(s), 45, 47, 55, 75, 142
  prices, 77
  production, 41, 90, 134, 137, 149, 185, 194
  transport, 57, 90, 126, 133, 145, 203
contractors, 133, 165, 277, 282, 284–85, 293, 297
convict labour. *See* forced labour
'coolies'. *See* labour
coolie depots, 237
copper, 143
cotton, 51–52, 75, 94, 96, 127, 134, 137n60, 139, 141, 143, 148, 159, 207, 210–14, 220, 230
  fabrics, 132, 162
  roads, 204, 211–12, 216, 223
Cotton, Sir Arthur, 47n73, 99–101, 221
Court of Wards, 275, 279, 282
cowries, 126n21, 135n56
'crime', 179–80, 187, 232–34, 286–87, 306
culverts, 184, 246
customs duties, 162–63, 165–67, 179
Cuttack, 60, 117, 119, 126, 128–32, 134, 140n68, 141n77, 146, 148–49, 151n107, 157, 162, 165, 172n71&73, 173, 178, 180–82, 189, 192, 195n30, 197, 201, 205, 207, 209–13, 215–16, 219, 222, 225–26, 230–32, 236, 238, 240, 242, 248–50, 253, 255–58, 271, 276–77, 288
"Cuttack hackeries", 138

Index

Cuttack–Ganjam Road, 178, 201n43

dacoits. See 'crime'
Dainik, 251
Dak. See mail roads, postal service
Dalhousie's "Minute on Railways" of 1853, 29n25, 39, 94, 109, 110n144, 206–7, 218
Danvers, Juland, 84
Das, Binod Sankar, 137n60, 179
Das, Sarangadhar, 298n102
Davidson, James, 142n79, 143
De, Baikuntha Nath, 249
Delhi, 11, 57n106, 68, 78
Deloche, Jean, 4, 120, 125n19
demilitarisation, 73
Derbyshire, Ian D., 98n104
Dhamra, 125n19, 202, 215, 225
dhangur coolies, 182
Dhenkanalgarh, 141n77
dikkus, 284
disarticulation, spatial, 150, 152, 193, 196, 213, 217, 248, 271, 303–4
Diwan-i-Bayutat, 88
dola yatra. See pilgrimage
Doyle & Co., 219
Dupuit, Jules, 74
Dutt, Romesh Chunder, 96n93, 99, 101, 233, 237, 263, 274n15, 280

earthworkers, 70, 88, 235, 285, 296
East Coast Railway, 33, 64, 223, 235, 238, 242–43, 247–48, 254–57, 261n130, 262, 264, 280, 287, 297, 303–4
East India Company, 7–8, 12, 43, 68, 71, 77, 83, 92–95, 99, 102, 103, 105, 110n144, 111n149, 117, 123, 138n62, 144, 149, 156–60, 164, 169, 180, 194, 198n37, 199–202, 207, 210
East India Irrigation and Canal Company, 159n25, 221

economic nationalism, 32, 54–55, 99, 233
embankments, 35, 48, 79, 100, 105n132, 111n149, 176, 178, 184–85, 201, 244–45, 291
encroachments, 178
engineering, 47, 80, 105n132, 124, 208–9, 245–46, 256–58, 304
Enlightenment, 78
entrepot towns, 143, 151
European travel accounts, 120, 150
evangelicalism, 165, 199, 263
"extra-ordinary" works. *See* productive public works

False Point Harbour, 201, 225, 238, 255
famine, 77, 186, 206, 227, 231
  of 1866 (in Orissa), 10, 12, 119, 133n47, 152, 186–96, 208, 222, 228n10, 234, 237, 242, 244
  of 1888–90 (in Western Orissa), 237, 239
  Parliamentary Commission on Orissa famine of 1866, 39, 151, 188–93, 205, 215–16, 219, 222
  protection, 95, 105, 111, 119, 250, 254, 257n115
faujdars, 88
Febvre, Lucien, 27, 43, 67n2
feeders, 97, 211, 240, 255
ferries, 112, 120–21, 126, 154, 163, 165, 175, 177, 203, 239, 260
Feudatory States. *See* princely states
food grains, 40, 53, 70, 89, 126, 132, 135n56, 138n62, 139, 148, 175, 188, 190, 192, 195–96, 214, 220, 227, 231–34, 257n115, 271, 273n15
  rice, 126n21, 127, 137, 139, 145, 152, 188, 191, 193–94, 217, 225, 227–35, 239, 249, 270, 273, 280, 294, 303–4
  wheat, 52, 141

* 354 *

Index

food riots, 231–34
forced labour,
   begar, 111, 172, 291, 294, 298–99
   bethi, 13, 46, 111, 130, 172–73, 180, 290–300, 306
   convict, 111, 180–82, 201
   famine relief works, 111
forts. *See garh*
France, 79, 82–83, 289
freight rates, 51, 57, 62, 89–90, 149
French physiocrats, 69

Ganges Canal, 45
Gandhi, Mohandas Karamchand, 262–63, 292
Ganjam, 117, 125n19, 126, 133, 141–47, 149–50, 161–62, 178, 181, 197, 213–14, 222, 226, 230, 237–38, 242, 253n97, 255n107
Ganjam Agency, 293–95, 300
garh (minor forts, fortified settlements) 86, 123n12, 126, 130n39, 131, 134, 154, 163–64, 166–68, 172, 184, 274, 277
Garhjat States. *See* princely states
Garhpada, 163
Ghani, Abdul, 219
Global market. *See* world market
Goswami, Manu, 21n7, 25n18, 32, 34n38, 37
Governor-Generals and Viceroys
   Lord Bentinck, 44, 92
   Lord Canning, 207, 210–11
   Lord Dalhousie, 29n25, 39, 52, 94, 103n126, 109, 110n144, 206–7, 209, 218,
   Lord Hardinge, 52, 77, 78n33
   Lord Mayo, 93
Grand Trunk Road, 45, 68, 76, 111n149, 145, 148, 176
Guha, Amalendu, 226n6
Gumsur, 134, 139n65, 160
Gurumahisani, 282

haats (periodic markets), 126, 135n56, 177

Hamilton, Alexander, 120, 165
Hariharpur, 132, 167
Harvey, David, 24, 41, 48–50, 53n91, 55–56
Heidegger, Martin, 26n19
Heine, Heinrich, 49n77
hides, 141, 228, 267
High Level Canal, 222–23, 242–43, 245, 255
Hopkins, A. G., 75n27, 91–92
hospital, 106, 183
House of Commons, 44n66, 85, 92, 104n127, 190n12&16,
House of Lords, 44n66
Hunter, W. W., 140, 150, 167–68, 193, 195–96
Hurd, John M., 3n4

Indian Engineer, 257
Indian Ocean, 63, 89, 132
Indian Road Development Committee (1928), 97
industrial capitalism, 40, 42, 46, 73
inland navigation, 6, 40, 62n123, 92, 99–100, 110, 126, 128–30, 138, 144, 148–49, 159n25, 163, 167, 191, 220–21, 239, 242–44, 246–47, 249, 258–59, 288n64
Institution of Civil Engineers, 208
Insurrection of 1857, 52, 76, 92–94, 96, 187, 205–7, 209, 276, 306
International Labor Organization (ILO), 298
iron ore, 123, 220, 253, 272, 282, 285
itinerant traders, 133, 139, 150. *See also* 'tribal' communities, Banjara
Iyer, G. Subramania, 32n32

Jabalpur, 146, 204
Jagannath temple, 165, 198–200, 262, 292, 302, 305
"Jagannath Pilgrim Fund Committee" of Balasore, 259

Index

Jagannath Road (incl. 'New Jagannath Road' and 'Orissa Trunk Road'), 60, 88n61, 119, 126, 131–32, 137n61, 145, 151, 157–58, 160, 162–63, 165, 176, 178–81, 184, 196–201, 208–9, 215–17, 221, 223, 225–26, 238, 240, 241n61, 245, 255, 263n136
Jagatsinghpur, 137n60
jagirdars, 88, 167
jails, 111, 180–82
Jajpur, 126, 131–32, 134, 260
jalkar (fishing tax), 35
Jamuna Canal, 45
Jamshedpur, 282–83
Jasipur, 175
Jomini, Antoine-Henri, 78n34
jute mills (Calcutta), 236

Kalahandi, 142, 283n54, 284n57
Kalinga Ghat, 141, 161
Kandarapur, 129
Kantilo, 130–31, 142–43, 151, 171, 260, 304
karkatch, 137, 230
Kendrapara Canal, 225, 238, 242
Kerr, Ian, 4n5, 6
Khan, Alivardi, 167
Khan, Asadullah, 163–64
Khandpara, 143
Kharagprasad, 141n77
Khariyar, 142
khoraki, 291
Khunta ghat, 140, 163–64
Kim, 68
Kipling, Rudyard, 68, 264–65
Kittoe, Markham, 134, 140n68, 141n77, 169–70, 172n73, 173–75, 180, 182–84
Konkan, 211
kos minar, 86
kotwal, 88
Kulke, Hermann, 261n128

Laak, Dirk van, 79

Labour. *See also* forced labour
abstract l., 42, 46
agricultural l., 63, 197, 232–33, 235
'coolie' l., 33, 139, 172–73, 182, 203, 212, 234, 236–37, 284n59, 285, 289, 293, 296–97
desertion, 173, 180, 183
history, 10n19
migration and mobility, 42, 63, 70–71, 98n104, 140, 177, 236–37, 271, 284–87, 306
recruitment, 39n52, 171, 173, 182, 202, 235, 237, 289–90, 293
surplus l., 90, 103
wage l., 22, 46, 173, 183, 203, 231, 234–35, 285, 296–98
Labour Corps, 289–90
laissez-faire, 105, 107, 190n12
Lancashire, 75, 207, 210, 230
land acquisition, 103n126, 110–11
land revenue, 102–3, 158–59, 175, 188–89, 198, 200, 221, 226
Leckie, Daniel R., 143, 162, 166, 184
Lefebvre, Henri, 9, 19n1, 20n5, 22n10. 23n12, 24–26, 30n28, 36–38, 41, 48, 54–55, 61, 62n125, 72, 113
Lenin, Vladimir I., 55
limestone, 283, 285
Lloyd, Henry, 78n34
London, 11, 31, 51, 62n123, 76n28, 95, 102, 187, 208
Lord Stanley. *See* Secretary of State for India
Löw, Martina, 26n18
Lyotard, Jean-Francois, 21n8

MacGeorge, G. W, 27–29, 59, 96n91, 105n132, 111n149, 207
Macpherson, Samuel C, 166
mahajans, 142, 233
Maharaja Sri Ram Chandra Bhanj Deo (of Mayurbhanj), 279–82, 298

Index

mail roads, 68, 127, 169, 173, 180, 182, 202–4, 216, 293
Madras, 46, 51, 117, 133, 150, 152, 157, 158n18, 161, 169n58, 172n71, 206, 214, 218, 242, 249–50, 255n107, 287, 293
Madras Irrigation Company, 221
Malapert, M. F., 83
malaria, 171, 245, 289
Malaya, 63
Manchester, 75, 92
Mangalpur, 141n77
Marwari traders, 228
Marathas, 54, 126n23, 132, 138n62, 150, 156–58, 162–64, 166, 168–69, 178, 184, 200–1, 302
Maritime transport, 4n7, 37, 39, 50–51, 61–64, 91, 125–26, 133, 138, 144, 149, 159, 191–95, 202, 216, 235–38, 246–47, 251, 258, 263, 270, 304
Marx, Karl, 24, 48, 50–51, 55, 73–77, 89–90, 206
Massey, W. N., 104
Mayurbhanj State Light Railway, 280, 282
McGuire, John, 76n28, 103
melas, 135n56, 140n68, 177
meli. *See* rural insurgency
merchants, 70, 87, 129, 132, 134, 137n60, 139, 142–43, 164–65, 167, 179, 194n29, 211, 228, 231–34, 241, 302
  capital(ism), 41–43, 89
  English, 162
meriah, suppression of, 139n65, 158n18, 289
Midnapur, 127, 182, 196, 202–3, 242–43, 255–56
Mill, John Stewart, 28, 105–8
Mills, A. J. Moffat, 160, 173
mineral resources, 158, 270–71, 283.
  See also coal and iron ore
Mirzapur, 146, 203

Mitchell, John W., 268–69
modernity, 22, 124
Mohanti (jati), 174
monetisation, 42, 73
moneylenders, 142, 233, 284
motorised road traffic, 8, 98, 124, 255, 261n128
Motte, Thomas, 165, 167, 170
mud forts. *See* garhs
"Mughalbandi" coastal area, 117, 157, 164
Mughal emperors, 87–88
mukhtars, 170, 174
Munsi, Sunil Kumar, 7, 56, 98, 207n63
Mysore (sultanate), 86, 157

Nagpur, 134, 146, 157, 179, 200n42, 202, 247, 302
Nair, Janaki, 24n15
Nandghat, 129, 148
Naoroji, Dadabhai, 32
navigable canals, 58, 60, 77, 90, 98, 128, 215, 222–23, 242, 249, 257, 305
nawabs, 164, 167
Nayak, Ganeswar, 8n16, 227n9, 236n41
Newton, Isaac, 20, 23n13, 41n57
  Second law of motion, 77–78
Nicolaus, Martin, 89n66
Nilamadhaba temple, 143
North India, 54, 98n104, 140, 145–46, 195, 213, 223. *See also* Awadh and Bihar
North-West Frontier, 77

oil seeds, 141, 145, 228
oriental despotism, 81n40, 106
Orissa Canal Scheme, 48, 221
Orissa Coast Canal (East Coast Canal), 60n117, 110, 238, 243–46, 255, 257, 263n136
Orissa States Enquiry Committee (1939), 292, 298n102, 299

Index

Orissa States People's Conference (1937), 292, 298n102
Orissa State Government, 123
Orissa Trunk Road. *See* Jagannath Road
Oriya,
    Chiefs (in 'tribal' areas), 158, 293–94
    language, 8
    literature, 133, 275
    newspapers, 33, 250, 288
    traders, 142, 228
    weavers, 148
Ouseley, J. R., 167

pack oxen, 5, 7, 51, 70, 89, 98n104, 131, 132n42&43, 133, 139, 141, 143, 147–49, 153, 161–62, 211, 214, 226, 273, 304
palaces, 86, 121, 277–78, 292
palki (palanquin), 138n62, 263
    bearers, 140, 171, 236
pandas, 261n130, 262, 264, 266–67, 305
panga (salt manufacture by boiling), 137
Paradip, 123, 177, 225n4
Parhi, Mothur Mohan, 241
parwana, 171
Pati, Biswamoy, 237n46
Patnaik, Jagannath, 281n72
peasants, 33, 70–71, 103, 135n56, 170, 176, 178, 180, 231–33, 246, 261, 271, 280, 283–84, 288, 292, 294, 299, 303, 305
peddlers, 37, 70
Pilgrimage, 12, 27, 61, 63–64, 70, 85, 88, 119–20, 126, 130–33, 140, 144–45, 151, 154, 162–67, 176, 178, 197–200, 219n95, 235, 241n61, 248, 250–54, 258–69, 271, 302–6
Pilgrim Committee Bihar and Orissa (1913), 261, 265–67

Pilgrim tax, 144, 162–66, 198–200
Pipili, 121n8, 125n19, 126, 197
plantations, 77, 218, 237, 285, 306
plebeian, 33, 175, 177, 283, 284, 287, 291, 296
police, 27, 171, 179, 258n121, 260n124, 286–88, 290
political economy, 6, 29, 82, 90–91, 101–9, 119, 190
polyvalence, 34, 154, 258, 285, 305
Popper, Karl, 80n36
ports (Orissa), 125, 132–33, 192–94, 202, 231, 235, 238, 255, 270
POSCO, 123
Postal service, 62, 67–68, 100, 172, 202–3
    dak chaukis/postal stations, 86, 156, 171
    dak runners (bearers), 59n113, 68, 70
Pouchepadass, Jacques, 73
prajamandal movements, 292, 300
'preventive' works, 77, 95
Principles of Political Economy, 105–8
princely states
    Angul (annexed in 1847), 129, 166–68, 192, 209, 212, 216, 288
    Athgarh, 168
    Athmallik, 276
    Bamra, 169, 203, 286
    Baudh, 134, 139n65, 141n77, 142, 166, 170, 183, 285
    Bonai, 169, 203, 286
    Daspalla, 166
    Dhenkanal, 285
    Gangpur, 283, 285–86
    Kendujhar (Keonjhar), 132, 139n63, 140n68, 160n29, 169, 172, 202, 213, 253, 272, 294–95
    Khurda (kingdom and town), 121n8, 131, 160, 165, 176, 178, 181, 197, 226, 256
    Mayurbhanj, 127, 129, 132, 140, 142n77, 161n32, 163–64, 167,

Index

169, 171n69, 174–75, 182, 202, 249, 277–85, 290, 293, 298–99
Nayagarh, 143n81, 168
Nilgiri, 163, 283
Pal Lahera, 169, 202, 288–89
Parlakimedi, 283
Patna, 142, 287n62
Ranpur, 143n81, 290n71, 299
Talcher, 271, 285, 290
'productive public works', 6, 93n82, 94–95, 243–44, 257, 304
'public works' policies,
  British and colonial, 8–9, 12, 31–32, 43n63, 46, 57, 68, 75–77, 82–84, 91–98, 102–12, 117, 123, 161–62, 175, 177, 180, 185, 190, 200–23, 238–49, 255–58, 270, 301–2, 305–6
  Indian nationalist critique of, 3, 6, 32–34, 98–101, 112n152, 251–52, 263, 292
  as a means of gaining political legitimacy, 5, 29, 83–84, 97, 224–25, 267, 269
  and military considerations, 29, 43, 52, 68, 77–78, 94, 96, 105, 156, 160–61, 197–98, 218
  of Garhjat rajas, 168–70, 273–83
"Puddam Talow" (*padmatola*), 166, 241n61
Punjab, 235, 258n119, 287n63
Puri, 33, 64, 88n64, 117, 119–21, 125n19, 126, 131, 133, 138n62, 140, 144–45, 149, 162–63, 165, 189, 195n30, 197, 199n39, 205, 216–17, 219, 229–32, 235, 240, 242, 250–51, 253, 258–65, 268, 271, 279, 302–5

Queen Victoria, 83

railway dividends, 102–4, 109, 206, 221, 254, 257, 305
Raipur, 127–28, 130, 133–34, 141–44, 211, 247

"Raipur Mail Road", 169, 173, 180, 182, 202–4, 216, 293
Raja Jadunath Bhanja (of Mayurbhanj), 174–75, 283
Raja of Rewah, 241n61
Raja Krushna Chandra (of Mayurbhanj), 249, 278–79
Raja Raghunath Bhanja (of Mahurbhanj), 167
Raja Ramachandra (of Khurda), 131
Raja Sukhamoy Roy, 198–200
Rajghat, 201, 226n6
Ramgarh (Baudh), 183
Ramgurh Light Infantry, 172
Ranchi, 127, 286
Rangoon, 63, 285
Rani Sumitra Bhanja (of Mayurbhanj), 164
rasad, 171–72, 183
rath yatra, 64, 140, 259n123, 261, 265.
  See also pilgrimage
Ravenshaw, T. E., 160–61, 275–76
Raynal, Guillaume T. F., 2, 31
relative distance, 48–49, 58–59, 61, 65, 220, 248
Rennell, James, 157
rest houses (*dharamsalas, sarais, sattirams*), 79, 85–88, 126, 154, 198–99, 241, 260
rhythm (of circulation), 61–65, 79, 134–44, 152, 193, 237, 261, 302–3
rice. *See* food grains
Ricketts, Henry, 137n61, 168, 201
rivers,
  Baitarani, 127, 131, 132n42, 221, 225, 242–43
  Brahmani, 127, 141n77, 213, 221, 242–43
  Burhabalang, 125n19&20, 127, 129, 132
  Debi, 125n19
  Dhamra, 125n19, 225
  Gamai, 125n19

Index

Ganges, 57n106, 89n67, 92, 146, 149
Godavari, 146–47, 221
Hugli, 236, 242
Jonk, 146
Kansbansa, 121n9, 125n19
Kharsua, 215
Krishna, 221, 255n107
Kuakhai, 131
Mahanadi, 8, 33, 35, 47–48, 127–31, 134, 137n60, 141–46, 148–50, 165–66, 172n71, 178, 183, 191–92, 209, 211–12, 215, 220–25, 238, 241n61, 242–45, 248–49, 253–56
Narmada, 146
Rushikulya, 125, 127, 131
Sheonath, 129, 146, 148, 220
Subarnarekha, 125, 127, 162–63, 226n6
river boats. *See* inland navigation
"Road and Improvement Committee" (1832), 176
road cess committees, 112, 239, 243
Robinson, Ronald E., 50n82
robbers. See *dacoits*
rumours, 33, 46–47, 234, 288–89
rural insurgency, 71, 289–90, 294–95

Sakchi, 282
sal, 167, 272–73, 279, 281–82, 304
salami, 172
salinisation, 245
salt,
  import of British salt, 149, 159, 189, 230
  manufacture, 125, 136–37, 142–43, 148–49, 151, 158–59, 189, 193, 229–30, 303–4
  trade, 70, 89, 125–26, 132–33, 135n56, 137, 139n65, 141–43, 147–50, 159, 161, 193–95, 201–2, 214, 216, 228–30, 238, 271, 302

  monopoly on manufacture and sale, 147, 149–50, 189, 193, 214
Sambalpur, 127, 130, 132n42&43, 134, 138n62, 146, 148, 151n107, 158, 167, 169, 172n71, 182, 184, 202–3, 209–12, 216, 238, 249, 253, 255–57, 271, 286
Second Anglo-Mysore War (1780–1784), 157
Secretary of State for India, 85, 187
Seeley, J. R., 69
Senapati, Fakirmohan, 132–33, 187n2, 193, 275, 294–95
Shankarakol, 161, 213
shellac, 139
Sher Shah Suri, 86
shifting cultivation, 273, 284, 297
shipbuilding, 159
ships. *See* maritime transport
siltation, 125, 202n48, 238, 241, 244
Singhbhum, 285
Sirguja, 134
Sir John Lawrence (ship), 251
Smith, Adam, 82n42, 90, 95, 101, 105–6
Smith, Neil, 19n1, 42, 48
Snan yatra. *See* pilgrimage
social savings of railways, 5
Sohela, 211
Soja, Edward W., 22n11
Sonepur, 127–28, 130, 134, 138n62, 142, 148, 161, 179, 211–12, 214, 249
Sonka Creek, 177
Sopher, David, 45, 70
space,
  absolute, 20, 41–43, 46, 48, 78, 87, 297
  abstract, 40–43, 46–48, 78, 152, 185–86, 244, 247, 283, 286, 297, 300, 301, 304
  conceived, 22n10, 30n28, 32, 40–42, 45, 53, 110, 113, 123, 206, 252, 267, 303

Index

differential, 38
production of social s., 9, 11, 23n12, 25–26, 29, 34, 36, 42, 62, 83, 110, 122, 150, 217, 224, 252, 297, 305–6
Stein, Burton, 37–38, 70–73
Stephenson, R. M., 109, 206, 249
Stirling, Andrew, 121, 135, 148–50
stonecutters, 88
Strachey, John, 28, 52n89, 92n80, 106–8
Strachey, Richard, 106, 107–8
Suez, 51, 62

Taldanda, 215,
Taldanda Canal, 225n4, 238, 242
Tamil region, 38, 54, 126n21
Tandas. See 'tribal' communities, Banjara
Tangi, 143n81
Tatas, 282
telegraph, 34, 50, 67, 290
telephone, 67, 290
Temple, Sir Richard, 128n29, 145, 147–50, 220, 223
temples, 64n127, 70, 88n64, 121, 129–30, 141, 143, 165, 198–200, 260–62, 266, 292, 302, 305
textiles,
British imports, 52, 63, 75, 230
commercial manufacture, 137, 148, 151, 159, 194. *See also* weavers
trade, 126, 139n65, 143, 151, 228–30
The Bridge-Builders, 264
The Lake of Palms, 263
The Times, 42–43, 99–100,
Thorner, Daniel, 6, 56n101, 103
Thornton, William, 28, 96, 100
Thrift, Nigel, 67
Tikerpara, 166
timber, 7, 129, 139, 148n98, 158, 167, 220, 228, 272–73, 276, 281–82, 292, 304

time-space
compression, 23n12, 48, 50–53, 58, 60, 65, 151–52, 248, 260, 303
dispersal, 53, 58, 60, 152
toll station, 27, 126, 140, 162–64, 166
Toynbee, George, 120–22, 124, 180n100, 199, 201
tramways, 100, 219n93&96
transport revolution, 4–5, 39, 58, 73
'tribal' communities
Banjara, 70, 89, 133–34, 141–42, 147
Bhuiyan, 284, 294–95
Kol, 284–86
Koravar, 287
Khond, 117, 139, 142, 158n18, 171n69, 166, 178–79, 289, 291n73, 284, 293–94, 300
Oraon, 284, 287
Pana, 284, 288–89, 296
Santal, 284–85, 290
Tributary Mehals/States. *See* princely states
'trunk lines'
railways, 76, 105n132, 109, 207
roads, 35, 45, 60, 68–69, 76, 110–11, 137n61, 145, 148, 158, 160, 163, 176, 196–97, 201, 208, 215–17, 221, 223, 225, 226, 238, 240, 255, 263n136
Tucker, Henry St. George, 111n149, 199–200
turmeric, 139
turnpike roads and trusts (in Britain), 62n124, 90, 112

uneven development, 3n4, 38, 53–58, 97–98, 100, 106, 213, 217, 231–32, 241, 271, 283
United States of America, 55–56, 103n126, 104
US Civil War, 207, 210
utilitarians, 44, 91–92, 181

Varady, Robert G., 145n89, 207n63

Index

Vijayawada, 255n107
village communities, 70, 74, 135, 177–78, 291
village headmen, 88, 171, 174
Vishakapatnam, 242, 253n97

watershed, 47–48, 152
water tanks, 126, 130, 142n77, 166, 199n37, 291–92, 297
weavers, 70, 71n13, 132n43, 137n60, 148, 150, 230
well-diggers. *See* earthworkers
wells, 79, 86, 126, 182, 199n37, 241
Western India, 57n106, 138, 211, 227–28, 235

works of "permanent utility". *See* "productive public works"
World Bank, 123
world market, 36–37, 48, 50, 52–55, 57–59, 76, 213
world wars, 39n52, 289–90

Yang, Anand, 5n10, 68, 86n56, 98n104, 149n100
Yatris. *See* pilgrims

zamindars, 35, 88, 130n39, 162–63, 166, 169, 171–77, 185, 188, 198–99, 219, 231, 233, 241, 249